Assessment of Writing: Politics, Policies, Practices

Edited by
Edward M. White,
William D. Lutz, and
Sandra Kamusikiri

The Modern Language Association of America
New York   1996

For information about obtaining permission to reprint material from MLA book publi-
cations, send your request by mail (see address below), e-mail (permissions@mla.org),
or fax (212 533-0680).

An earlier version of Edward M. White's essay "Power and Agenda Setting in Writing
Assessment" appeared in *Writing Assessment* 1 (1994): 15–31. Reprinted with permission from Ablex Publishing Corp. An earlier version of portions of Roberta Camp's
essay, entitled "New Models for Writing Assessment and New Views of Measurement,"
appeared in *Validating Holistic Scoring for Writing Assessment: Theoretical and Empirical
Foundations* (ed. Michael M. Williamson and Brian A. Huot), published by Hampton
Press, Inc. Used with permission.

Library of Congress Cataloging-in-Publication Data
Assessment of writing : politics, policies, practices / edited by Edward M. White,
     William D. Lutz, and Sandra Kamusikiri.
          p.   cm. — (Research and scholarship in composition, ISSN 1079-2554 ; 4)
     Includes bibliographical references (p.) and index.
     ISBN 0-87352-581-7 (cloth). — ISBN 0-87352-582-5 (pbk.)
     1. English language—Rhetoric—Study and teaching. 2. English language—Ability
testing. 3. Academic writing—Ability testing. 4. College prose—Evaluation.
I. White, Edward M. (Edward Michael), 1933– . II. Lutz, William. III. Kamusikiri,
Sandra, 1949– . IV. Series.
PE1404.A88   1996
808'.042'07—dc20   96-40971

ISSN 1079-2554

Set in New Aster. Printed on recycled paper

Published by The Modern Language Association of America
10 Astor Place, New York, New York 10003-6981

AJN 4039

Contents

Preface to the Series   ix

Introduction   1

PART I: Political and Legal Issues

Introduction   7

Power and Agenda Setting in Writing Assessment   9
   Edward M. White

Writing Assessment in Florida: A Reminiscence   25
   Gordon Brossell

Legal Issues in the Practice and Politics of
   Assessment in Writing   33
   William D. Lutz

Response: Why Do We Test Writing?   45
   John Trimbur

PART II: Validity and Reliability

Introduction   51

The Politics of Validity   53
   Maurice Scharton

Essay Reliability: Form and Meaning   76
   Doug Shale

Response: The Politics of Methodology   97
   Roberta Camp

PART III: Models of Writing Assessment: Old and New

Introduction   105

Essayist Literacy and Sociolinguistic Difference   108
   Marcia Farr and Gloria Nardini

Writing Assessment: Do It Better, Do It Less   120
  Peter Elbow

New Views of Measurement and New Models for
  Writing Assessment   135
  Roberta Camp

Upper-Division Assessment and the Postsecondary
  Development of Writing Abilities   148
  Stephen M. North

The Need for Clear Purposes and New Approaches to the
  Evaluation of Writing-across-the-Curriculum Programs 158
  Gail F. Hughes

Response: Testing as Surveillance   174
  Kurt Spellmeyer

PART IV: Issues of Inclusion and Equity

Introduction   185

African American English and Writing Assessment:
  An Afrocentric Approach   187
  Sandra Kamusikiri

Gender, Feminism, and Institution-Wide
  Assessment Programs   204
  Deborah H. Holdstein

The Challenges of Second-Language Writing Assessment 226
  Liz Hamp-Lyons

Response: Awareness of Diversity   241
  Marcia Farr

PART V: A Look to the Future

Introduction   247

Computer-Assisted Writing Assessment:
  The Politics of Science versus the Humanities   249
  Hunter M. Breland

The Pedagogical Implications of a
  College Placement Portfolio   257
  Donald A. Daiker, Jeff Sommers, and Gail Stygall

Portfolios in the Assessment of Writing:
  A Political Perspective   271
  Richard L. Larson

Portfolio Approaches to Assessment:
  Breakthrough or More of the Same?   284
Sandra Murphy and Barbara Grant

Response: Assessment as a Site of Contention   301
  Edward M. White

Works Cited   305

Index   333

Preface to the Series

The Research and Scholarship in Composition series, developed with the support of the Modern Language Association's Publications Committee, responds to the recent growth of interest in composition and to the remarkable number of publications now devoted to it. We intend the series to provide a carefully coordinated overview of the varied theoretical schools, educational philosophies, institutional groupings, classroom situations, and pedagogical practices that collectively constitute the major areas of inquiry in the field of composition studies.

Each volume combines theory, research, and practice in order to clarify issues, synthesize research and scholarship, and improve the quality of writing instruction. Further, each volume reviews the most significant issues in a particular area of composition research and instruction; reflects on ways research and teaching inform each other; views composition studies in the larger context of literary, literacy, and cultural studies; and draws conclusions from various scholarly perspectives about what has been done and what yet needs to be done in the field.

We hope this series will serve a wide audience of teachers, scholars, and students who are interested in the teaching of writing, research in composition, and the connections among composition, literature, and other areas of study. These volumes should act as a lively orientation to the field for students and nonspecialists and provide experienced teachers and scholars with useful overviews of research on important questions, with insightful reflections about teaching, and with thoughtful analyses about future developments in composition studies. Each book is a spirited conversation in which you are cordially invited to join.

Series Editors

Introduction

The essays in this collection address, in different ways, the central issues of the politics, policies, and practices of writing assessment in postsecondary education. In this volume *assessment* does not mean simply testing, which is a much narrower activity. Leo Ruth and Sandra Murphy offer a good working definition of *assessment*:

> An *assessment* may occur formally or informally whenever one person seeks and interprets information about another person. An "assessment of writing" occurs when a teacher, evaluator, or researcher obtains information about a student's abilities in writing. This information may be gathered in classrooms through observations, class assignments, or formal tests. Assessment information may be gathered without tests or without any kind of measurement that implies fixed standards. Assessment procedures do not require the comparison and ranking of students, or the attaching of a letter or number score to the performance. Assessments can be descriptive without being evaluative. In everyday usage, however, the two terms—assessment and evaluation—tend to be synonymous.   (6)

The term *assessment* as used in the essays here includes the idea of evaluation, the use of assessment information to judge or appraise the knowledge or skills of those who are the subject of the assessment.

The politics of writing assessment is a central concern of all the essays in this volume because assessment is unavoidably a political act. All authoritative decisions that affect the lives and conduct of individuals and groups, such as the decisions made in writing assessment, are political. John Trimbur provides in his essay a working definition of politics that applies to the other essays in this volume: politics "[foregrounds] conflicts of interest, asymmetrical relations of power, hidden motives, and unforeseen consequences." That is, assessment helps determine what programs are approved and offered, who receives opportunity, who gains power and privilege, and who is successful. Assessment asserts a specific concept of what kinds of writing are acceptable and what kinds are not. Assessment expresses a hierarchy of values, and those who control assessment determine the values that prevail. Assessment results identify those who most fully internalize

1

and support the prevailing values and who thus are most entitled to the best rewards. Such is the nature of assessing writing: whether its purpose is formative or summative, whether it decides placement or measures achievement, or whether it is carried out in the classroom or statewide—it is political.

The essays in this volume are concerned also with the policies, the guiding principles, that instigate writing assessment, determine the form and conduct of assessment, and control the interpretation and use of the results of assessment in postsecondary education. In this sense policy is, of course, closely connected to politics, so much so that it is sometimes difficult to separate the two. As far as it is possible to distinguish politics and policy, these essays discuss the policies that determine who or what—student, teacher, institution—participates in any writing assessment and what its conditions and purposes are. Crucial, too, is the issue of who determines the policies that control any writing assessment and who defines the uses to which the results of the assessment are put.

The authors in this volume are concerned also with writing assessment as practice, as an activity that produces information that is used to evaluate, among other things, the writing skills of students. They are concerned too with writing assessment as an instrument and result of broader postsecondary educational policy. The politics and policies of writing assessment are intimately entwined, and its practice is joined to them. Indeed, practice is informed by and necessarily flows from politics and policy. The practice of writing assessment—our means, how we go about assessing writing—cannot exist apart from the politics and policies that are the driving force of any assessment.

It is perhaps the next logical step in the growth of writing assessment as a field that we should question the implications of what we do. By so doing we come to ground assessment practices more accurately in what we know about writing, about the teaching of writing, and about the contextual nature of learners and their environments. The twenty-two essays in this volume, including responses, advance writing assessment theory in this direction by exploring the outgrowth of those issues—policy.

The authors come from a variety of disciplines—English, education, law, sociolinguistics, program evaluation, institutional research, and statistics—and are based at two-year and four-year colleges, as well as in professional testing services. In examining the politics, policies, and practices of writing assessment in postsecondary education and the effects of such assessment on students, faculty members, the teaching of writing, the curriculum, and institutions at large, the authors pose complex questions. For example, since political decisions are grounded in the decision maker's worldview, what are some of the underlying values, ideologies, and assumptions that we who assess writing hold, and in what ways are they embedded in our policies? Do our assessment policies exist to defend, if only unconsciously, the status quo of American academic life? What kind of writing do we expect of our students, and why do we expect it? Does writing assessment favor certain economic, social, and political arrangements of discourse? What assumptions about the test taker do we make when we assess writing, and do our current methods privilege a particular social and cultural mindset? Finally, what does the future hold for writing assessment? What are the views of those in the assessment community about the changes that are needed and the proper tactics to achieve those changes? While exploring these questions, the authors in this volume present a range of perspectives, methodologies, approaches, and solutions.

As the editors of the book, we strove to create a volume the whole of which functions as a colloquy. Although we grouped the essays into sections, we did not allow these groupings to restrict the authors' discussions. Therefore, all the authors in the volume address the global issues of politics and policy. Similarly, each explores issues of race, class, and gender and suggests the future direction of writing assessment. The dialogic quality of the book is enhanced further by the inclusion of a response that comments specifically on the essays in each section.

We have divided the book into five parts focused on (1) political and legal issues, (2) validity and reliability, (3) old and new models of writing assessment, (4) issues of inclusion and equity, and (5) writing assessment in the future. Part 1 defines the issues and provides the background for the central focus of the book by analyzing the theoretical, practical, and legal context for the politics, policies, and practices of writing assessment. The two fundamental but often omitted issues considered in part 2 are included to challenge the belief held by some professionals that there are certain absolute standards transcending politics and that to discuss the politics of writing assessment is to surrender or compromise those standards. The essays in this section discuss in detail the significant political implications of topics usually considered the domain of the mathematician and thus beyond politics. In part 3, authors who have designed and administered assessment programs describe models of writing assessment in detail. The descriptions highlight the political assumptions and consequences of each program, as well as the basis of its policies and practices. The contributors to part 4 address race and gender, pointing out that writing assessment involves serious and complicated implications for women and minorities, two groups that are traditionally disadvantaged by assessment. Finally, part 5 investigates some of the directions in which writing assessment is advancing and needs to advance. Again, the essays in this part focus on the political issues involved in any direction in which writing assessment might move, pointing out the ramifications for policy and practice of each development.

Writing assessment does not exist in its own sphere, as a simple instrument of educational or public policy, but rather is an integral part of the field of composition. We cannot assess writing until we know what we mean by writing, what it is we are trying to assess. Likewise, we must have some notion of what constitutes acceptable writing for the purpose of our assessment. In sum, any form of or procedure for writing assessment must be based on a sound knowledge of the writing process, of the theory of composition, and of the function of rhetoric in composition. Thus, this collection builds on the discussion of composition studies, writing, and rhetoric that was begun in such volumes as *Perspectives on Research and Scholarship in Composition* (McClelland and Donovan), *Into the Field: Sites of Composition Studies* (Gere), *Contending with Words: Composition and Rhetoric in a Postmodern Age* (Harkin and Schilb), and *Writing Theory and Critical Theory* (Clifford and Schilb).

Politics focuses on the making of vital decisions that affect the lives and conduct of individuals and groups in a sphere of human relations. Most students and teachers imagine that writing assessment in the classroom is free of ideology and linguistically objective and that student writing is measured against the rhetorical and mechanical norms of Standard American English—norms that are politically neutral. Such objectivity is a pretense. Writing assessment is inherently and inevitably political, not just in its trappings of essay topics and classroom methods but also in its vitals of grammar and rhetoric, in the very concept of what constitutes acceptable writing. The essays in this volume highlight some of the political issues in writing assessment, the impact these issues have on the policies surrounding assessment, and the current practices in the field. We believe that the essays will be useful and informative for researchers, teachers, and graduate students—specialists and nonspecialists—involved in the teaching of writing, in the administration of composition programs, and in composition research, as well as for all those engaged in the assessment of writing.

Edward M. White
William D. Lutz
Sandra Kamusikiri

PART I

Political and
Legal Issues

Introduction

The essays in this section explore the political and legal ramifications of writing assessment. In "Power and Agenda Setting in Writing Assessment," Edward M. White examines the conflicts that can occur when members of discourse communities with different values and interests collaborate in the assessment of writing. Because disciplinary and professional divisions, with their distinct political concerns, are a matter not merely of vocabulary or perspective, White argues, but of worldview, they form distinct ways of seeing that divide us from each other and make communication difficult. These differences in turn affect the types of assessment policies and practices we prefer and the ways in which we would like to see writing assessment implemented and interpreted. White suggests that we become familiar with the discourse communities within our discipline and without, to overcome the limitations of perception we all experience.

Gordon Brossell's "Writing Assessment in Florida: A Reminiscence" is a case study of the discord among participants in a large-scale writing assessment who did not share the same language or worldview. Reporting on the accountability movement in Florida education and its effect on teachers, the teaching of writing, and students, particularly nonmainstream students, Brossell contends that the lack of operational consistency in the state-controlled writing-competency tests is due, in a large measure, to a failure to take into account the paradigm shift in writing pedagogy. Brossell suggests that Florida's "idiosyncratic efforts in the testing of writing skills" can be improved by a reconciliation of assessment practice and current writing theory.

In "Legal Issues in the Practice and Politics of Assessment in Writing," William D. Lutz analyzes the present and potential legal issues in writing assessment policy, discussing relevant recent court cases. Of particular legal concern is the relation of assessment practices to the rights of minority students. Lutz discusses the procedures that testing programs should follow to comply with key legal rulings.

John Trimbur's response argues that by focusing on political issues, these essays "foreground conflicts of interest, asymmetrical relations of power, hidden motives, and unforeseen consequences. From this perspective, political analysis should be able to help us read between the lines, so we see what's really going on in writing assessment." The effort to see behind assessment leads to social and historical concerns: "What are the politics that authorize the assessment of writing?" Trimbur's answer speaks to the persistent "literacy crisis" in the United States, which he connects to social anxieties. These anxieties are displaced into a preoccupation with testing literacy: "The ideological work assigned to literacy has supercharged writing instruction and led to the desire to measure it."

Each of these essays is keenly aware that assessment, whatever its intention, is an exercise of power and that the teaching of writing as well as its assessment is necessarily political. But the different conceptions of the political that emerge in this section point to the extreme complexity of the politics of writing assessment.

Power and Agenda Setting in Writing Assessment

Edward M. White

As we move into a new century, the issues and problems in writing assessment have shifted and become more complicated. Or perhaps it would be more accurate to say that the complicated issues and problems behind writing assessment have finally become evident, after a century in which they were concealed by special interests and technical problems. Teachers' concern for assessment that reflects their teaching has often hidden an unwillingness to risk any assessment at all; testing firms' devotion to multiple-choice tests has in part protected investments in expensive instruments; reliability coefficients and faith in the "true score" have concealed the naive positivism inherent in the use of statistics to discover reality. As Anne Gere points out, the first English placement test, at Harvard in 1874, served to define university writing instruction as an administrative nuisance rather than as a college field of study ("Empirical Research"); and, as James Berlin argues, that test also served to protect the social status of the university (*Rhetoric*).

By calling for essay testing and more recently for portfolio assessment, teachers have hoped to gain power over assessment and hence over the definition of what is to be valued in education; they have attempted to impose the educational vision in which assessment is a vital support for the learner onto the institutional vision in which assessment is a sorting and certifying device. This was a bold power grab indeed, far more subversive to institutional purposes and structures than was collective bargaining over salaries or faculty control over the curriculum. For assessment defines goals and expresses values more clearly than do any number of mission statements. When our students ask us whether a class topic will be on the test, they express the same view: if you really value it, you will assess it. The converse is also true: what you assess *is* what you value, whatever you assert. A transfer of real power over institutional goals, values, and priorities from those who now wield it to teachers would seem to many, as a California State University trustee put it in a frank moment, like letting the inmates run the asylum. We should not be surprised to see teachers' drive for power frustrated.

9

I do not mean to suggest wickedness by proposing that attitudes of self-interest lie behind the varying approaches to writing assessment issues that have emerged over the last century. Self-interest is an inevitable and proper result of having a profession, belonging to a language community, and seeing the world a particular way. We need to recognize the differences self-interest creates, and our own situatedness, if we are to come to terms with perspectives other than our own—as we must, since no single group is likely to set the agenda for assessment by itself. Whatever our perspective, it determines how we define the issues and problems in our field. And we tend to see others' limitations and self-interest more clearly than we do ours; the view from our vantage point seems simple common sense to us and to those standing in the same place. Thus writing teachers take it for granted that writing must appear in any writing assessment, while those immersed in the business of testing assume that test items must be scored by computer if they are to yield reliable information.

Furthermore, each group sees itself not as one among a variety of interested parties but as the sole guardian of truth. Commercial and "nonprofit" test administrators are prone to scoff at teachers' preferences for direct writing measures, while many teachers see statistical issues like reliability as mere technicalities that even interfere with useful measurement (e.g., Elbow, Foreword). Teachers become furious or frustrated when an assessment takes away their teaching time for what they see as useless bureaucratic purposes, while those conducting the assessment may see the teachers' opposition to it as self-serving and destructive. We need to move beyond such attitudes to recognize the appropriateness and value of views other than our own, and we should recognize that conflicts must be mediated for new agendas to be defined. Until we come to understand the play of political forces and the need for conversations among those representing them, the dialectic will remain constricted.

Certainly, the key political and policy problem in writing assessment is beyond specific issues, problems, or technical concerns: which group or groups will accumulate the power to define the issues and problems of writing assessment, to set the agendas for research and the paradigms for practice? The diverse and often conflicting stakeholders differ in not only their perspectives on assessment but also their definitions of the purposes of writing. For example:

○ Writing teachers concerned about individual student growth and the writing process as a means of discovery are at odds with state and local governing bodies interested in reducing costs and identifying minimally proficient individuals and the programs that produce them.

- The conservative tendencies of the commercial and nonprofit testing firms conflict with the innovative tendencies of theorists.
- The needs of researchers for precise measurement tools contradict the experience of generations of creative writers, which suggests that writing is more an elusive art than a measurable skill.
- The practical demands for reliable scores, cumulative data, and short turnaround time put enormous pressure on the more theoretical requirements for validity, particularly those for a sufficiently complex definition of the construct "writing" and for attention to the consequences of assessment on the teaching of writing.

I propose here to set out the assumptions, perspectives, and demands of several of the principal interest groups concerned with writing assessment: teachers; researchers and theorists; testing firms and governing bodies; and students, especially those from minorities and other marginalized groups. I hope this book can begin to promote a respectful conversation among them and thus foster orderly progress in writing assessment, which over the last several decades has reflected political power struggles and educational faddism as much as it has the findings of research.

What Do Writing Teachers Want from Writing Assessment?

I begin with the interest group that has been most vocal over the last two decades—and to which I happen to belong—the teachers of writing in American schools and colleges. Their concern is understandable, for writing assessment not only sets out to measure the effectiveness of their work but defines to a considerable extent the content of their work; teachers speak disparagingly of "teaching to the test," but in fact they have no choice but to do so. Teachers feel the power of assessment all the more keenly because they often have little influence over assessment criteria, instruments, or scoring. Many teachers are aware that composition theory has been developing at a rapid pace recently and that writing assessment has not kept up; they also tend to see themselves as powerless, overworked, and underappreciated by their institutions and society at large. Add to this emotional mix a general ignorance of statistical thinking, particularly among those in higher education, and it is no wonder that writing teachers have emerged as the most threatened as well as the most articulate opponents of most writing assessment (see, e.g., Elbow, Foreword; Mahala and Vivion).

Writing teachers usually experience writing tests as irrelevancies imposed from outside the classroom by administrators, researchers, textbooks, or test personnel unfamiliar with the teaching situation. The widespread use of indirect measures such as multiple-choice mechanics and usage testing is a particular irritant, since it drives the curriculum in the schools away from writing by emphasizing the editing of test prose, undermines the theoretical basis for English teaching, and reinforces social bias from earliest schooling through many university programs (White and Thomas). Even though scores on these tests tell little about mastery of the curriculum, the test results are routinely used to attack the schools or to suggest that the students, the teachers, or both are incompetent.

Teachers generally experience two purposes for assessment: evaluation as an administrative sorting device, to make institutions more efficient, more accountable, and more objective; and evaluation as a personalized teaching device, to help students learn more effectively. Not all evaluation devices fall neatly into these categories, of course, and some of the most useful can work at both the institutional and the personal levels. For instance, most colleges and universities have developed a first-year writing curriculum that provides instruction starting at several different levels and thus requires a means of placing students into the course that is most appropriate for them. A good placement test is institutionally efficient, since it arranges students in convenient teaching groups, and is also valuable for teachers, since—when the test is driven by the curriculum—it gives them relatively homogeneous groups to work with.[1] But most of the testing devices that bother writing teachers have strict institutional purposes and only negative effects on students: proficiency tests designed to identify failures, admissions tests to screen out the unworthy, "value-added" tests to convince legislators that students have accumulated information, and the like. Such tests seem to teachers to have little to do with the curriculum, their students, or their goals as teachers of writing, though other interest groups find the tests of value. When teachers are forced—as they often are—to choose between teaching to an inappropriate institutional test and helping their students learn how to write, they are bound to consider evaluation an intrusion into the classroom.

But writing teachers also experience considerable internal conflict

because they probably do more evaluation of student work than anyone else on the faculty. At the same time that they condemn assessment, they know that some sort of evaluation is crucial for learning
("How'm I doing?"), and most teachers of writing spend many hours a
week assessing work in an attempt to help students write better.
Clearly, despite their usual dislike of tests and grading, writing teachers
need and use assessment to do their jobs. Some kinds of evaluation are
more valuable—and less offensive—to them than others. Teachers are
perfectly ready to adopt assessment—perhaps even too ready—when
they are convinced that it will enhance student writing and support
their teaching. Most writing teachers have a relatively uncritical faith
in their own assessments of student work, on which they spend inordi-
nate amounts of time.[2] It is not unusual for writing teachers to spend
the greater part of their evenings and weekends grading papers and
writing comments on them in the hope that an individual personal response will lead a student to revision or, more likely, to better work on
the next paper.

Many writing teachers resent as well as honor this time-consuming
and onerous responsibility, for which they receive no additional compensation, and express an undifferentiated anger about it in their metaphors, speaking, for example, of "bleeding all over a set of themes."
The grading of papers is a potent aspect of what Stephen North calls
teachers' "lore," the way things are done by the profession. This lore
has a power of its own, connected with professional identity as much
as with assessment: the red pen, the mystifying abbreviations (*k, fs*)
scrawled in the margins, the grade at the end, accompanied by avuncu-
lar advice and cautions—all define the writing teacher as much as they
describe the writing. Writing assessment that fails to recognize the
depth and meaning of this lore will have little effect on teacher practice. Although assessment research can make writing teachers more effective in the classroom and reduce their excessive workload, they are
rarely able to overcome their resistance to assessment and to use some
assessment concepts in their teaching.

Perhaps teachers' thorniest objection to assessment challenges the
very nature of the activity, at least in its psychometric form: its need to
simplify and sample phenomena in order to measure them. If there is a
common bond among writing teachers at all levels, it is their sense that
writing and its pedagogy are exceedingly complex, that ever-shifting individual and group contexts govern effective communication. What
works in one class fails in another; a student turns out fine work today
and abysmal stuff tomorrow; a piece of writing strikes me as wonderful

and you as ordinary. And yet it is of the essence of traditional assessment to sample a universe, to reduce variety to measurable units, to present meaningful comparative data. Anyone seeking the support of writing teachers for assessment must deal with this resistance to simplification and reductionism.

What kind of writing assessment, then, do teachers want?

○ Assessment that supports their work or at least does not deny its importance
○ Assessment that recognizes the complexity of writing and of the teaching of writing
○ Assessment that respects them as professionals and their students as individuals
○ Assessment that will not be misused to provide simple, damaging, and misleading information

If writing teachers controlled assessment practice, the ideal assessment would likely be an expanded version of classroom assessment—such as we see now in portfolios. Such an assessment would be performative and direct, include many kinds of writing, resist numerical reduction, be time-consuming and expensive, and incorporate such matters as revision, creativity, and discovery as part of the construct evaluated. Teachers would participate heavily in the scoring of the assessments and give student writers individual responses, which would reflect the current curriculum and its underlying writing theory. Although teacher-driven assessment design would provide immediate useful feedback to students and qualitative information, it would not likely produce the kind of data that most other interest groups value.

The issues and problems emerging from such a design would focus on pedagogical implications like these:

○ How can large-scale assessments be consistent with teachers' judgments of individual students?
○ How can students and teachers receive useful and constructive feedback from assessment?
○ How can assessments support collegial work among faculty members and supportive relations between teachers and students?
○ How can assessments provide or give the appearance of providing the data sought by other interest groups without becoming reductive or interfering with teaching and learning?
○ How can teachers control writing assessment so that it is not used for purposes contrary to their interests?

However much sympathy I have for this perspective, I do not think the nation can or will allow writing teachers to set the entire agenda for writing assessment—any more than it will allow physicians to determine health-care policy. Teachers' predominant concern for teaching and learning excludes too many financial and outcomes issues, and the influence of current educational theories and patterns inhibits innovation. The teacher's perspective is important, but it is one among many, and it omits too many matters of urgent importance to other interest groups.

What Do Researchers and Theorists Want from Writing Assessment?

I group researchers and theorists here not because they have identical interests but because both groups necessarily oppose the view of assessment I have just described. They are united by discomfort with current practice and are accustomed to asking questions that make teachers uneasy, particularly questions about what goes on in classrooms. Any assessment model that accepts, reflects, and rewards current practice seems inadequate to those seeking to interrogate that practice from a different perspective—an intention that unavoidably leads to conflict with teachers, who distrust assessments that do not reflect the teaching and learning going on in their classrooms.

Although most researchers and theorists also happen to be teachers, they tend to be university scholars with primary commitments to their fields of study rather than to their students. They are thus ready to notice, as most teachers are not, the usual failings of classroom assessments: for example, unclear assignments, inconsistent responses to student writing, arbitrary grading, formulaic comments, and hostility to weaker students. They also notice theoretical inconsistencies in grading (such as teachers' demands for careful editing of material to be revised or even deleted in later drafts) and in dominant concepts of measurement (such as the "true score" [White, *Teaching* (2nd ed.) 142–44]). The positivism behind most measurement theory, the belief that a skill construct or a student text is fixed and can be observed and measured, is an assumption much under attack in writing theory, just as positivism is under attack in many fields, from literature to physics to assessment itself (see Guba and Lincoln).

Most traditional research in writing or assessment depends on some kind of measurement device that can deliver reliable data. Although not all such research is empirical, much of it is, and the quest for accurate and objective measurement has consumed much energy during this century. As Anne Gere demonstrates, the research tradition in writing has been empirical for a century; almost all assessment research has been based on statistical manipulation of experimental data. This quest for reliable measurement has led to much multiple-choice testing and to other quantitative measures, such as Kellogg Hunt's "T-Units," for measuring syntactic complexity, or trait scales based on Francis Christensen's theories of levels of abstraction in paragraph development (White and Polin). The history of social science research paradigms, particularly those derived from educational psychology, weighs heavily on writing research. In a recent overview, Michael Williamson speaks perhaps too hopefully of writing assessment's "tearing itself loose from the theoretical foundations of psychometric theory and establishing itself with a foundation based in a theory of writing" (38).

Even when research that does not depend on the evaluation of data, such as a clinical or ethnographic study, comes up with findings that may be generally applicable, the findings are usually subjected to experimental and statistical tests from empirical methodologies designed to demonstrate—or undermine—claims of generalizability. If an ethnographic study was to argue that, say, certain kinds of classroom arrangements help create a writing community, the question of whether students write better because of the arrangement would be bound to arise. As soon as we seek to document that some writings are better than others, we must look for reliable measurement.

While not usually as concerned with measurement as are researchers, theorists too have interests that are antithetical to the teachers' agenda. A historically oriented theorist like Robert Connors, for instance, takes issue with teacher practice based on lore rather than on sound theory; his essay "The Rise and Fall of the Modes of Discourse" disputes one of the most common curricular designs. But the most pressing concerns of theorists have to do with the grounds of assessment in textuality. The working assumption of most writing assessment —and reading assessment, for that matter—is that a text's meaning resides wholly in the text; but almost all reading and writing theory contests that assumption, maintaining that the meaning lies in some kind of negotiation between the reader and the text. Some theorists place the meaning entirely in the minds of the readers (Holland). Since the reader (teacher, essay scorer, portfolio reader) is situated somewhere—in time, a gender, a class, a race, a dialect, and so on—writing assessment is context-bound and not open to generalizations supported by statistical manipulation. Teachers grading papers are at least in part (and perhaps only) grading their own reading; the multiple-choice test with its supposed correct answers simply privileges some possible readings (those of the test developers) over others. While theorists disagree on many of these matters, of course, on one point agreement is total: the least we should expect is that our assessment theory be consistent with our theories of reading, writing, and pedagogy.

What kind of writing assessment, then, do researchers and theorists want?

- Assessment that supports the gathering of reliable data
- Assessment that recognizes the complexity of writing and of the teaching of writing but that allows focus on particular subskills or processes
- Assessment that does not privilege existing practice but that explores a variety of potential practices
- Assessment that leads to the production of new knowledge and theories

If researchers and theorists were to control and define assessment practice, the ideal assessment would likely consist of a wide variety of specialized instruments, some of them indirect, meant to generate the most reliable data. An example of such a design appears in a 1991 article in *Research in the Teaching of English* with the nicely typical title "Conceptualizing and Measuring Knowledge Change Due to Writing" (Schumacher and Nash). The researchers interrogate the familiar argument for writing-across-the-curriculum programs—that students will know more about a subject if they write about it. What, the researchers ask, does the word *know* mean in such a context, and what kinds of tests can ascertain whether knowing has occurred? After defining with narrow precision the kinds of knowledge involved (drawing on theories of knowledge change), the authors propose specific tests—which do not involve writing—on such matters as "ordered trees from recall," "multi-dimension scaling," and "hierarchical clustering analysis." In general, researcher assessments would likely be indirect, include many kinds of writing subskills, allow numerical reduction, be time-consuming and expensive, and focus on outcomes as a major part of the construct evaluated. Teachers would not participate in the scoring of researcher assessments, since as interested parties they would be presumed less reliable than disinterested researchers. Students would not receive individual responses to their writing, since group findings would be the main concern. Although researcher-driven assessment design would produce data to support a certain kind of research and theorizing, it would not provide useful feedback to students or to writing programs, and the data would be too complex and specialized for institutional or governmental use.

The issues and problems emerging from an assessment paradigm reflecting theorists and researchers would focus on questions like these:

- How can writing assessments accurately measure particular, isolated subskills?
- What kinds of assessment can yield the most accurate information at the least cost in time and money?
- How can assessments reflect and measure the application of theories?
- How can assessments provide the data to test theories without becoming reductive or simplifying teaching and learning?
- How can researchers control writing assessment so that it is not misused for political purposes or unproven pedagogies?

While a tiny group compared to teachers, researchers and theorists have a powerful voice. However, creators of knowledge, as the atomic scientists in the Manhattan Project learned all too well, do not determine the use of their work. The research agenda will surely play itself out in funded projects and continue to make its influence felt. But its agenda is even less likely to dominate than that of teachers, since the practical demands made of writing assessment seem to be increasing in size and scope.

What Do Testing Firms and Governing Bodies Want from Writing Assessment?

The testing firms have a proprietary attitude toward assessment, rather like that of certain religions toward heaven: they think they are the only ones with the right to be there. But what outsiders see as arrogance, those on the inside take to be professionalism; if your livelihood and that of your many employees depend on timely delivery of reliable and valid scores, you had better get assessment right. The test firm's existence depends on producing tests on time, selling them to users, getting scores and data back to the user quickly, and standing behind the accuracy of the data produced. Let others worry about such peripheral concerns as teaching, abstract theorizing, or the making of knowledge. Sometimes the testing firms attempt to ensure proper use of test results—in one extraordinary instance, the Educational Testing Service (ETS) refused to provide National Teachers Examination scores to a state that intended to misuse the data—but usually the job is seen as finished once the data are produced and the customers are satisfied.[3] Even the nonprofit firms must attend to the bottom line more carefully than to any other concern, and, like businesses in general, they are unlikely to take risks or overspend on research and development.

Despite the conservative and professedly atheoretical nature of the testing business, it nonetheless has produced some of the most important innovations in writing assessment—perhaps as an inevitable byproduct of trying to please customers concerned about the implications of tests. Two important research studies undertaken by ETS demonstrated early the value of essay testing (Godshalk, Swineford, and Coffman; Diederich), and a more recent ETS study draws the same conclusion (Breland, Camp, Jones, Morris, and Rock). Roberta Camp conducted important work promoting portfolio assessment while employed at ETS in the 1980s, and in this volume her careful analysis of the problems of both multiple-choice and essay testing shows her theoretical grounding and independence of mind. Both holistic scoring of essays and large-scale use of portfolios began at ETS, whose strong domination of the commercial field continues to allow it to seek advances in testing practice.

Yet an eye to the future of testing practice is not the same as a genuine concern for theoretical soundness. The technological innovation called computer-adaptive testing (which uses computer programs to zero in on a candidate's ability level, thus abbreviating the number of items that must be answered) depends on the accumulated test items in the ETS item bank—a vault of treasures dating back many years, heavily weighted toward surface features of edited American English. Theories disputing the value of this Fort Knox of testing get short shrift at ETS; the items have shown they "work," and thus they will be used. Like phrenologists in former times (Gould), the testing firms rely on their ability to produce measurements that meet current needs, and theoretical niceties are expensive fringes only sometimes attended to. ETS is so prominent that it makes an easy target, but it is more responsible than most of its competitors in the business of testing, whose profit lines are even more tenuous and whose commitments to theory even slimmer.

The governing bodies that use the tests produced by ETS, the American College Testing Service (ACT), and dozens of other commercial or nonprofit testing firms want scores and are not particularly concerned about how the scores are obtained as long as the cost is not too high. These bodies want to know how many students failed a particular test and who should be blamed; or they want to know what steps might improve scores at no expense. One example of this cavalier attitude toward tests is the widespread use of the SAT (formerly the Scholastic Aptitude Test, now the Scholastic Assessment Tests, sponsored by the College Board and administered by ETS) as a writing placement test—an entirely improper use, not proposed by the tests' authors and for which the tests were not designed.

What kind of writing assessment, then, do testing firms want for the use of governing bodies?

- Assessment that produces scores quickly and cheaply
- Assessment that reduces the complexity of writing and of the teaching of writing but that allows the data collected to imply complex measurement
- Assessment that weighs heavily surface features of writing and dialect features of edited American English
- Assessment that leads to the sorting of students according to existing social patterns
- Assessment whose meaning depends heavily on statistical explanations, of sufficient complexity to invite misuse of scores

If testing firms and their institutional clients were to control and define assessment practice, the ideal assessment would likely consist of a series of multiple-choice tests, with occasional impromptu essays added (as they are now in several programs such as advanced placement) mainly as window dressing and a public-relations effort to please the teachers. (Many testing professionals are convinced that indirect measures are sufficient for accurate measurement, and test-scaling procedures in some programs even now minimize the contribution of direct measures to the student's total score.) The assessments would be passive and indirect, focus on surface scribal and dialectal features, allow numerical reduction, be efficient and cheap, and use correctness as a major part of the construct evaluated. Teachers would participate in the scoring of essay portions (which would count for little in the final scaled scores), and individual students would receive scores but no responses to their writing. Although testing firm–driven assessment design would produce data to support governmental and institutional policy, it would not provide useful feedback to students or to writing programs, and teachers would ignore it as irrelevant to their instructional aims.

The issues and problems emerging from such a design would focus on institutional problems like these:

○ How can writing assessments accurately measure particular, isolated subskills?

○ What kinds of assessment can yield the most useful information for policy makers at the least cost in time and money?

○ How can assessments reflect and measure the social and economic needs of society?

○ How can assessments provide data that maintain the current educational priorities and privileges?

○ How can professional testing firms control writing assessment so it is not turned into an expensive proving ground for untried theories or pedagogies?

Once again, it is obvious that enough forces are opposed to the power of the testing firms to keep them from setting the national agenda, despite their great influence with those running American institutions. But the firms' voice is ever present, reminding teachers, researchers, and theorists that the testing of writing is big business in America, with important links to economic and political conservatism.

What Do Students, Especially Those from Minorities and Other Marginalized Groups, Want from Writing Assessment?

Some years ago, a friend of mine assigned the topic "Why Write?" as the first paper for her remedial English class. She received one brief response that summed up the student perspective on writing assessment in a way I find unforgettable. "They make you write," the student put down in a struggling hand, "so they can *getcha!*" For this student, as for many others, writing assessment is a danger, an almost physical threat, and writing is so caught up in the assessment of it that the two blend into one anxiety-filled action. The demand most often uttered by students about assessment is that there be less of it. A secondary, almost plaintive, request is that the results of assessment help students learn rather than be used punitively and arbitrarily.

Various marginalized groups among students, including not only racial and ethnic minorities but also the middle-aged, women, and athletes, tend to see assessment as part of the oppressive apparatus that has traditionally worked to their detriment. Some of their spokespersons, unaware of the research showing that multiple-choice tests seem more racially biased than essay tests (White and Thomas; Mitchell and Anderson; Koenig and Mitchell), consider direct measures of writing as the particular agent of oppression, perhaps because of bad experiences with English teachers. A more sophisticated version of this argument asks those scoring writing samples to heighten their awareness of contexts and of the force of dialect (see Sandra Kamusikiri's essay in this volume).

What kind of writing assessment, then, do students want?

○ Assessment that stresses the social and situational context of the writer
○ Assessment designed to provide maximum and speedy feedback to the student
○ Assessment that breaks down the complexity of writing into focused units that can be learned in sequence and mastered by study
○ Assessment that produces data principally for the use of learners and teachers
○ Assessment that focuses on critical thinking and creativity and that places surface features of dialect and usage in a large social context

Something like the following issues would be of moment to this perspective:

○ How can writing assessment overturn the exclusive patterns of the past and open opportunity to the deserving in marginalized groups?
○ What kinds of writing assessment display the least bias toward the underprivileged or the oppressed?
○ How can writing assessment draw on and value the rich experiences of nontraditional students and still treat traditional students fairly?
○ How can those scoring writing assessments overcome the various biases inevitably part of their privileged positions?
○ How can assessment in context become part of learning and not be misused to exclude individuals or groups from educational opportunity?

Many of these issues have already become part of the national assessment agenda, but it is by no means clear that they will receive the attention required to resolve them. Indeed, this assessment design is so sharply at odds with that of other interest groups that conflicts are sure to develop. After the reduction in funds for education in recent years, an unspoken alliance seems to be developing between conservative governing bodies, who seek to limit educational costs by reducing enrollments and increasing fees, and relatively liberal faculties, who seek to maintain educational quality. This alliance seems likely to restrict access to higher education and to oppose—in the name of standards—assessment design that reflects the interest of students, especially those from marginalized groups.

The Needed Miracle: Restoring Hearing to the Dialogue of the Deaf

No easy solution to the conflict of interests that I have just sketched (and I have used only a few of many possible examples) is possible or desirable. Indeed, I have tried to point up the inevitability of the conflicts that often lie concealed beneath the surface of many debates on writing assessment. There is no possibility of convincing writing teachers to like multiple-choice tests, just as it is a waste of time to urge commercial testing firms to accommodate poststructuralist theories of reading. The stakeholders stand at wholly different positions and are bound to see writing assessment from where they stand. And with so much at stake, they cannot shift position without sacrificing what they are and do.

But we can recognize the importance of views other than our own, even if we feel them to be wrong on some counts. In fact, opposing interests frequently cooperate on campuses developing new writing assessment programs. If the teachers in charge of the assessment are wise, they immediately recruit a test officer or someone else who brings in the businesslike perspective of the testing firm. They cannot accept the multiple-choice test that this person finds most comfortable, but they need to design efficient and cost-effective ways to administer the assessment. In addition, every assessment program requires its own evaluation, a research project often assigned to a specialist. A test-development subcommittee deals with the most important theoretical concerns as it comes up with assessment goals and criteria before selecting an instrument. In short, an assessment program with wide concerns can be successful only if it incorporates varied perspectives.

In the same way, scholarship in writing assessment needs to set agendas through negotiation by interested parties. We should state overtly where we are coming from and why we select the issues we do, we should make our invisible agendas visible, and we should consider how those in different places might view our data, theories, or findings. Referees for journal articles should be chosen from different areas of study and centers of interest, and articles that ignore all perspectives but their own should state clearly why they do so or perhaps be sent back for revision.

Until now, however, those of us working in this field have been able to maintain our enclaves, even in our published scholarship. A glance at the works cited in our journal articles shows that we rarely go beyond the boundaries of the comfortable. The compartmentalization has been narrow indeed; sources cited in *Research in the Teaching of English* rarely appear at the ends of articles in *College Composition and Communication*—both official publications of the National Council of Teachers of English. The same polarization is comon in journals in education, psychology, and statistics.

But those boundaries must be crossed if the future of writing assessment lies, as I believe it does, in negotiating and compromising among the interest groups involved. Discussions about values in writing assessment concern the most complex act of our species. We ought never to expect the discussions to be a simple matter of persuading others or of conversing comfortably with those who think as we do.

California State University, San Bernardino

NOTES

[1]Even this apparently benign use of assessment has been arousing substantial opposition from some writing teachers, who argue that placement creates negative groupings and labels for which the usual weak instruction does not compensate (Elbow, "Writing Assessment"; Haswell).

[2]Teacher reliability in grading is probably not high (Diederich; Sommers, "Responding"), but students obviously value teachers' comments and appear to learn from them. See Lunsford and Straub for an analysis of patterns in teachers' responses.

[3]This unusual concern by a testing firm for the consequences of a test and of the scores the firm produces echoes a pervasive teacher interest as well. It further reflects an evolving notion of validity, sometimes called "consequential validity," advanced by such scholars as Messick ("Meaning") and Cronbach ("Perspectives").

Writing Assessment in Florida: A Reminiscence

Gordon Brossell

Retrospection

Sometime during the last half of the 1970s, Florida began to acquire a reputation as a national leader in testing. The reputation grew more from the state's sheer enthusiasm for testing than from the effectiveness, quality, or design of Florida's programs. Reacting to increasing public outcry over students' perceived command of basic skills, the state enacted laws requiring minimum-competency tests for elementary and secondary students (the State Student Assessment Test, or SSAT), one of which was a barrier test governing high school graduation; for college sophomores, in the form of the College-Level Academic Skills Test (CLAST), a check on basic reading, writing, and math abilities that controlled entrance to upper-division study; and for elementary and secondary school teachers seeking certification in Florida for the first time.

Politicians and public officials cheered this general movement toward accountability in Florida education. The commissioner of education hailed the "Functional Literacy Test," the part of the SSAT governing high school graduation, as the greatest advance in the history of public education in Florida. The testing programs, state leaders maintained, would help ensure that decent standards of academic competence would be upheld across the spectrum of Florida's schools and colleges.

State testing officials made decisions concerning the nature of particular assessments. In the case of writing assessment, both the CLAST and the Teacher Certification Examination were earmarked to contain holistically scored essays prompted by topics specially developed for, and field-tested on, writers from the groups to be tested. (As Florida State University faculty members, James Hoetker and I collaborated on a good deal of this developmental work and the research on which it was based. See, as examples, Brossell and Ash; Hoetker and Brossell,

25

"Effects.") The SSAT, in contrast, contained no compositional task of any sort. Students' knowledge of writing was measured by multiple-choice, objective tests of grammar and usage.

A curious division thus came to exist between the procedures for assessing the writing skills of postsecondary school students on the one hand and those used for precollegiate students on the other. State testing officials were not unaware of the inconsistency and even took action in the early 1980s to inaugurate a pilot program for a writing production test for elementary and secondary school students. But the effort had nothing of the urgency that marked early development, and the prototype test was inadequate, calling for no more than a sentence or two of composition. Except for an official review of this prototype, which the Florida Department of Education commissioned me to do in 1984, the issue lay dormant until the late 1980s, when the development of a composition test as part of the SSAT was finally undertaken. (It was instituted in 1993.) I remember hearing that cost was one of the factors that delayed the creation of such a test. But cost alone explains neither the lack of political will to make the test operationally consistent with the others nor the lack of protest from all but a few interested parties (myself included) about the continuation of the practice of assessing writing performance solely through indirect and, in fact, oblique methods.

Unfortunately, the act of writing remains a relatively uncompelling social issue. While most Americans would support the notion that students ought to acquire some decent measure of writing ability, most do not write enough to be motivated by so seemingly remote an issue as how student writing performance should be assessed. Furthermore, public concern over academic issues is typically spurred by aggressive media coverage. But except for periodic, routine reporting of test results, the media in Florida have not paid more than casual attention to state testing programs. As a result, most Floridians are unaware that writing tests can differ and that the differences are manifest in their own state. But even if they were aware, it is doubtful whether the issue would stimulate much interest: writing assessment is simply not important enough to get most people politically excited. The lack of any real public pressure to make Florida's writing tests operationally consistent helps explain how a state whose political leaders prided themselves on leaping to the forefront of the national accountability movement in the 1970s has taken so long to begin preparing a writing assessment that requires elementary and secondary school students to produce a piece of writing.

Disjunction

At the same time that Florida was accelerating its idiosyncratic efforts in the testing of writing skills, the teaching profession was being swept up in a wave of new theories of written discourse, based largely on models of the processes writers use in creating texts and on analyses of the rhetorical and cognitive demands associated with such processes. Research in written composition exploded after 1970 and helped shift the dominant paradigm of writing instruction significantly. College and university writing programs became the focal point for the changes wrought by the process model, changes so swift and determinative that they constituted a virtual revolution in the conception and practice of writing pedagogy in America. In place of the assign-compose-correct syndrome that dominated most classrooms previously, students were asked to engage in the transactive processes of the new pedagogy: pre- and free-writing for discovery; drafting for differing rhetorical purposes; sharing and conferring about drafts with teachers and peers; revising in the light of personal response; and editing for power and expressiveness as well as for the elimination of error.

In a handful of states around the country (New York and Wisconsin are two examples), testing officials took notice of the paradigm shift and responded by incorporating process assumptions and strategies into their writing tests. Most states, including Florida, did not and have not. Conceptually, the effect in Florida has been to segregate writing assessment from writing pedagogy.

This disjunction will not startle anyone familiar with the making of education policy. State legislators are woefully uninformed, by and large, about the theoretical and research bases of academic matters like writing assessment and writing pedagogy. And having more-politically-charged issues to contend with—taxes and funding, school prayer, voucher systems and school choice—they are not usually motivated to explore a problem that goes largely unrecognized outside the English-teaching profession. Besides, there are other inconsistencies in Florida policy (for example, it requires minimum SAT or ACT scores, predictors of freshman-year performance only, for admission to teacher-education programs that begin in the junior year), and they appear to bother only a handful of cantankerous professors.

Teachers who recognize the unwholesome split between pedagogy and assessment find it politically difficult and professionally risky to do much about it. State-sponsored testing has the power of law and strangles school practice by placing test results ahead of responsible teaching. So most teachers who care console themselves with the thought that while they may not be providing the best writing experiences in the classroom, they are at least helping their students to jump an academic hurdle.

Nonetheless, the effect on students is pernicious. The CLAST program involves all college sophomores, whether they attend one of the ten four-year state universities or the twenty-eight two-year community colleges. Students in the state university system meet higher admission standards than students in the community colleges and as a group get higher average scores on the CLAST. Community college students, many of whom aspire to upper-division work at state universities, are thus at greater risk as test takers than their university counterparts. (Recall that all students must pass the CLAST to advance to junior standing.) Community college writing teachers are constantly aware of the importance of the CLAST to their students' academic futures. So they take to doing what the assessment system in its current configuration inevitably encourages: they prepare their students by assigning, continually and as part of regular classroom work, the kind of writing required by the CLAST—fifty-minute extemporaneous essays on topics resembling those on the exam or even previously used on it.

It is my impression from having talked and listened to countless students and writing instructors, from having worked on numerous topic-development projects, and from having close contact with the administrators of the CLAST that across the state, in community college after community college, teaching to the test has become the accepted norm in composition classes. The unfortunate result is that for many students the concept of writing ability has become synonymous with skill in impromptu theme writing on predetermined topics, a condition that mocks our best professional theory and practice.

Politics

Testing inevitably influences teaching to some extent, especially in situations where success on tests is prerequisite to academic promotion or program completion. Florida's CLAST, however, provides an ironic twist on the politics of writing assessment. It represents a brilliant example of what state-controlled writing-testing programs in American colleges are threatening to become: a watchdog industry in the service of public relations.

Testing programs like the CLAST are, after all, established and run by elected officials and their appointees, who are accountable to the voting, tax-paying public. It is therefore important that citizens have the right impression of the educational system they support, and a good deal of state effort goes into seeing that they do. Just as Florida's agriculture and tourism industries tout oranges and vacations, Florida's government touts public education. If students are passing state tests in large numbers, they must be learning something in school. And if schools are demonstrably successful in teaching students, citizens are more likely to feel that they are getting a decent bang for their tax bucks and less likely to hassle their state legislators. This is not political cynicism; it's political reality.

The passing rate for the CLAST essay exam is consistently around 95%, for a testing population that numbers in the thousands every year. Students who fail the test may take it over until they pass. The standards that govern the test's holistic scoring system are not especially rigorous, though they have been carefully monitored and amended to give the appearance of becoming more stringent. In the early 1980s, the minimum passing score for a CLAST essay was raised from 5 to 6 points, but the scoring-scale range was concurrently increased from 1–4 to 1–6. An essay's final score is the sum of two evaluators' ratings. Thus virtually any essay would receive a higher final score on the new scale than on the old. The passing standard is, in effect, no different.

Should there be further raising of CLAST standards, real or apocryphal, Florida taxpayers will no doubt greet the news with approval and applaud the state's determination to improve the writing performance of its college sophomores. But in all likelihood the game will not really change: any increase in the passing score will be enacted only when testing officials determine that it will not appreciably affect the percentage of students failing the exam. Then as test writers and test readers adjust to the new, higher standards, certification of student writing competence will continue at a high level.

But what if estimates prove wrong and more students begin to fail the test? One answer would be to roll back the standard by tinkering with the scoring scale again, in effect admitting publicly to a decline in student writing skills and inviting criticism of college writing teachers, of the test, and of those responsible for it. Given the established pattern of changes in the standards, actual or apparent, such a step would be unfeasible and politically unwise.

A more effective response, politically speaking, is the one the state took in 1988 in asking Hoetker and me to create a system for providing diagnostic assistance to writers who fail the CLAST essay exam. The system we developed yields a profile of each failing essay in terms of the specific discourse features associated with the holistic scoring of

CLAST essays. The profiles are based on trained readers' "analytic judgment" of the discourse features and result in a series of statements intended to give writers a sense of their essays' deficiencies: "A central idea or intention is not detectable," "The thesis is inadequately developed," "Word use is seldom effective and is often uneconomical and inappropriate," and so on. On receiving such a report, writers would be encouraged to seek the assistance of local teachers and writing laboratories, which would use the analytic feedback in helping writers solve individual compositional problems and, of course, in getting them ready to retake the test.

This system—which resembles efforts in other states (West Virginia, Texas, and Illinois, for example) to provide diagnostic responses to student writers through analysis of their compositions—is ready to be put into operation. Its economic viability was confirmed in a successful field test and a separate feasibility study. The system received high praise from the readers who served in its field test (all veteran CLAST raters), some of whom intended to use it in their classes. But as of this writing, it has been officially put on hold, ostensibly because of tightened budgets. If, in the future, students begin to flunk the CLAST writing assessment in sufficient numbers to occasion concern, there is little doubt that money to implement the system will be found. Current and projected passing rates, however, make that development seem unlikely. As far as I am aware, no thought has been given to, and no funds have been allocated for, the remedial work that would necessarily follow from the diagnostic summaries of student essays—work that would invariably fall back in the hands of writing teachers.

Litigation

Florida's sensitivity to maintaining the good will of its citizenry with respect to the assessment of educational outcomes can be traced back to the beginnings of the state's efforts to certify the minimum competencies of its students. The Educational Accountability Act of 1976, which mandated passage of the SSAT as a requirement for a high school diploma, ushered in an era of legal challenge to the notion of state-controlled competency testing, an era whose distant thunder continues to rumble menacingly in the background.

In October of 1978, a year after the initial administration of the SSAT (including the so-called Functional Literacy Test) had resulted in a 36% failure rate (80%–90% among minorities), the first federal lawsuit attacking the use of minimum-competency tests was filed against

Florida's commissioner of education (*Debra P. v. Turlington*). The suit, a class action, was brought by ten African American high school students in the Tampa Bay area who had failed the test. It contended that the test, having a disproportional failure rate among black students, was racially biased and violated the equal-protection clause of the Fourteenth Amendment to the United States Constitution. It maintained further that students were given inadequate time to prepare for the test and that the test was not valid and was being used to resegregate Florida's public schools. The plaintiffs sought a permanent injunction to prevent the state from using test results as a prerequisite for high school graduation and as a means of assigning students to special remedial classes (M. McCarthy; Pinckney).

In July of 1979, the federal district court rendered a kind of split decision that called the state's competency-testing program into question while permitting the program to continue. Judge George C. Carr ruled that the test indeed violated the constitutional rights of black students and that their diplomas could not be withheld, but he tied the issue to the schools rather than to the test. His decision called for a four-year lapse in the implementation of test results as a graduation requirement, so that the schools could rid themselves of the last vestiges of racial segregation (Pinckney). The test itself the court found valid and not racially biased and upheld its use in the identification of students who were deficient in basic skills and thus of candidates for remedial classes. When the 1982–83 school year began, SSAT results were legally sanctioned as a means for withholding high school diplomas in schools that were officially free of racial segregation. That condition has continued to the present day.

At the time the *Debra P.* case was tried, it was clear that the SSAT produced lower scores among black and other minority students, but it was just as clear that competency-testing programs like the SSAT were fast becoming a national phenomenon. Most states had one or more in some stage of implementation or development. Judge Carr rendered his decision in full consideration of the inevitable clash between the increasing general acceptance of large-scale state testing and its undeniable effects on minority students. A decision favoring either side of the divisive issue would have set off a political firestorm of protest and ensured years of continued judicial wrangling with no chance of altering the political reality of the situation and the dilemma it produced. A decision verifying the merit of each side and mandating a lengthy period of adjustment—Carr's crafty solution to the dilemma—allowed all concerned to claim a measure of victory and directed attention to the future, encouraging a clear view of the test and its consequences.

It would take a considerable stretch of the imagination to conclude that Judge Carr honestly believed that Florida schools would become completely integrated in four years. Schools in Florida are essentially no better and no worse than others in their treatment of minority students. But increasingly reflecting the ills of an ever more racially and culturally diverse society, Florida schools are, and were in Carr's decision, a convenient and plausible surrogate for the cause of the dilemma of competency testing and minorities.

Since the decision took effect, large numbers of black and other minority students (80%–90%) have flunked the SSAT on the first attempt; many of those who remained in school and continued to retake the test, as the law allows, ultimately passed it and received their high school diplomas. Barbara Lerner, an education critic who testified before Judge Carr and who has defended minimum-competency testing in American schools, claims that better than 90% of minority students pass the SSAT by the fifth try. If this figure is true, it is also deceptive. The dropout rate in Florida high schools is among the nation's highest, something like 38% or 40%, and most dropouts are from minorities. So minority students who graduate are a greatly reduced percentage of those who enter high school. It is difficult to believe that the SSAT, with its legal sanction to withhold diplomas from low-achieving high school students, has no effect on the dropout rate.

University of Illinois, Chicago

Legal Issues in the Practice and Politics of Assessment in Writing

William D. Lutz

From 1977 to 1979, Rutgers University "loaned" me to the New Jersey Department of Higher Education to serve as the first executive director of the New Jersey Basic Skills Assessment Program. I left my position as director of the writing program and moved to a state-level position in which I was charged with designing and then administering placement tests in reading, writing, and mathematics for all first-year students entering all New Jersey public two-year and four-year colleges and universities. Since the assessment program was newly created, I began with a tabula rasa and an opportunity to design entirely new tests. I plunged into the world of testing with enthusiasm and naïveté, knowing nothing of the traps and challenges that were waiting.

I received my first lesson in conducting a large-scale assessment program when I was assigned an office in the corridors of power in the Department of Higher Education. Others in the complex quickly noted that my office was close to the office of the chancellor of higher education, a clear sign of the importance he attributed to the assessment program. This was an important message, and I was keenly aware of the political implications of my location.

I learned many political lessons during my two years in that office, but I think some of my most important lessons were legal ones. While my office was close to the chancellor's, it was even nearer to the office of the general counsel for the department. I was right next to the department's lawyer. I quickly learned to visit that office frequently.

No proposal, no program, no policy statement could go forward in the Department of Higher Education unless it was first reviewed by the department's lawyer. At first I found this procedure awkward and just a little intrusive on my professional judgment. After all, as a tenured faculty member and the director of the writing program at Rutgers University, Camden, I had pretty much done what I judged to be academically reasonable, necessary, and desirable. For some initiatives, such as instituting a placement testing program or proposing new writing courses, I had to seek the approval of my colleagues in the English department and of the faculty senate. However, I needed only academic approval. It had never occurred to me that the placement testing program I had designed for Rutgers, Camden, might need any kind of legal review, since I believed that academic policy belonged in the hands of the faculty, not of lawyers. My experience administering a statewide assessment program quickly changed my thinking about the need for legal review of assessment programs.

I learned much about the law of higher education during my two years administering the New Jersey assessment program. Indeed, I became fascinated with law, so fascinated that on my return to Rutgers I enrolled as a part-time student in law school and earned my juris doctor degree three and a half years later. In a few of my law courses, I explored the legal aspects of testing, and the more I studied the subject, the more I realized that few people involved in assessing writing have any idea of the legal implications of their actions or the legal liability they incur when they conduct an assessment program.

I do not have the space in this essay to explore in any detail or depth the full complexity of the legal responsibilities of a writing assessment program. The legal implications of an assessment program depend on who are affected by it and how it will affect them. However, I will outline briefly the major issues with which every person involved in assessing writing should be concerned. I will also suggest some guidelines that every writing assessment program should follow. They are based on a review of the most significant court decisions affecting testing. Finally, I will suggest what every writing assessment program should do to ensure that it meets its legal responsibilities. We live in a litigious age, and prudence suggests that writing assessment administrators take every reasonable care to see that they comply with all legal requirements.

Writing assessment programs may be divided into two kinds: those conducted within the institution and those conducted outside the institution. External testing programs, such as those conducted by a school district or a state agency, are governed by a series of court decisions and by any applicable state and federal law. Internal testing programs, such as course-placement and proficiency testing, come under fewer unambiguous legal constraints and exist at present in a kind of legal limbo. Nevertheless, there is enough legal precedent to warrant caution by anyone involved in an assessment program within an institution, whether the institution is public or private or two-year or four-year.

Judicial Restraint

I do not mean to suggest that courts, especially federal courts, are eager to review assessment programs. Quite the contrary. Courts have long exercised a strong, self-imposed restraint, holding to the view that courts are not the place to second-guess professional educators, at least in the public sector.

> Judicial interposition in the operation of the public school system of the Nation raises problems requiring care and strength. . . . By and large, public education in our Nation is committed to the control of state and local authorities. Courts do not and cannot intervene in the resolution of conflicts which arise in the daily operation of school systems and which do not directly and sharply indicate basic constitutional values.   (*Epperson v. Arkansas*)

On the other hand, students, teachers, and others do not give up their constitutional or statutory rights when they enter the educational environment, and courts will intervene when school authorities act arbitrarily, capriciously, beyond their authority or in violation of constitutional or statutory rights. (See, for example, *Board of Curators of the University of Missouri v. Horowitz,* in which the Supreme Court upheld the expulsion of a student from medical school but reaffirmed that courts will intervene if warranted, and *Fiacco v. Santee,* in which the court, finding that school authorities had acted arbitrarily, ordered the awarding of a diploma.) The same legal restraints hold true for private schools. "As a practical matter, the application of a legal remedy to the use of standardized tests in public education probably would carry over to private institutions as well" (Beckwith 799).

Recent decisions by federal courts indicate that courts will not hesitate to intervene in an assessment program if the basis for judicial action exists. In some instances, state law or constitutional provisions provide a basis for challenging an assessment program. More frequently, however, challenges to assessment have been founded on a combination of federal statutory and constitutional grounds. For example, the famous case of *Debra P. v. Turlington* was founded on the due-process and equal-protection clauses of the Fourteenth Amendment to the United States Constitution, on Title VI of the Civil Rights Act of 1964, and on the Equal Educational Opportunities Act of 1974. (In *Debra P.,* Florida high school seniors who were predominantly minorities challenged the state's minimum-competency test after being denied diplomas for failing it.) Similarly, *Larry P. v. Riles* was founded on section 504 of the Rehabilitation Act of 1973, the Education for All Handicapped Children Act of 1975, and Title VI of the Civil Rights Act of 1964. (In *Larry P.,* a minority student who was placed in a lower ability group because of a standardized IQ test challenged the test and its results.) Thus a number of court decisions provide ample grounds for challenging an assessment program.

There are three main bases on which a challenge to an assessment program can be founded: Title VI of the Civil Rights Act of 1964 and the equal-protection and due-process clauses of the Fourteenth Amendment to the United States Constitution. There are other grounds, but I will limit my discussion to these three areas because my review of the relevant cases indicates they are the most frequently used.

Title VI of the Civil Rights Act of 1964

Section 601 of Title VI of the Civil Rights Act of 1964 provides that "[n]o person in the United States shall, on the ground of race, color, or national origin, be excluded from participation in, be denied the benefits of, or be subjected to discrimination under any program or activity receiving Federal financial assistance." The statute also authorizes federal agencies to formulate appropriate regulations that make federal financial assistance contingent on the recipient's prohibiting discrimination. Since most colleges receive some form of federal aid and thereby come under Title VI regulations, a writing assessment program that affects minorities may well come under Title VI review.

The regulations of the Department of Health and Human Services declare that Title VI is violated by any practice or procedure that has a disproportionate racial impact (45 Code of Federal Regulations §80.3 (b)(2)), a regulation the United States Supreme Court upheld in *Lau v. Nichols*: "Discrimination is barred which has that effect even though no purposeful design is present" (568). Moreover, a 1975 memorandum written by the acting director of the Office for Civil Rights in the former Department of Health, Education and Welfare requires schools "to adopt and implement procedures to insure that test materials and other assessment devices used to identify, classify and place exceptional children are selected and administered in a manner which is non-discriminatory in its impact on children of any race, color, [or] national origin . . ." (qtd. in McClung 692). Thus, it can be argued that a writing assessment program, especially a proficiency assessment program, that has a disproportionate effect on minority students can be challenged in the light of Title

VI standards, "especially where there is evidence of racial bias in the test itself or in the administration of the test" (McClung 692).

It is important to note that a challenge brought under Title VI does not have to conform to the stricter standard for intent to discriminate that was enunciated by the Supreme Court in *Washington v. Davis*. In *Davis*, a challenge to an employment test was brought under the equal-protection clause of the Constitution. The court held that a racially discriminatory purpose was now essential to invoke Fourteenth Amendment protection and that a demonstration of racially disparate impact alone was no longer sufficient to establish a claim of racial segregation. Thus, plaintiffs must now establish a racially discriminatory purpose when invoking Fourteenth Amendment protection. However, the court stated that disproportionate racial impact could be evidence of a discriminatory purpose. As Justice John Paul Stevens noted in his concurring opinion, "Frequently the most probative evidence of intent will be objective evidence of what actually happened rather than evidence describing the subjective state of mind of the actor. For normally the actor is presumed to have intended the natural consequences of his deeds" (*Washington v. Davis* 253).

Davis and a number of other cases, such as *Griggs v. Duke Power Co.* and *Albernarle Paper Co. v. Moody*, have provided the method of analysis many courts now use in Title VI cases to determine the discriminatory impact, if any, of a test: (1) plaintiffs must establish a prima facie case of the test's discriminatory impact on minority students; (2) those administering the test must then show that the test is valid for the purposes for which it is used; and (3) plaintiffs then have the opportunity to show that there are alternative means that would serve the same legitimate interests as the test but without discriminatory effects. This analysis was essentially adopted by the court in *Debra P. v. Turlington*.

Thus assessment programs with disproportionate effects on minority students are subject to close judicial scrutiny. In an action brought under Title VI, those conducting the assessment have to provide evidence of legitimate educational objectives behind the assessment. They also have to demonstrate that the assessment has a high degree of educational usefulness and that there is no alternative program with less of an adverse impact on minority students.

Since American society produces minority students with disproportionate numbers of writing problems, virtually all writing assessment programs are subject to this challenge. Therefore, those in charge of an assessment program need "to avoid foreseeably discriminatory policy choices when it is educationally feasible to do so" (D. Lewis 170). Officials must offer educational justifications for any assessment program that adversely affects a disproportionate number of minority students. Discriminatory purpose is established if the assessment program does not further an educational goal such as increased proficiency or a designated competency or "if there exists no alternative means of ensuring attainment by students of those skills with less disparate impact on minority" students (Lewis 170). Test administrators should keep careful records of their efforts to identify and eliminate any bias in their tests, and they should document carefully the educational purposes of their tests.

Equal Protection

The Fourteenth Amendment to the Constitution states that "no State shall . . . deny to any person within its jurisdiction the equal protection of the laws." While state laws may for various purposes treat citizens differently by classification, persons who are similarly situated with respect to the purpose of a law must be treated equally by it (*Jenness v. Fortson*). Since tests classify individuals into groups, the equal-protection clause of the Constitution may be invoked if such classifications are not legitimate and are discriminatory.

Equal-protection analysis begins with two questions: (1) has the state acted with an unconstitutional purpose, and (2) has the state classified together all and only those persons who are similarly situated? Courts always begin such an analysis with a strong presumption of constitutionality if the method of classification is rationally related to a valid public purpose. However, when the basic interests of individuals are involved, officials must justify the classification and must demonstrate that the classification is necessary to achieve the state's purpose. "A classification 'must be reasonable, not arbitrary, and must rest upon some ground of difference having a fair and substantial relation to the object of the legislation, so that all persons similarly circumstanced shall be treated alike,' " stated the United States Supreme Court, quoting one of its earlier decisions (*Reed v. Reed*).

In *Armstead v. Starkville Municipal Separate School District*, the court found that the use made of the test scores bore no rational relation to the purpose for which the test was designed. Clearly, a test not designed to measure the qualities that the test users claim to be testing lacks the "fair and substantial relation" to the purpose of classification required by equal-protection analysis. Test validity becomes a crucial factor in this analysis, as does any evidence establishing how the test's validity was established.

A test might be also challenged as lacking the precision necessary to classify adequately those who take it. For example, students may challenge a writing test that determines whether they may advance beyond sophomore-level courses by arguing that (1) while testing may be a legitimate means of classification, this particular test is inadequate for measuring whether individual students are ready for or have the ability to do junior and higher-level work and (2) while the means used to classify students may be legitimate, these means are too imprecise to classify students correctly. These arguments are directed not at the state's methods of classification, nor do they assert that the plaintiffs have been included in the wrong class. Rather, these arguments are directed at the precision of the method of classification. They are directed at an imprecision that is inherent in the test. Thus, there can be no fair and substantial relation between students' ability and their test scores, a point that was argued effectively in *Davis v. Washington,* in which a written examination of verbal skills was used to select recruits for the Washington, DC, police department.

Measured against an individual's strong personal interest in education, the use of test scores to hamper or hinder students' attempts to avail themselves of educational opportunities may be difficult to justify. A plaintiff may well argue that a test purports to measure abilities that in fact are impossible to assess directly, so the rationale of *Armstead* applies. Additionally, the plaintiff may argue that although the test has a degree of predictable accuracy in measuring what it purports to measure, it may be so imprecise that the rationale in *Eisenstadt v. Baird* applies. In that case the court invoked a strong presumption against state-created classifications that were based on suspect criteria and that burdened a fundamental interest. The court required the state to carry the burden of proof and demonstrate that a fair and substantial relation existed between its classifications and a legitimate state purpose.

Due Process

The Fourteenth Amendment states that "no State shall . . . deprive any person of life, liberty, or property, without due process of law. . . . " Historically, the doctrine of due process has protected those rights recognized by the courts as fundamental but not delineated in the Constitution. However, before the due-process requirements of the Fourteenth Amendment can apply to a cause of action, two questions must be answered: (1) do the concepts of "liberty" or "property" encompass the asserted interest, so that the procedural requirements of due process apply, and (2) if due process applies, what formal procedures does it require to protect the interest adequately? In other words, an individual must have a legitimate claim of interest to a benefit before it can be characterized as a property interest to which the safeguards of due process apply (*Board of Regents v. Roth*).

Students obtain a property right to education through state law (*Ingraham v. Wright*; *Board of Curators of the University of Missouri v. Horowitz*; *Goss v. Lopez*). A state may make a constitutional or statutory guarantee of a public school education to all its citizens. Such a guarantee creates a property interest in education that meets the property requirement of the Fourteenth Amendment (*Goss v. Lopez*). Additionally, a student's right to an education is created when a state has compulsory attendance laws that are coupled with the promise of a free education. Such laws create the property interest necessary to invoking the protection of the Fourteenth Amendment. While the Supreme Court has indicated conclusively that high school students have a property interest in education (*Goss v. Lopez*; see also *Gaspar v. Bruton*), the courts have not yet found a college education to be a benefit for which a plaintiff can assert a claim of entitlement and invoke due-process procedural safeguards, since the concept of property does not include a "unilateral expectation" of a benefit (*Board of Regents v. Roth*). "An individual still must have a 'legitimate claim of entitlement' to a benefit before it will be characterized as a property interest to which the procedural safeguards of due process apply" (Beckwith 813). College students who claim that an adverse test score has deprived them of a property right would most likely not find a favorable judicial response at this time. However, once the benefit is conferred on an individual, procedural due process must be afforded before state action can revoke the benefit (*Dixon v. Alabama State Board of Education*).

While a claim of a property interest may well fail, a claim of a liberty interest may be received more favorably by the courts. The Supreme Court has held that the due-process safeguards of notice and opportunity to be heard apply whenever a person's good name, reputation, honor, or integrity is at stake and that an individual has a liberty interest in freedom from a state-imposed stigma (*Wisconsin v. Constantineau*; see also *Board of Regents v. Roth* and *Goss v. Lopez*). Students already have a property interest in being free of the stigma associated with receiving less than a standard high school diploma (*Debra P. v. Turlington*). "This stigma is very real and will affect the economic and psychological development of the individual" (266).

In *Constantineau*, the local police chief, pursuant to state statute, posted in retail liquor establishments a notice naming the plaintiff and forbidding the sale of liquor to her for one year. Since the posting was done without notice or hearing, the plaintiff sued for injunctive relief. The Supreme Court affirmed the federal district court's grant of relief, pointing out that the posting imposed a "stigma" on the individual. While it may be argued that testing does not impose a stigma—in the sense of public embarrassment—on a student who receives a low score, it can be argued that a low test score can impair a student's reputation. Moreover, to the extent that the test score and the effects of it are revealed, the student is embarrassed to the extent that the plaintiff in *Constantineau* was embarrassed.

In *Willner v. Committee on Character and Fitness,* the Supreme Court held that procedural due-process safeguards apply to the decision to deny an individual the right to practice law. It can be argued that a test makes a similar determination about a student's capacities to pursue a course of study that is a prerequisite for certain professional degrees. Moreover, a college degree is a prerequisite for many kinds of employment. Since an adverse test score could substantially impair employment opportunities, the safeguards of procedural due process may well apply in some fashion to any testing that acts as a barrier to possible employment.

Technical Issues

Depending on the circumstances of individual cases, courts may address such technical issues as reliability, validity, bias, and the calculation and use of cutoff scores. If the assessment program involves proficiency, the court will examine the match between instructional content and test content. The court will also examine whether a test is norm-referenced or criterion-referenced. For each of these issues, a court will consider whether those who constructed the test and used the test results followed professionally acceptable procedures.

While the court's approach to these questions is straightforward, those who administer assessment programs should bear in mind that, as Maurice Scharton and Doug Shale discuss in their essays in this volume, such issues as validity and reliability are not as settled or as clear-cut as we would like them to be, especially if we have to explain and defend them in court. Validity is a particularly difficult issue, open to probing questions during any legal challenge. In designing any assessment program, test administrators need to pay particular attention to all these issues to ensure that the program can, if examined, prevail against any legal challenge.

Test content may also be subject to legal review, particularly if the content covers value systems or beliefs. Questions that appear to be innocent may involve problem areas of coerced belief, invasion of privacy, or unmeasurable content. When the state is involved, answers to test questions that touch individual opinion and personal attitudes must not be judged right or wrong (*West Virginia State Board of Education v. Barnette*). Questions dealing with values or beliefs may also be unconstitutional invasions of privacy. Questions that assume certain views about their subjects or that imply correct answers or questions that penalize students for refusing to disclose their opinions may also be unconstitutional.

While this brief discussion of some of the legal issues involved in assessment is cursory, I hope it suggests the range of relevant legal issues. I hope also that I have demonstrated that those involved in assessing writing need to pay some attention to the legal issues related to their programs. I offer, therefore, the following guidelines and procedures.

Some Legal Guidelines for an Assessment Program

A review of case law suggests these recommendations for those charged with conducting a writing assessment program:

○ The test instrument must be properly validated and reliable. The methods used to establish the test's validity and reliability must conform to current, professionally accepted procedures and standards, and these methods should be fully documented. Validity and reliability should be reviewed and reestablished regularly. As a minimum, the guidelines in the American Psychological Association's *Standards for Educational and Psychological Tests* should be followed.
○ The purpose of the test must be clearly delineated, and items on the test must match specific skills taught in courses or specific curriculum objectives.
○ Mere correlation between the test and the curriculum is not sufficient. There must be additional evidence, obtained from a regular, continuing, and documented procedure, that classroom activities are related to curriculum goals and test specifications.
○ All test items must be carefully developed and evaluated to ensure that they conform to curriculum and to instructional practices. Moreover, there must be no evidence of bias related to racial, ethnic, or national origin status.

○ If possible, other measures of performance and ability should be used in conjunction with test results.

○ Cutoff scores should be the result of a well-documented process of deliberation that conforms to state and federal statutory requirements. There should be no suggestion of arbitrariness or capriciousness in the setting of cutoff scores.

○ Students should be informed far in advance about what they need to know to perform well on the test. Students should also be informed in advance about the nature of the test.

○ Students should have access to their test scores and have a full explanation of their scores and how their scores are used.

○ Options should be available to the students who fail the test, including the opportunity to retake the test and institutional help with preparing for the test and correcting deficiencies.

Reviewing an Assessment Program

Prudence and professionalism suggest that anyone conducting an assessment program should take the following steps:

○ Conduct a full, impartial review of all aspects of the assessment program, and document this review.

○ Examine all program documentation—such as reports and records on test design and development, on how cutoff scores were derived, on what methods were used to detect and eliminate test bias, and on what procedures are followed to monitor the test and the testing program, as well as the results of such monitoring—and write the documentation that should be there but is not.

○ Correct all the deficiencies identified in the program, and then document the processes by which they were identified and corrected.

○ Institute these two procedures as permanent parts of the assessment program: a formal, fully documented process for administering and conducting the assessment program and a formal review of the program carried out regularly by an impartial, professionally qualified outside reviewer, who prepares a written report that becomes part of the program documentation.

○ Conduct longitudinal studies of the students who take the test, determining what correlations, if any, there are between the students' test scores and measures of achievement such as the students' performance in subsequent courses.

A Final Note and a Caution

In 1993 a group of students at Wayne State University in Detroit, Michigan, filed suit, challenging the English proficiency examination. This examination had been a graduation requirement in some of the colleges in the university for more than thirty years, but in 1983 it became a university-wide requirement. Students who do not pass the examination are denied their degrees, even if they have successfully completed all the other degree requirements.

Attorneys for the students asked these questions in the lawsuit: Is the test a demonstrably valid measure for helping determine students' graduation? Does completing courses at the university adequately prepare students to pass the test? Is it fair to maintain the test as an obstacle to graduation for students who have completed all other requirements and who had assumed they were making satisfactory progress toward a degree? Why is the test, normally taken in the junior year, administered so late in students' careers, instead of being used to provide an earlier assessment of their writing skills? Is there a fairer method for judging students' competence? (Richardson; "Testing").

These are valid and important questions to ask of a testing program that so significantly affects the lives of students. However, the attorneys for the students chose to seek the answers not in federal court but in a state court, basing their suit on Michigan law and not on federal law or on constitutional grounds. The state court was not receptive to their arguments that the test violated university regulations and a state guarantee to an education. While the students did not prevail, their lawsuit prompted a wide discussion in the press of the test, its fairness, and its effects on minority students.

Those who administer a writing assessment program usually see nothing wrong with their test. Yet writing assessment administrators must ask themselves and their institution whether, if their program was challenged in federal court, they would be prepared to present to the court documents demonstrating that the program was professionally responsible. I cannot help but wonder how many writing assessment programs are vulnerable to a legal challenge based on the grounds I have discussed here.

Rutgers University, Camden

Response:
Why Do We Test Writing?

John Trimbur

As I read the three essays in this section, I realized once again how problematic the terms *politics* and *political* are in the study, teaching, and assessment of writing. As the contributors indicate, virtually every aspect of writing instruction is political, from the kind of prose we ask students to write in class assignments to large-scale state-mandated testing programs.

To say that the activities of writing instruction are political and therefore subject to political analysis, however, only labels a set of practices. It doesn't go far toward explaining what is political about teaching and testing writing or what we might learn by unraveling the politics that seem to be woven into the fabric of writing programs. The terms *politics* and *political* are hard to get a handle on.

Perhaps one way to get some critical purchase on them is to say that they foreground conflicts of interest, asymmetrical relations of power, hidden motives, and unforeseen consequences. From this perspective, political analysis should be able to help us read between the lines, so we see what's really going on in writing assessment. As Edward White suggests, political analysis of writing assessment can help us identify how various groups—teachers, researchers, testing agencies, government bodies, minority groups, and student groups—bring different interests and values to discussions of testing. Political analysis, moreover, can help us see, as Gordon Brossell does, the "disjunction" between teaching and testing (which leads to attempts to close the gap by "teaching the test") and recognize the political uses of testing by state legislatures as a form of public relations. Finally, William Lutz shows how testing gets entangled in the legal apparatus of the state and in notions of equal protection and due process. But notice, once again, how the terms *politics* and *political* seem to diffuse throughout writing programs, implicating themselves in every nook and cranny and leaving us to contemplate the idea that everything we do is political.

As useful as these political analyses are, they take politics to be a way of reading the world, of interpreting experience. However, if we think

45

of politics not only as an analytic technique that is learned—a means of clarification in a beclouded world—but also and more fundamentally as the situation of human life, encompassing us all, then we might be able to say something about the apparent ubiquity of politics, as the social and discursive practices individuals and groups draw on to inscribe their motives and aspirations in the world. This account follows Aristotle's idea that human beings are political animals and that they find themselves time and again in rhetorical situations, where various exigencies move them to speak and to act, in an effort to cope with the imperfections and contradictions of their lived experience. To look at *politics* and *political* this way is to read the contributions to this section not only as political analyses but also as political statements in their own right, interventions to change how we think about and enact assessment in the study and teaching of writing.

But then the question becomes, What are these acts of persuasion about, and what are they urging people to do? One answer to these questions begins by recognizing that the exigence to which the contributors respond, whether they acknowledge it or not, is the growing pressure from university administrators, state legislatures, and national panels of experts for accountability, for hard data to convince the public that writing instruction merits the resources devoted to it. This line of thought holds that unless we devise ways to assess writing, someone else will do it for us.

There is a good deal of merit to this view, which aims to preserve the professional autonomy of writing instructors and program administrators at a time when downsizing is the rage in the corporate world and "profscam" is shorthand for a conventional belief that college faculty members don't work very hard. In other words, we need to explain ourselves and our work if we want to keep our jobs. But this way of thinking about the politics of assessment concedes that writing abilities, unlike, say, the ability to read literature, ought to be assessed regularly according to minimum competencies and measurable standards to which all reasonable persons might assent. You can test and rank student-written products, but literature is something students are simply exposed to. On the one hand, it doesn't seem to matter much whether students are good at reading literature, whether they catch the irony in a turn of phrase, as long as they acknowledge (whether as an act of piety, social allegiance, or personal self-development or from some combination of these motives) literature's importance and affirm its cultural weight. On the other hand, students need to demonstrate that they are at least functionally literate in writing or, as employers of college graduates often put it, can "communicate effectively" in the workplace.

Now, I happen to believe that college graduates should indeed be able to "communicate effectively" in the workplace, as well as in public forums. My point is that something—some set of hopes and interests—is invested in writing instruction and testing but apparently not in the teaching of literature (or of other academic subjects) in the same way. After all, we don't just expose students to writing; we expect them to acquire some demonstrable skill at it, and we have spent a lot of time and effort figuring out how to measure this skill. We have constituted writing less as a subject matter (like literature) than as a measurable skill. We have chosen, that is, to evaluate student performances in writing rather than their knowledge of what writing is and does. To get to the politics of assessment, it seems to me, we need to ask why this is the case: what are the politics of designing writing instruction in such a way that student-written products can be evaluated?

This question may appear at best naive. More likely it will seem in some quarters impertinent, an evasion of pedagogical responsibility and institutional accountability. But to my way of thinking, the question is important because it probes what goes without saying, the reigning assumption that writing can and should be measured. I do not wish to be misunderstood on this point. I'm not opposed to writing assessment, and I can imagine a number of ways it can serve worthwhile educational goals. I simply want to ask why assessment is taken for granted as a necessary part of the study and teaching of writing. What are the politics that authorize the assessment of writing?

There are many possible answers to this question, and in the space I have here I can only make the most general response. In part, the representation of writing as a measurable skill is embedded in the history of English studies around the turn of the century, when literary studies arose in the modern research university, rhetoric and poetics were separated, and composition was created to train a newly emerging professional-managerial class in writing. Robert J. Connors, James A. Berlin, Richard Ohmann, and others have treated this history in detail. For my part, I want to extend a point I make elsewhere ("Literacy"), that what authorizes and in a sense produces (and is produced by) writing assessment is the persistence of literacy crises in American education.

To my mind, these crises have less to do with how well students read or write than with the cultural anxieties that are attached to literacy and with how educational discourse serves to displace social tensions into the realm of literacy. Just as the literacy crisis of the 1890s and early 1900s gave a name to cultural anxieties about immigration and the rise of corporate capitalism or just as the crisis of the 1970s served to galvanize a backlash against the "permissiveness" and antiauthoritarianism of the 1960s, so do the political forces calling for accountability in writing instruction today thematize current cultural tensions—arising from such phenomena as the "new" immigration, the changing demographics of the workforce, the widely heralded shift to an information and a service economy, and the United States' competitive position in the global market—under the rubric of declining literacy standards. In this sense, the desire for accountability and the call for higher standards that underwrite writing assessment are ideological to the extent that, in Althusser's terms, they bear an imaginary relation to the conditions of existence. To put it another way, literacy—and particularly the ability to write—is being called on to provide a common means of communication in a divided culture, to promote national economic recovery, and to explain the success and failure of individuals in a class society.

What I suggest here is that the ideological work assigned to literacy has supercharged writing instruction and led to the desire to measure it. Moreover, writing teachers, theorists, and program administrators have conspired in the supercharged discourse of the literacy crisis by using the crisis to justify funding and support of their studying, teaching, and assessing of writing. The contributions to this section, however, it seems to me, have not given way to this temptation. Rather, they maneuver in a kind of guerrilla operation at the margins of power, complicating the notion of what it means to teach and assess writing. If we think of the politics of writing assessment as the result (as well as the cause) of the great ongoing American literacy crisis, then the role composition studies has in the public debate about standards may be to keep the meaning of writing fluid and indeterminate—a subject of cultural contention as much as a measurable skill.

Worcester Polytechnic Institute

PART II

Validity and Reliability

Introduction

Maurice Scharton and Doug Shale challenge the notion of political neutrality sometimes associated with writing assessment. Evaluation selects, marginalizes, and excludes by its very nature. By providing artifacts such as grades and writing assessment scores, according to Scharton in "The Politics of Validity," assessment serves the social status quo, for it tends to reproduce ideologies that preexist in the minds of those who control social institutions. In writing assessment, we will always measure the validity of a test against our subjective sense of how well the results square with our beliefs about writing. Assessment can help us to recognize that we may have "an investment in one belief system" and that the concept of validity has as many avatars as it has contexts. Scharton examines validity in the context of the groups who use assessment, analyzes their beliefs, and proposes five basic questions as a heuristic for exploring issues of validity.

In "Essay Reliability: Form and Meaning," Doug Shale shows how classical test theory is not an appropriate measurement model for a concept of reliability in writing assessment and maintains that generalizability theory offers a far better means of determining the reliability of writing measurement on essay tests. Moreover, Shale argues, the political ramifications of forcing classical test theory onto a concept of the reliability of essay scoring are wide-ranging and subtle. In this context, Shale asks how essay assessments derived from fundamentally flawed premises should be regarded and questions the consequences for students who are affected by decisions based on such scores. Finally, he speculates on what might be the effects on the role and professional status of composition teachers of a measurement theory that privileges measurement specialists and that embodies a view of writing contrary to the view of those directly concerned with teaching composition.

In a response to these essays, Roberta Camp asserts that assessment and evaluation are value-laden, that they require negotiation among a number of parties with different perspectives and concerns, and that methodology counts. The essays demonstrate, she notes, that the misunderstandings and confusion that have become typical cannot be minimized without a systemic and collegial perspective on assessment. Echoing Edward White's call in the first essay of this book, she sees cross-disciplinary understanding as the practical solution to problems with validity and reliability, as well as with assessment itself.

The Politics of Validity

Maurice Scharton

In peaceful times, educational assessment simply keeps the gate of academe, granting and denying entrance in the name of the ruling party. But in troubled times, when underprepared students, budget-minded legislators, or other vandals begin storming the gate, ambitious academics can mobilize assessment to impose order on the turmoil and, not incidentally, to acquire power for themselves. By declaring a state of academic emergency, the politically astute can authorize the imposition of a martial purpose on assessment: instead of advising teachers who wish to evaluate instruction, assessment must lead the charge for ideologues who wish to reform instruction; instead of counseling administrators who wish to allocate resources, assessment must subvert established authority on behalf of insurgents who wish to seize resources. Naturally, each party to the ensuing political conflicts cherishes the belief that it serves a just cause whose truth valid assessment can demonstrate.

Validity and Truth

We often define the validity of an assessment as its truth-value—the degree to which the assessment measures what it claims to measure. At first, this criterion may appear easy to meet. One assessment provides a multiple-choice measurement of writing ability, while another assembles essay portfolios, and both succeed by their own lights, giving different yet valid views of writing ability. But the simplicity of this definition belies the political nature of assessment's effects. As Pamela Moss observes, assessments "provide potent and value-laden models of the purposes and processes of school, of the appropriate roles for teachers, students and other stakeholders in the discourse of teaching and learning, and of the means through which educational reform is best accomplished" ("High Stakes Writing Assessment" 124). Rarely does everyone agree that an assessment has provided truth. Indeed, it is not reasonable to hope for truth from an assessment. The best one can hope for is that an assessment faithfully represents

53

one's values, thereby facilitating the best return on one's educational investments. If a teacher must cut material from a course, placement tests can show what students have already mastered. If an administrator must decide which programs to fund, an external assessment can provide comparative data on program effectiveness. People often blame assessments for the sacrifices consequent on value judgments, forgetting that an assessment only brings to the surface the axiological issues that underlie education.

Perhaps the most disagreeable consequence of assessment is that after an assessment has produced its results, we can no longer nurture the comforting illusion that everyone has the same beliefs, abilities, or opportunities. By generating test scores, an assessment hypostatizes a value judgment, which becomes a fact everyone must cope with. In coping with assessment results, we may try to explain away the evidence of our differences as an artifact of the political agendas of particular teachers, departments, administrators, and institutions. We may even set up a new, competing assessment program or technique to generate scores we like better. Still, however we rationalize assessment products, we cannot avoid the sad realization that assessments define opposing political camps. The history of assessment is rife with technically based political movements, each promoting its dream of the ideal technique that will satisfy and unify everyone. Yet one person's dream is always another's nightmare. We have no godlike vantage point beyond our own perspectives from which to perceive or construct the ideal assessment. We measure the validity of a test against our subjective sense of how well the results square with our values. If an assessment does anything, it helps us to recognize that we have values, an investment in one belief system.

Validity and Belief

The English profession has been accustomed to allowing measurement theorists and writing assessment experts to define validity, often in statistical terms that appear irrefutable to the naive. While validity must be expressed mathematically for some purposes in assessment, the profession need not allow technicians and scientists an entirely free hand to define its beliefs. Creating validity is in fact not so simple as establishing a satisfactory curve of scores or statistical correlation. Rather, the issue turns on the beliefs of the affected parties. Students, teachers, program administrators, test designers, parents, legislators, and the general public all participate in the educational process, and each of their perspectives bears on the issue of validity.

The term *validity* is derived from the Latin *valere,* meaning "to be strong." The derivation from the concept of strength suggests that validity is an axiological matter of degree, not a positivistic dichotomy of valid versus invalid. Even positivistic measurement theory affirms the axiological nature of validity. Norman Gronlund, one of the most authoritative measurement theorists, defines validity in terms of what observers may properly infer from a test score (125–26). That is, validity is an attribute of one's reasoning about the data that tests produce. Strictly speaking, it is nonsense to assert that a given assessment is valid or invalid. Assessments are simply mechanisms that produce data about which human observers draw more or less believable conclusions. For example, we can reason with some validity that an essay test in a literature course assesses a student's understanding of the course content. We can also draw more-general conclusions about the student's writing ability from the essay-test performance, but they will probably be less credible than the conclusions about the student's knowledge of the course content.

Classical assessment theory suggests that belief in an assessment grows from four perspectives on validity. When we can argue credibly for a logical relation between a student's performance on the test and a theoretical underlying factor (in the present case writing ability), we demonstrate *construct validity.* When we derive test content from the curriculum students experience, we promote *content validity.* When the results of a test correlate with an independent measure of ability, such as grades, we have established *concurrent validity.* When a test accurately forecasts the quality of a student's future performance of the target activity, we may presume *predictive validity.* These four perspectives represent commonsensical questions an intelligent observer might ask concerning a writing assessment. "How do you define writing ability?" "What writing curriculum do you assume that test takers have experienced?" "Does this test give the same results as other tests?" "Does performance on this test accurately forecast the test taker's degree of success as a writer?" Of course, one evaluates the answers to these questions from one's experience of assessment and of writing instruction. In short, anyone who observes and measures writing ability does so from an interested, political perspective.

Preference for a particular perspective on writing ability and for a consonant definition of validity naturally entails the view that other perspectives and definitions are inferior. Thus a pedagogical writer

argues that assessment designers should pay greater attention to instructional priorities (e.g., Lunsford, "Past" 8), while an assessment authority argues the converse: that classroom teachers would profit from
studying large-scale assessment methods (e.g., White, *Teaching* [1st ed.]
130–32). We may refer to these two lines of thought as the *instructional
perspective* (derived from small systems such as individual writers, peer
groups, individual classes, and small numbers of classes taught by a
single instructor or a like-minded group of instructors within a program) and the *programmatic perspective* (derived from large systems
such as writing programs, colleges, and associations of writing programs and colleges). To those taking the instructional perspective, validity is synonymous with advocacy of writing instruction. A good test
supports teachers' efforts to help students produce their best writing.
To those taking the programmatic perspective, validity is a matter of
usefulness in resource allocation. A good test provides decision makers
a simple, reliable numerical score to use in determining how to spend
money.

The Instructional Perspective

The advocates of the instructional perspective, here represented by the
portfolio movement, seek to change the political situation in assessment so that the classroom teacher rather than the institution wields
the real power. The instructional perspective implies a narrative in
which right-minded teachers struggle against ruthless big-company
test designers who merely want to sell a test score to administrators interested in a quick fix. Instructional writers on assessment tend to express their opinions in process-oriented terms of construct and content
validity: the more a test resembles a valued ideology and writing experience, the more we can believe in its results.

Construct Validity

The instructional perspective privileges what is sometimes called "process writing," involving significant invention, multiple drafts, and peer
interactions. This political move all but excludes traditional writing assessment tasks from the construct of writing ability on the assumption
that traditional assessment, a primitive and brutal force, unnecessarily
interferes with expression and learning in the classroom. In the instructional view, construct validity rests on three important premises:
theoretical currency, authenticity, and home rule.

Theoretical Currency Theoretical currency is defined by the elite of the English profession. Quite simply, a "valid" test conforms to theory about writing instruction currently discussed in the most prestigious professional circles. Members of the English profession, quick to implement the latest idea from the journals, have no patience with assessment's tendency to change slowly. Several essays in the collection *Writing Assessment: Issues and Strategies* seek to defend instructional rights and prerogatives against perceived encroachments by the old-fashioned goals and methods of traditional, multiple-choice assessment. The writers of these essays tend to value the theoretical currency of an assessment more than its reliability or its utility (e.g., Lederman 41; Brown 46–49; Conlan 110–11). Charles Cooper and Lee Odell (Introduction viii–xii) represent most commentators in flatly asserting that standardized multiple-choice instruments are not as valid as essay assessments. Important members of the writing-research community seem to have accepted the instructional imperative to define construct validity politically (Charney 76–79; Lauer and Asher 140–41). Since a major goal of research is to reconcile findings about writers' processes with findings about instruction (Hillocks 223), it would appear that research-oriented writers also consider it important to foster solidarity between research and teaching. In "Changing the Model for the Direct Assessment of Writing," Roberta Camp exemplifies the theoretical-currency line of argument in suggesting that assessment privilege construct validity above all other forms, that the construct privileged in assessment design be drawn from reformists in curriculum and assessment, and that portfolio assessment be designed in harmony with prevalent theory. Portfolio research has just begun to address technical problems, such as reliability, that are basic to all forms of assessment (e.g., Nystrand, Cohen, and Dowling), and many technical debates and difficulties are unresolved. Nevertheless, both higher education and the public schools have outstripped assessment research to implement portfolio assessments, as the two dozen essays in the volume *Portfolios: Process and Product* indicate (Belanoff and Dickson). Camp's proposal would authorize the implementation to continue at its present pace.

What fuels the urge to implement theory? Stanley Fish suggests that the English profession is motivated by "theory hope," a drive to discover a highly abstract paradigm that will reintegrate the profession ("Antifoundationalism"). Paradoxically, theory is precisely the cause of the profession's disintegration. In science, a theory describes how a process works. Scientific research uses experimental procedures to test a theory against data before allowing it much credence. Hence, scientific theory develops slowly. In English, on the other hand, a "theory" follows a different trajectory, moving rapidly from hypothesis to political system. Humanists motivated by theory hope require only theoretical currency to transform an intuition into a set of prescriptive axioms and thence into a movement with strong political and, occasionally, religious overtones. Because theory in English develops with little empirical basis and at great speed, a credibility gap often opens, separating a conservative corps of practitioners from an avant-garde research element.

In *The Education of Henry Adams,* Adams speculates that a culture built around a medieval tradition such as worship of the Virgin may, under the influence of a modern technology such as the dynamo, accelerate until it flies apart of its own momentum. At times, the English profession seems perilously close to realizing Adams's vision. To some people, writing assessment has the power to allay a fear of change like Adams's and to realize the hope for a new faith, like the one Fish notes, that will bring dilatory curricula, textbooks, and practitioners into line with the orthodoxies of the powerful. Assessment could reform curriculum, curriculum reform textbooks, and textbooks eventually reform the most recalcitrant practitioners. Clearly this is magical thinking. Consider the axiomatic disdain of modern compositionists toward teaching traditional grammar. Grammar served, along with the modes of discourse, as a pivotal element of the current-traditional paradigm. Then in 1963 Richard Braddock, Richard Lloyd-Jones, and Lowell Schoer—rather like Luther nailing his theses to the door at Wittenberg—asserted that teaching grammar was a waste of time, since generations of research had failed to demonstrate a relation between the teaching of grammar and improvements in writing ability. After 1963, research on grammar and writing dwindled. In the years since, many assessments from ACT and ETS have incorporated writing samples with multiple-choice questions. Readers for holistic scoring programs across the country have learned to discount surface errors in arriving at judgments. In process-oriented classrooms, peer responses have largely replaced that mode of instruction prevalent in American colleges until the early 1960s. In short, the modern view minimizes traditional grammar. Yet so many teachers and administrators nurture an implicit faith in the power of grammatical knowledge to transform student editing abilities that grammar is taught from elementary school through college; and handbooks that provide explicit instruction in traditional grammar continue to outsell rhetoric textbooks in every market. While modern composition thought despises both multiple-choice assessments and traditional grammar as vestiges of the ancien régime, current-traditional practices still define the very concept of writing instruction for most of the public and for many writing teachers. In short, though postmodern theory reigns at court, grammar is still god in the provinces.

Will some set of beliefs comparable to grammar or the modes of discourse reunite the profession of writing instruction? As James Berlin's *Writing Instruction in Nineteenth-Century American Colleges* suggests, college writing research and instruction have sought restlessly for some catholic belief system to replace the current-traditional paradigm. National conventions have proposed mottoes valorizing "process, not product," "getting back to the basics," "problem solving," "discourse communities," and "resistance." Still, the profession's theory hope is probably vain, for English has undergone a protestant reformation and is unlikely to be reunited by any single belief system. Given humanists' historical distrust of positivism, the criteria for construct validity will continue, unfettered by empirical information, to vary directly and rapidly with the political developments in the journals.

Authenticity In expressivist composing theory, authenticity is an ineffable, affective quality, usually related to personal voice, that persuades the reader the writer believes in, has a personal stake in, or is otherwise intrinsically invested in the writing. While no one has quantified the discourse features that signify authenticity, it has been associated in the work of people like Peter Elbow, Donald Murray, and Ken Macrorie with self-sponsored writing topics, personal narrative forms, invention work in dialogue journals, conferencing, and peer-group revision.

Authenticity in writing assessment may be defined as faithful replication of the circumstances of process-oriented writing instruction, especially as those circumstances are defined in expressivist composing theory. Presumably, authentic processes will produce authentic products. Thus defined, authenticity may become an important criterion by which to judge the validity of an assessment. For example, Leo Ruth and Sandra Murphy call on assessments to "honor" elements of the writing process (240–42), as if the writer's processes were a sacred event. Given the expectation of authenticity, Davida Charney can express dismay rather than satisfaction that writing samples often correlate well with multiple-choice tests: the correlation evokes suspicion that the essays were composed and evaluated only to demonstrate their authors' command of grammar (75).

While writing instructors differ over the precise nature of the construct "writing ability," they concur in the opinion that whatever writing ability is, it cannot be measured (or, perhaps, appropriately honored) with a multiple-choice instrument. A multiple-choice instrument's concurrent or predictive validity—the fact that it correlated well with grades or placed students satisfactorily—would not excuse its failure to provide an authentic experience of the writing process. Of course, because traditional essay assessment has usually worked with assigned argumentative topics and allowed scant time for invention or revision, holistic scores represent little improvement over multiple-choice scores in the minds of those who require authenticity in assessment programs, despite Brian Huot's 1993 findings that holistic techniques promote a receptive reading of student work.

In defining the authentic experience of writing to exclude assessment writing, critics of programmatic assessment techniques exclude from curricula much important writing instruction. The English profession suffers a corresponding loss of credibility among the powerful people who do not share its orthodoxies. Among that constituency, one might number surviving practitioners of the current-traditional pedagogy; undergraduate-admissions officers who ask for autobiographical essays; all the colleges and universities that use the SAT, the ACT, the AP, the CLEP, and similar exams; the graduate programs that use the GRE, the LSAT, the MCAT, the GMAT, and other tests like them; the boards of education of populous states—such as Illinois, Florida, New York, and California—that have instituted mass literacy assessments; the various local, state, and federal government agencies that use tests to screen applicants for employment; and many parents and legislators. In addition, one would probably find that most graduate programs in English use comprehensive examinations based on one-draft essays. These people and programs control an enormous amount of political power and considerable money.

Perhaps an uninformed public needs to be made aware that writing is a complex activity and that writing ability involves far more than a one-draft essay can reveal. However, so long as society continues to sponsor competitive tests of writing ability, the English profession would do well to ascertain why society values the writing measured by such tests and to make instruction in it available to students. Perhaps one might take as an analogy the teaching of Standard English or of academic discourse. Most teachers have their pedagogical and ethical quarrels with Standard English and the academic idiom, but few deny their political utility. On utilitarian grounds, most students probably should receive instruction in the use of those codes.

Home Rule   I want to distinguish academic freedom from home rule. The exercise of academic freedom implies an individualistic right to think, write, and teach according to the dictates of one's conscience and to be protected in the exercise of that right by the institution. Home rule involves a far more limited sociopolitical privilege to control the educational enterprise within one's classroom. In practice, home rule forbids an assessment to cause inappropriate "teaching to the test." Teachers perceive any interference in their personal teaching agendas by an assessment as prima facie evidence that the assessment has compromised construct validity.

In the classroom, teachers are accustomed to the prerogatives of a benevolent despot or philosopher-ruler: their judgment embodies the law, is intrinsically valid, and is practically unlimited. A teacher's evaluation standards may not even be written down except as commentary on papers. Like sovereign states that insist on home rule, teachers resist assessment initiated from outside, and they particularly resist being measured by the standards and results of outside assessment. The argument is that outside assessment cannot take into account the situation of a particular student, class, teacher, or school. As a member of the committee that oversaw the development of the writing assessment for the state of Illinois, I continually heard teachers object to assessment in general: "Tests take too much time away from instruction," or "The trouble with tests is then you have to teach to them." Setting aside the obvious rejoinders that instruction is blind without assessment and that tests can legitimately cause or prevent change in instructional practice, I find those objections reasonable in some ways. Unfortunately, people operating from the instructional perspective exhibit an exasperating tendency to use home-rule arguments to polarize education and the larger society, authorizing English departments to isolate themselves intellectually in order to engage in technically amateurish evaluation of their programs.

While one may not wish to limit academic freedom, one must accept reasonable limits on home rule in the classroom. Society—from colleagues to the department chair to parents all the way to state and federal funding agencies—has a legitimate interest in what one does in one's classroom. The public has for years accepted the good intentions of the educational community as security for the payments appropriated for education. As recent taxpayer revolts indicate, people have begun to view educational-funding requests with suspicion. In fact, taxpayers are entitled to measurable results for educational expenditures, unless one redefines education as a form of art or religion whose benefits lie entirely in the realm of the spiritual. When requesting concrete assistance in the form of funding, educators would do well to provide concrete proof of achievement rather than abstract hope for the future.

Content Validity

We know that educational curricula exist to prepare people to function in society. We also know that, historically, writing courses have appeared in response to faculty demands that student writing skills be improved. In the interest of testing the content students need, it would seem reasonable that assessment ought to model itself on classroom writing and that classroom writing ought in turn to model itself on real-world writing; thus we would complete a circle drawing together assessment, academe, and the real world. But instructional perspectives on validity in assessment usually advocate a political agenda aimed at remaking both academe and the real world into the ideal composing environment. Instructional assessment seeks to test a curriculum that is better than the one students experience, to establish a utopian community that actualizes the writing potential of all its members.

We can see utopianism in the way Odell defines appropriate conditions of assessment: giving writers more than one kind of assignment, supplying information about audience and purpose, ensuring that writing assignments have reasonable demands, and basing any judgment on an adequate amount of writing (113). Odell's guidelines conflict with his assertion that students should write in circumstances comparable to those in which professionals do important writing. Many people in careers both in and out of academe do much important writing without the nurturance of a teacher who imposes and adjusts assignments in conformance with an instructional code of ethics.

Portfolio assessment is the most successful example of idealistic and progressive instructionally oriented assessment. As Camp explains, in the discourse on portfolios, assessment is called on to act as a causal agent for educational reform—in the form of staff development, student learning, and broad "systemic" support of educational improvement. Teachers often argue that assessment will drive curriculum, so it makes sense to use a test that will improve the curriculum. This reasoning seems to be predicated on a conflation of axiological and methodological priorities: since curriculum reform is of first importance, the reformed curriculum should take precedence over the actual curriculum in test design. However, if the test is designed to lead the curriculum, students will not have experienced the instruction for which they are being tested, rendering the test meaningless with respect to the present curriculum. Further, teachers who are in positions of authority will be allowed to promulgate their educational theories among their less powerful colleagues. This is a clever but dangerous political move that enables those who control the test to shrug off the burden of proof that usually falls on advocates of reform. Recently, the notion of "consequential validity" has been proposed as a technical way of conceptualizing reformist views of assessment (Cronbach, "Perspectives"; Messick, "Meaning"; P. Moss, "Conceptions"). An assessment can be attacked on grounds of consequential validity if it causes or promises to cause social effects someone finds undesirable. An obvious political danger is that consequential validity conveniently rationalizes the practice of using a test to achieve a personal end.

If an assessment is designed to achieve an effect rather than to measure an effect, politics drives assessment. If one uses a test to rectify injustices, one runs, at best, a considerable risk of deceiving oneself concerning the ability of test takers to compete successfully in the status quo. At worst, one may unwittingly cooperate with the forces one opposes. To reduce these risks, people have traditionally had validity represent the relation of assessment to the status quo. Thus the criteria for validity have been based on the values of the status quo as those values are represented by accepted educational theory and curriculum and by external criteria such as test takers' success with other relevant tests and tasks. If certain students don't do well on the test, it has revealed something either about them (that they lack a necessary competence) or about the status quo (that it discriminates against them).

To the concerns I have outlined, traditional content validation responds with a pragmatic model of the classroom, including traditional instruction and assessment, both of which hold a place in the curriculum, in textbooks, and in the views of practitioners. A line of reasoning that might appeal to those adhering to the instructional perspective maintains that students learn not only from process-oriented instruction but also from instruction in writing for tests. Teachers might reason that to compete successfully in our culture, a writer needs to understand how all sorts of tests are constructed and scored. At a simple, practical level, a student who does not learn by taking a multiple-choice test might likely pick up information by writing one. A student for whom writing impromptu test essays is excruciating might well find that designing a topic and participating in a holistic-scoring session provide information about how to make value judgments about writing. This sort of training might in time affect the student's attitude toward and performance on the essay tests one encounters in competing for a place in society. Teachers who wanted curricular change could pursue it through channels more regular than assessment, by seeking office in professional organizations and assuming administrative positions in their schools.

The Programmatic Perspective

Programmatic assessment implies a narrative in which a skeptical scientist uses sophisticated statistical techniques to test hypotheses generated by observations of natural phenomena. In this narrative, science provides the educational enterprise with hard data able to correct the misapprehensions and rebut the anecdotal evidence of naive practitioners. More efficient and accurate than the classroom teacher, the scientific test-development specialist can sample a narrow range of writing behavior or even writing-related knowledge, infer from the sample information about knowledge and behavior not sampled, and then establish facts, criticize theories, and offer and test new hypotheses about writing ability. The test developer assumes an integral relation among all aspects of writing ability. A single piece can, like DNA, generate an organic whole.

Basically scientific in its orientation, programmatic assessment privileges externally oriented forms of validity that help establish objective viewpoints. Concurrent validity and predictive validity are instances of *criterion-related validity*, which, as W. James Popham suggests (120–21), requires test scores to be correlated against an independent, external criterion (such as grades, class rank, or a multiple-choice score). For test-development specialists, the most important practical difference between writing assessment and the usual content-area multiple-choice assessment is that content areas have a content domain, or canon. I use *canon* in the broad sense of a valued body of knowledge, beliefs, principles, and practices. The canon is the profession's received wisdom, the source of the external criteria with which a test is compared. For example, designers creating a mathematics or geography assessment can obtain advice from a panel of experts about the items the assessment ought to include. Once designers have sampled the content domain, a set of well-defined technical procedures guides them toward the final product. Thus a content-area assessment score will correlate well with other assessment scores (suggesting concurrent validity) and will accurately predict a student's level of success beyond the immediate context (suggesting predictive validity).

Unfortunately, today writing instruction cannot provide external, independent measures useful for establishing criterion-related validity. Though a multiple-choice assessment such as the ACT can examine test takers on rhetorical concepts and writing-process issues, writing instruction enjoys no widely accepted canon of knowledge and practices. The problem is further complicated by the fact that writing is a practice one performs, not simply a knowledge one recalls. Over the last thirty years, the profession has seen a constant reconstruction of the theoretical base of writing, from the current-traditional paradigm to an expressivist movement to a cognitivist movement to a social-constructionist movement, among others. Though the more avant-garde journals give the impression that certain ideological stances have been supported and others refuted, the variety of textbooks available makes clear that many theoretical bases retain followings among teachers. Given the lack of a canon, there is a theoretical mismatch between traditional assessment technique and the subject of writing. Nevertheless, in the cause of scientific efficiency and precision, programmatic assessment has attempted to transfer to writing assessment a set of methods and assumptions developed for multiple-choice assessments of subject-area knowledge. Like the categories of Latin grammar, the techniques we use in writing assessment were derived from another situation and overlaid on writing instruction. On the whole, traditional measurement transferred to writing assessment about as comfortably as Latin grammar did to English. That is, the system fits well enough to be of some use while frustrating attempts to capture writing ability within its perfectly ordered categories. In consequence, concurrent and predictive validities become problematic. Writing assessment has responded to this problem somewhat illogically, by focusing intense attention on *reliability*: the consistency with which a given writer's ability is ranked at a single level.

Concurrent Validity

Fred Godshalk defines the concurrent validity of an essay assessment as the degree to which the assessment correlates with a multiple-choice test (Godshalk, Swineford, and Coffman). Godshalk's study established a pattern for the holistic assessments now associated with college-admissions, placement, and competency testing, as well as for professional-school tests such as the MCAT and the NTE. For Godshalk's research, students wrote essays in the modes of discourse—descriptive, narrative, expository, and argumentative—and were encouraged to take a competitive attitude toward their writing. Trained readers evaluated the essays, distributing their scores along a range comparable to the range of grades traditionally given in classrooms.

Godshalk's model probably produced valid decisions, given English-teaching methods in the current-traditional paradigm of the early 1960s. Since instruction and evaluation in writing courses at that time placed significant emphasis on proofreading skills, a multiple-choice test of these skills was, from the standpoint of content validity, a rationally defensible assessment method for that context. Mode-based textbooks and competition for grades would also support the validity of reasoning from data produced by such models. Happily, then, given two acceptable yet distinct evaluation instruments, one could during the 1960s establish concurrent validity by measuring their correlation.

Contemporary theorists would argue that the mode-based competitive model of writing makes some questionable assumptions about the nature of writing and of writing instruction, but contemporary theory, which may change its orientation twice in a decade, cannot provide test designers with an up-to-date, stable political consensus on which to build a test. Progressivism often characterizes the thinking and rhetoric of reform-minded authors of journal articles: a new theoretical paradigm must raze all the old ideas in order to prepare the ground for the latest "advances" in pedagogy, theory, or curriculum. One should not be surprised to discover that insofar as measurement specialists can tell, the modes of discourse and traditional grammar still supply writing instruction with its closest approximation of a canon. Writing instructors have little in common ideologically beyond an agreement that final products should exhibit a recognizable organizational pattern and an error-free surface, so there is some justification for measurement experts to continue to construct tests that require students to make appropriate language choices within a genre. This current-traditional canon can readily be assessed in a multiple-choice format, and one multiple-choice score can be correlated with another to test concurrent validity. These measurement advantages do not impress practitioners, who require writing samples and reject multiple-choice tests out of hand.

Criterion-related validation is hard to come by. For example, from 1982 to 1992, I measured the correlation between the ACT English subscore and a writing sample students produced for placement at my university. In over 35,000 tests, the correlation (Pearson product-moment r) hovered at or below .35. This correlation suggests statistically that the ACTE does not measure about 88% of what readers of the writing sample would define as evidence of writing ability. Can I therefore reason that the ACT results are of no interest? Certainly not, for other analyses have established that the ACT correlates with course grades, a very important measure of writing ability, better than writing samples do. Instead, I must acknowledge that no single assessment captures all the qualities that enter into the evaluation of individuals' learning processes. In education, the problems of measuring writing ability are inextricably bound up with the politics of learning.

Quasi Validity

Since it is unfeasible for an assessment to satisfy the criteria of both in-struction and traditional measurement, one's confidence in a writing assessment's objectivity must rest on approximations of concurrent va-lidity. The various forms of reliability provide a not altogether satisfac-tory substitute for correlations with independent external criteria, establishing a sort of quasi validity.

Interrater Reliability Reliability limits validity: one can make mean-ingful statements about assessment results only to the degree that the results remain consistent. Holistic-assessment specialists have devel-oped well-defined, efficient methods of achieving high *interrater relia-bility*—that is, agreement among readers on the scores appropriate to a range of papers.

Holistic assessments achieve reliability by means of an essentially political process of coalition involving scoring criteria, sample essays, and negotiation. The criteria take the form of a "scoring guide" that de-scribes in some detail the qualities of essays at various levels of perfor-mance on the assessment assignment. Before the scoring guide is composed, highly experienced readers may examine and rank a sample of essays from the assessment to be scored. The guide would then in-clude descriptions of these readers' perceptions as the criteria for scores, from as few as two scores (pass and fail) up to as many as the readers can distinguish consistently. Later, when the entire corps of readers is assembled to evaluate all the essays, the expert readers would lead small groups of them in discussion of both the scoring guide and the sample essays to achieve consensual interpretations. This intersubjective agreement, though useful, is only a sop thrown to the dragon of objectivity.

Other Forms of Reliability Crucial measures of reliability developed in other assessment contexts have not yet been widely applied to essay assessment. An important reliability question is how well assessment scores will hold up when the assessment occasion or topic differs. A study by the Association of American Medical Colleges suggests that on MCAT essays two writing samples are required to establish a score that will remain constant from test to test (Mitchell and Anderson). Except for that study, little is known about *test-retest reliability,* the measure of whether someone will achieve approximately the same score on each attempt at a test of writing ability, or about *alternative-form reliability,* the measure of whether a writer will achieve comparable scores on two different versions of the same test. To make that sort of information widely available would require research techniques as practicable as those for establishing interrater reliability. Even if several forms of reliability could be established, reliability could not be logically equated with concurrent validity.

Triangulation   Given these empirical and political problems, can one look to holistic or portfolio assessment or some as yet undeveloped form of assessment to provide a single definitive score? Both political reality and the state of knowledge about writing assessment discourage implicit faith in any single form of writing assessment. One sensible, practical choice in this situation is to borrow a technique from qualitative research and to *triangulate* information, using multiple sources of data about writing ability and trusting no single measure, since different sources are not usually well correlated. Decision makers already use such a practice. Admissions officers, for example, use high school rank, a writing sample, and a multiple-choice score to make informed decisions about a candidate. In college competency assessments, one might reasonably triangulate a holistic score with grades in writing-intensive courses (in the writing program and the student's major) and the score on a professional writing portfolio. These scores would provide perspectives on writing ability in controlled competitive situations (the holistic score), in learning situations across the curriculum (the grades in writing-intensive courses), and in "real world" situations of unlimited access to assistance with revision (the professional portfolio). One could not expect correlations comparable to those between Godshalk's essay and multiple-choice scores, but one would cross-reference the judgments of students' writing ability instead of assuming ethnocentrically that English departments deserve all the political power on this issue.

Predictive Validity

Like the competitive culture for which education prepares writers, programmatic assessment assumes writing to be a competitive exercise in which arbitrary constraints of time and subject matter serve as rules and in which varying configurations of those constraints produce the various methods of assessing competence. The competitive configurations produce hierarchies, and most important for predictive validity is the hierarchy produced by the bell curve. The bell curve is usually represented as an ineluctable mathematical fact of nature. If one acquires a large enough sample of any human phenomenon, from birth weight to IQ to writing ability, the people in the sample will arrange themselves in a bell curve, a few at the top and bottom and a great many in the middle. Whether fact or artifact, as the bell curve governs writing assessment, it exercises political influence over the topics students may write about, and it creates ethical dilemmas for those who administer assessments and use their results.

The Bell Curve and Topic Choice   For influential testing authorities, predictive validity requires a normal distribution of scores—a bell curve in which most writers' work falls in a middle range and the upper and lower scores taper off on either side of the middle (e.g., White, *Teaching* [1st ed.] 100–19). Edward White sees it as an unequivocal indicator of the validity of a topic if the topic yields a range of scores similar to the range produced by other measures of writers' abilities (111). In natural conditions, repeated measurements or very large samples may be required to produce a bell curve. If circumstances do not permit the luxury of infinite measurement, the curve can nevertheless be produced, if one exercises great care. To produce the curve, one must rigorously formulate assignments for the competitive assessment environment. Ruth and Murphy list over thirty criteria for formulating an assessment assignment (238–89). Even White's comparatively simple list of four criteria makes clear the elaborate premeditation involved in scientifically designing an assignment for assessment (104–10). Designers must pretest assignments to be sure that students are given a single topic that they can read easily and write on with interest, a topic that allows scorers readily to perceive and agree on levels of performance and that produces papers whose scores approximate the bell curve created by other measures of student writing ability.

Assessment administrators take such pains with topic construction to help students demonstrate their authentic ability, usually presumed to be the best they can do. Those experienced in writing assessment know that some topics seem to cause good students to produce dreadful writing and that the most reliable way to minimize unwanted and "irrelevant" topic effects is to construct topics carefully and to pretest them thoroughly. Designing topics to produce best work is more important to *summative assessment,* which occurs at the end of instruction and is intended to evaluate its net effects, than to *formative assessment,* which occurs during instruction and is intended to guide the teaching-learning process. I suggest elsewhere ("Models of Competence") that students' best work may not necessarily be either their most representative work or the most useful information an assessment can produce. For example, a teacher who wants to see the limits of students' competence may deliberately elicit less than their best work by giving them a diagnostic essay more challenging than the work for the course. Summative assessment could provide teachers with information about the essay topics that cause students to perform erratically and with speculations about the sources of the difficulty with the topics.

The profession enjoys considerable understanding of how to design writing assessment to produce summative evaluations. Interrater reliability and bell-curve validity are solved problems. Practicable procedures guide assessment administrators in engineering prompts and training raters. It is time to begin attempting to understand how more-relaxed procedures and more-naturalistic conditions can be brought into the discourse of assessment. As research moves assessment closer to the authentic conditions of learning and writing performance, assessment and instruction will enter into a less adversarial relation, creating a more credible place for assessment in schools.

Ethical Implications of Using the Bell Curve   Considered a fact of nature, the bell curve seems to authorize social Darwinism. If natural law dictates that any group has a top, middle, and bottom, it's no one's fault if some people fail. Instead, it is the eugenic responsibility of academe to purify itself of those who are the bottom and thereby to improve the species. After each purification cycle, a new bell curve emerges from nature, supplying more misfits against whom campaigns for rigor and higher standards can be mounted. Again it's no one's fault if these campaigns require that some grow richer, others grow poorer, and still others are sacrificed altogether. This specious formulation bears enough resemblance to a basic academic value—competitive striving for improvement—to be easy to use and reuse as a political strategy. Though the bell curve may be a fact of nature, the decision to use it is ethically dangerous.

As we have seen, building a curve is assessment's raison d'être. Any good effects of a bell-curve hierarchy will derive from the wisdom and experience of those who set the curve. In situations where an unambiguously right choice is almost never apparent, assessment authorities must attempt to distinguish better choices from worse so that the sacrifices they impose on others will be meaningful. Since ethical dilemmas are a personal issue, I will illustrate this point with an anecdote concerning a situation in which I tried and failed to solve a political problem with an assessment. Social Darwinism combined with ulterior motives to create a nasty outcome.

In the early 1980s, factions of the Academic Senate at Illinois State University approached the English department chair with a proposal for an exit writing examination. The chair solicited my support as writing assessment coordinator. I had originally taken the coordinator job because I was interested in working with the test used to place students in writing courses. In designing and implementing that test, I had enjoyed serving what I believed to be good academic values and useful purposes—previewing instruction for new students, advising students on appropriate classes, supporting instruction, giving administrators a snapshot of the entering class. The exit examination turned out to be quite another matter. It was clear to me that the chair's interest in assessment stemmed from the promise of additional power and resources. It was equally clear that the people outside the English department who sought the examination had no inkling of what writing ability constituted and, in fact, planned to use the exam to punish certain departments and groups of students in a way that I abhorred. I told myself that if I maintained control, I could create a "valid" examination and in the process educate faculty members. I could transform their petty turf wars into a higher good, the promulgation of correct knowledge and attitudes about writing. I thought, as many people before me have thought, that the only problem with power was getting enough of it into the right hands.

During the debate in the Academic Senate, the main issue seemed to be that graduates might embarrass the institution by committing surface errors in the workplace. I found the Academic Senate's bourgeois parochialism more embarrassing than my students' surface errors, but I was evidently successful in concealing my feelings, for those who proposed the examination prevailed and even managed to levy a fee on students who would take it. Eager for the technical challenges of developing the exam and hoping to stimulate interest in writing across the curriculum, I dutifully researched the attitudes and practices of faculty members who taught writing or used it in content courses. I found to no one's surprise that the most common forms of student writing outside writing courses were essay answers to examination questions and summaries of reading passages. I also found that the faculty believed an exit examination should test students' ability to avoid the sort of surface errors that mortify the middle class. I designed a two-hour examination: the essay prompts were reading passages drawn from various subject areas, and a multiple-choice examination assessed students' ability to identify and correct surface errors in a prepared passage. In due course, the examination began identifying questionable writers who had slipped through the system and delaying their graduation until they could provide a presentable writing sample, reassuring us that they would not embarrass the institution.

As chair of the University Writing Examination Board, I tried to make the exit exam lead the curriculum beneficially. I published sample essays, scoring guides, and analyses of failing essays. I led scoring sessions for faculty members, gave talks at meetings, and wrote reports about the meaning of the assessment. I secured reading passages from faculty members in all five colleges of the university. I gave analytic feedback to students whose essays had failed to pass muster, and I trained tutors in the writing center to work with those students. In time, some departments began requiring additional writing courses. The freshman English course began to include some work on test writing, which I regarded as a responsible change, given the results of my survey. Informal comparisons of the first-year's exit examination essays with later years' suggested some improvement in students' writing abilities insofar as the examination measured them.

Nevertheless, I felt more and more conflicted as time went by. My initial perceptions about the motives of the exit examination's advocates turned out to be right on the money, as it were. Each year, English department coffers were enriched by funds—examination fees and grants—that were designated for the writing examination but used to finance activities not remotely relevant to it. I still was told all too often by faculty members—including some in the English department—that it was good to know we had a writing examination to catch those illiterate students their lazy colleagues were letting through the system. Too often, the students found by the test to write less well than the norm were ones whom the academic system in general and the writing program in particular had already marginalized, even terrorized. They were minorities or immigrants or athletes or students in half a dozen applied technological majors. Whereas the placement test had served meaningful ends, even doing some good for such students, the exit exam did not serve a meaningful purpose for anyone. Not justified by any higher good, it was merely imprisoning students, holding them hostage to the vanity and venality of the faculty. My discomfort with the situation grew and, after a particularly nasty series of interactions over the examination, I decided to resign my position as coordinator of assessment and lord high executioner.

A year after my resignation, at a meeting of the state English teachers' organization, a brief conversation with the chair of a high school English department in a western suburb of Chicago crystallized the experience for me. I told him that I worked with writing assessment, and he angrily described his feelings of victimization by assessments. He said that the Chicago newspapers were using assessment scores to rank high schools. His school had recently absorbed a number of Hispanic immigrants, and it was now ranked near the bottom of Chicago-area schools. He was sure his budget was going to suffer because of tests that did not accurately measure the abilities of his students. A little taken aback by his vehemence, I advised him to write letters explaining that no one could draw valid conclusions from newspaper rankings, but I was not able to believe in my own arguments. He said that his letters would be perceived as "sour grapes," and I knew he was right. It was the ethical responsibility of the assessment's designers and administrators to confront and rebut uses of their data that contributed to unfair and inaccurate reasoning. The conversation drove home to me at the ethical level a practical fact I had always known about assessments: that they may acquire predictive validity by tautological designs that serve political ends and that reinforce preexisting inequities. While the proposed new category of "consequential validity" may appear to provide an angle of attack on assessments that perpetuate the sort of abuses I have described, it seems both more elegant and more logical to construe this issue as a simple ethical one related to predictive validity, which is consequential in its nature. Practically, since one cannot design an apolitical test, one had better be able to present good reasons for subordinating the interests of a person to those of an institution. The predictive validity of an assessment should be based, at least in part, on the procedures assessment administrators have established for informing the public and controlling the public's interpretations of assessment results. Any published version of assessment results should present those who use the information with the caveat that the assessment's administrators will pursue every available means, including legal action, to prevent misuse of their data. Such practices would go a considerable distance toward remediating the tendency of assessments to operate tautologically, producing self-fulfilling prophecies.

I have tried in this essay to convey my confidence that good assessments can help an institution to evaluate its past accurately and thereby reason about its future intelligently. I have also tried to convey my deep misgivings about putting assessment in the service of educational reform. It seems to me appropriate to use assessment to establish the necessity for reform. Once the curriculum is reformed, it also seems appropriate to use assessment to determine the degree of success the new curriculum has enjoyed. And it is always appropriate to bear in mind the political consequences of assessment. However, when awareness of political consequences shades into furtherance of political ambitions, including selfless zeal for educational reform, one can be sure that sound assessment practice will be compromised. I believe it is best that writing assessment remain as aloof as is practicable from political activism: two steps behind composition theory and one step behind teaching practice, operationalizing the logic and quantifying the consequences of what researchers and teachers have done, solving the technical problems of measurement, feeding back data to inform valid educational decision making in classrooms, schools, colleges, other institutions, and communities. If assessment has a role to play in the development of theory in English, that role is to supply empirical grounding like that which experimentation supplies to the sciences.

In closing, I propose some guidelines for productive discussions of validity—five red herrings to avoid and five questions to discuss.

The following propositions, effective as distractions from important issues, tend to subvert reasoning and promote quarreling.

- *Assessment is absolutely necessary.* Particularly in situations beset by political conflict, assessment is often not worth the trouble it causes.
- *Assessment should be pursued for altruistic ends.* Altruists are often more dangerous than criminals. A self-deceived altruist can override personal scruples and technical priorities in the interest of achieving some nebulous future benefit for humankind.
- *Teachers are the victims of assessment, and administrators are the perpetrators.* In defining the instructional and programmatic perspectives, I have attempted to suggest that the holders of both views share the patient and agent roles and that neither can see assessment clearly without taking the other's perspective.
- *One assessment technique is inherently superior to another.* Discussants of this proposition will exchange extravagant and unsupportable claims for their favorite technique, generating more heat than light.
- *Assessment is the source of unfairness in education.* This obfuscating move, available to any desperate debater, is analogous to blaming the weather report for the weather.

Among the questions relevant to an interesting discussion of validity are the five that follow. These questions may also be useful in generating relevant dialogue about the political viability of an assessment, for, practically speaking, the validity and the viability of an assessment rest on the same grounds.

- Whose construct of writing ability underlies the assessment's design?

○ What cooperative measures have assessment and curricular designers undertaken to ensure integration between assessment and curricular content?
○ How are credible triangulating sources of information used to improve the accuracy of an assessment's results?
○ How does the assessment handle conflicts between the need to obtain authentic writing samples and the need to produce usable
scores?
○ What specific policies and procedures have assessment administrators established to prevent inaccurate or unfair use of assessment
results?

Illinois State University

Essay Reliability:
Form and Meaning

Doug Shale

Much of what has been written about essay reliability is predicated on the application of classical test theory to the scores awarded to essays. The dominance of this traditional psychometric view of reliability has far-reaching consequences for writing assessment. I believe that one of these is what Michael Williamson calls "the stasis in writing assessment" (4). In fact, the premise of this essay is that classical test theory is not an appropriate measurement model for elaborating a concept of reliability for the assessment of writing. Moreover, I believe that the political ramifications of developing a concept of essay reliability through classical test theory are wide-ranging and subtle. Why do we persist in our view of classical test theory when the dysfunctional and deleterious consequences of doing so confront us boldly and continuously? What of the professional relation between those concerned with teaching writing and those who are the keepers and interpreters of a measurement theory that exerts on teachers a view of writing antithetical to classroom experience? How should we regard quantified assessments of essays derived from fundamentally flawed premises? What are the consequences for students affected by decisions made on the basis of such scores? These questions reflect a political side to the measurement of writing performance that is often not apparent to those who are affected by the measurement process.

The concept of reliability has been well worked out for multiple-choice tests and seems well understood. However, the application of the concept of reliability to essay marking has been considerably less clear (see, e.g., McCleary; Thompson, a reply to McCleary). Partly, this is attributable to imprecise usage of the term *reliability*—which may reflect an imprecise understanding of what things possess the quality that the term designates. For example, in the literature on the subject, the term has been applied to scoring procedures, to classes of scoring procedures (as in the "reliability" of direct or indirect assessment), to criteria used in analytic marking, to essay scores, to writers, and to inter- and intramarker agreement. Problems of interpretation have not been helped by deterministic references to *the* reliability, which imply that there is just one common understanding of the term. There simply is "no single, universal and absolute reliability coefficient" (Stanley, "Reliability" 363). Moreover, as Roy Cox observes, regarding the concept of reliability in testing, "the use of 'reliability' in this context is not quite the same as its common use." The term refers in testing to an absence of differences "when we repeat what is meant to be exactly the same measurement. . . . Even with this use, however, the term is still vague and there may be some point in dropping it and only thinking in terms of particular aspects of reliability like homogeneity, stability or [lack of] marker variability" (71).

Considerable ambiguity arises also because the full sense of reliability as understood within the context of multiple-choice testing does not transfer well to the world of essay testing. Reliability in multiple-choice testing is a matter of assessing the consistency of results over a period of time (which is a measure of the stability of scores) and over different forms of the instrument (which is a measure of equivalence) and of assessing consistency within the instrument itself (internal consistency). The measurement model that elaborates this sense of reliability is known as classical test theory.

Undoubtedly, the major factor responsible for the complexity of the concept of reliability in the context of essay testing is the subjective scoring process. It has long been known that marks awarded to essays may vary considerably from marker to marker when multiple markers are used and from occasion to occasion when the same marker is used (see, e.g., Hartog, Rhodes, and Burt; T. Hopkins; Huddleston). This variation has naturally led to a concern that the measurement procedure does not yield reliable results. Rater disagreement (or inconsistency) is important insofar as it limits the reliability of essay measures —and unreliability in these measures, in classical terms, limits their validity. (We shall see later in the essay that there is another dimension to the relation between validity and reliability in writing assessment.) Thus, we are faced with something of a dilemma. We value the essay because it can reveal "information regarding the structure, dynamics and functioning of the student's mental life" (Sims 17). On the other hand, we have difficulty contending with the effect that such freedom of response has on judgments of quality.

For this reason, measures of intermarker and intramarker agreement have often been calculated and cited as indexes of reliability. However, to use indicators of rater consistency as estimates of reliability is confusing and misleading. As Douglas Finlayson, among others, observes, rater consistency is not a measure of reliability in the usual sense of that term. Even in instances in which it is explicitly recognized that the dependability of a measure of essay scores is attenuated by inconsistency in rater judgments, there typically has been no direct calculation of the effect that the disagreement has on the dependability of the measure—other than through a general eyeballing of whatever index of marker agreement is available and occasionally through the application of some rule of thumb regarding what constitutes "too much" disagreement.

A major consequence of classical test theory has been a fixation on marker disagreement, and efforts to improve the "reliability" of essay measures have been directed primarily to eliminating marker variability. This emphasis is not necessary and has led to distortions in essay assessment practices. In this essay I attempt to develop a fuller understanding of the concept of reliability as applied to essay testing and then argue that alternative views are available to us. In particular, the framework of generalizability theory offers a more satisfactory measurement model (Cronbach, Gleser, Nanda, and Rajaratnam). In elaborating on generalizability theory, I pay especial attention to the issues of marker agreement and the essay topic.

Although I emphasize essay marking, the measurement view I present here is equally appropriate to the wider class of performance assessments that "typically permit students substantial latitude in interpreting, responding to, and perhaps designing tasks; they result in fewer independent responses, each of which is complex, reflecting integration of multiple skills and knowledge; and they require expert judgement for evaluation." By this characterization, an essay would be a performance assessment, but so too would be "work exhibits, portfolios, or other products or performances" (P. Moss, "Conceptions" 230, 229). The concept of generalizability and the statistical treatment of quantitative assessments derived from the assessment of writing portfolios would be similar. In fact, the notion of a portfolio anticipates a requirement within generalizability theory that we identify the universe to which we wish to generalize our quantitative assessment.

The Concept of Reliability

Ted Frick and Melvin Semmel state, "Reliability has been defined classically as the consistency with which something is measured by maximally similar methods" (158). In practice, this requires obtaining at least two measurements, typically by retesting an individual on the same test, by the use of parallel forms of a test, or through measures of internal consistency. We should recognize, in addition, that the estimation of reliability depends not only on the test itself but also on such factors as the characteristics of the individuals being tested and the conditions under which the test is administered.

With essay tests, the presence of a rater (or raters) has clouded the issue, and there is often confusion about what attribute *reliability* refers to. In this essay, the term refers to a measure (or, alternatively, a measurement)—a measure being a procedure for producing a score for each examinee. Characterizing reliability in this way has a number of advantages. In particular, it underscores the fact that "a single instrument can produce scores which are reliable, and other scores which are unreliable. Even one measure may be reliable or unreliable, depending on the manner in which the instrument is used, the subjects observed . . . " (Rowley 53). Thus, this characterization calls attention to the fact that it is essential to specify the conditions constituting the procedure whereby an instrument is used. One aspect of the procedure whereby measures are generated from essays has to do, of course, with markers and marking conditions. It follows, then, that it would be extremely useful to have some structural theory to support this specification of conditions. A case can be made that generalizability theory provides such a structure.

As indicated above, "the formal definition of reliability has been phrased in terms of the correlation between parallel sets of measures . . . " (Stanley, "Reliability" 404). The parallel-measures concept entails a number of important assumptions that bear on the meaning and sufficiency of calculations of reliability coefficients. Tests are assumed to be parallel if they are equivalent in content, means, variance, and intercorrelations of items (Cronbach, Rajaratnam, and Gleser). In practice, this is widely regarded as a stringent definition of parallelism that is seldom satisfied even when traditional psychological tests are used. Moreover, as Julian Stanley observes: "it seems obvious that the procedure for reliability determination which makes use of parallel forms will measure up to logical requirements. This is in fact true, provided satisfactory procedures for preparing parallel tests can be established" ("Reliability" 404). Whether or not satisfactory procedures can be established is arguable (for example, see the preceding essay, by Maurice Scharton). More will be said on this point later.

Calculating a reliability coefficient, then, is a matter of determining "how much of the variation in the set of scores is due to certain systematic differences among the individuals in the group and how much to other sources of variation that are considered, for particular purposes, errors of measurement" (Stanley, "Reliability" 369). In the classical formulation, an observed score is seen to be the sum of a "true score" and a purely random "error." In the classical context, a reliability coefficient is estimated as the ratio of the variance of true scores to the variance of observed scores. The issue essential to determining the reliability of a measure relative to a particular group of individuals is defining what should be thought of as true variance among individuals and what as error variance, given the investigator's purpose.

The hypothetical true score for an individual is classically defined as the average score that would result if the individual took similar tests many times under similar conditions. However, "a difficulty with the term 'true score' is that the statistical concept of a limiting value approached through extensive observation is readily confused with some underlying in-the-eye-of-God reality" (Cronbach, Gleser, Nanda, and Rajaratnam 19). In effect, a true score "is the score resulting from all systematic factors one chooses to aggregate, including any systematic biasing factors that may produce systematic incorrectness in the scores. . . . The heart of any treatment of reliability involves recognition that the true variance is *wanted* variance and that what is wanted will depend on the interpretation proposed by the investigator" (Stanley, "Reliability" 361).

Specifying what would constitute "similar tests" and "similar conditions" given the systematic factors one chooses to aggregate is problematic. In classical theory, the concept of parallel forms and parallel measurements provides a framework for addressing this issue. However, when a measurement procedure is based on the essay, the matter becomes even more complicated, largely because of the effects of implicit assumptions about markers (who they are) and about how they should regard the marking task. While the exercise appears rational—an appearance shored up by the application of an apparently rational classical measurement model—in effect the marking process (and its results) can be politically determined in subtle, wide-ranging ways. This is an issue I return to later in the essay. G. Gosling approaches this dilemma from the classical-measurement point of view by distinguishing a *candidate's* true score ("his mean score on an infinite number of tests") and a *script's* true score ("the mean of the marks [awarded a script] by all qualified judges"). He concludes, "Ideally, then, to arrive at a perfect assessment of the ability we wish to measure, we should administer an infinite number of tests, each marked by all qualified judges" (8). Such an approach begs two critical conceptual questions. First, there simply is no satisfactory theory to support the construction of parallel essay forms (Scharton, in his essay, refers to "the lack of a canon" in writing instruction). Second, how should one regard markers as a condition of measurement? Are they "parallel instruments" in the same sense that different forms of a test can be parallel? Classical test theory would hold that they are, with the strong equivalency requirement that, in theory, alternative markers should produce perfectly consistent assessments of writing quality. Both of these points are elaborated on in later sections.

On the other side, it has long been recognized that there are many ways to define "error." In general, though, error variance is the variation in a particular set of measurements that will not be reproduced on another occasion (for example, error due to the sequence in which essays in a set are marked). Error variance is considered a consequence of unreliability in a measurement procedure, and the magnitude of this variance relative to total variance is a measure of the unreliability. However, as Stanley points out, "not every type of error, not every discrepancy from the 'true' value that would register for the specimen in question, qualifies as a part of the error variance" ("Reliability" 360). What appears as error variance in a set of measures depends on how they are defined and carried out.

The variance that is "wanted" with respect to individual differences is usually the lasting general variance (Thorndike)—for example, variance due to differences in writing tasks. The other category of errors consists of chance errors of measurement "that are unrelated to the future performance of the individual to which one wants to make inference" (Stanley, "Reliability" 361). This is random error, the type of error that typically is of most concern in reliability considerations.

About essays William Coffman points out:

> The sources of error in essay examinations are complex. Some error arises because the questions in an examination are only a sample of all the possible questions that might be asked. Some error is the result of differences between raters. Some is due to the variability in the judgments of a rater from one time to another. Both interindividual and intraindividual variability can be further broken down into at least three components. The extent to which any of these various sources of error are present depends on how the essay questions are prepared, on how the responses are rated, and on how the scores are used. (7)

The degree of concern appropriate for each of such sources of error depends on the aims of the investigator (and, concomitantly, on the design of the study).

The Correlational Approach

As mentioned previously, the traditional approach to assessing reliability is to calculate the correlation between two sets of scores that, theoretically, are produced by "maximally similar methods." Again, under this approach, it is postulated that measures are strictly parallel—that in addition to the instruments' being equivalent in content, test forms have equal means and variances, and there is no interaction of subject with test form. Variance is considered to arise as a result of true differences among subjects combined with random variation among observations (i.e., error). While this approach is reasonable for carefully equated parallel forms of tests, it is not appropriate for measures that depart from these assumptions or that differ qualitatively. As Lee Cronbach points out, the assumption of parallel measurement procedures "is not likely true for work samples, observations, or ratings from different acquaintances" (*Essentials* 154). For example, in essay testing, markers may differ in the central tendency of the scores they assign (a main difference among markers), in the distribution of their scores across the grading scale being used, and in the attributes they attend to (a difference giving rise to a subject-marker interaction).

All of which shows that there are many sources of systematic variation in essay measures. The classical approach to reliability cannot properly reflect these influences. As Coffman states, "A product-moment coefficient of correlation between two sets of ratings does not adequately assess all of these sources of errors in ratings. It takes into account only the fluctuations in relative standing" (3). The classical approach deals with error variance as an amorphous single source of variance, typically leaving two or more sources entangled (Cronbach, *Essentials*). Moreover, when a study correlates two sets of measures, the value of the study is much enhanced if we can ascertain how much the observed correlation is attenuated by errors of measurement. For essays, we are concerned with how much effect inconsistency in marking has on the dependability of the obtained measures of writing proficiency. Classical theory cannot address this question directly. In addition, the standard correlational approach does not generalize well when more than two sets of measures are being considered.

Under the classical approach, any two sets of measures may be correlated, and the result is expressed as a reliability coefficient. There is no simple way to interpret each coefficient, because it is not usually apparent what factors contributed to the error variance. Consequently, these reliability coefficients may appear nominally similar, even interchangeable. To state this in a converse form, coefficients that seem nominally the same may in fact be based on extremely diverse information and sometimes may suggest contradictory conclusions.

Finally, as Kenneth Hopkins observes, classical measurement theory has "ignored latent random effects in the relevant universe of inference." Consequently, "classical test theory ordinarily underestimates the degree of measurement error in the appropriate universe of generalization; that is, the inferences are not statistically congruent with those addressed by the reliability coefficient because undefined random sources of variation in the system are not acknowledged" (703). As we see later in this essay, an alternative view of markers in writing assessment reveals their role as a major latent effect ignored "in the relevant universe of inference."

The Analysis-of-Variance Approach

Under the classical measurement approach, the observed score is regarded as the sum of the true score and an error component, and reliability is estimated as the ratio of the variance of true scores to the variance of observed scores. Researchers have long recognized that analysis-of-variance (ANOVA) procedures could be applied to the estimation of components of variance (see, e.g., Burt; Hoyt) and that these components could be used to calculate correlation coefficients. Under certain assumptions, the classical correlational approach and the ANOVA approach coincide (Stanley, "Reliability"; Cronbach, Gleser, Nanda, and Rajaratnam).

In general, Ronald Fisher's analysis of variance (*Statistical Methods*)

> revolutionized statistical thinking with the concept of the factorial experiment in which the conditions of observation are classified in several respects. Investigators who adopt Fisher's line of thought must abandon the concept of undifferentiated error. The error formerly seen as amorphous is now attributed to multiple sources, and a suitable experiment can estimate how much variation arises from each controllable source.
>
> (Cronbach, Gleser, Nanda, and Rajaratnam 1)

In spite of the power of the analysis-of-variance framework, it has not seen extensive use in research based on essay measures. Early applications of the analysis of variance to essay marking were made by B. M. D. Cast; Douglas Finlayson; Albert Pilliner; and Julian Stanley ("Analysis-of-Variance Principles"). A more contemporary example is by Hunter Breland and his coauthors.

In summary, then, in efforts to characterize the reliability of measures, the ANOVA approach represents a major advance over the classical correlational approach because ANOVA allows us to represent multiple sources of variation systematically in an experimental design and to estimate the effect of each—instead of dealing with such variance as an undifferentiated, amorphous whole. This in turn permits a more refined appreciation of the factors that affect our sense of true variance and error variance; that is, we can advance our understanding of how a change in study design affects each component of observed-score variance. And having specific components of variance permits the formulation of different estimates of reliability that are appropriate to particular research questions.

However, an approach based strictly on the ANOVA framework also has shortcomings. First of all, the traditional ANOVA approach emphasizes testing for the statistical significance of experimental effects, although this emphasis is not necessary. Furthermore, the traditional applications of ANOVA in agricultural studies permitted direct measurement of variables and an exhaustive enumeration of experimental conditions—conditions that rarely, if ever, prevail in social science research. As Kenneth Hopkins points out:

> The numbers associated with bushels, pounds, pigs/litter, and so forth differ fundamentally from cognitive and affective measures in ways that have important implications for statistical analysis and interpretation. Items on tests and inventories are only a sample of the universe of items to which an inference is intended, whereas there is no sampling in the agricultural measures per se.   (704)

Hopkins goes on to say that the development of the distribution theory for "fixed," "random," and mixed ANOVA models has done much to improve matters.

However, the analysis-of-variance framework is silent about how to generalize appropriately from a study. That is, it is left entirely up to the investigator to consider *at the time of designing a study* whether a particular factor should be designated as fixed (that is, as a specific condition not representative of a population of such conditions and hence not interchangeable with another similar condition) or random (that is, as a sample condition drawn from a population of such conditions and hence interchangeable with other such samples) and to be aware of the implications of this specification. As a result, as Hopkins notes,

> Inferences drawn in education research are frequently not congruent with the statistical analysis because an important source of error is hidden and ignored in the statistical model employed. That

is, a factor is implicitly treated as a fixed effect, yet the results are interpreted as if the factor had been employed as a random factor.
(703)

Moreover, unless one attends closely to the details of the design of an ANOVA study, it is not apparent from the study's results just how the factors involved ought to be regarded and, most important, how the results should be interpreted. For example, the variance components given in Pilliner's analysis of a three-factor design (subjects, markers, essay form)—and, in particular, the estimates of coefficients of reliability based on these components—differ from those given in Stanley's analysis of the same three factors ("Analysis-of-Variance Principles"). An examination of the details of the experimental design indicates that Stanley considered an effect with respect to the order in which the essays were written, whereas Pilliner did not. Moreover, Stanley assumed that the subjects and the markers used were samples from populations (that is, were random effects), whereas Pilliner seemingly regarded them as fixed. The important point to be made is that although Stanley and Pilliner present estimates of reliability that are nominally the same, one would conduct each study differently, and consequently one also ought to qualify appropriately the inferences that can be properly drawn in each study.

The analysis-of-variance framework per se does not support the elucidation of such distinctions. So, although ANOVA has provided the means for a more refined analysis of components of variance, there remains the problem of illuminating "the subtle inconsistency between the statistical analysis and the related universe of inference . . . " (K. Hopkins 704). Generalizability theory is widely viewed as a comprehensive structural theory for dealing with the dilemmas arising from classical reliability theory and from the application of ANOVA procedures to estimating reliability. As Robert Brennan points out, "To an extent, generalizability theory can be viewed both as an extension of classical test theory and as an application of certain analysis of variance procedures to measurement models involving multiple sources of error" (1).

Generalizability Theory

The foundations of generalizability theory were set out in early work by Cronbach and his associates ("Theory") and were culminated in a book by Cronbach, G. C. Gleser, H. Nanda, and N. Rajaratnam entitled *The Dependability of Behavioral Measurements*. Readers may find this source or one like Brennan's *Elements of Generalizability Theory* help-ful, for, as Brennan points out, "the power of generalizability theory is purchased at the price of some conceptual and statistical complexities" (2). There is a substantial literature regarding generalizability theory, and the account that follows here is necessarily abbreviated.

A measure has value to the extent that it gives us information about some larger context. An observed score should at least represent the collection of measurements that might have been made, and the ob-tained score is of interest because it tells us something about the ex-pected value of other measures taken under equivalent conditions. This is the essence of the traditional understanding of the concept of reliability. If it were possible to do so, an investigator would measure a subject exhaustively over equivalent conditions and take the average of all the measurements. As mentioned earlier, such an average is referred to in classical measurement theory as "the true score." It has already been noted that it is particularly difficult to define when conditions are equivalent. In contrast, observed-score variance is computed on scores obtained under a set of conditions that may differ from one another:

> Using another set of questions, or repeating the same measure on another occasion, as was done traditionally, inevitably introduces sources of systematic variation. . . . When conditions of a mea-surement situation can be maintained equivalent, the variability between one result and the next is likely to be limited. When mea-surement conditions are allowed to vary in one or several respects, the results are likely to be modified by the intervention of the cor-responding sources of variation.
>
> (Cardinet, Tourneur, and Allal 121)

Under the requirement for equivalency, an investigator would need to determine the range of conditions over which true-score variance ought to be estimated, doing so by some procedure that yielded repro-ducible results. But, as Cronbach notes, there is no clear basis on which to do this (*Essentials* 14).

Generalizability theory was formulated to address directly the concep-tual difficulties inherent in the classical measurement approach. In gen-eralizability theory, the concept of the true score, with its connotations of absoluteness, is replaced by the concept of a "universe score," which Cronbach, Gleser, Nanda, and Rajaratnam characterize as follows:

> The score on which the decision is to be based is only one of many scores that might serve the same purpose. The decision maker is

almost never interested in the response given to the particular stimulus objects or questions, to the particular tester, at the particular moment of testing. Some, at least, of these conditions of measurement could be altered without making the score any less acceptable to the decision maker. That is to say, there is a universe of observations, any of which would have yielded a usable basis for the decision. The ideal datum on which to base the decision would be something like the person's mean score over all acceptable observations, which we shall call his "universe score." The investigator uses the observed score or some function of it as if it were the universe score. That is, he generalizes from sample to universe. The question of "reliability" thus resolves into a question of accuracy of generalization, or generalizability. The universe of interest to the decision maker is defined when he tells us what observations would be equally acceptable for his purpose (i.e., would "give him the same information"). He must describe the acceptable set of observations in terms of the allowable conditions of measurement. This gives an operational definition to the class of procedures to be considered. (15)

Under this concept of the universe score, generalizability (or reliability) can be regarded as the expected value of the correlation between the set of obtained scores and other sets of obtained scores that could be drawn from the universe of interest. If the obtained scores derived from a particular measurement agree closely with the universe score, the observation may be regarded as reliable or generalizable. Because such observations necessarily also agree well with one another, they are considered dependable or consistent.

The counterpart of the traditional reliability coefficient is the coefficient of generalizability, which Cronbach, Gleser, Nanda, and Rajaratnam define as "the ratio of universe-score variance to the expected observed-score variance" (17). In the framework of generalizability theory, a set of measures is not necessarily reliable or unreliable in the traditional absolute sense. "One can simply generalize, to different degrees, from one observed score to the multiple means of the different sets of possible observations. It follows that there are as many generalizability coefficients as sets of observations" (Cardinet, Tourneur, and Allal 122).

Cronbach coined the term *generalizability* because it "immediately implies 'generalization to what?'" (*Essentials* 154). As he points out, generalizing over markers is not the same thing as generalizing over written passages. So it is important to note that a marker usually has a different universe score for each universe and that there is typically a different degree of generalizability for each universe. Consequently, the investigator's responsibility for defining the universe of concern is a considerable one. Typically, an investigator should choose a set of observations that represent this universe. Conversely, the conditions under which measures are obtained constrain the universe to which the measures can be generalized.

Someone conducting a generalizability study obtains two or more measures per person and determines how well they agree. Certain conditions (both known and unknown) will vary from measurement to measurement, and their influence will be accounted for in the "error" variance. Other conditions may be held constant from measurement to measurement. An analysis that treats this effect as part of the universe-score variance is incorrect unless the universe definition calls for holding that particular condition constant.

For example, if two raters mark every essay, the agreement of their scores provides an evaluation for only one source of error—that originating from the markers. In this case, the coefficient of generalizability tells us how well we can generalize from one marking to the score a universe of judges would assign to the same performance. It tells us how well we have sampled judgments, but it cannot tell us anything about how well we have sampled a person's writing. An intraclass correlation among raters may be calculated, but it ignores differences in marker means. Therefore, this coefficient is of relevance only in studies in which markers rate all essays. But in a study in which the markers differ from essay to essay, the relevant intraclass coefficient is the one that treats marker leniency or severity as a source of error.

Generalizability theory has not been used much in writing research, to which it is well suited because of the multitude of variables that must be contended with in that area. Generalizability theory is drawn on in studies by Joe Steele; Kari Tormakangas; and Suzanne Lane and D. Sabers.

Choosing an appropriate experimental design for a generalizability study is largely a matter of deciding which facets to incorporate and in what interpretive context to incorporate them. Because we know that interrater disagreement can significantly affect measures obtained with essays, all studies in this domain ought to specify markers as a facet (a facet being the set of all possible conditions of a particular kind). We also know that individual writing performance can vary considerably from writing sample to writing sample (begging for the moment the issue of the specification of writing samples); consequently, the study design should also include a facet for writing samples. The objectives of the study dictate the need for other facets, but the facets of markers and writing samples are ubiquitous.

Identifying appropriate universes seems much more problematic for these two facets than for others. Since we must be aware of what these universes are before we can select an appropriate experimental design, it may serve us well to look at the matter in some detail.

Universes of Writing Samples

Seldom is an investigator interested only in a single piece of writing. Typically the intent is to generalize to writing samples of a particular kind and perhaps occasionally to writing samples in general. There are a variety of universes of writing samples to which one might generalize, and it is important to distinguish among them.

As a first look at the problem, let us take the variability that appears when measures are obtained for a person's performances on what is intended to be essentially the same writing task. This traditionally was a matter of the person's responses either to the same writing task on two (or more) occasions or to two (or more) writing tasks that could be considered to be in some sense equivalent. This universe of generalization is of limited interest. While it is true that by repeatedly presenting the same writing task we may enhance the reproducibility of the measures obtained from it, we do so at the expense of the extent to which we can generalize the results of the study. And this is basically the point made by the American Psychological Association standards: "Aside from practical limitations, retesting [an individual with the same test] is not a theoretically desirable method of determining a reliability coefficient if, as usual, the items that constitute the test are only one of many sets (actual or hypothetical) that might equally well have been used to measure the particular ability or trait"(48). As noted earlier, there is also the considerable difficulty of establishing formal equivalence between different writing tasks (where a particular writing task or its equivalent would result in the same score, all other things being equal). How does one go about prescribing conditions of equivalency in writing assignments—particularly with respect to content? Or is it even possible? Under the classic concept of reliability, such equivalency was of course vital.

The viewpoint of generalizability theory makes the issue of the selection of a writing sample more manageable. All one need do is address the question of what observations would be equally acceptable for the investigator's purpose. In this framework, we would be prepared to accept a specification that the sample should be like the universe of writing tasks. We are not forced to establish formal equivalency—we need only establish the basis on which a sample may be taken from the universe. This requirement could reduce to defining a universe in terms of topics or of mode of discourse or whatever. However, because any set of equally acceptable observations identified in this way is likely to be heterogeneous (either in itself or because of the varying interaction between writer and task), a sample of one observation is less likely than a larger sample to represent the universe. Therefore, one ought to incorporate more than one writing task in any study using essays. To state the matter simply, we know that individuals' writing performance varies in response to the writing task. Thus two or more writing tasks derived from the universe of interest can yield a more dependable measure for an individual than one can.

This approach rationalizes many practices that have been shown to enhance the dependability of measures obtained with essays. For example, it has been demonstrated in a variety of ways that "reliability" (granting that the meaning of the term was inconstant) improves when the number of samples is increased (Steele). In addition, it is well known in sampling theory but not widely appreciated in research in writing that results derived from a sampling of observations that is too small are likely to be unstable. Finally, such an approach can do much to mitigate the kinds of issues raised by Davida Charney, among others, regarding the selection of writing topics. For example, Charney, in the context of the reliability of ratings, asks, "Specifically, should writing samples representing different aims of discourse be compared?" (70). The answer according to generalizability theory is, If essay topics representing different modes of discourse are equally acceptable for the investigator's purpose, it does not matter whether writing tasks vary in this way. However, if this is so, the investigator must be interested in some overall, general indication of writing performance, and a single writing sample representing only one mode clearly is not sufficient. The proper sample should reflect the diversity inherent in the universe of interest—and consequently ought to comprise writing samples in all modes. Observations obtained for a writing sample representing only a single type of mode justify one in generalizing only to the universe defined by that particular mode.

However one chooses to address such matters as these, it is important to realize that we in fact sample from universes of writing tasks. An implication of this is that a writing task must be regarded as a "random" effect in a study design. Treating it as a "fixed" effect would be incorrect.

Finally, although generalizability theory may appear indifferent to the quality of writing tasks, it is not. The theory is robust enough to encompass poorly designed writing assignments as well as ones that are well designed. However, poorly specified writing assignments typically exacerbate the problem of nonsystematic variation among respondents. Even though we may be able to isolate and estimate error of this kind, the precision of our measures diminishes as the error term increases.

Universes of Markers

Much of what has been written regarding "unreliability" in essay testing is really concerned with marker inconsistency, and much of this concern is directed at intermarker disagreement and to a lesser extent intramarker disagreement. As noted earlier, inconsistency in marking attenuates measures obtained with essays. However, calculating indexes of rater inconsistency tells us only about rater disagreement, and there is a substantial inferential step between this and the concomitant effect produced by rater inconsistency on the dependability of observed scores—an inferential step that has not been much aided by the measurement methodologies applied to date.

A major consequence of the fixation on marker agreement has been that efforts to improve the "reliability" of essay measures have been directed primarily to ways of eliminating intermarker variability. This emphasis has led to further distortions in measurement procedures based on essays. Such practices as analytic scoring have been introduced largely because they were viewed as a means of securing rater agreement, not because they were viewed as congruent with a philosophy of composition. But perhaps the most questionable of the practices is what in some cases has been an almost blind commitment to seeking homogeneous groups of markers, which has sometimes led to the exclusion of markers who deviated from group norms. We know from research that there are likely to be systematic differences among raters in the marks they award (e.g., Blok). It follows that the variation in scores is greater with a group of raters than with a single rater. Consequently, we can obtain more-dependable (i.e., "reliable") scores by using one marker. This method would not be satisfactory because we would be haunted by the knowledge that had we selected a different rater (who also could have been highly self-consistent), we might have obtained different results.

E. D. Hirsch, Jr., offers an interesting perspective in this regard: "critics have disagreed for centuries in their holistic judgments of texts, and, since the time of Plato and Aristotle, the fundamental grounds for their disagreements have been known. The structure of the problem has remained the same, in all of its many guises, throughout the centuries." He concludes that the "problem of holistic assessment has been studied by some of the greatest thinkers of history. They have not solved the problem because it is not susceptible of solution. For that reason, and for purposes of research, we must restrict ourselves to judgments where agreement can be reached in principle, that is, to intrinsic judgment" (182, 185). Hirsch's conclusions seem both unnecessary and unfounded. To elaborate on this assertion and to explain how generalizability theory renders the problem "susceptible of solution," it is necessary to digress briefly to review Hirsch's distinction between intrinsic and extrinsic judgments of writing.

Hirsch characterizes extrinsic evaluation as a Platonic mode of judgment, "because it is based on criteria that are extrinsic to the writer's intentions, and even includes judgments about the quality of those intentions." Intrinsic evaluation, on the other hand, "is a mode that begins and ends in the *telos* or implicit intention of the kind of writing that is judged. The quality of the text is judged according to its success in fulfilling its own implicit intentions, and these are not, by and large, to be measured against different intentions" (182). Building on this distinction, Hirsch deduces three characteristics of writing that are assessed: (1) the quality of intentions, (2) the quality of their presentation, and (3) correctness. The quality of intentions Hirsch subsumes under extrinsic evaluation. The quality of the presentation of intentions and correctness are subsumed under intrinsic evaluation (186). According to Hirsch, judgments in general consist of some indeterminate mix of extrinsic and intrinsic evaluation—but it is the nature of extrinsic evaluation that is at the heart of the age-old predicament of disagreement in judgments of texts. He feels that by fixing attention on the intrinsic quality of presentation, we have "at least a sporting chance of solving the assessment problem—if the problem can be solved" (187). Hirsch's emphasis on judging the quality of intentions may lead, though, to the kind of situation that Edward White describes:

> These markings almost universally treat the student text as simultaneously a finished product with editing faults and an unfinished part of the writing and thinking process. It is as if our confusion about evaluation is somehow bound up with a confusion about the nature of the student text, an odd form of literature created for the sole purpose of being criticized. Sommers finds that writing teachers tend to say the same things about student writing even though the texts in front of them change, as do the writers ["Responding"].
> (*Teaching* [1st ed.] 95)

Hirsch, like many others, views "the assessment problem" as caused by disagreement among judgments of texts, and naturally he sees the elimination of such disagreement as the solution to the problem. This point of view may be ill founded for philosophical reasons alone. From a measurement perspective, there are grounds for another resolution to the conundrum.

Throughout this essay, I have advanced the proposition that the principle of eliminating rater variability has its roots in the classical measurement approach to "reliability." The classical approach ill accommodates multiple sources of variation, so it eliminates them (in theory, at any rate) by invoking strong conditions of equivalency. Elliot Mishler describes this effort as "context stripping," an attempt to formulate universal laws "free of the specific constraints of any particular context and therefore applicable to all" (2). By this line of thought, then, a necessary condition for equivalency would be (in theory) identical marker behavior. However, as I have argued, there is no logical or philosophical basis (independent of the measurement context) to support such a proposition. Does it not make more sense to accept that markers *naturally* vary in their judgments of texts and to settle on a measurement theory that allows us to accommodate this reality? Generalizability theory provides this structure, permitting us to specify markers as a facet in a study and to estimate the variation that is due to them—and to remove the effect of this variation from our considerations of other factors that may be of more direct interest.

Being able to accommodate variance due to markers is not enough, though. Marker variability, as noted earlier in the essay, is composed of systematic variance and of random "error"—variance that is not reproduced. In general, an increase in random "error" adversely affects coefficients of generalizability. Consequently, the amount of random "error" should be minimized. Up to a point, past practices in marker training have served this purpose (and to some extent so has the principle of selecting only experienced markers). "Calibrating markers" through such procedures (White) is especially important if we consider our sample of markers to be selected from a large, heterogeneous population of markers. However, other universes are possible. One of the most intriguing possibilities, which could address the issue of extrinsic evaluation raised by Hirsch, is that of the "interpretive community." As White points out:

> Fish defines an interpretive community as made up of those whose common agreement about how to read texts becomes an agreement about how they will in fact "write" for themselves those texts: "Interpretive communities are made up of those who share interpretive strategies not for reading (in the conventional sense) but for writing texts, for constituting their properties and assigning their intentions. In other words, these strategies exist prior to the act of reading and therefore determine the shape of what is read

rather than, as is usually assumed, the other way around." As Fish develops this concept, it serves a number of purposes. "This, then, is the explanation both for the stability of interpretation among different readers (they belong to the same community) and for the regularity with which a single reader will employ different interpretive strategies and thus make different texts (he belongs to different communities)" [*Is There a Text?* 171].   (97)

How one goes about specifying an interpretive community and identifying its constituents is a difficult problem. Peter Smagorinsky and Michael Smith present an interesting line of inquiry that also appeals to the notion of interpretive communities, proposing we examine "the extent to which different [writing] tasks require particular knowledge and the extent to which different interpretive communities require specific understandings" (279).

Efforts at standardizing marker behavior are conceptually ill founded, and the philosophy driving them is at odds with the reasons for using writing samples. Moreover, the general approach that requires (in principle) perfect marker agreement distorts the theory and practice of essay assessment. Perfect marker agreement is not—as it has generally been thought to be—a necessary precondition for high reliability in writing assessments (assuming the proper sense of "reliability"). Therefore, we need no longer cling to the old mythos in which essay reliability has been embedded. Generalizability theory provides a more satisfactory way to look at the issue of essay reliability, one that allows us to accommodate the reality that people vary naturally in their judgments of writing. Given this different way of looking at essay reliability, it is nonetheless possible to achieve acceptable levels of consistency for assessments of writing.

Why, then, does the classical test theory model continue to hold sway, and why do investigators persist in their efforts to control marker (and writer) behavior to force a fit to the model? Undoubtedly, a major reason is the emphasis that the classical model received as educational and psychological measurement theory and practice developed in the United States. The research tradition in the social sciences in America has been dominated by an experimentalist, quantitative view resulting from the hegemony of the field of psychology. Those who would undertake research and systematic inquiry in composition have too readily and needlessly bought into the assumption that numerical measurements are a sine qua non for research. As Louis Guttman points out, there is no rational basis to support the preconception "that assigning numerical values to phenomena is a necessary preliminary to finding laws of formation relating them" (335). It seems significant that much of the early work on essay reliability that came out of the United Kingdom (and extended to other systems derived from the British model, such as in Australia) was predicated on the principles of multiple marking and of minimizing temporary and specific kinds of variance. Reliability estimates were largely produced from analysis-of-variance procedures. Admittedly, similar work took place in the United States, but it has been negligible in amount and impact compared to the classical correlational approach.

Why have classical measurement practice and theory almost excluded all other thinking in the assessment of writing? Part of the answer may be that the correlational procedures used in the classical approach to estimating reliability are simple to apply and calculate (simple to the point of being simplistic). Ease of use undoubtedly contributes substantially to the ubiquity of the correlational conceptualization of reliability. Another part of the answer likely derives from the fact that those concerned with substantive understanding of the writing process have assumed an unequal partnership with an epistemically privileged class of researchers. Lorrie Shepard notes this state of affairs: "If subject-matter experts had always had equal say, how can we imagine that teachers of English would have given up essay tests in deference to inter-judge reliability coefficients"? (12). In this partnership, the research professionals have become the determiners of truth and knowledge, handing over the results of their investigations to teachers of composition, who are viewed as technicians "who must somehow absorb the results of this research and introduce it into the very same contexts of practice that have been derogated and ignored" (Lieberman 11). In any event, we ought to be aware of Elliot Eisner's warning that "socialization in method is a process that shapes what we can know and influences what we value. At base it is a political undertaking" (15). To date, the politics of classical measurement methodology has dominated the research-and-practice agenda in writing assessment.

The politics of educational achievement testing also exerts an inexorable pressure for the continuance of present practices in essay assessment. As Scott Paris and his coauthors note, "Educational achievement testing is 'high-stakes' assessment because the consequences are profound for the participants."

These authors go on to say that, among other effects,

> assessment drives the design of curriculum and instruction by signalling the valued objectives of education. These two goals, rein-

forced by public pressures for reform and accountability and by commercial interests to sell materials to schools, provide traditional psychometric and political perspectives for understanding educational assessment, particularly standardized achievement testing. (12)

Paris and his colleagues point out that the persistence of this undesirable state of affairs can be attributed, on the one hand, to the substantial vested interests of commercial bodies for whom testing is big business and, on the other hand, to an "equally powerful force that fuels the demand for achievement testing": "the public faith in quantitative comparisons" (13).

In addition, "there are considerable threats to the validity of tests and the interpretation of the results which undermine the usefulness of the test for students and teachers, who should be the prime consumers of test information" (19). Not the least of these threats comes from those who force a measurement model to fit for the sake of producing reliable results inexpensively while playing loose with the meaning of the results. How ironic that the unquestioning pursuit of reliability in essay marking, classically regarded as a necessary condition of validity, should in this larger view prove to be a threat to validity.

So we have an ethos in which there has been an apparently irresistible requirement for testing to be large-scale and cost-effective. Such a climate is antithetical to the measurement practices necessary to support the line of development given in this essay. As Paris and his colleagues state, the problems that have arisen from large-scale educational achievement testing are so substantial and damaging to educational practice that we need to reconsider the whole matter. They propose that "a developmental perspective on testing may prevent students' counterproductive reactions and may help to guide reforms in educational assessment" (12). Such a perspective would need to address the constant tension that exists "between the requirement to make assessment decisions" and the fact that assessments "are considered to be acts of interpretation which do not easily accommodate the notion of correctness" (Delandshere and Petrosky 11). A developmental perspective on educational assessment based on essay writing begins with an appropriate view of the concept of essay reliability and with the will to invest proper effort in attending to this issue.

University of Calgary

Response:
The Politics of Methodology

Roberta Camp

Maurice Scharton and Doug Shale have written from different situations and different kinds of expertise. Yet as readers, we can find a number of commonalities in their essays, especially if we look beneath the surface issues and consider underlying concerns.

What drives the writing in these essays, gives them force? Without being simplistic, I think we can say that the frustrations described and the issues raised are related to three major concerns and to the way these concerns play out in the assessment of writing.

Motivating Concerns

Assessment is a value-laden activity. Assessment involves making important and often difficult decisions about the kinds of learning to be addressed, the kinds of performances and behaviors to be considered for evidence of learning, the perceptions and judgments to be exercised in evaluating the evidence, the kinds of analysis to be conducted, and the formats and forums in which results will be reported. Writing assessment in particular requires that judgments be based on performances and behaviors and on criteria and standards compatible with the perspectives on writing and writing pedagogy found in research and in a range of classroom practice. As is clear from the two essays, this is no easy matter.

Assessment requires negotiation among a number of parties with different perspectives and concerns. Within any context in which writing is assessed, different kinds of expertise are required, and different audiences must be served. If the negotiation among interested parties is conducted openly and throughout the various phases of design, implementation, analysis, and reporting, then power and responsibility are shared. Unfortunately, negotiation more typically occurs among a handful of individuals designing and conducting the assessment, who then exercise power more or less unilaterally. In such instances, further negotiation is likely to be necessary after the fact about the assumptions made, the meaning of results, and the responsibility for acting on results. Post hoc negotiation may be characterized by misunderstandings and disagreements that could have been prevented or diffused by earlier discussion.

The outcome of this negotiation, however it occurs, is a set of inferences or interpretations about students' current or anticipated learning. These inferences and interpretations—not just numbers or scores—constitute the public meaning of the results. Although the process of creating assessment in which all interested parties are fairly represented and their concerns taken into account can be arduous and challenging, it is essential to shared, public understanding about students' learning. Assessment, that is, is political in the fundamental sense—it requires dialogue among the citizens of the community in which it occurs.

Methodology makes a difference. Much is at stake in decisions about methodology in assessment. Methodology shapes and colors the gathering of evidence for learning and for behaviors related to learning, the performances that are evoked or observed, the judgments made about evidence and performance, the information created, the procedures for monitoring the quality of information, and the interpretations that can be derived. Clearly, measurement specialists alone should not at any point assume complete responsibility for decisions about method; but neither should teachers of writing, especially if the assessment results are likely to have significant impact on students' lives or on the use of educational resources.

As Shale points out, measurement specialists or teachers of writing who act in isolation are likely to rely too heavily on one or two familiar methods applied without reference to purpose and without recognition of their limitations. Thus we see the curious fixation, reported by Scharton, on a bell-curve distribution of essay scores irrespective of the decisions to be based on the scores. Or we find all too often the practice of using a single essay as the entire sample of writing, then basing unwarranted generalizations about writing ability on the single-essay scores. Or we consume time and print in unproductive and misleading speculation about the reasons for low correlations between single-essay scores and other indicators of ability (such as scores on other tests or grades in academic courses), with little or no acknowledgment that a single prompt, however complex the writing it evokes and however reliably the writing is scored, is in effect a one-item test yielding a single data point.

If specialists in writing and in measurement can successfully cross the boundaries of their communities of discourse, they can together ensure that methodology is appropriately chosen and applied. Their willingness and ability to create shared understanding may determine, in fact, whether interpretations based on the assessment can be trusted and made intelligible to the various audiences concerned with student learning. The need for such understanding is apparent, I think, in the essays in this section.

Implications for Practice

What should we do about the concerns identified above? What are their implications for practice? The essays here tell of frustrations; failures of communication, if not outright abuses of power; conceptual dead ends. Scharton protests more directly against these shortcomings, but concern about them also stands behind Shale's careful argument.

Each essay proposes a partial solution, within its own context. Describing oppositions, Scharton is able to reconcile them in practical terms without denying the tensions between them; Shale finds in generalizability theory an alternative to the dilemmas for writing assessment he observes in classical test theory. As a reader, though, and an individual with long-term interests in writing assessment, I wonder whether we can draw from these partial solutions and these particular contexts an understanding that will frame other solutions in other contexts.

I think we can, if we are willing to see the issues and frustrations described in these essays, and others of our own, within a broader perspective. We can then identify what we need in order to address both immediate and long-term concerns in the assessment of writing. I have three suggestions for creating a sense of perspective.

Take a systemic and integrated view of assessment and learning. Writing assessment is more than a test instrument or a method of scoring. The technical apparatus of assessment is important; its quality determines whether the information it yields can be trusted. But equally important is coherence among the components of an assessment, their relation to goals for learning and to the social and institutional context in which the assessment activities are conducted (Frederiksen and Collins; Graue, "Integrating Theory"; Guba and Lincoln; P. Moss, "Conceptions"; Murphy and Camp).

Taking a systemic view requires clear statements of purpose and explicit understanding of what is to be measured, what kinds of statements about learning are to be supported, and how students, teachers, and institutions are to be served. These are issues that require discussion, negotiation, and consensus building—activities I would argue are central to assessment and conducive to the long-term well-being of educational institutions.

Recognize multiple audiences for assessment and establish dialogue among them. The value of assessment lies in its potential to inform educational decision making. As issues of power become increasingly apparent in assessment, there is greater need for understanding and responsibility to be shared among all parties who have a stake in students' learning—students themselves, teachers, administrators, other members of the educational and social community (Darling-Hammond and Ascher; Guba and Lincoln). Shared understanding requires at least that information and interpretations resulting from assessments be provided in formats and through channels accessible to all (e.g., exemplars, narrative descriptions, nontechnical reports, face-to-face meetings, newspaper releases). More substantive understanding and greater sharing of responsibility are possible if the interested parties are consulted while the assessment is under development—teachers, students, and administrators early on, other members of the community later (see Camp, "Thinking"; LeMahieu, Eresh, and Wallace; Murphy and Smith, "Talking"; Rothman; Sheingold, Heller, and Paulukonis). If such discussions are conducted around examples of student work, the assessment can promote common and increasingly acute perceptions about learning and encourage the development of a shared vocabulary for describing evidence of learning (Camp, "Assessment in the Context"; Gitomer; Howard, "Portfolio Culture").

Cultivate collegial and collaborative relationships and scholarly activity across disciplines and institutions. In the real-world situations where most professional practice occurs, the most challenging problems are messy, indeterminate, and unlikely to fall neatly within the boundaries of academic disciplines and institutions, as Donald Schon observes (4–5). Writing assessment is not exceptional in this respect. The problems that are most challenging and persistent are not well solved by mere technical application of expertise, whether from writing pedagogy and research or educational measurement. Such application often misses the "wisdom" and "artistry" (Schon's terms) of thorough, well-grounded understanding. Some of our current challenges in writing assessment—for example, the need for assessments that better capture what we consider important about writing performance—call for cross-disciplinary insight into the implications of current approaches and for insightful, collaborative exploration of alternatives (see my essay in this volume).

The foundations for such work have not been fully established, although we have made a start. We have the beginnings of a scholarly literature, as the pace of recent publication suggests. We need to create from these beginnings a more public arena for discourse. Published work in writing assessment needs to become more accessible and better integrated into critical discussion among audiences of our peers, within and across disciplines—through better use of refereed journals, for example, like *Assessing Writing, Research in the Teaching of English,* and *Written Communication.* In addition, the discourse about assessment conducted in journals like *Educational Assessment, Educational Researcher, Educational Measurement: Issues and Practice,* and *Phi Delta Kappan* needs to be more generally taken into account by writing assessment practitioners.

A comprehensive, well-organized, and widely accessible database would help, especially for locating essays on writing assessment that have been published in books of essays by diverse authors. The Conference on College Composition and Communication recently developed an annotated bibliography on writing assessment at the postsecondary level. More of this kind of effort is needed, across all levels of writing assessment, across disciplinary boundaries, and across divisions between teachers and researchers, if knowledge from current research and development is to be sorted out and widely shared.

Projects and proposed solutions are likely to improve if awareness of previous work in writing assessment and in related fields is increased and combined with a commitment to cross-disciplinary scholarship. Many of the problems described in this section, for example, could be profitably examined in relation to recent publications that cross discourse boundaries. For example, on correlations between essay scores and course grades, see McKendy. On validity in writing assessments, see Williamson. On the limits of psychometric approaches based on classical test theory, see Camp ("Changing"); Graue, "Integrating Theory"; Murphy and Ruth; Williamson; Wolf, Bixby, Glenn, and Gardner. On reliability in writing assessment and in college placement, see Cherry and Meyer; W. Smith. On instrument reliability of single and multiple essays and on topic effect, see Breland, Camp, Jones, Morris, and Rock; Murphy and Ruth. On qualitative, interactional approaches to assessment, see Johnston; P. Moss ("Conceptions," "Can There Be?"). On shared responsibility and accountability within educational institutions, see Darling-Hammond and Ascher; Guba and Lincoln.

Beyond scholarship, we need collaboration on projects, especially if we hope to develop assessment directly informative to teaching and learning. Projects in which content specialists work with measurement specialists and across educational institutions on real-world problems can bring genuine advances, including new forms of assessment, new test theory, and new methodology. This is evident, for example, in the work using FACETS, a method of statistical analysis that not only separates rater and topic variance on performances such as essay examinations and portfolios but also provides within-group data sufficiently specific to pinpoint sources of unwanted variance and identify bias toward populations of test takers (Engelhard; Linacre and Wright). Such advances are also apparent in the Arts PROPEL project in Pittsburgh public schools and in the work on the California Learning Assessment System. In both of these projects, teachers and researchers collaborated on the design and scoring of writing portfolios and created new approaches to score analysis (*Arts PROPEL: A Handbook*; Camp, "Assessment in the Context"; Wolf, "Assessment as an Episode"; LeMahieu, Gitomer, and Eresh; Mislevy; Sheingold, Heller, and Paulukonis).

This kind of dialogue among content and measurement specialists, teachers and researchers, all focusing on real-world applications, is the most likely context for progress in our understanding of what's possible in writing assessment. Without it, we are likely to accept prematurely, as Scharton and Shale indicate, the constraints of narrowly construed and merely technical applications of expertise.

PART III

Models of Writing Assessment: Old and New

Introduction

While research on writing assessment as a practice has grown rapidly over the past few years, our understanding of how our ideologies and views of the world impinge on the ways we assess writing has not. Historically, practice in the field of writing assessment has outpaced theory, and as a result we have either ignored or denied the theoretical basis for writing assessment. In our movement from multiple-choice exams to such direct measures as single-sample impromptu essays to portfolios, we have developed complex and manifold means of assessing writing but have yet to focus extensively on the assumptions behind our activity and on their implications. Our focus on practice has resulted in a number of schisms. Assessment practice does not reflect consistently the recent shifts in writing pedagogy. Testers and teachers of writing do not share the same views about how writing should be assessed. Views about the nature of writing assessment vary among teachers, researchers, theorists, testing firms, governing bodies, minorities, women, and students. The future of writing assessment requires that we articulate a theoretical basis for our assessment practices.

In this section Peter Elbow, Roberta Camp, Stephen North, Gail Hughes, and the coauthors Marcia Farr and Gloria Nardini challenge widely held assumptions about literacy and question the efficacy of writing assessment models that have long been in common practice. In "Essayist Literacy and Sociolinguistic Difference," Farr and Nardini trace the political implications of "essayist literacy," the model of discourse dominant in classrooms and textbooks and "associated primarily (although not exclusively) with educated white European-origin men." Farr and Nardini posit that essayist literacy is a social and political construct that is neither universal nor objective. They find that while essayist literacy is certainly valuable as a model of academic discourse, it may not be the only one. Farr and Nardini attend to the political implications of writing assessment modeled on essayist literacy and to its effects on culturally nonmainstream groups and propose research that would help develop "metalinguistic awareness of sociolinguistic difference, an awareness that can facilitate the teaching of essayist-literacy conventions."

In "Writing Assessment: Do It Better, Do It Less," Peter Elbow criticizes current quantitative writing assessment policies and shows ways to minimize the unfairness and untrustworthiness of assessment. He recommends that we reduce the frequency of our assessment and improve the quality by adopting portfolio assessment and at the same time avoiding conventional holistic scoring. Doing so, Elbow argues, will produce more-trustworthy evidence of writers' ability and allow more-accurate judgments about that evidence.

Citing the major advances in our understanding of the practices of writing and writing instruction, Roberta Camp, in "New Views of Measurement and New Models for Writing Assessment," makes clear the need to develop models of assessment compatible with our new construct for writing. She asserts that the validity of traditional approaches to writing assessment is called into serious doubt by the mismatch between the construct they imply and the current theoretical constructs for writing. She proposes an expansion of the concept of validity to include the effects of assessments on the educational systems in which they occur—an assessment should demonstrate "systemic validity," derived from direct and contextualized assessments of writing rather than indirect assessments. She proposes approaches to writing assessment that are influenced by cognitive psychology, reflect the current construct for writing, take into account differences among test takers, and are more closely integrated with instruction and more immediately useful to teachers and students.

Stephen North turns his attention to the relation between upper-division writing assessment—particularly the barrier exam—and our understanding of the postsecondary development of writing abilities. He contends that although we have increased our involvement in writing assessment, we have done so without any real understanding of development and lack, therefore, any "clearly articulated theory, grounded in either practice or research, about the emergence of postsecondary literacy regarding which we purport to be judging students." He asserts that by taking part in an institutional practice with "what amounts to professional ignorance, we abdicate our ethical and political responsibilities."

Gail Hughes, in "The Need for Clear Purposes and New Approaches to the Evaluation of Writing-across-the-Curriculum Programs," asserts the necessity of improving the evaluations of writing-across-the-curriculum programs by better defining the goals of such projects, by developing new ways to assess on a large scale, and by assessing the system-wide impact of WAC. To these ends, she proposes that we coordinate our efforts, give WAC research high enough priority to attract the resources it needs, and design assessment projects that function effectively in the political framework of their institutions and funding agencies.

Kurt Spellmeyer's response to these essays reminds us that "debates about who's literate and who's not are actually about ownership of 'cultural capital'" and points to the vast social changes in access to power that have occurred in this century. His concerns about the destructive policies of standardized testing are based on his opposition to those uses of assessment that weaken public confidence in teachers and programs. When testing is used in these ways, it undermines the unique American experiment in educational opportunity that he describes: "Testing is surveillance, first and last, and if we neglect to ask who is surveying whom and for what ends, we will have no one to blame but ourselves." The necessary response, Spellmeyer argues, along with the other authors in this section, will come from informed teachers, willing to take responsibility for assessment.

Essayist Literacy and Sociolinguistic Difference

Marcia Farr and Gloria Nardini

Cultural and linguistic diversity has always existed in the United States but has not always been widely recognized. In the academy in particular, diversity has generally been little acknowledged. In fact, the model of discourse taught formally in educational institutions, and represented in virtually all composition textbooks, is associated primarily (although not exclusively) with educated white European-origin men. In this style of discourse, termed "essayist literacy" by Ron Scollon and Suzanne Scollon, high value is placed on language, either oral or written, that is rational, decontextualized, explicit, and carefully ordered internally (Farr, "Essayist Literacy"). Scollon and Scollon characterize essayist literacy as an idealized exchange between fictionalized readers and writers. John Trimbur refers to essayist literacy as a "rhetoric of deproduction" in which all traces of the actual production of the language by a contextualized human being are erased ("Essayist Literacy"), and Clifford Geertz calls this kind of prose "author-evacuated" (9). In such rational text, emphasis is placed not only on exactness of expression but also on well-planned and highly marked arrangement of propositions—for example, transition words indicate the logical relations between propositions (Walters, "Writing").

But essayist literacy has become increasingly vulnerable to criticism, especially by ethnic minorities and women who claim it to be ethnocentric and elitist. Jane Tompkins even describes the critical essay as a vehicle used to inflict "violence," likening the essayist-literacy practice of attacking other scholars to a Western shoot-out ("Fighting Words"). Part of the basis for such criticism lies in the postmodern concept of construct, which means the encoding over time of a particular set of ideas and writings that eventually come to be viewed as the standard of significance against which all other ideas and writings are measured. This standard is not arbitrary; for some critics its covert political stance is exposed by the very choice of the term *construct*. According to Paul Lauter, "the works generally considered central to a culture are *those composed and promoted by persons from groups hold-*

108

ing power within it" (10; emphasis added). It is important, therefore, to realize that essayist literacy is a historical and social construct, not the "natural" way to make a point. It is equally important to recognize that a problem occurs when this kind of literacy standard is the only one used to assess writing, as it is in our current testing.

Several questions come to mind:

o What assumptions does essayist literacy make (about the writer and the writer's point of view, for instance)?
o Is a particular social and cultural mind-set privileged in the negotiation of this kind of literacy?
o Is what essayist literacy asks students to do culturally problematic for some of them?

In the answers to these questions lie important implications for assessment, which we address in the following sections.

Essayist Literacy as Construct

A number of researchers have deconstructed the notion that there is only one kind of literacy. Brian Street, for example, identifies two models for conceiving of literacy: the "autonomous" and the "ideological." In what he calls the "autonomous" model, literacy is represented in the essay test and is constitutive of progress, civilization, individual liberty, and social mobility. In his "ideological" model, in contrast, literacy is located in specific and constructed social practices. The basic argument of Street's *Literacy in Theory and Practice* is that the skills and concepts accompanying literacy acquisition do not stem from inherent qualities of literacy. Rather, they are aspects of specific ideologies that, when turned into theoretical precepts, pass for objective truth.

Particularly important is the way in which Street deconstructs the meaning of *literate* as fixed and unchanging. Before the Norman Conquest, according to the historical research by M. T. Clanchy that Street reports (Clanchy described the shift from memory to written record in medieval England), land ownership was passed on through some sort of symbol—for example, a sword handed from the old owner to the new or a family seal affixed to parchment—or through the witness of "twelve good men and true." The Normans sought to impose their power on the conquered Anglo-Saxons by introducing written pacts for the codification of land ownership. According to Street, our notion that seals were just so much medieval decoration is an ethnocentric assumption that the literate mode was thought of as more important than other modes. In fact, the Normans realized that paper deeds for land were open to forgery, so they continued to use the older practice of affixing seals as well, for safety. Contrary to the idea that the shift to literacy caused a radical shift in thinking, the continuing mix of literate and nonliterate modes exemplified in the seal stamped on top of the land deed shows how written forms adapted to oral and other practices. Thus, the literacy of the Normans was embedded in a practical view of how best to sustain their claims to land they were stealing from the indigenous peoples of Great Britain (81–82).

Street's ideological model stresses the political and socially constructed character of literacy. Harvey Graff's analysis of a "literacy myth" similarly shows that in nineteenth-century Canada social mobility and freedom from poverty were determined by class, gender, race, and ethnicity—not by literacy, as commonly claimed (347). Street cites other examples that show how people using oral and literate modes invest them with beliefs. In India, Brahmans control ancient oral texts recited according to guarded pronunciation codes; this arrangement reverses our privileging of literate over oral texts (99).

Also concerned with deconstructing the assumptions of literacy, David Bartholomae addresses the literacy that he sees as necessary for students to "invent the university." In a now canonical piece, he argues that every time students sit down to write English papers, they must position themselves both within and against academic discourse to prove their worth as members of the university community ("Inventing the University"). The following example takes a stance suitable for a literary paper, Bartholomae says: "While many critics have said that Mark Twain's main purpose in writing *Huckleberry Finn* was to represent the innocence of America in the late 1800's, a closer reading really reveals a darker viewpoint about the malignant habit of riding on barges on the Mississippi River." Although both Bartholomae and Street depend on community-constructed truths, the two authors' concerns differ somewhat, because Bartholomae wants to empower students to see the academic frame of reference. He means to show that the literate essay is a sort of song and dance in which the writer must use the appropriate steps (canonical truths) to create a new ballet (originality in using the discourse). In this way student writers validate what the professor knows and show that they also know the sanctioned method of adding to that knowledge. Bartholomae therefore sees literacy as a specific social practice used to further the political and ideological ends of the academy.

Other theorists challenge the supposed objectivity of essayist literacy.

Richard Ohmann views academic writing as a tool for power. His thesis in *English in America* is, simply, that English departments carry out the agenda set by the dominant groups in society. He claims that no institution can ever not be political and that the university, despite its ivory-tower pose of choosing not to involve itself in the ideological fray of industrial values and economic power, is especially political. Ohmann maintains that college writing textbooks are written as if the authors were alone and without historical or social origins. Academic argument such as is taught in freshman composition he sees as divorced from anything that matters: he calls it "pseudo argument" particularly well suited for a society with "pseudo politics" (158). The rhetoric of the university exists to defend the status quo of American political life without affirming, or perhaps even being aware of, such a goal.

Lester Faigley is concerned with the student concept of self in the academic discourse community. His view is a somewhat pessimistic one: while it would seem that the assumptions underlying the evaluation of writing are much more complex now than they were fifty years ago, Faigley claims that not much has changed. Students are still judged by their teachers, who still look for a replication of themselves—the teachers' "implicit cultural definitions of the self"—in students' autobiographical writing. He cites, for instance, the examples from William Coles, Jr., and James Vopat's *What Makes Writing Good*, which are sixty percent autobiographical and which use the "before I didn't know but now I do" model of reasoning. The implied purpose of most writing assignments, according to Faigley, is that students should achieve the unified rational self by analyzing the former self as lacking, or at least pretend to do so.

Sociolinguistic Difference

While students from all backgrounds may find some of the practices of essayist literacy strange, those from culturally nonmainstream backgrounds have an additional burden: they must learn as well the sociolinguistic conventions of academic discourse. Marcia Farr and Harvey Daniels show how some difficulties students have in learning to write may originate in a conflict between standard and nonstandard linguistic domains, which reflect class distinctions. Not pronouncing the *r* may lead to not writing it; not articulating the copula in speaking may lead to omitting it in writing; African Americans may use *attitude* to convey "negative attitude" rather than the mainstream neutral sense of the term; and only mainstream students may interpret "Have you finished your math?" to mean "Sit down and get to work." Despite the fact that William Labov long ago criticized as racist the notion that African American English was linguistically deprived, establishing that it was just as rule-governed and "logical" as Standard English ("Logic"), his view does not yet generally obtain in the school community. So students who do not share the mainstream, middle-class frame of reference may be handicapped in writing and understanding by a literacy that excludes them. This notion of class extends the definition of *literate* to include talking, as well as writing, like the people in power, a definition that most people with power choose not to admit.

Shirley Brice Heath, in her classic and groundbreaking ethnography of literacy, *Ways with Words*, also explores sociolinguistic differences, by examining the effects of the preschool home and community environment on how children learn language. Her study of Roadville, a rural community of working-class whites, and Trackton, a rural community of working-class blacks, both in the Piedmont area of the Carolinas, discloses community language practices that contrast sharply with language use at school. Trackton children are expected to absorb knowledge holistically from observing and experiencing; flexibility and adaptability are highly valued in learning to be and to talk. "Whatcha *call* it ain't so important as whatcha *do* with it. That's what things 'n people are for, ain't it?" is the overarching notion for both language use and worldview in Trackton (112). In Roadville, in contrast, adults think themselves responsible for teaching children to talk. Lives are rule-based, and knowledge, too, is viewed as bounded and fixed. Roadville's children are "brought up" while Trackton's kids "come up." In school, however, neither group does particularly well.

Heath uses notions of story in accounting for both groups' lack of scholastic success. To Roadville residents, *story* can mean "lie." Their children are discouraged from "what if" considerations and told to stick to the point. This rigid adherence to a literally true narrative with a concluding moral point stands the children in good stead in the initial years of school, when establishing routine and following directions are important. Ultimately, however, when school requires an inventive use of facts and an extension of knowledge, many Roadville students flounder and drop out.

In Trackton, stories are seen as imaginative ways to compete for audience attention. They do not address points explicitly and seemingly continue for as long as anybody wants to hear them. They follow no particular formula and close in no particular way. The best, a "true story," may start with a germ of truth and then become more and more exaggerated in the telling. It would seem that this kind of linguistic creativity would be rewarded in school, where elaborate language play is frequently expected. But in actuality Trackton children's dissonant conception of language as holistic and self-expressive—as well as their seeming inability to follow directions, work individually, and sit quietly in their seats—turns them off to school long before they receive the rewards of imagination. In the initial years of school, they experience difficulty in analytically separating wholes into parts—for instance, in focusing on explicit names for colors and shapes. In later years of school, when their creative abilities would stand them in good stead, they are "behind" in the subskills and generally discouraged. Therefore many Trackton students, too, flounder and drop out.

Heath also documents the literacy habits of the adults in these communities. She establishes that both communities are oral and literate but that their customs differ from each other's and—more significant— from those of the mainstream townspeople. Trackton residents understand the exercise of literacy as a community event, exemplified by a church service and the communal reading of the newspaper on the front porch. Composing formulaic letters to relatives, Roadville residents see writing as private and rule-bound. In Roadville the written word limits alternatives for expression, whereas in Trackton people use it as a jumping-off point for further construing. (For the people of Roadville, Trackton's stories would be lies, while for the people of Trackton Roadville's stories wouldn't even count as stories.) Neither community's "ways with words" prepare its members for the ways of school. Heath concludes that patterns of language use in these two communities are in accord with and reinforced by the residents' other cultural patterns.

The problem is compounded by the fact that different styles of language involve different ways of thinking (Hill; Walters, "Language"). Patricia Bizzell posits that joining the academic discourse community requires taking on a particular identity, a site of possibly painful changes after which the writer "can't go home again" ("What Is?"). James Berlin argues that no rhetoric is ever neutral, because rhetorical choices always favor certain economic, social, and political arrangements of discourse. Rhetoric therefore becomes a kind of ideology in which language forms the conceptions of ourselves, our audiences, and the reality in which we exist. That is, from an epistemological point of view, language is not neutral but part of the interpretive and discursive practices of rhetoric. Crucially, these culturally embedded patterns often directly conflict with those taught in school, especially with essayist literacy. As studies of writing assessment have found (e.g., Ruth and Murphy; Purves), a single set of discourse standards cannot validly be applied across cultures.

Literacy and Oral Traditions

Unfortunately, it is easy to be unaware of how deeply ingrained some cultural traits are, especially those reflected in the use of language, either oral or written. Because everyone makes sense of the world—and of language—from a particular cultural framework, only an experience of dissonance will jar someone into considering meaning from another point of view. Often, even dissonant experiences result only in culturally comfortable interpretations. For example, Asian students who have learned not to reveal opinion may be misinterpreted by non-Asian teachers as being shy or lacking in knowledge. An important goal of research in culturally nonmainstream communities, then, is to uncover alternative cultural frameworks, ways of using language that may contrast with essayist literacy.

Since ways of using language are generally part of speakers' unconscious knowledge, such research is especially important because it provides the means of developing metalinguistic awareness of sociolinguistic difference, an awareness that can facilitate the teaching of essayist-literacy conventions. We do not suggest that traditional essayist literacy should always and exclusively be maintained as the preferred model of academic discourse. One could argue that much is lost, for example, in the overprivileging of expository, as opposed to narrative, style. Peter Elbow, in fact, argues passionately for teaching "a larger view of human discourse" ("Reflections" 137), one that makes room for the rendering of experience as well as for vernacular explanations of textbook prose. It is nevertheless true that some uses of essayist literacy are socially, economically, and politically powerful, and it is vitally important that students from all backgrounds have equal access to the power such uses confer.

Toward this end, the Chicago Language and Literacy Project, at the University of Illinois, Chicago, promotes studies of literacy practices and oral-language traditions among specific populations in various Chicago communities. These studies are carried out within the framework of the ethnography of communication, a field that evolved from anthropological linguistics and that was conceptualized primarily by Dell Hymes. The methodology used in this kind of research includes participant observation (long-term associations with the people whose communicative conduct one is studying), ethnographic (usually open-ended, informal) interviewing, and informal audiotaping. Data thus consist of field notes and transcripts of audiotapes. A key characteristic of this research is the attempt to understand meaning holistically and from the "emic" point of view—the perspective of those studied. Thus the research emphasizes long-term involvement and context-based interpretation.

One major project in this program is the Mexican-Origin Language and Literacy Project. Supported by the National Science Foundation Linguistics Program and the Spencer Foundation, this project is an ongoing study of literacy and oral genres in both Spanish and English among a social network of Mexican immigrants in Chicago (about forty-five people in seven households). An important finding from this work is that a wide range of literacy practices is carried out by adults with limited formal educations (Farr, "Biliteracy," *"En los Dos Idiomas"*; Guerra). The adults' oral genres include culturally distinct strategies for persuading others through witty, humorous, emotive performances (Farr, "Essayist Literacy") and through narrative (Elías-Olivares). In another part of the larger research program, graduate students (PhD candidates in English specializing in the Language, Literacy, and Rhetoric program) carry out dissertation research in African American, Mexican-origin, Puerto Rican, female Italian American, white working-class, and other culturally cohesive communities in the Chicago area.

Beverly Moss's study of the sermons of three African American ministers reveals a model of discourse that clearly contrasts with essayist literacy. By focusing on middle-class churches, Moss identifies cultural rather than class-based differences in language. Though these ministers have extensive formal educations and thus are highly literate, their sermons are virtuoso oral performances. Even the "manuscript" minister, who writes out his sermon several days before the service, performs it without reading (and does so verbatim). These ministers, then, use language according to norms shared within their community: they draw on means that are persuasive within their cultural framework—for example, personal testimony and "call and response"—to achieve what their congregations judge excellent performances.

Ralph Cintron's research details community language and literacy practices in the Mexican-origin population of a small midwestern town ("Use"). Reading all sorts of texts both inside and outside homes, including gang graffiti, signs, and other environmental print, Cintron illuminates the cultural, social, and economic forces that entrap residents and influence these texts (Pues Aquí).

Jabari Mahiri's study of sports discourse among preadolescent male African Americans also describes ways of speaking that represent community-wide cultural practices but contrast with school-based norms for language use. Moreover, Mahiri documents literacy practices among basketball-team members that evidence a range of cognitive processes not often assumed to be part of such students' lives. Although these cognitive processes are valued in school, they are not developed there, because school practices do not build on student capabilities in the necessary way. Calling for bridging of the gap between community and school, Mahiri finally recommends that teachers act as "coaches" and use pedagogical approaches based on "game" and "play" metaphors.

Virginia Young's research on cross-cultural communication during videotaped university writing conferences clarifies the role of culturally based politeness systems (Brown and Levinson) in the criticism of student writing. Three groups of students were compared: rural whites, urban African Americans, and Taiwanese. The white rural students dealt more easily with criticisms of their writing by white middle-class female teachers than other students did. This was partially due to the similarity in "solidarity" politeness systems between these students and the teachers. The African American students, while generally sharing features of solidarity politeness, did not deploy them as the teachers did, so communication was less than optimal. The Taiwanese students generally used deference politeness, suitable to a hierarchical rather than an egalitarian social structure, and contrasted the most sharply with the teachers. Thus, ways of speaking politely can differ significantly from one cultural group to another, and the differences can seriously undermine the communication that is crucial to teaching and learning.

Research is being done to identify and describe the oral traditions of various populations whose natural styles of discourse may differ from the academic essayist model. For people from such traditions, learning academic literacy—when both they and their teachers lack a metalinguistic awareness of sociolinguistic difference—can be a confusing and frustrating process, one often resulting in failure. Members of culturally nonmainstream groups document this predicament in their low levels of achievement on tests that rely on models of essayist literacy (Kirsch and Jungeblut; Natl. Assessment of Educ. Progress, *Reading* and *Writing*). Clearly, the political implications of such models of assessment are striking.

What assumptions does essayist literacy make?

The primary assumption of essayist literacy seems to be sameness of context—that is, that all writers are or should be (explicitly or implicitly) aware of the academic frame of reference and that decontextualizing therefore has the same meaning for everyone. This assumption sets rules for topic choice, point of view, use of conventions, and expectations about the discourse community. But research shows that literacy is located in social, cultural, and historical practices that have changed over time, not in anything objective or universal. John Swales relates a relevant example from his experience teaching English at the University of Khartoum in the Sudan. By emphasizing the narrative structure of legal case reports to teach his students reading comprehension, Swales inadvertently worked at cross-purposes with the criminal-law professor, who was teaching the same students to "spot the crucial fact on which the decision (rightly or wrongly) rested" (73). Thus, in different contexts, even the same genre can give rise to different assumptions about communicative purpose.

Taking note of the arbitrariness of standards will permit teachers to interpret more accurately the results of assessment and, in turn, to improve practice. Gloria Nardini tells of a Filipina student who, tutored in a writing center, had no idea what her white middle-class instructor meant by asking her to "respond to" a piece of literature. For the student, essay answers ideally reported a teacher's response to a piece of literature (presumably provided in class lectures). Even when the writing-center tutor told her that "respond" meant to give her own opinion, the Filipina student was unable to comply with the instructions. They were simply at odds with her context for academic writing.

Is a particular social and cultural mind-set privileged in the negotiation of essayist literacy?

The social and cultural mind-set that construes rationality, explicitness, and order as fundamental values of literate text—namely, the (primarily white and male) Anglo-American analytic orientation—seems to be privileged in essayist literacy. Teachers, again, need to note the conflict in identity that a student can experience when writing posits a mode of thinking different from the modes embedded in the student's home community.

Is what essayist literacy asks students to do culturally problematic for some of them?

It would seem that, at the least, miscommunication could occur when cultural systems collide. If we posit communities defined by different "ways of speaking" (Hymes) and acknowledge that these ways are important sites of identity for their speakers, then it is easy to see that issues in assessment could parallel those in translation. That is, students might understand our words without comprehending what we are asking them to do, and they might interpret and perform the task according to their own ways of thinking and speaking.

Jeanne Weiland reports that at a writing center a Mexican-origin female student presented a first draft of an assigned essay that was poetic in rhetorical structure and syntax (e.g., the essay began, "Aware of who I am and where it was I came from, I am"). Although the writing-center tutor was taken with the writing, she reluctantly advised the student that this probably was not what the teacher expected in this essay. Subsequent drafts moved toward language that was rational, explicit, and ordered but that completely lost the appealing poetic qualities of the first draft. Although there clearly is a place for both styles of writing in contemporary society (and within essayist literacy as well), this student may well have concluded that her inclinations in writing were neither valuable nor desirable and that only the model the teacher expected was worth learning.

While our purpose is not to reject essayist literacy as an academic discourse style—we have used it in writing this essay, after all—we mean to caution that assuming it to be the only appropriate means of discourse too frequently denies voice and identity to those whose ways of speaking are different. In the classroom such denial may mean lower literacy scores, higher drop-out rates, and the loss of potential talent. Elsewhere it may mean that those who are simply different are seen as deficient—or, worse, ignored as if they didn't matter at all. Further, assessments by academics who fail to take into account sociolinguistic research on nonmainstream populations may be undermined by ethnocentricity. It is important to note that these issues obtain whether assessment is carried out through multiple-choice, impromptu, or portfolio methods, although portfolio assessment allows more time for revision and editing, during which cultural issues can be addressed. Teachers of essayist literacy—like literary scholars, in view of the recent movement to redefine the American literary canon—must not assume cultural norms but, rather, self-consciously locate and evaluate them. While we proceed to teach and evaluate some, but not all, writing according to essayist-literacy standards, we must acknowledge that essayist literacy is changing, possibly as a result of the meeting of different cultures.

As we enter our third century as a nation, the United States is experiencing extensive demographic change that heightens sensitivity to cultural and linguistic differences among populations. The argument of this essay is ultimately not about linguistic standards but about whether or not we grant as much "power" to, for example, narrative structure as to analytic, to personal tone as to impersonal, or to writing (or speaking) that persuades through involvement (Tannen) as to writing (or speaking) that persuades through detachment. In other words, the issue is whether we should teach exclusively the traditional model of text or should be open to change in what we consider the meaning of literate.

University of Illinois, Chicago

Writing Assessment:
Do It Better, Do It Less

Peter Elbow

I start from our dilemma. On the one hand, we know too much about reading and writing to trust the quantitative scores on large-scale writing assessments: about reading, we know the immense contribution of the reader to the meaning and value of the text; about writing, we know the immense influence of audience, situation, and the writer's mood or even health on the quality of the text. On the other hand, we probably cannot forgo all large-scale writing assessment. Even if such tests are often unfair—for example, to students with nonmainstream cultural backgrounds—they can also increase fairness. In the 1950s, College Board exams played a crucial role in opening up higher education to Jews, who were subject to highly restrictive quotas in many colleges and universities (Riesman).

My goal in this essay is to explore ways to minimize the untrustworthiness of quantitative writing assessment. My conclusion is in my title: we can assess better; but that will take more time and money, so we must do it less; yet, paradoxically, less will be better.

Do It Better

I have two proposals here. First, to get more trustworthy evidence of a writer's ability, use portfolios. Second, to get more trustworthy judgments about that evidence, avoid conventional holistic scoring. I will suggest two alternatives to regular holistic scoring.

Use portfolios. Portfolios are not perfect: they suffer from being a fad and thus are sometimes used in ill-considered or degraded ways. But they represent a huge improvement over assessment based on single samples of writing. Because students perform differently on different occasions, we simply cannot trust evidence about a student's writing ability unless we see different pieces of writing, produced at different times, in different genres, directed to different audiences—and most of them not written under exam conditions. This principle holds whether we are testing for writing ability in general (if that makes any sense) or for more-restricted skills such as writing clear sentences (or giving reasons, or revising, or copyediting). As teachers we are perfectly accustomed to saying, "Why did you write such a weak essay, John [or such tangled sentences], when we both know you can write better?" But as testers we too often take John's text as a picture of his ability. We have known about this problem for a long time (Braddock, Lloyd-Jones, and Schoer; Breland, Camp, Jones, Morris, and Rock). But we have tended to ignore it—probably because it has seemed intractable.

There's no need to sing the praises of portfolios these days. But there's still crucial work to do: using all our professional influence and rhetorical skill to persuade institutions to refrain from making significant assessment decisions except on the basis of well-furnished portfolios. Of course, portfolio assessment takes more time and money, but we know enough now to insist to policy makers and the public that any other method of writing assessment is unfair, untrustworthy, and unprofessional. And we don't need to ask for more money; we can ask for something more precious—namely, prudence: less frequent and more selective assessment. (More later about less.)

Don't use holistic scoring. I abbreviate my argument for portfolios because they are so widely admired. But I must take longer to argue against holistic scoring because it is so entrenched.

We have long known that readers bring their own diverse value to what they read—indeed, they help construct the very meanings they find in a text. Louise Rosenblatt gives the classic formulation: the meaning in a work is a "transaction" between reader and text (*Literature*, "Transactional Theory"). Thus we shouldn't be surprised that even the most skilled readers characteristically disagree with one another not only in their valuings of a text but even about its meanings.

Up to now, the profession's solution has been to *get* agreement by "training" scorers and making them use "scoring guides." But these are not solutions; they just hide the problem. The high rates of reader agreement that testers sometimes brag of do not reflect the way the readers value texts but only how they rate them under special conditions with constraining rules. (Thus the sardonic comment I once heard from a scorer: "I'm bringing a peculiar reading process to bear on a peculiar writing process.")

A number of people have been criticizing holistic scoring for a while (see app. A of this chapter, "Works That Question Holistic Scoring"), but we have portfolios to thank for finally getting more of the profession to listen to these critiques. For portfolios increase and highlight disagreements among readers. In the same portfolio, some pieces are stronger than others, some dimensions of writing are better than others (e.g., ideas, organization, syntax, mechanics), and a single dimension may be strong in one piece and not in another. Even one reader of a portfolio tends to get into fights with herself trying to settle on a single-number score she can trust. The disagreements escalate when we ask several readers with different values to agree.

Yet this very conflict and confusion is a more accurate picture of the student's writing ability. That is, the only accurate answer to the question "How good is the student's writing?" is something like this: "It depends—pretty good in playfulness and creativity; pretty bad in giving evidence and thinking logically; pretty good in mechanics and usage when the student takes the trouble and perhaps gets some help; pretty bad when the student is careless or in a hurry; pretty good for reader 1; pretty bad for reader 2."

Any other kind of answer would be skewed. If we "trained" the readers, we might get them to agree, but we would have a correspondingly less accurate decision about the value of the student's writing (that is, about how it is valued by readers as they normally read). Thus holistic scoring locks us into giving scores that are inherently untrustworthy.[1]

The long-running critique of holistic scoring has become noisier in recent years as portfolio scorers have shown themselves to be less tractable or trainable than scorers of single samples. Portfolios don't lend themselves to single numbers. In addition, portfolio scorers are harder to handle because the diverse writing in a portfolio gives them more trust in their sense of the writer. Thus they fight harder for their judgments. When scorers see only a single sample that was written under exam conditions, they are more liable to think, at least unconsciously, "Why fight for my judgment when I have no evidence that this text is typical of the student's other writing—especially the writing done in more natural writing situations." (For three recent, vivid studies of scoring sessions where test administrators had great trouble training portfolio scorers to agree, see app. A: Broad; Despain and Hilgers; Hamp-Lyons and Condon.)

We seem to be stuck, then. We need portfolios to give us better evidence of students' ability, yet this better evidence makes it harder for readers to agree and harder for us to trust any single holistic score. We can't just wish away the variability in how human beings read, and it seems problematic to try to train it away. Nevertheless, the fact remains that sometimes we need a holistic score—a concrete, single-dimensional decision about whether, say, a student should get credit for a course, be exempted from a course, move on to upper-division status, graduate—or perhaps be placed into a basic course. We don't need many or even most of the scores we get, but sometimes we need some, and we can't just beg off and say, "Our readers won't agree." In the face of this dilemma, let me suggest two alternatives to holistic scoring.

1. *Minimal holistic scoring.* Just as portfolios highlight the problems with conventional holistic scoring, they also suggest a better alternative: a peculiarly simple, minimal or marginal holistic scoring. Portfolios are vexing because they are usually too mixed for agreement on one score. But what about a full and rich portfolio where readers agree that most of the pieces are excellent? Are we not more than usually justified in giving a "score" of "excellent" or "notably strong for this population" or some such label? Similarly, what if most readers agree that most of the pieces are weak or unsatisfactory for this setting? Are we not more than usually justified in giving a "score" of "unsatisfactory" or "failing" or "notably weak"? Admittedly, this implies a third, middle score, "neither excellent nor unsatisfactory," but this middle range would be larger than the other two and thus not symmetrical with them.

Readers would not need to be trained for this minimal scoring process. They would simply be shown ahead of time a sample of papers reflecting the range of the students' work so they could decide better which papers were among the best or worst they would encounter during the session. Readers wouldn't even have to meet for this preparation.

Readers sometimes agree about middle scores too, but as LaRene Despain and Thomas L. Hilgers show (30 [cited in app. A]), most disagreements are about middle-range portfolios; moreover, middle-range holistic scores on portfolios are often compromise verdicts when readers experience some papers as strong and others as weak. Middle scores depend on a concatenation of accidents: on the values that happen to be embodied in the scoring guide or on the random compromises readers make between conflicting standards and weightings.

It may sound like theoretical folly to give holistic scores to some portfolios and not to others, but I would insist that the only theoretical wisdom is to restrict holistic scores to the portfolios where a single-number verdict has any justification and to refuse them to the range of portfolios about which readers cannot agree—where readers cannot assign holistic scores without making compromises inside themselves or between each other.

This minimal or marginal holistic scoring epitomizes my theme of both better and less because it involves fewer dubious evaluations. Thus it also permits substantial saving in time and money. A major cost in holistic scoring comes from giving scores from 1 to 6 to *all* portfolios—yet our needs are usually only to identify students who fail or need special help. Sometimes we also want to identify exceptionally skilled students for exemption.

At the State University of New York, Stony Brook, when we started using minimal holistic scoring, we discovered that most portfolios can be read quickly. Most soon disqualify themselves by being too weak to be excellent or too strong to be unsatisfactory. What a pleasure it is to save all the money we normally spend on giving indefensible and misleading middle-range scores. (For more about using minimal holistic scoring in writing programs—that is, letting the scoring procedure grow out of a pragmatic acknowledgment that usually we are trying to identify relatively few students—see Belanoff and Elbow; Elbow and Belanoff, "State University"; W. Smith; Haswell and Wyche-Smith.)

The general principle here is that boundary decisions are always arguable. Therefore, making fewer boundary decisions means making fewer unfair decisions. And when we make fewer boundary decisions, we can make them better in two ways. First, we can put more resources at the boundaries. Richard Haswell and Susan Wyche-Smith shrewdly applied this approach at Washington State University by simply letting the best readers take more time on borderline cases, which were fewer. They also let these readers talk to each other since the readers were making inferences about abilities in writers, not just about qualities in texts. Second, we can adjust the boundaries according to whether we want to emphasize the goal of excellence and gatekeeping or the goal of opportunity and opening doors. If we want to emphasize excellence (such as when we certify pilots or doctors), we must set the boundary "too high" and acknowledge that some good candidates will probably fail. But if our most important goal is to increase opportunity (as surely it must often be in many school and college settings), we must set the boundary "too low" and acknowledge that some weak candidates will probably pass.

Many people defend all the scores and ranking we use by appealing to the "real world": "It's a bottom-line, dog-eat-dog world out there!" But real-world results seldom consist of fine-grained ranking as in holistic scoring or standard grading. More often they consist of minimal "scores" like the ones I have been suggesting: being hired or fired, having a grant application approved or disapproved, getting a manuscript accepted or rejected for publication. People often get feedback about strengths or weaknesses of their work, but they seldom get a holistic, single-quantity rating unless their performance is good enough to be special or bad enough to be a problem. Most real-world "evaluators" know they don't have the time or money to give rankings to everyone, and they realize instinctively that judgments at the extremes are more trustworthy.

2. *Another alternative to holistic scoring: multiple-trait scoring.* In our culture, we seem to suffer from a pervasive, popular assumption that evaluation isn't trustworthy, hardheaded, or honest unless it consists of a single number. As professionals, therefore, we need to convince people that evaluation isn't trustworthy unless it *avoids* the distortion of a single number by distinguishing strengths and weaknesses in the same performance or portfolio. Fair evaluation, then, requires something more descriptive or analytic.

In suggesting multiple-trait scoring, I'm not asking us to go back to the crude and mechanical process called analytic scoring, where various writing dimensions or features are scored on a scale of 1–4 or 1–6 and the subscores are added up into a holistic score. I'm suggesting something in the minimal spirit of this essay—where readers score a writing trait or dimension only if they feel it is notably strong or weak. Thus there are only two scores ("strong" and "weak"), along with a large, third, default middle range. The traits might be traditional ones (such as ideas, details, organization, clarity of syntax, voice, mechanics) or rhetorical features (such as finding a subject, contact with readers, etc.). Readers might even use this procedure on individual pieces in a portfolio. (See app. B for a list of features that readers can quickly check off as they read a portfolio—features that Robert Broad derived from actual scoring-and-anchoring sessions.)

This multiple-trait scoring can easily be combined with the minimal holistic scoring I described earlier. Readers would look not only for writing traits or dimensions that are notably strong or weak; they would also look for portfolios that are notably strong or weak as a whole. Naturally, they would arrive at these minimal, bottom-line, holistic verdicts not just by adding up trait scores. For example, a reader might judge a portfolio to have only one notably weak feature (perhaps ideas and reasoning) yet judge the whole portfolio notably weak. The reader might judge another portfolio to have two or more notably weak features (perhaps organization, voice, and mechanics) yet not judge the whole portfolio notably weak.

When I suggested minimal holistic scoring, I was addressing the unfairness in conventional holistic scoring. To address the following additional problems with holistic scoring, I am suggesting this:

○ Holistic scores give no feedback. A holistic score is nothing but a single point on a yea-boo applause meter and provides no evidence

about what the scorers considered strengths and weaknesses. (Sometimes testing administrators supply "scoring guides" that purport to
describe the strengths and weaknesses of papers for each score. But
these Platonic descriptions seldom describe actual papers.)

○ Holistic scoring encourages the dangerous assumption among
many writing teachers that there is a true score for any piece of
writing or portfolio—and feeds the general cultural hunger for ranking by single numbers. (For a warning about true scores, see White,
"Language" 192.)

○ Holistic scoring fuels what is probably the biggest enemy of
thoughtful evaluation: judgment based on global or holistic feelings
("I like it" or "I don't like it") rather than judgment that tries to describe and to discriminate between strengths and weaknesses.

The crucial point is that multiple-trait scoring adds an element of description to the mere yea/boo of holistic scoring. Thus it has the enormous advantage of giving at last some useful feedback and meaning to
the audience of students, teachers, parents, administrators, legislators,
employers, and others. Even though some students will complain if
their bottom-line score is merely "neither excellent nor poor," most of
them will also receive something more useful and descriptive than the
B– or 4 they are more accustomed to: some indication of particular
strengths and weaknesses. Even students with an "excellent" will almost invariably see features they need to work on. And students with
"unsatisfactory" or "failing" will almost invariably get some much
needed encouragement by seeing features or pieces that readers did
not rate unsatisfactory. Moreover, failing students will see more clearly
the basis of their failure, not just receive an empty number.

Finally, multiple-trait scoring can sometimes even increase fairness
by increasing agreement among readers. Though much disagreement
among readers is inevitable, some disagreement comes needlessly
from the process of holistic scoring. For example, consider a portfolio
full of strong, interesting thinking, clear focus, and pertinent examples
and reasons—but much unclear language and many surface errors.
Consider also two scorers with different tastes: one of them cares more
about the thinking and focus and less about unclear language and mistakes; the other has the opposite values, caring more about clear, idi-
omatic, and correct language and worrying less about writing that says
little or says what is foolish. If these two readers score this portfolio
with conventional holistic scoring, they will almost inevitably disagree
about the score—despite their training (especially since most scoring
guides don't give much help on writing that mixes strong and weak fea-

tures). If they use multiple-trait scoring, they have a good chance of agreeing that the thinking is strong and the language is weak. Even if they disagree in their bottom-line scores, readers will be able to see the grounds of the disagreement—to see that the high score came from a scorer who cares more about thinking and focus. When the values of scorers are not hidden, outside readers have a better chance of making an informed decision about the student's abilities in terms of their *own* values or needs. (Freedman, in app. A, provides evidence that analytic scoring gives higher reliability.)

People often assume that multiple-trait scoring is unfeasibly expensive. But when I last checked, nine states were using some form of analytic or multiple-trait scoring for their statewide tests. Besides, we can save money by switching from full holistic scoring to minimal scoring (and in some other ways that I describe in my next section).

Two objections to multiple-trait or analytic scoring are sometimes raised. One is this: "Readers always see individual traits or features through a holistic halo. When they like a portfolio or paper as a whole, they will see the language and ideas as strong; when they hate it, they will see the same language and ideas as weak." Yes, this is a problem. But what it highlights is something larger—a pervasive bias toward holism in human perception: the path of least resistance in human information processing is to sort things into binary piles of like/dislike, friend/enemy, us/them, familiar/other. This is why people fall so easily into snap judgments. Liz Hamp-Lyons and William Condon found that holistic scorers often decided their scores for a portfolio early.

What looks like a problem, therefore, is really the strongest argument *for* multiple-trait scoring, since that technique attempts to fight the reductive tendency in human perception or information processing. Of course, the attempt must always fail to some degree, but that's all the more reason to persist with it.

While the first objection is that multiple-trait scoring doesn't work, the second is that it does work. This objection might be put as follows: "When readers judge by multiple traits or analytic features, they tend to miss the *essential* quality of the paper. The whole is more than the sum of its multiple parts—thus we need something 'holistic.' Analytic reading is completely artificial and fails to capture the real reactions of real readers. For example, multiple-trait scoring tempts readers to give good scores to papers that are proper or obedient on the specified criteria but that real readers find flat, unsuccessful, or even repellent and to give poor scores to papers that fail the criteria but that real readers find satisfactory or even attractive."

Yes, this too can happen. But let's pause and analyze why. The problem

In addition, we can emphasize a multiple-trait approach that distinguishes strengths and weaknesses instead of giving a single holistic number. Students in my classes are much more willing to forgo middle-level holistic grades on their papers when they know I will notify them if I find their work notably weak or strong. And we can emphasize the classroom as a place for fine-grained feedback—not large tests. Most of all, we need to emphasize the real bottom line: the blunt fact that professionals simply cannot make fair or trustworthy holistic decisions about whether someone is a B level or C level writer. Good readers cannot agree on which portfolios fit those scores or about what skills distinguish B and C level abilities in writing.

4. *Placement exams.* There are more placement exams than any other kind of writing assessment in higher education (CCCC Committee on Assessment, *Post-secondary;* Greenberg, Wiener, and Donovan, *Writing Assessment;* Lederman, Ryzewic, and Ribaudo). The goal of these exams is to identify weak or poorly prepared writers so as to give them extra help (and also sometimes to identify skilled writers so as to exempt them). But is this approach the best way to give these students extra help—trying to identify them ahead of time and then segregating them into basic courses away from skilled and middle-range writers? There are lots of ways to give supplemental help rather than help by quarantine. If we opt for supplemental help, there is no need for placement testing.

The University of South Carolina Writing Program has taken this approach and dropped the placement exam along with all sections of the remedial or basic writing course (though not the ESL course). Entering students are asked to bring a portfolio of precollege writing to their first-year writing course, and on the basis of this and of lots more writing they do during the first week, teachers decide which students should attend the supplemental Writing Studio. Students in the Writing Studio meet weekly with an instructor in groups of four, where they get help with the assignments of the regular course and also work on the writing process and their past experiences with writing. At the end of the first year, all but five or six of the Writing Studio students passed the regular course—many of them with good grades. Teachers and administrators were even more pleased with the results of the second year (Grego and Thompson). After experimentation and research, Washington State University also eliminated its basic writing program.

There are various models for supplementary help given in place of segregation: extra tutorials, workshops, work in a writing center. New York University and Washington State University have one-credit supplementary courses that poorly prepared students can take alongside the regular first-year course. Princeton recently let students make their own choice about whether to take a more basic writing course. We can also require students to stay longer in the first-year course if they don't achieve good enough skill by the end of the semester—instead of pretending we can decide ahead of time which ones cannot make it in one semester. We have uncharted territory here that we need to explore (Elbow, "Writing Assessment").

The enormous amount of placement testing on campuses around the country rests on the pervasive assumption that more testing and segregation of students into different levels will create better learning. This assumption is beginning to be powerfully questioned (Bartholomae, "Tidy House"; Adams). If we look carefully, we may find that even when remedial courses are good (often they are problematic; Greenberg, "Politics" 67), the potential learning is undermined by a host of side effects: some students internalize the label "stupid"; some students are angry because the course delays their progress and adds to their costs and sometimes doesn't even give them credit; and all the students lose the opportunity to work with students who are more skilled.

Placement testing is a growth industry, even though the number of students placed outside the regular first-year course on most campuses is relatively small. Is it really useful to spend so much time and money on these tests when there are other ways to give unskilled writers the help they need? Do we really intend the message we send by insisting that students' first encounter with a university is to undergo writing assessment in order to be segregated into ability groups? Do we really want to exempt some students from any writing course—thereby sending the message that writing instruction is a punishment for not being good enough instead of the message that a writing course is what everyone does as part of the liberal arts? Why are we trying harder and harder to achieve more sophisticated segregations of students into different classrooms at the very time when English teachers in schools around the nation are learning to teach heterogeneous classes? The money used for placement testing and developmental courses could be much better spent to give poorly prepared writers extensive help in individual or small-group tutorials, to pay for longer stays in the course, to pay for currently exempted students to take a writing class, and above all to provide substantial workshops for teachers that help them learn to handle heterogeneous classes.

We can afford to improve assessment by doing less of it. In the first section of this essay, I argued for better testing, making a case for portfolios and against standard holistic scoring. Portfolios give us better evidence of writing abilities or skills; minimal holistic scoring increases the fairness of our judgments about that evidence (if only by forcing us to make fewer judgments). Multiple-trait scoring also helps with fairness, but most of all it gives substantive feedback to students about their strengths and weaknesses. It's true that minimal holistic scoring and multiple-trait scoring are quantitative, but they still help push against the current mania for reductive, one-dimensional quantification. They do this by yielding many fewer reductive, bottom-line scores (most will be "neither excellent nor poor") and by providing a grid of multiple-trait scores that cannot be simply added up. In the last section of the essay I began the kind of policy analysis required for figuring out which tests and scores we need and which we don't.

University of Massachusetts, Amherst

NOTES

I appreciate the helpful comments I got on various drafts of this chapter from various readers, particularly Karen Greenberg, Brian Lavendel, Ed White, and Kathleen Yancey.

[1]There is no reason why we cannot report the divergent holistic scores of different readers *as* the student's score—and indeed every reason why we should do so. Divergent holistic scores would not only give a more accurate picture of how the writing is valued. They would also help students and others gradually come to terms with the intractable truth that even the most professional readers often cannot agree.

Appendix A
Works That Question Holistic Scoring

Belanoff, Pat. "The Myths of Assessment." *Journal of Basic Writing* 10.2 (1991): 54–66.

Broad, Robert. " 'Portfolio Scoring': A Contradiction in Terms." *New Directions in Portfolio Assessment: Reflections, Practice, Critical Theory, and Large-Scale Scoring*. Ed. Laurel Black, Donald A. Daiker, Jeff Sommers, and Gail Stygall. Portsmouth: Boynton-Heinemann, 1994. 263–76.

Buley-Meissner, Mary Louise. "Reading without Seeing: The Process of Holistic Scoring." *Writing on the Edge* 4.1 (1992): 51–65.

Charney, Davida. "The Validity of Using Holistic Scoring to Evaluate Writing: A Critical Overview." *Research in the Teaching of English* 18 (1984): 65–81.

Despain, LaRene, and Thomas L. Hilgers. "Readers' Responses to the Rating of Non-uniform Portfolios: Are There Limits of Portfolios' Utility?" *WPA: Writing Program Administration* 16.1–2 (1992): 24–37.

Elbow, Peter. Foreword. *Portfolios: Process and Product.* Ed. Patricia Belanoff and Marcia Dickson. Portsmouth: Boynton-Heinemann, 1991. ix–xvi.

———. "Ranking, Evaluating, and Liking: Sorting Out Three Forms of Judgment." *College English* 55 (1993): 187–206.

———. "Will the Virtues of Portfolios Blind Us to Their Potential Dangers?" *New Directions in Portfolio Assessment.* Ed. Laurel Black, Donald A. Daiker, Jeff Sommers, and Gail Stygall. Portsmouth: Boynton-Heinemann, 1993. 40–55.

Freedman, Sarah Warshauer. "The Registers of Student and Professional Expository Writing: Influences on Teachers' Responses." *New Directions in Composition Research.* Ed. Richard Beach and Lillian S. Bridwell. New York: Guilford, 1984. 334–47.

Gorman, Thomas P., Alan C. Purves, and R. E. Degenhart. *The IEA Study of Written Composition I: The International Writing Tasks and Scoring Scales.* Oxford: Pergamon, 1988. Vol. 5 of *International Studies in Educational Achievement.*

Gould, Stephen Jay. *The Mismeasure of Man.* New York: Norton, 1981.

Hamp-Lyons, Liz. "Scoring Procedures for ESL Contexts." *Assessing Second Language Writing in Academic Contexts.* Ed. Hamp-Lyons. Norwood: Ablex, 1991. 241–76.

Hamp-Lyons, Liz, and William Condon. "Questioning Assumptions about Portfolio-Based Assessment." *College Composition and Communication* 44 (1993): 176–90.

Hanson, F. Allan. *Testing Testing: Social Consequences of the Examined Life.* Berkeley: U of California P, 1993.

Huot, Brian. "Reliability, Validity, and Holistic Scoring: What We Know and What We Need to Know." *College Composition and Communication* 41 (1990): 201–13.

Lucas, Catharine Keech. "Toward Ecological Evaluation." *Quarterly of the National Writing Project and the Center for the Study of Writing* 10.1 (1988): 1+.

———. "Toward Ecological Evaluation, Part Two: Recontextualizing Literacy Assessment." *Quarterly of the National Writing Project and the Center for the Study of Writing* 10.2 (1988): 4–10.

Scharton, M. A. "Models of Competence: Responses to a Scenario Writing Assignment." *Research in the Teaching of English* 23 (1989): 163–80.

Smith, Barbara Herrnstein. *Contingencies of Value: Alternative Perspectives for Critical Theory.* Cambridge: Harvard UP, 1988.

Appendix B
Check Sheet for Portfolio Scorers

Developed by Robert Broad
(from Broad's essay "Portfolio Scoring" [274], given in app. A)

Paper # _____   Grader #_____   Grade _____

The criteria below were derived from the anchoring-session responses. Some of the qualities are specific to particular assignments (i.e., discourse analyses and reflective narratives); others are more general, for the entire portfolio.

Check 3–5 qualities that were key in the grade determination.

+

- ❏ asks good questions
- ❏ aware of methodological influence on research
- ❏ clear
- ❏ challenging topic
- ❏ complex ideas
- ❏ contextualizes
- ❏ depth
- ❏ describes method used
- ❏ engaging
- ❏ focused
- ❏ includes data
- ❏ incorporates discourse in analysis
- ❏ in-depth analysis
- ❏ interesting topic
- ❏ interesting use of language
- ❏ locates/positions self in relation to social
- ❏ mechanical competence
- ❏ organized
- ❏ provides examples
- ❏ reflective
- ❏ resists generalizations
- ❏ resists pat ending
- ❏ specific
- ❏ style
- ❏ takes risks
- ❏ thoughtful
- ❏ uses humor
- ❏ uses research or data
- ❏ uses quotations
- ❏ voice
- ❏ well developed
- ❏ other _____
- ❏ other _____

−

- ❏ appropriates research
- ❏ clichéd
- ❏ difference denied
- ❏ difference not examined
- ❏ disjointed
- ❏ disorganized
- ❏ doesn't explore issues raised
- ❏ doesn't consider own location
- ❏ doesn't fulfill assignment
- ❏ ends where it should begin
- ❏ essentializes
- ❏ formulaic
- ❏ generalizes
- ❏ importance of topic unclear
- ❏ incompetent mechanical skills
- ❏ location is superficial
- ❏ "normal" goes unexamined
- ❏ not self-reflective
- ❏ overstated conclusions
- ❏ passes judgment without considering location
- ❏ plagiarism
- ❏ proofreading
- ❏ repetitious
- ❏ superficial
- ❏ surface analysis only
- ❏ takes on too little
- ❏ takes on too much
- ❏ topic nebulous
- ❏ undefined terms
- ❏ unfocused
- ❏ unorganized
- ❏ voice
- ❏ weak connections
- ❏ other _____
- ❏ other _____

New Views of Measurement and New Models for Writing Assessment

Roberta Camp

It is no secret that our ideas about writing have changed in the last two decades. Many of the essays in this volume clearly indicate that change. I have argued elsewhere that the concepts of writing evident in current research and practice constitute a major shift in what is to be measured in writing assessment, a shift in the very construct for writing ("Changing," "Place"). Like others, I have pointed to our understanding of writing as a rich, multifaceted, meaning-making activity that occurs over time and in a social context, an activity that varies with purpose, situation, and audience and is improved by reflection on the written product and on the strategies used in creating it. This understanding, I contend, is not well served by our traditional testing formats; it requires new approaches to assessment, such as portfolios, classroom-based performances, and documentation over time.

The necessity for change is not unique to writing assessment. New views of learning, and consequently of teaching and assessment, are evident across the disciplines. The perception of students as active learners, the interest in cognitive processes involved in learning, the recognition of differences in learning that arise from social and cultural contexts—all have led to exploration of new assessment approaches in mathematics, science, social studies, and the arts, as well as in writing (see Berlak et al.; Mitchell, *Testing*; Wolf, Bixby, Glenn, and Gardner). These developments, combined with new perspectives on accountability and on the place of assessment in our educational institutions, have given rise to new models for assessment and the beginnings of new measurement theory.

It is time to consider the current issues of writing assessment in the context of changes occurring elsewhere in measurement. To that end, this essay offers a survey of current thinking about validity and the movement toward contextualized assessment. From the vantage point of the survey, the essay then suggests resources and promising directions for responsible and informed approaches to the assessment of writing.

New Views of Validity

In recent years the educational assessment community has given considerable attention to the concept of validity. As a result, validity is now seen as a single, unified concept in which the construct to be measured—the theoretical understanding of the knowledge and skills targeted in the assessment—is central to all other considerations (Cole and Moss; Cronbach, "Perspectives"; Messick, "Meaning," "Validity"). At one time the validity of a test would have been discussed in terms of one or more kinds of validity, each independent of and more or less equal in value to the others: content validity, construct validity, criterion-related validity (including predictive validity and concurrent validity), and face validity. In the last two decades, however, validity theory has increasingly focused on the inferences about a test taker that are derived from performance on a test. Using evidence from multiple sources and arguments, investigations of validity involve the ongoing evaluation of such inferences. The investigations may draw on methodologies associated with earlier approaches to validity, but to be consistent with current views they must consider validity in integrated and comprehensive terms and always in relation to the theoretical construct—what the assessment is intended to measure. Moreover, the evidence for validity must be examined in relation to the social consequences of inferences made about test takers and of actions taken on the basis of those inferences (Cole and Moss; Messick, "Meaning," "Validity").

Thus investigations of validity now include far more than traditional content validity studies, which were essentially examinations of a test's coverage of the subject, and more too than the comparisons of performances within and across tests (often correlational studies) that characterized many studies of predictive validity. Most important, however, is that all evidence for validity is to be interpreted in relation to the theoretical construct, the purpose for the assessment and therefore the inferences derived from it, and the social consequences.

This new understanding of validity suggests that our concerns about the validity of traditional writing assessments are legitimate (see Camp, "Changing," "Place"; Greenberg and Witte; Scharton, this volume; Williamson). The mismatch between the current theoretical constructs for writing and the construct measured in traditional formats for assessment casts serious doubt on the validity of traditional approaches. That doubt is not entirely allayed by the familiar arguments for the content validity of the multiple-choice writing test (that it is a broad sampling of writing subskills) or for its criterion validity (that it shows a high statistical correspondence with writing samples in corre-

lational studies). Furthermore, our concerns about the possibly deleterious effects of conventional writing assessment formats on students
outside the mainstream of academic culture no longer appear peripheral; they are central to validity, especially if those effects result from
misrepresentation of the construct of writing.

Current thinking suggests that problems with a test's validity, especially those associated with adverse social consequences, be investi-
gated by looking at how the construct to be measured is represented in
the test. That means we should think about whether our assessments
adequately represent writing as we understand it. If an assessment fails
to include important and relevant dimensions of the construct—as traditional writing assessments do—it is said to suffer from "construct un-
derrepresentation." If the assessment is more difficult for some test
takers than for others for reasons irrelevant to the construct—as may
be the case with writing assessments using traditional formats—then it
is said to exhibit "construct-irrelevant variance" (Messick, "Meaning"
7). Similarly, if the information derived from an assessment is more
valid for some groups of the test-taking population than for others—if
it exhibits "differential validity"—the assessment is said to show test
bias (Cole and Moss 205).

These criteria for validity can be useful as we evaluate traditional formats for writing assessment and search for new ones. They suggest
that our assessments and the inferences about writers' abilities we derive from them must take into account both the current construct for
writing and the possible distortions in our estimates of writers' abilities
that result from the limitations of our assessment formats.

Also useful to our evaluations of traditional and new assessment formats is a shift in methods employed for construct validation (Messick,
"Meaning"). The historical development associated with emerging
views of validity is moving the field away from primary emphasis on
patterns of relations such as correlational studies and toward methods
more favorable to complex performances in writing. Studies of predictive validity still contribute to construct-validity investigations, but
there is considerably more interest now in insights to be gained from
studies of the processes underlying performance and from studies of
test takers' performances over time and across groups and settings.

Additional expansions of the concept of validity have recently become evident. Following on the concern about social consequences,
they open possibilities for complex, context-rich assessments. They
have far-reaching implications, especially for new constructs of writing.

John Frederiksen and Allan Collins, pointing out the unfortunate effects of indirect assessment (e.g., multiple-choice tests) on teaching

and learning, suggest that our notions of validity be expanded to include the effects of an assessment on the educational system in which it occurs. For an assessment to demonstrate "systemic validity," they argue, it must support instruction and learning in the cognitive skills it is intended to measure. In this view, indirect assessment, despite its purported economy, efficiency, and objectivity, exacts a high price; it emphasizes isolated, low-level skills and displaces skills and strategies necessary to higher-order thinking, problem solving, and metacognitive awareness. Direct assessment, in constrast, is based on performances that address the intended cognitive skills and that can incorporate not only the product to be created but also the process of its creation. Through the procedures and discussions involved in conducting and scoring the assessment, direct assessment also develops awareness among teachers and learners of the characteristics important to good performances and products.

The expansion of the concept of validity to include systemic effects has implications for writing assessment. It means not only that the legitimacy of direct assessment has been established but also that the procedures associated with direct assessment of writing are now exemplary for assessments in other areas of the curriculum. The setting of representative tasks; the identification of criteria and standards for judging performance of those tasks; the development of libraries of sample performances that illustrate how the scoring criteria have been applied; the involvement of all parties to the assessment, including classroom teachers and students—these procedures emphasize the skills and strategies that the assessment is intended to address. The procedures involved in the direct assessment of writing, that is, have great potential for enhancing systemic validity.

A second expansion of the concept of validity addresses the criteria by which assessments are to be evaluated. Recognizing that the criteria traditionally applied—which emphasize reliability, efficiency, and comparability—do not reflect current conceptions of validity, Robert Linn, Eva Baker, and Stephen Dunbar argue for an enlarged set of criteria. In addition to "fairness," "transfer and generalizability," "content quality," "content coverage," and "cost and efficiency," which are reformulations of traditional concerns, they include criteria such as "consequences" ("the intended and unintended effects . . . on the ways teachers and students spend their time and think about the goals of education" [17]), "cognitive complexity" ("emphasis on problem solving, comprehension, critical thinking, reasoning, and metacognitive processes" [19]), and "meaningfulness" (having a basis in "meaningful problems that provide worthwhile educational experiences" [21]).

The enlarged set of criteria allows new approaches to assessment, especially those based on more complex kinds of performance, to be judged in terms that take full account of their value. The advocacy of such criteria by respected members of the assessment community strengthens the case for new forms of writing assessment. Their advocacy goes far toward eliminating the disparity between the requirements of the emerging theoretical construct for writing and the requirements of good measurement.

A third expansion of the concept of validity focuses on the methods used to evaluate assessments. In a comprehensive review of recent developments in validity, Pamela Moss ("Conceptions") has analyzed the new theoretical arguments (including those of Frederiksen and Collins; and Linn, Baker, and Dunbar) that call for balance between traditional, technical concerns and consideration of social consequences. She finds that investigations of validity, even those based on new theoretical arguments, must allow new methods and new kinds of evidence if they are to recognize the value for learning of teacher-and-student discussions related to assessment. She argues for inclusion of epistemological strategies that value participants' perspectives, like those used in qualitative research and interpretive inquiry. Classroom teachers' interpretations of student work, for example, could then be viewed as credible sources of evidence. In this way, Moss suggests, investigations of validity will be better able to take into account the benefits of teachers' and students' discussions of student work and their discourse about standards and criteria for performance. The information about students derived from assessments can in turn be interpreted in the light of teachers' knowledge about students' day-to-day classroom performance (P. Moss, "Can There Be?," "Conceptions").

Within the broad outlines of these expanded concepts of validity, whose central focus is on the construct to be measured and whose emphasis is on consequences for teaching and learning, we can find accommodation, even direction, for the writing assessments of the future. If we take from these discussions of validity the sense of assessment as a set of contextualized performances and procedures, examples of which are found in the best direct writing assessments, and if we merge that sense with our recently expanded constructs for writing and with our growing awareness of the value of teachers' and students' discussions of writing performance, we can begin to address the challenges for assessment we now experience. At the very least, we can gain a clear indication of the rationale we will need if we are to establish the legitimacy of assessments that are consistent with our new understanding of writing, closely integrated with writing instruction, and immediately informative to teachers and students.

The Movement toward Contextualized Assessment

The development of new theories of measurement is stimulated in part by a movement within curriculum and school reform toward alternative models of assessment (Berlak et al.; Gardner; Glaser; Graue, "Integrating Theory"; Haney and Madaus; Mitchell, *Testing*; Perrone; D. Resnick and L. Resnick, "Standards"; Stiggins; Wiggins). In many of the alternative models, assessment is based on performances of complex and meaningful tasks that are related to real-world situations and are themselves valuable to learning (Archbald and Newmann; Gitomer; Mitchell, *Testing*; Wiggins). These performances draw on knowledge and skills integrated in the context of purposeful problem solving, which may be accomplished collaboratively and within a relatively extended and flexible time frame. The tasks are challenging, but support is provided, in some assessments as needed, enabling all performers to demonstrate some degree of success.

The performances central to such models of assessment are likely to culminate in production of discourse or artifacts that yield evidence of achievement, but the products are not the exclusive focus for evaluation. The evaluation requires informed judgment by knowledgeable witnesses to the performance (teachers, for example), who attend to the essentials of the performance, including the strategies and processes used to bring it about. Judgments are expressed as multiple scores corresponding to multiple dimensions or multiple facets of achievement. The criteria informing the judgments are public, shared, and eventually internalized by performers and evaluators alike. The tasks for the assessment are consistent with individual and institutional goals for learning, and the purpose of the assessment is to enable learners to discover and demonstrate what they can do and what they might work on in the future.

Models for contextualized assessment are being explored, as are the issues regarding their implementation, across academic disciplines and educational institutions. Some of the new assessments are built around projects that involve hands-on problem solving or sustained inquiry, as in the science projects developed by the National Assessment of Educational Progress and the Connecticut Assessment of Educational Progress; in the New York science and mathematics assessments; in Educational Testing Service's PACKETS for mathematics; in the graduation requirements for Central Park East in New York City and for Walden III in Racine, Wisconsin; and in numerous other instances (*Arts PROPEL: An Introductory Handbook*; Berlak et al.; Lesh and Lamon; Mitchell, "Sampler," *Testing;* Wolf, "Assessment as an Episode"). Other assessments are based on carefully articulated procedures for documenting, interpreting, and discussing evidence of student learning. The most fully developed examples of this approach focus on emerging literacy (the Primary Language Record; see Barrs, Ellis, Hester, and Thomas) and on the literacy of young adults (the California Learning Record; see Cheong and Barr). Significant work has also been done with documentation in mathematics and science (Chittenden and Kanevsky) and in schoolwide assessment across the curriculum (Chittenden and Wallace).

Some assessments, especially in reading and writing but increasingly in mathematics, science, and other areas of the curriculum, engage students in the creation of portfolios (e.g., the California Learning Assessment System, Arts PROPEL in Pittsburgh, Vermont's writing and mathematics assessments). The portfolios often draw on work completed in projects sustained over time; sometimes the development of portfolios and their evaluation involve teachers, or teachers and students, in discussion about goals for learning, about evidence of learning in student work, and about the criteria and standards by which students' work will be evaluated (*Arts PROPEL: An Introductory Handbook*; Belanoff and Elbow; Camp, "Assessment in the Context," "Thinking," "Portfolio Reflection"; Daiker, Sommers, and Stygall, this volume; Gitomer; P. Moss et al.; Zessoules and Gardner). Schools, school districts, states, and college writing programs from Juneau, Alaska, to Fort Worth, Texas, and from California to Vermont are developing portfolio assessments that deal specifically with writing or literacy (see Belanoff and Dickson; Daiker, Sommers, and Stygall, this volume; Murphy and Camp; Murphy and Grant, this volume; Murphy and Smith, *Writing*; Tierney, Carter, and Desai; Yancey).

Such models—classroom projects, documentation, and portfolios—have strong potential for addressing the limitations of traditional approaches to literacy assessment. They represent a movement toward assessments that are "ecological" in the ways described by Catharine Lucas ("Toward Ecological Evaluation, Part Two"): they have a positive effect on the learning environment, they take into account the whole environment of the learner, and they increase the amount, quality, and usefulness of the information provided to teachers and students. They point toward assessment that exhibits the qualities Sheila Valencia, William McGinley, and P. David Pearson indicate are necessary to literacy assessment, toward assessment that is "continuous, multi-dimensional, collaborative, knowledge-based, and authentic" (134). Such assessment involves teachers and students in what Peter Johnston calls the "constructive evaluation of literate activity"; it takes into account the meaning-making aspects of evaluation, the social interactions inherent in evaluation, and the consequences and political implications of evaluation. Such assessment embodies the constructivist paradigm described in this volume by Sandra Murphy and Barbara Grant.

The use of such models reflects a significant transformation in the expectations for assessment held by the institutions that use them, a transformation consistent with current discussions of school reform and restructuring (Berlak et al.; Camp, "Assessment in the Context"; Darling-Hammond and Ascher; Newmann; Perrone). The change is especially telling where assessments specifically designed to be used in classrooms and to be directly informative to teachers and students are also used to shape decisions at the institutional level (*Arts PROPEL: A Handbook*; Camp, "Assessment in the Context," "Place"; Chittenden and Wallace; LeMahieu, Eresh, and Wallace; LeMahieu, Gitomer, and Eresh; Murphy and Camp).

Moving toward New Models for Writing Assessment

The challenge of developing models of assessment compatible with our new understanding of writing will not be met easily or quickly. Clearly, though, we are not alone in our effort. Educators and designers of assessments in other academic disciplines face the same challenge, and researchers in educational measurement are engaged with the same issues. It may be helpful to consider briefly here the resources available to us, both in the research literature on measurement and in our previous experience with writing assessment.

The work of several of the researchers already cited in this chapter provides guidelines for new approaches to assessment. Frederiksen and Collins set out "principles for the design of systemically valid testing" (30). Doug Archbald and Fred Newmann identify critical issues for alternative assessments, as well as criteria for the tasks presented (vi, 2–4). Grant Wiggins describes "criteria of authenticity" for contextualized assessment (711–12). Valencia, McGinley, and Pearson indicate "important attributes of classroom and individual assessment" (134), and Lucas describes criteria for ecological validity in writing assessment ("Toward Ecological Evaluation, Part Two" 5). In addition, assessment practitioners have begun to articulate guidelines based on their experience with performance assessment (Baron; Lane, Parke, and Moskal). Although these guidelines arise from different perspectives and experiences, they are remarkably similar. In combination

with such fully articulated approaches to literacy assessment as Johnston's constructive evaluation and the whole language evaluation of
Kenneth Goodman, Yetta Goodman, and Wendy Hood, they constitute
the beginnings of a literature to which we can refer in our efforts to
shape writing assessments compatible with the construct of writing as
we currently understand it.

The principles behind such established psychometric concerns as reliability and validity can guide us as we design and evaluate new approaches to assessment, although those principles need to be understood
and applied in new ways. Fairness, equity, and generalizability still pertain to assessments based on complex performances in writing; the challenge now is to apply them in ways that go beyond the narrow focus on
score reliability and beyond the narrow definitions of validity that characterized earlier discussions of measurement (Gitomer; P. Moss, "Can
There Be?"; Shale, this volume). In this effort we will eventually be supported by new measurement theory and new methodologies (see Frederiksen, Glaser, Lesgold, and Shafto; Frederiksen, Mislevy, and Bejar).
Meanwhile, we can proceed, as cutting-edge development in assessment
now does: we can consider what kinds of performances are central to students' learning about writing, what kinds of information can legitimately
be derived from those performances, what generalizations about students' ability and development can be made on the basis of the information derived, and whether the writing performances required for our new
assessments are equally appropriate for students who draw on different
cultural and linguistic experiences.

A further resource in our attempt to create richer forms of assessment lies in the research done on the processes and strategies of writing. The work of Linda Flower and John Hayes; Robert de Beaugrande;
Arthur Applebee; and Marlene Scardamalia and Carl Bereiter, for example, will help us develop models for assessment that inform both
teachers and students about how writing processes and strategies contribute or fail to contribute to the success of the writing performance.
In moving toward richer assessments, we will be building on and enlarging the scope of research like that of Leo Ruth and Sandra Murphy,
which analyzed the demands that tasks used in assessments make on
writers.

Our earlier experience with direct assessment of writing can also
help us in the design and evaluation of assessment based on more complex performances. Catharine Lucas and Sybil Carlson, creating a
prototype for alternative assessment strategies, indicate how the understanding gained from previous experience can be applied. They

describe the procedures of development, evaluation, and analysis now familiar to those who have been involved in creating direct assessment systems and suggest that the procedures can provide "some systematic control" while accommodating performances on more open-ended tasks (14–16). The procedures encompass several stages in the development of an assessment system, each stage drawing on the understanding of individuals experienced in the teaching and assessment of writing. The first stages are identifying the competencies to be assessed, translating the expectations for performance into specifications for the tasks, and developing the tasks. The next stages are trying out the tasks, evaluating them, exploring preliminary scoring systems, and refining both tasks and scoring systems. The final stages are training readers, scoring the samples that result from the performances, and conducting statistical and qualitative analyses to establish reliability, validity, and generalizability and to determine the assessments' feasibility, cost effectiveness, and social consequences.

The experience gained from decades of writing assessment can be extremely helpful to those developing and trying out new assessments (see Faigley, Cherry, Jolliffe, and Skinner; Greenberg, Wiener, and Donovan; Spandel and Stiggins; White, *Teaching*). Understanding based on experience is essential, in fact, if we are to move forward in an orderly and responsible way. The procedures refined by practitioners in creating the assessments of the past can be adapted, with care and vision, to accommodate complex and long-term performances. Those procedures can help the shapers and users of assessment focus on skills and strategies as well as on the performances themselves. What is more, if the assessment-creating activities involve teachers in the development and refinement of assessment design, in the evaluation of student performances and products, and in the examination of the effects of the assessment on teaching and learning, and if the activities result in articulated criteria and standards for performance and their application to classroom work, then the assessment system can become a means of promoting the kinds of learning it addresses (Camp, "Assessment in the Context," "Place"; Howard, "Portfolio Culture"; LeMahieu, Gitomer, and Eresh; P. Moss, "Can There Be?"; Sheingold, Heller, and Paulukonis). In short, the activities involved in building and using an assessment, activities that create and require informed dialogue among participants, can help establish systemic validity.

It is no accident, then, that the procedures associated with direct assessment of writing are seen as exemplary. If we are wise, we will consult them and what we have learned from them as we press beyond the constraints of current forms of assessment.

Probable Characteristics of New Models for Writing Assessment

It is too early to describe definitively the forms of writing assessment to come. Nevertheless, if we consider both the needs that lead us to search for new assessments and the exploratory activity evident in classrooms, schools, school districts, universities, and state departments of education, we get a sense of possible approaches and—more to the point—of the qualities to look for in writing assessment that is compatible with our current understanding of writing.

The most obvious example of forward-looking writing assessment is the portfolio. In their potential for addressing traditional measurement concerns about sampling and in their potential for accommodating the new constructs of writing, portfolio approaches seem especially promising. Portfolios provide evidence for complex and varied performances in writing, for writing generated in rich instructional and social contexts, for the processes and strategies that students use, and for students' awareness of processes and strategies (*Arts PROPEL: A Handbook*; Camp, "Portfolio Reflection," "Thinking"; Camp and Levine; Daiker, Sommers, and Stygall, this volume; Mitchell, *Testing*; Murphy and Grant, this volume; Murphy and Smith, "Looking," "Talking," *Writing*; Paulson, Paulson, and Meyer; Wolf, "Assessment as an Episode," "Portfolio Assessment"; Zessoules and Gardner).

The procedures associated with portfolio design, implementation, and evaluation provide valuable opportunities to discuss goals for writing instruction, to discuss the writing skills and abilities that portfolios are intended to measure, and to discuss the criteria and standards used to evaluate writing performance. Through such discussions portfolios can enrich and refine teachers' perceptions of student writing and development while enlarging participation in the assessment to include the entire educational community (Belanoff and Elbow; Camp, "Assessment in the Context," "Place," "Thinking"; Daiker, Sommers, and Stygall, this volume; LeMahieu, Eresh, and Wallace; LeMahieu, Gitomer, and Eresh; P. Moss, "Can There Be?"; Moss et al.; Murphy and Camp; Murphy and Smith, "Looking," "Talking," *Writing*; Roemer, Schultz, and Durst; Tierney, Carter, and Desai). If portfolios are designed to encourage students to reflect on their work, they can also help them learn to evaluate their writing and assume increased responsibility for their development as writers (*Arts PROPEL: A Handbook*; Camp, "Portfolio Reflection"; Camp and Levine; Daiker, Sommers, and Stygall, this volume; Gold; Howard, "Making," "Portfolio Culture"; Murphy and Smith, *Writing*; Reif; Tierney, Carter, and Desai; Wolf, "Assessment as an Episode").

Approaches to writing assessment that are consistent with the larger movement to contextualized assessment and that complement portfolios—approaches like classroom-based projects and documentation—are also being explored in literacy assessment in school sites and research projects. Some of this exploration involves extended classroom projects that integrate instruction and assessment and emphasize writing as a tool for discovering ideas and techniques or for solving problems (*Arts PROPEL: A Handbook*; Levine; Mitchell, *Testing*). Some of this exploration addresses procedures for documenting evidence of developing literacy (the Primary Language Record and the California Learning Record).

What does all this tell us about probable directions for writing assessment? It is clear that many questions are yet to be addressed and many discoveries are yet to be made in the exploration of new approaches. Only recently have we been able to gather and examine data from large-scale use of new writing assessments (see, e.g., LeMahieu, Gitomer, and Eresh; Mislevy). It will be some time before we understand fully what is possible in the new approaches. Nevertheless, on the basis of our collective experience to date, our understanding of the current constructs for writing, and current developments in measurement, several tendencies now seem likely:

○ Use of assessment approaches employing different methods and formats and serving different purposes and educational contexts
○ Sampling of writing performance and products generated on multiple occasions, for multiple purposes, over extended periods of time and under various circumstances
○ Increased attention to the cognitive processes involved in writing, with awareness of the connections among the processes used and the skills, abilities, and strategies available to the writer
○ Encouragement for writers to reflect on the processes and strategies they use in single and multiple pieces of writing and over time
○ Increased attention to the knowledge required and cognitive processes involved in evaluating writing products and performances
○ Increased attention to the procedures used in developing and conducting writing assessments and to the opportunities they provide: to examine goals for learning, to reflect on curriculum and instruction, and to arrive at shared standards and criteria for student work
○ Development of formats for reporting on writing performance that are more informative to teachers and students than are single numerical scores—formats such as profiles and qualitative descriptions of processes and strategies

○ Use of caution in generalizing from single performances in writing to performances that call on substantially different knowledge, skills, and strategies; that make different resources available to the writer; or that draw on different kinds of linguistic or cultural experience
○ Creation of assessments that take into account the evolving needs of the educational systems within which assessment occurs

By creating assessments of writing that incorporate these characteristics and practices, we will be better able to provide accurate and useful information to the various constituencies we serve—students, teachers, parents, and community. In addition, if we build thoughtfully and carefully, calling on what we have already learned about writing and writing assessment and on what we are learning from assessment practice in other disciplines, we will generate new models for assessment and the data and experience through which new methods and theories of measurement can be grounded and refined.

Educational Testing Service

NOTE

This chapter is an abbreviated and updated version of my essay "Changing the Model for the Direct Assessment of Writing."

Upper-Division Assessment and the Postsecondary Development of Writing Abilities

Stephen M. North

In this essay I argue that while we have increased our involvement in upper-division writing assessment—particularly, although by no means exclusively, in the form of various barrier tests—we have acquired no substantial corresponding understanding of the postsecondary development of writing abilities: no clearly articulated theory, grounded in either practice or research, about the emergence of the postsecondary literacy regarding which we purport to be judging students. By thus participating in an institutional practice from a position of what amounts to professional ignorance, we abdicate our ethical and political responsibilities.

We have become involved with upper-division writing assessment more slowly than we have with either entrance examinations or assessments that are more course- and program-specific, for understandable reasons. After all, for the first two or even three decades after World War II—years of radical change for higher education—most institutions tended to be preoccupied more with who should be (or, under later, "open" admissions policies, who in fact was being) admitted than with who might graduate. Properly rigorous selection and placement, reinforced by strict grading, were expected to obviate graduation problems. From a narrowly programmatic perspective—our view as an emerging corps of writing assessment professionals—entry-level and program-specific assessments were closely tied to matters we could control: finding appropriate placements, initiating diagnostic work, altering curricula, and so on. That pragmatic connection, coupled with our tendency to be institutionally insecure (and, always, the problem of limited resources), conspired to keep much of our assessment work focused on the lower division.

Nevertheless, the idea of writing assessment for upper-division students has had institutional proponents since at least the 1960s, and it has had a minor but visible place on our professional agenda (Purnell; Freedman and Robinson; White, *Teaching* [1st ed.] 40–50; Elbow and Belanoff, "State University" 96). It is not hard to understand the conditions that gave rise to interest in the subject. The same postwar increase in access to higher education that gave such a boost to large-scale assessment of writing abilities in the first place (a boost best indexed, perhaps, by the burgeoning fortunes of the Educational Testing Service) also eventually caused a crisis of confidence in the value of undergraduate education. To some extent, that crisis can be characterized as a distrust of the "normal" curriculum and of the faculty members who offer it: if it and they were doing the job properly, the literacy of upper-division students would never be questioned (White, *Developing* 126). More fundamentally, though, the crisis represents a distrust of a democratized higher education—a distrust, finally, of the students, this new "raw material" gumming up the heretofore perfectly serviceable curricular works.

For much of the country's history, a college education had been primarily a process of social certification, not transformation. Early on, the goal was to prepare the sons of a white elite to take their "rightful" places as the leaders of the next generation; later, the goal gradually became to prepare the sons of the white middle class for different but no less expected places. After World War II, the pace and demographic scope of change was dramatic enough to transform longstanding anxieties—class- and race- and gender-based—into more widely articulated fears. If colleges that these students never could have attended before were going to admit them or if new institutions were opened for them, could future graduates possibly be as "good" as past ones? Could the baccalaureate mean what it once meant, serve the purposes it once served? One response to such questions as they pertain to writing—which has, of course, its own venerable status as a discriminator in education (Berlin, *Writing Instruction* 61)—was the barrier exam: "Nobody graduates from here," it could be imagined to declare, "who cannot write."

Given these causal conditions, it is no surprise that interest in upper-division assessment has continued to grow. The democratization of higher education has perhaps slowed, but we are still dealing with its impact. Witness, if nothing else, the growth of two-year colleges and the corresponding phenomenon of the transfer student. And continued democratization has meant a continued undermining of the baccalaureate's credibility, accompanied by increasing demands for accountability, most recently in response to the nation's economic difficulties. It is somewhat ironic that as writing professionals we have contributed to this interest, especially by our successful promotion of writing across the curriculum. Thus, while we have gradually won institutional security for our writing programs, we have also made it clear that responsibility for student literacy cannot fall exclusively on them and particularly not on the course or courses traditionally constituting freshman composition. Rather, we have argued, students must have many opportunities to work on their writing, in a variety of disciplines, throughout their undergraduate years: writing is, in short, an institutional responsibility. From there it isn't much of a leap to the notion that the responsibility for assessing writing is also institutional.

Most often, the impulse for institution-wide upper-division writing assessment seems to manifest itself as the desire for some sort of test (Purnell; Elbow and Belanoff, "State University" 96; White, *Developing* 126–29; CCCC Committee on Assessment). The current appeal of assessment tests is made most visible, perhaps, by the 1990 publication of likely the first book-length treatment of the subject: Norbert Elliot, Maximino Plata, and Paul Zelhart's *A Program Development Handbook for the Holistic Assessment of Writing*, which describes the rising junior essay assessment program at East Texas State University. According to Karen Greenberg, director of the National Testing Network in Writing (NTNW), the book meets a real demand. Response to presentations by its authors at NTNW meetings were "so enthusiastic," she writes in her foreword, that "we received numerous requests for copies of their material. Thus we are delighted that it is being published in its entirety." Such testing has not gone unopposed. Peter Elbow and Pat Belanoff, for example, outline its disadvantages, proposing the increasingly popular portfolio system as an alternative ("State University" 96–97); and White offers probably the most comprehensive critique—on grounds from political to methodological (*Developing* 126–29)—before suggesting that a required upper-division course makes more sense (128).

However persuasive these two critiques of barrier tests are, the fact that both preface alternative proposals for upper-division assessment—and are not, say, outright dismissals of any need for it—demonstrates the power of the basic impulse. Whether the method of choice is a rising junior assessment, a proficiency test, portfolios, or a required course, the essential message is the same: we expect "that students receiving college degrees will be able to read and write better than they did upon entrance" (White, *Developing* 157–58), but we cannot trust that, left to their own devices in our curricula, students will satisfy that expectation. Rather, we need "a kind of quality control—not only to avoid inconsistency but to hold up standards" (Elbow and Belanoff, "State University" 97). In short, this impulse to defend the baccalaureate is well on its way to becoming institutionalized. And the forces that have brought us this far show no signs of letting up (Winston).

The connection between upper-division assessment and knowledge about the development of writing abilities isn't very complicated. In effect, such assessment stops people half or three-fourths of the way along an imagined trajectory toward postsecondary literacy to make sure they are more or less where they are "supposed to be" in terms of textual production: that they are writing "better," have achieved a certain "quality"—determinations that obviously presuppose a developmental model. The notion of development is more complicated. On the nature-nurture continuum that shapes much of our thinking about education, development has most commonly been associated with nature, in what might be called its biological sense, involving the movement (usually "progress") of an individual organism from one stage of maturation to the next, with the further understanding that this movement is fundamentally (usually genetically) programmed. But development has resonances at the nurture end of the continuum as well, a more social or cultural dimension. While no one seems prepared to deny that human beings, as organisms, develop in a programmed biological sense, there is much disagreement about how large a sphere of human activity such programming can account for. And surely no area has been more contested than language, where notions about what counts as natural—or, the more usual form of the term in education, "normal"—are clearly implicated in a society's political dynamic.

Unfortunately for us and for our students, however, we can claim only a meager understanding of postsecondary development in either sense. We can plausibly point to only two substantial research traditions that feature both college-level ambitions and anything like a consistent developmental focus, and even they are most noteworthy for the peculiarity of that focus when they deal with upper-division writers. The older of the two—dating from the early 1960s—is the work on syntax and syntactic "maturity" usually identified with Kellogg Hunt and later with the sentence-combining movement (see Hillocks 142–51 for a full review). Hunt's extensive body of studies mostly passes over the college years, focusing on grades 4, 6, 8, 10, and 12, then jumping to "skilled adults," authors "who recently had published articles in *Harpers* or *Atlantic*" (96). Subsequent studies, even including collateral work (e.g., Christensen and Christensen; Pitkin; Hake and Williams), have done little to plot the missing college-year points along this trajectory. Instead, the studies that move beyond grade 12 (e.g., Morenberg, Daiker, and Kerek; Stewart; Maimon and Nodine, "Measuring") are generally restricted to a single course, freshman composition. Oddly, this holds true even for a pair of key studies in which the students were no longer freshmen. Elaine Maimon and Barbara Nodine ("Words") and Andrew Kerek, Donald Daiker, and Max Morenberg retested students involved in earlier experiments—in one case, a year later; in the other, twenty-eight months later. But these studies were clearly seen more as follow-ups than as new developmental work: as asking, "What has happened to the syntax of those freshmen?" rather than, "What can we say about the syntax, or the writing in general, of sophomores and juniors?" Interest in syntax as an index of development has faded, but not because we have ever had a comprehensive account of syntactic development through the college years.

Even more striking is the way this developmental blind spot shows up in the research tradition that relates insights from cognitive-developmental psychology, broadly conceived, to writing. Like the work on syntax, this line of inquiry can be understood in part as an effort to extend a trajectory plotted for younger writers (Britton et al.; Graves). Although also often restricted to freshman composition (Odell, "Piaget"; Slattery), this tradition has covered a somewhat broader spectrum, especially when it has borrowed from William Perry's *Forms of Intellectual and Ethical Development in the College Years* (Haisty; Hays; Anson). However, the overall trend in such inquiry, even when it uses Perry, has been to look not so much at development through the college years as at how models of development apply to "basic" writers. Thus, from Andrea Lunsford's "Cognitive Development and the Basic Writer" (1979) to Patricia Bizzell's "What Happens When Basic Writers Come to College" (1986) to Kathleen Dixon's "Intellectual Development and the Place of Narrative in 'Basic' and Freshman Composition" (1989), more and more such work has centered around people understood as somehow precollege, at least in their writing. (See Winchell for a fuller discussion.)

This account of our literature on writing development in the college years is not, to be sure, exhaustive—not in the way that a bibliographic essay would be. Indeed, readers current in the literature will note that I have omitted two recent books, to be discussed later: Robert Ochsner's *Physical Eloquence and the Biology of Writing* and Richard Haswell's *Gaining Ground in College Writing*. Nevertheless, I believe that this summary represents the general state of our knowledge about the subject and, equally important here, portrays the status of development in our professional consciousness. If this essay were a bibliographic essay on development, it would be the only one: the sourcebook *Research in Composition and Rhetoric* (Moran and Lunsford) features an essay on psychology, but the text's section on development—two pages out of thirty—mainly argues that "composition has only very recently begun to address seriously the subject of development, so there was very little research to cite" (Phelps 57). *Teaching Composition* includes no essay on development (Tate). The term does not appear in the index of the exhaustive *Research on Written Composition* (Hillocks). Even in the annotated bibliography in *Research in the Teaching of English*, "Development" falls under "Language"; the major heading "Writing" has no parallel subcategory. Or consider, finally, that the last book on writing development in college before Haswell's was Albert Kitzhaber's *Themes, Theories, and Therapy*, published in 1963 (Haswell 4).

In short, although we have compiled a substantial body of research and a rich practical lore concerning the writing college students do in writing courses (from Sommers ["Revision Strategies"] to Shaughnessy, from Connors and Lunsford ["Frequency"] to Coles) and, thanks to an invaluable body of more recent work, in courses across the curriculum (Walvoord and McCarthy; Herrington; H. Fox), we have done so with only a limited consciousness of development or, more accurate, with a consciousness of development in only a limited sense. The longest operative temporal unit for nearly all researchers and practitioners in composition—even on the relatively rare occasions when they have focused on upper-division writers—has been the course: in the standard system, some 135 hours of a student's time (45 in class, 90 outside) spread over fifteen weeks, usually as one of five courses. Often shorter spans are considered—the assignment, the composing session—but rarely anything longer. The result: we have little sense of development over a year or two, let alone three or four or more.

We could argue, perhaps, that this limited consciousness is not our fault, that given the conditions under which we have traditionally taught writing, we have had neither the opportunity nor any particular need for a broader perspective. Nearly all colleges, we could point out, operate on some version of the semester plan; students take from three to six courses a term, each course with a different instructor. And while in theory this system needn't preclude longer-than-one-term relationships between teachers and students, in practice the exigencies of writing-program life dictate that writing teachers at all but the smallest institutions are unlikely to work with students more than once in the students' careers, let alone for two or three consecutive semesters. Our experience of college writers, therefore, is grounded primarily in discontinuous fifteen-week chunks. We see students for maybe 40 classroom hours, spend perhaps 10 more with each of them responding individually to their writing . . . and then they are gone: to different teachers, different majors, different colleges. Wherever they go, we don't teach them again, and the result is that our lore lacks any significant longitudinal dimension. The same constraints affect our research: because our classroom experience doesn't have this dimension—in the absence, that is, of something approaching testable longer-term hypotheses from writing teachers or at least in the absence of a troubling ignorance—researchers who are, in any case, often studying their own teaching have tended not to focus their efforts longitudinally.[1] Moreover, even a researcher determined to take on a longer-term study faces pretty severe logistical difficulties along similar lines.[2]

But while there may have been a time when such an explanation-cum-excuse would have been marginally acceptable, that time is past. Had we been content to quietly teach those discrete fifteen-week courses, maybe our ignorance concerning the subsequent development of the students who took them wouldn't matter very much, and we could claim—however Pilate-like—not to be implicated in any political or ideological schemes to protect the baccalaureate from devaluation by democratization. As the first section of this essay indicates, however, we have not been thus content and have long implicated ourselves in such schemes. The most damning feature of our participation is what might be termed a developmental pseudologic: the collection of notions and prejudices about the development of writing abilities that we sanction, if only by default, because we can offer no viable alternative. For assessment purposes, the lineaments of this pseudologic often remain tacit, hidden in the neat round numbers of holistic scoring. Still, it's possible to identify at least some of them (and I do so here with help from Haswell). On a junior-assessment essay, then, we generally expect the more developed writers to produce longer essays formed from longer paragraphs. We likely expect the essays to have titles of greater relevance and (what we regard as) wit. We expect more logical schemes of organization, with clear sections and transitions marked by paragraphing, subheadings, and the like. As Haswell suggests, we likely expect "more transitions everywhere—between paragraphs, sentences, independent clauses—a change in cohesion that, along with a greater control of introductions and conclusions, will show a clearer awareness of purpose and audience" (36). Generally speaking, we expect a greater overall correctness (standard usage, spelling, etc.), even as we expect evidence of greater fluency (more variety in syntax and punctuation, wider vocabulary, etc.).

These expectations are problematic on at least two grounds. First, there is the status of these "more developed" writers we imagine as an end point, albeit not always explicitly or fully. Who are these people, where are they, and why have we chosen or, more accurate, constructed them? It is true that we can claim somewhat greater contact, especially in the research we read, with what might be called "skilled adults" than with the college-age writers they once were (e.g., Sommers, "Revision Strategies"; Flower and Hayes, "Cognitive Process," "Dynamics"; Odell and Goswami). But to advance that claim only begs the question, a political question (Clifford, "Subject") but with methodological resonances as well: Why these people—these constructs—and not others? What (or, to put it more politically, whose interests) do they represent? Whatever status we might grant these writers at our trajectory's end point, we have no way of knowing what the shape of the trajectory was, let alone whether or how that trajectory or their movement along it might be generalizable.

All of which is not to say that I don't believe in development or assessment: that, for instance, the changes we characterize as development are beyond institutional comprehension in their subtlety (Knoblauch and Brannon, ch. 7) or that assessment activities will always be, by definition, objectionably oppressive, the machinations of the state's language police at their worst (Clifford, "Subject"; Vitanza). On the contrary, I contend that as college writing teachers we must—inevitably do—meddle with development and impose forms of assessment all the time. The activity our culture calls teaching requires both, and the culture, operating through our students and our institutions, would extract them from or read them in even our most practiced passivity. Thus, while I'm never likely to support the kinds of large-scale, anonymous testing we currently favor—they appear to me about as useful as sending snapshots of my children's heads to expert phrenologists for advice on career aptitudes—the political complexities of higher education and the depth of our developmental ignorance make it seem unwise to preclude now any possibility of such testing.

This cultural position is neither narrow nor immutable, however; we have considerable latitude in shaping it and have a corresponding responsibility to do so ethically. In letting our involvement in upper-division assessment outstrip our understanding of development, we have abdicated that responsibility: moved near, if not into, the realm of fraud and misrepresentation, where what we don't know harms the people we say we are trying to help. The best way to redress that imbalance is to move quickly to end our ignorance. To that purpose, our top priority—just once, let us have the practice horse lead the research cart—must be to alter our institutions' teaching patterns so as to create a practice-based knowledge of development: we must make it possible for teachers to work with students often enough over the students' careers to gain a grounded sense of what happens with and to them as writers.

There are any number of ways to go about this. Given the practical difficulties involved, I recommend the simple strategy of concentrating the bulk of our writing programs' resources on a smaller proportion of our institutions' students. Let us create writing majors, writing minors, writing tracks through the English major: institutional structures that generate their student credit hours through repeat business, if you will, rather than through the high-volume, one-time "sale" of freshman composition. And in fact a recent survey reports that there are more than two hundred such programs across the country, most of them new and, so far, successful (Jenseth). Programs like these will provide the experiential base we need to transform our thinking about the development of writing abilities.

At the same time, albeit as a lesser priority, we need to adopt other modes of inquiry as we intensify our exploration of development. Two books can serve as models. The first, Robert Ochsner's *Physical Eloquence and the Biology of Writing,* has a distinctly biological focus. It is not a book I wholeheartedly agree with; parts of its methodology and many of its conclusions seem to me problematic. But Ochsner persistently reminds us—in defiance of what he rightly calls "the contemporary and more fashionable cognitive and social approaches to writing research"—of Whitehead's "maxim for educators: Allow that your students have bodies" (2). For developmental purposes, no reminder is more important.

Second, and with even more enthusiasm, I recommend Richard Haswell's *Gaining Ground in College Writing.* I would place this book nearer the nurture than the nature end of the continuum in its focus, but Haswell tries to deal with both: development is "any human change that both lasts and leads to further change of a similar cast." Development can include "some but not all instances across the entire range of changes: physical accidents, experiential growth, physiological maturation, cultural maturing, skills expertise, book learning" (5). I disagree with some of this book's methodology and conclusions, as well, but I have especial admiration for Haswell's tireless interrogation of our developmental pseudologic and for his equally relentless effort to articulate, in its place, a vision of "*growth,* of ordinary complex creaturely experiential growth" (55). As Haswell makes clear, we have a great deal to learn; his book marks only a kind of fresh beginning. But *Gaining Ground* can, I think, direct and reenergize our research on development, doing for that endeavor what Mina Shaughnessy's *Errors and Ex-*

pectations did (and still does) for work in basic writing: shake us out of our fixed metaphors and upset the tales we habitually tell about where writers come from, where they go, and—most important—how they get there.

State University of New York, Albany

NOTES

[1]To some extent, these constraints explain why development in basic writing programs has attracted interest. Although such programs often operate under adverse circumstances, they frequently place their teachers in longer, more intense contact with students. These conditions favor the emergence of practice- and research-based perspectives that are longer-term and so more plausibly developmental.

[2]For a rare and impressive exception, see L. McCarthy's study, which tracks one student over two years, with some follow-up in the third. Even this study, though, is limited to one course in each semester.

The Need for Clear Purposes and New Approaches to the Evaluation of Writing-across-the-Curriculum Programs

Gail F. Hughes

In response to complaints that college graduates don't know how to write, writing-across-the-curriculum (WAC) staff development programs have been proliferating in high schools and colleges. These programs are designed to prepare faculty members in all disciplines to incorporate into their classroom teaching instructional writing activities such as journals, five-minute exercises, and essay exams. The hope is that more writing experience will improve students' learning of course material and also improve their general writing proficiency.

Although many WAC programs have been accompanied by some form of assessment, few program evaluations do as much as they might either to validate the potential of WAC or to improve its effectiveness. Toby Fulwiler's 1988 statement could have been written today: "At this time, no comprehensive evaluations of writing across the curriculum programs have been completed, though several books do examine particular components of such programs and provide models that might be useful in evaluating them" ("Evaluating" 61). Research on writing has been conducted primarily at the classroom level; it compares the effectiveness of competing instructional methods in one classroom or several (Hillocks; Young and Fulwiler; Davis, Scriven, and Thomas; Beason). Most program-level evaluations focus on composition programs in English departments rather than on WAC (Witte and Faigley; see also Fulwiler, "Writing"), or the evaluations describe the authors' ideas and impressions based on their experience with WAC at their institutions (Fulwiler, "How Well"; Farris).

Problems in Program Evaluation

Fulwiler notes that WAC programs are "extremely complex, multifaceted, and idiosyncratic—characteristics that make evaluation most difficult" ("Evaluating" 62). WAC programs are amorphous and change-able, and they vary in content, meaning, and administration from institution to institution. Stephen P. Witte and Lester Faigley comment that the conclusions drawn from the studies they reviewed are program-specific and may not apply to any other program (35).

The most common approach to evaluation is to have writing experts give their opinion after visiting a site. But they use idiosyncratic criteria and have no special training in the assessment of WAC programs. This observation also applies to evaluations of WAC staff development programs.

Many evaluations are superficial—designed, perhaps, to fulfill a legal, political, or bureaucratic requirement, and nobody is very interested in the results. They appear to assess a program without really doing so. Reports sit unread on administrators' shelves. The chief purpose of such window-dressing evaluations seems to be to reassure people that all is well. The program may continue unimpeded. After all, the evaluation report says that faculty members really liked the staff development workshops. The analysis does not mention that participants would probably have liked anything at the idyllic lakeside resort where the workshops were held and that they may have returned to their teaching-as-usual routines once back in the classroom.

Part of the problem is that it is difficult, expensive, and time-consuming to go beyond the superficial. To assess the effectiveness of WAC programs, we need to collect and measure a representative sample of student work from across the college or system. Course grades won't do, because different teachers have different goals, give students different assignments, and grade according to different criteria. Thus when the effect of WAC on students' writing and subject learning is examined, program evaluation becomes a form of systemwide instructional research involving large-scale writing assessment.

Another problem is that evaluation must operate in a complex and often hostile political environment. This environment includes priorities and assumptions in an educational research community that favors the use of quantitative, experimental methods; the need to please funding agencies whose rules and regulations may or may not be helpful; and campus politics. Faculty participants may view evaluation as a threat to their WAC program. Moreover, evaluation projects and the program's activities are likely to be competing for funds.

Methodological difficulties also are involved. Most evaluations undertaken have not been able to provide statistically significant evidence of the benefits of WAC for student writing. Evaluators have begun to question whether it is possible to provide such evidence. Many, after

battling the idiosyncracies among institutions, a large number of uncontrollable variables, and the failure of earlier projects, have given up
on this form of instructional research. Their despair may be understandable, but it is not a constructive response to the problems that beset the evaluation of WAC programs. We must identify the problems
and find ways to solve them.

Evaluation can be greatly improved by clarifying the need for WAC
programs, developing new approaches to the large-scale assessment of
student learning, and coordinating efforts. WAC research must be
given sufficient priority to attract needed resources, and evaluation
projects must be designed to operate effectively within the political
constraints of their campuses and their funding agencies.

The Need for Substantive Program Evaluation

Given the difficulties, why should we bother with WAC program evaluation? If we have trouble obtaining the research outcomes we've been
looking for, why not rely instead on the informal responses of participants and on the intuition of program coordinators?

One answer is that many granting agencies demand program evaluation that is more credible than intuition. Continued funding may be at
risk if convincing data are not provided. The issue is a deeper one, however, involving the long-term health and reputation of WAC as a professional area. If we invest hundreds of thousands of dollars and a great
deal of energy in WAC staff development because we assume that students will benefit, then it is our duty to test that assumption and to obtain the feedback required to make our programs more effective. If
evaluators say that existing educational research methods are not powerful enough to measure the effects of WAC programs, then they must
develop research tools that are designed for our needs rather than use
ones borrowed from other times and other fields.

A key element of such new research is the development of a series of
evaluation projects that build on one another. It is necessary to demonstrate the link between instructional writing and student performance
not for every WAC program but only for WAC as a whole. If we can establish the potential of WAC for improving writing performance and identify
the key criteria and conditions for fulfilling that potential, most subsequent evaluation projects will need demonstrate only that the programs
examined meet those criteria. The important things are that evaluations
be substantive, that they address appropriate goals, and that at some
point underlying assumptions be tested by projects that have the re-

sources to test them. If evaluators build on one another's work and share professional responsibility, evaluation will become more cost-effective.

To develop more substantive agendas for evaluation projects, we must consider the phases of program implementation. Different types of assessment are needed to address the goals of each phase and to test the underlying assumptions of the WAC program at each phase.

Clear Purposes and Appropriate Agendas

Purposes for evaluating WAC programs will differ according to the program, situation, funding, and so on. Not every evaluation project will have a research agenda that examines student learning or the quality of student writing, but every evaluation project should consider how it can build on the results of previous evaluations and how it can best contribute to our knowledge of WAC programs.

To identify appropriate purposes and agendas, let us examine a model of how a WAC program works to attain desired outcomes. The model has three phases:

Phase 1	*Phase 2*	*Phase 3*
Staff development activities	Classroom implementation	Student impact

In phase 1, staff development activities, program participants are taught how to use instructional writing; during phase 2, classroom implementation, they act on what they have learned, augmenting or improving the writing assignments used in their classes; and in phase 3, student impact, there is improvement in the quality of student writing, in student learning of course material, and in student attitudes toward writing. It is important to note that the WAC program has a direct effect only on phase 1, the assumption being that phases 2 and 3 will follow.

Program evaluation incorporates three types of assessment, each addressing a different phase of the program:

Phase 1	*Phase 2*	*Phase 3*
Assessment of program activities	Assessment of classroom implementation	Assessment of student impact

Each type of evaluation has a different focus, and each builds on the one before. A WAC evaluation project that assesses only phase 1 is termed a "program activities assessment"; one that assesses only phases 1 and 2 is termed a "classroom implementation evaluation"; and one that assesses all three phases is termed a "program validation."

WAC Program Activities Assessment

When people think of program evaluation, they're perhaps most likely to think of the survey distributed at the end of a workshop that asks participants to rate the speakers, the food, et cetera. Too often, program evaluation is top-heavy with the collection of participant-satisfaction responses of this type. Although end-of-workshop surveys can be useful in improving organizational features of activities, they usually do not address what we most need to know. Did the workshop improve participants' skills in instructional writing and increase their motivation to use it? If not, why not? If the workshop was successful, what contributed to its success? Answering these questions entails identifying the objectives of all the major activities of the program; understanding the components, design, and distinctive features of the program; and seeing how various activities should work together to achieve such program goals as empowering students and promoting active learning. A comprehensive assessment also includes a description of the broader context—the goals and organization of the WAC program as a whole, its educational setting, and the philosophy of its leaders concerning WAC and staff development.

WAC Classroom Implementation Evaluation

We cannot assume that what is presented and learned from program activities will effect change in the classroom. Yet anything short of such change represents a failure to achieve the major goal of most WAC programs: increasing the amount of instructional writing students experience in courses across the curriculum. For this reason, program evaluations must include but go beyond the activities assessment described above; they must examine the effect of those activities on classroom teaching.

To determine whether a WAC program has discharged its responsibility to funding agencies and to those who invest their time and energy in it, we need to know whether faculty members use more instructional writing than before, whether they use new types of instructional writing, and whether they design or use writing activities differently as a result of their participation in the WAC program. To get a feel for the quality of classroom implementation, we can compare the specifics of how faculty members use instructional writing with WAC principles and research results on composition instruction.

A classroom-implementation evaluation includes a program activities assessment, described above. If the WAC program succeeds in stimulating instructional change, people will want to know how to replicate that success. Alternatively, if the program does not achieve its goals, well-focused data about program activities will provide the diagnostic information organizers need to improve the program. As Witte and Faigley caution, however, differences within an instructional method are perhaps no less important than differences between methods (55). "Group discussion," for example, may mean different things to different people. Therefore, both staff development activities and classroom instructional activities should be described in enough detail that readers can reconstruct them if they wish to do so.

WAC Program Validation

Program validation tests WAC's underlying assumption that WAC benefits students. Validation examines the implied link between phases 2 and 3, the belief that an increase in the amount, types, or design of instructional writing used in classrooms across the curriculum will improve the quality of students' writing, their learning of subject matter, and their attitudes toward writing. If WAC cannot demonstrate its potential to benefit students, its raison d'être evaporates.

WAC personnel are not accountable for the validity of the program's theoretical assumptions. If they organize staff development activities that have the desired effect on classroom instruction, they will have fulfilled their mission. Educational researchers and evaluators must assume responsibility for validating the program. However, an attempt at validation makes sense only where there is a chance of success. If program activities don't attract participants or if teachers participate but nevertheless don't make changes in their teaching, there's no reason to suppose that the program will have an impact on students. In this situation, if an evaluation is done anyway and fails to yield positive results, that failure doesn't necessarily mean that the program cannot benefit students; it may mean only that the program wasn't implemented well. To make justifiable interpretations, it's important to know what is being validated. For this reason, validation projects must include assessment of student impact as well as assessment of program activities and classroom implementation.

Once the positive potential of WAC is established and conditions for its effectiveness delineated, we have a basis for assuming that a program that adheres to those conditions will be effective. With that basis, evaluators can focus their attention on ensuring that WAC programs meet the criteria for successful implementation; evaluators don't have to wrestle with the more difficult task of measuring the impact of those programs on students.

A WAC program validation project in the Minnesota Community College System found that instructional writing benefits students but probably only under certain conditions (Hughes-Wiener and Martin). The caveat is that programs differing significantly from the Minnesota model may not achieve the same results. For example, Minnesota used a collaboration-leadership approach, in which the program coordinator served as a facilitator rather than as an instructional writing expert. In the collaboration model, the emphasis is on developing the leadership skills of a core group of faculty members who organize WAC activities such as workshops and follow-up meetings but bring in outside speakers and consultants to conduct most of these activities. In contrast, the expertise-leadership model has WAC coordinators conduct the program activities themselves. It is possible that programs using an expertise model are as successful as ones using a collaboration model, but that assumption should not be made (Hughes-Wiener and Jensen-Cekalla). There are probably a number of different WAC programs that can be effective. The point is that each type must be described and validated independently, and the results may be generalized only to programs whose key features correspond to those of the type validated.

New Methodological Approaches to Large-Scale Assessment

Once we decide what purposes and strategies are appropriate, we need to consider the practice of WAC assessment, that is, how to design and conduct our evaluation project and how to interpret the results. Methods of WAC assessment derive legitimacy from the educational research community—the political context in which professional evaluators must operate. The ineffectiveness of generally preferred methods challenges the values promoted and assumptions made by this community.

Educational research perforce differs from research in the physical sciences, medicine, or even other social sciences. In the physical sciences, researchers can control context, variables, and treatments. Medicine must deal with individual differences but can standardize treatments (e.g., "take two aspirin and call me in the morning"). Even many of the social sciences can standardize at times through lab experiments; they usually can at least obtain a good statistical sample. Educators are rarely able to proceed so quantitatively, and even if they could, it probably wouldn't make sense. Educational contexts are different, there are many variables that affect outcomes, and many programs and techniques may succeed in one setting but fail in another.

Writing evaluators need to have enough confidence to develop their own type of research and set their own standards of evidence for program evaluation—standards based on what is reasonable and convincing for their field rather than on what is reasonable and convincing for the scientific fields they might wish to emulate. Our field may never permit us to obtain results as conclusive as those in the physical sciences, but such results are not necessary. What is necessary is that our questions address the needs and problems of teachers; that our research is as sensible and systematic as our field permits; and that our answers are reasonable and convincing when the body of evidence on which they are based is considered.

Research Designs and Methods

The ultimate question concerning WAC is not the one usually of greatest interest to WAC sponsors and evaluators, namely, Is the program effective in achieving desired outcomes? Even if we can demonstrate to everyone's satisfaction that a WAC program has been successful in improving students' writing at Rural America College, it won't necessarily work at Central City College. On the other hand, if it's a miserable failure at Rural America College, that doesn't mean Central City College should eliminate its WAC program. WAC programs are a response to an underlying need—the need to improve students' writing and active learning. If they don't work, we must find some other, better way of addressing that need. Therefore the key question isn't does it work, but, rather, can it be made to work, or, how can I get it to work at my college.

Traditional research paradigms are inadequate. We need to test clusters of variables that relate to each of the three phases of program implementation described above and to use evaluations that enable us to examine the effects of WAC programs across an entire educational organization. We need to draw on qualitative methods to hypothesize conditions for success and on quantitative methods to measure the strength of the relations among variables.

We also need to consult a variety of sources. The literature in sociology offers findings about complex organizations (Etzioni), organizational development (Bennis et al.), the diffusion of innovations (Rogers), and leadership (Argyris). Social psychology also provides information about leadership and leadership training (Fiedler, "Contingency Model," "Effects"). Kenneth Eble and William J. McKeachie describe the features that differentiate successful staff development programs from unsuccessful ones. Research on the design of writing assignments (the "assignment variable" identified by Braddock, Lloyd-Jones, and Schoer) is skimpy but relevant to the classroom-implementation phase of WAC programs (Ruth and Murphy). George Hillocks provides a summary and meta-analysis of research results on composition instruction. And Edward M. White gives guidance on the assessment of student writing (*Teaching* [2nd ed.] and *Developing*).

Such eclectic, multimethod, and multidisciplinary reading provides a rich mine of diagnostic information. With some thought and planning, the evaluator can use that information both to improve the particular WAC program being evaluated and to address more general questions about what kinds of WAC programs succeed, at what kinds of colleges they succeed, and under what conditions. Ultimately, we'll be able to answer the question How can I get WAC to work at my college? on the basis of empirical data rather than untested assumptions or the preferences of the politically powerful.

Examination of Evidence

Since evaluation research can never take into account all possible factors affecting college-wide program outcomes, no single study or evaluation project can conclusively prove or disprove the effectiveness of WAC. Results must be compiled into a body of evidence and examined in combination. Information should be collected from a variety of sources, using multiple methods, and a data bank of WAC evaluation findings should be started, to serve as a basis for identifying the conditions under which they vary. Blind ratings should be used whenever possible. Analysis should consider negative results and counterexamples as well as positive results and exemplary cases.

Standards of Statistical Significance

The standards of statistical and educational significance (used to determine how likely the results are to be due to chance) presently used in educational research are the same as those in the physical sciences. But in education—unlike the physical sciences, where variables and conditions can be controlled, and unlike medicine, where even a small error can have dire consequences—we should not dismiss results that have seven-percent error, say, rather than the traditional cutoff of five percent or less. Instead, we should look carefully at the outcomes and decide, judging them on their own merits, whether they are convincing. We should consider the evidence and the quality of the research design in combination and in context.

Program Replication and Validation

In the physical sciences, replication (i.e., repeating an experiment) is the criterion used to determine whether results are valid and generalizable. In education, replication of an innovative project may provide an indication of its robustness. However, since WAC programs are almost never the same in their components, design, or educational context, replication is rarely possible or, for that matter, relevant. To test generalizations about program effectiveness, it may be more useful to make predictions about what results will be obtained under specific conditions. The ability to predict accurately is more appropriate for program evaluation than is confirmation of results through replication.

The Political Context of Funding Agencies

A WAC program is usually funded by a grant from the federal government or a philanthropic organization; it competes with WAC proposals from other colleges and with other programs in its own college. Funding agencies almost always request that some form of evaluation be conducted to see whether the program was implemented as described in the proposal and to determine the extent to which program goals have been achieved. This evaluation is designed to assess the effect of a staff development program on a college or system, on faculty participants, and on students, for the purpose of ensuring accountability and making decisions about the future funding of that or subsequent programs.

The seriousness of program evaluation depends on the funding agency. It is often a formality, requiring only participant-response surveys and a report that is more a public relations document than a professional paper. But some agencies, wanting an assessment that goes deeper, ask for evidence that the program has influenced classroom instruction or student learning. Even if funded internally, staff development programs such as WAC must justify themselves to obtain funding.

Funding agencies expect that someone will be assigned to conduct the program evaluation and write a report. Often an external evaluator—usually an expert in the subject area rather than a professional evaluator—is sent by the funding agency to the institution for a brief but intensive visit. Sometimes a college internal evaluator will be designated as well. To preserve some measure of objectivity, the internal evaluator will not be the grant director or WAC program coordinator, though the internal evaluator typically reports to the grant director.

Having both an internal and an external evaluator is ideal, because they complement each other. External evaluators are usually experts in English or composition; they are hired directly by the funding agency and therefore represent its interests. They are in a position to be objective vis-à-vis the program, but since they are only visiting, they cannot know a great deal about its intricacies. Internal evaluators are hired by the college (although their salary may come indirectly from the funding agency) and report to the grant director. They are participant-observers who have in-depth knowledge about the program and are ideally situated to provide diagnostic information that can be used to improve it.

As with other forms of assessment, evaluation can be threatening to those responsible for designing and implementing the WAC program, especially the program coordinator and the grant director. When the program is strong, an evaluation can document its benefits and give visibility and prestige to its administrators. Information gathered is seen as helpful feedback that can further strengthen the program. When the program has serious problems, however, there may be an effort to censor the internal evaluator and engage in a cover-up, out of fear that the evaluation will damage the reputations of program personnel and cut off the program's source of funding.

There is also the possibility that the evaluators will not give the program the credit it deserves because they do not share the program's philosophy or understand the organizational constraints the program works under. Evaluators are human, too, and vary in competence and perceptiveness. Inasmuch as evaluators or assessment projects represent a source of power that program coordinators cannot completely control, evaluation will—and probably should—generate a degree of apprehension.

The best way to avoid unfairness and alleviate apprehension is to clarify at the outset the goals of the program and the responsibilities of all administrators—the funding agency representative, grant director, program coordinator, and program evaluators. Both the program and the evaluation should focus on those goals—to improve student writing and student learning—as directly as possible. However, as explained above, assessment of student impact involves systemwide or collegewide instructional research—research that requires considerable time, expertise, and energy. Most WAC grants cannot provide the funding and structure necessary to undertake such a major instructional research project. As a result, program evaluations generally measure the attainment of intermediate goals like the participation and positive perceptions of faculty members, making the assumption that these goals will have the desired effect on students. Such measuring is all right—in fact, it is more efficient than program validation—as long as assumptions are examined in some evaluation projects and the results are coordinated to build on one another. But if major assumptions about the effect of WAC on student writing and learning are never tested with feedback, programs can veer silently off course for a long time without correction.

The Political Context on Campus

Unlike many kinds of assessment, WAC program evaluation is never conducted by evaluators exclusively. It requires cooperation from program leaders, faculty participants, various committees, funding representatives, and so on. Often evaluators work with people who know little about evaluation and do not value its potential usefulness. Some of those people may feel threatened by an assessment project, particularly if the program is weak. Even if it is strong, participants may fear that evaluators will not understand the program. They may think that the role of evaluators is to criticize.

How can a program evaluation obtain funding and political support without sacrificing the independence and objectivity required to maintain professional standards? Some guidelines follow.

Generating Support

Evaluators and program planners need to discuss the purpose of evaluation in general and of their project in particular to build trust and ensure that participants understand the potential benefits of evaluation. Faculty participants need to gain confidence that the evaluation will serve the program—if things go well, by documenting its good results and providing visibility and rewards for a job well done; if not, by helping organizers redesign a program that has problems. In addition, if the evaluation either validates the effectiveness of a program or identifies how the program can be improved, the college may find it easier to obtain subsequent funding.

At the same time, evaluators need to gain confidence that they will not be subject to censorship or retribution if they should happen to be the bearers of bad news. Support for the evaluation also means support for the evaluator's role. It is essential to clarify roles at the outset, since the committees that oversee the WAC program and plan staff development activities are likely to have members with no interest in or knowledge of program evaluation and since evaluators are certain to be in the minority. Most often decisions on crucial methodological matters should be made by those who have the expertise and the responsibility for conducting the evaluation project—usually the internal evaluators. If a dispute arises, someone external to the project but having the expertise—an external evaluator or perhaps the funding agency—might be asked to arbitrate the matter.

As the program gets under way, internal evaluators should regularly attend program events and discuss the program's objectives, problems, and activities with organizers. This participation will help ensure that the evaluators understand what the program is trying to accomplish and will enable them to ask the right questions, so that the data collected are relevant and useful. Program organizers and participants as well should be involved in the design and implementation of the evaluation project. Their involvement will enhance their ongoing understanding of and support for the evaluation project and will increase the likelihood that the project's findings are taken seriously and used for program improvement.

It helps if the evaluation project includes some dual-purpose activities—such as planning workshops that benefit the program as well as the project—or shows how assessment activities such as holistic rating give participants skills that can be adapted for use in the classroom. It is much easier to generate support for a project that provides some practical assistance along the way than it is for a project whose activities seem unrelated to program goals. People will not support an evaluation project if they feel that it's using money that could be spent on more WAC workshops or more release time for faculty coordinators.

Obtaining Funding

Most agencies that fund educational programs want to know whether or not their money was well spent. They will expect about ten percent of the grant money to be spent on an ordinary classroom-implementation evaluation. But a program validation is likely to cost almost as much as the program itself. A college will probably need to obtain a separate grant for it. A small institution might consider collaborating with others that have similar WAC programs to make a validation project cost-effective.

For political purposes, evaluation funding should avoid competition with program funding. If evaluation is viewed as diverting money from the program, it is likely to generate resentment and undermine its basis of support. Applying for a separate grant may be a good idea, or having the funding agency earmark a specific percentage or amount for the evaluation project.

Enhancing the Credibility of Results

If the evaluation results aren't as favorable as anticipated, program advocates may say that the evaluators didn't understand the program or that they are being overly critical. If reports are glowing, however, program critics may remain unimpressed, believing that the evaluators were co-opted by the program. If evaluation is to have credibility, it is important that most people—especially the funding agency—believe the evaluators to be honest and competent.

Evaluators will enhance their credibility if they adhere to key norms of program evaluation. They should describe observed problems in a direct, matter-of-fact way; give reasons and evidence for their judgments and inferences, favorable or not; and insist on maintaining a voice that is independent from both program funders and program planners. Maintaining an independent voice generally is not difficult for external evaluators; but internal evaluators, if problems arise, may come under pressure from program organizers. It is in the best, long-term interest of the program that the WAC director respect the independence of internal evaluators by allowing them to take responsibility for reports and by resisting the temptation to sanitize those reports. After all, if the reports omit attention to major problems and at any later point those problems are revealed, then the evaluators will not be believed when they report subsequently that things have improved—even if the program now is Shangri-la.

Methodologically, the best way to maximize the credibility of results is by using blind ratings of essays or using other procedures that prevent bias. For example, if essay raters do not know which students have had more instructional writing, it is impossible for the raters either unconsciously or deliberately to give higher scores to those students than to students who have had less writing experience.

If the evaluation is large enough to warrant it—and validation projects certainly warrant it—it is customary to recruit a national expert in writing assessment to serve as an external evaluator. Internal and external evaluators will have somewhat different perspectives, and the perspective of each can serve to check the biases of the other. If both internal and external evaluators are favorably impressed, the funding agency will have more confidence in the report, as will the skeptics. But if both internal and external evaluators pan the program, the program will be in great trouble. To minimize the likelihood of such an outcome, program planners and evaluators should make sure they agree on goals and criteria and that they keep each other informed every step of the way. Internal evaluators in particular can serve as an early warning system to alert the program to pitfalls and encourage it to make mid-course corrections.

Enhancing the Utilization of Results

Michael Patton has written extensively about how program planners can enhance the use of evaluation results. The basic two principles are that the evaluation should be designed to meet the needs of the program and that everyone who has a stake in the outcome of the evaluation should be involved in as many facets of the evaluation as possible. Such involvement will ensure their understanding of and their sense of ownership in the results. It will also increase political support for the evaluation project.

The requirements and expectations of the funding agency are likely to set the broad framework of the evaluation. In that framework, program organizers should work with the evaluators to identify goals, and evaluators should use those goals as the basis for designing an appropriate evaluation project. Organizational and instructional design factors considered important to program effectiveness should be identified, so that assumptions about them can be tested. The evaluation project should train faculty members to do the holistic rating, interviewing, et cetera, and meetings or discussion sessions should be organized for faculty members and administrators to consider the implications of evaluation results for program improvement. Without this type of involvement, the evaluation is likely to be an academic exercise, a report left on the shelf to gather dust.

WAC programs have become popular as a collegewide effort to increase the amount and quality of students' writing experiences in all subject areas. Questions about the systemwide effect of WAC should be addressed by program evaluators who have clear purposes and relevant agendas. However, because of the expense involved and the lack of appropriate research methods, little attention has been given to conducting substantive evaluations of the effectiveness of these programs. We need the political will to generate the energy, support, and funding required to develop WAC program evaluation as a distinctive genre of large-scale assessment. We must find ways to assess the merit of WAC programs as programs; to identify the factors that contribute to the achieving or inhibiting of good results in different types of programs; and to look at a variety of results in combination to see whether the preponderance of evidence presents a convincing argument—an argument of reasonable "probablies" rather than scientific "probabilities"— that writing-across-the-curriculum programs can make a difference.

Minnesota State Colleges and Universities

Response:
Testing as Surveillance

Kurt Spellmeyer

> *In 1983 Ceauşescu ordered that all typewriters be registered with the police.*
>
> Gale Stokes

As Stephen North suggests in his essay, assessment is a conservative response to democratic trends in higher education. Even now, with more than half our college-age population actually going to college, we still hear words like *crisis* and *decline* spoken everywhere, while people increasingly point to standardized tests as our last, best hope. But before signing on with the testing industry, we should take a second look at the crisis itself. We might ask, for one thing, if it actually exists, or if we are dealing with an illusion produced by a perspective that erases history. Those who accept the rhetoric of collapse uncritically would do well to recall that until the mid-1930s no more than forty percent of the children entering this country's elementary schools ever made it to high school graduation: in 1931–32, for example, only 833,000 students, out of the roughly three million who began, left with diplomas (*Biennial Survey 1930–1932* 3, 7). Figures like these strongly argue that we are doing much better than our predecessors did, but the perception of decline is often just that, a perception unaffected by realities. Even in the 1930s, when college doors were opened just wide enough to let in the very brightest—supposedly—many of those lucky few were derided as poor writers once they landed their first full-time jobs. One researcher of that decade, Burges Johnson of Syracuse University, found widespread dissatisfaction with the literacy of college graduates; among the editors, lawyers, and executives interviewed for his Carnegie Foundation Report, thirty-eight out of thirty-nine believed that our colleges had failed in the "field of writing" (11, 21).[1]

Of course, these college graduates were far from illiterate, and a few of the business leaders had complained not that the graduates wrote ungrammatically but that they wrote in prose too purple and oblique for everyday communication. Yet the real source of interviewee discontent was less the preparation that the students brought from college than the backgrounds of the students themselves. In their encounters with these young college men, Johnson's editors, lawyers, and executives were forced to deal with people who had typically come from below. At the turn of the century, after all, only 695,903 students were enrolled in high school nationwide. Thirty-two years later, that number had climbed to 5,592,872, an eight-hundred percent increase. College enrollments also went through the roof, from 237,592 in 1900 to 1,154,117 three decades later, a five-hundred percent increase, well surpassing the growth in population generally (*Survey* 6).

So successful was America's experiment in mass public education that observers today tend to forget its unnerving, disruptive social consequences several generations ago. For the first time in world history, millions of children born to working-class families confronted, on something like an equal footing, the moneyed class their parents had been taught to obey. In the closing decades of the nineteenth century, a hundred thousand Americans *were* our society—the ones, that is, who made the big decisions for everyone else. Thirty years later, this aging elite found its power and influence perceptibly ebbing, and so has every subsequent generation of college-educated Americans. Today, conservative critics charge that educators no longer teach the things they need to teach. What these critics really mean is that too many "inappropriate" people have gained access to education, and to the privileges that education brings.

Under conditions such as these—when education works to level the sociopolitical playing field—standards are notoriously relative. Academic intellectuals might prefer to believe, for example, that literacy goes hand in hand with the qualities they value most in themselves: a capacity for critical thinking, an ability to persuade, a certain "negative capability." Yet the shortest of stays on any campus will show that the reality is at variance with the idealized self-image. Debates about who's literate and who's not are actually about the ownership of "cultural capital," as ordinary citizens understood long before that term enjoyed its current vogue. From the historical record it seems safe to conclude that working parents in America a century ago gave their children all the schooling they could (not always in the English language, it should be said), and no sooner did communities have the needed funds than they built their own schools and colleges. In *Seventy Years of It*, the autobiography of the sociologist E. A. Ross, Ross remembers the seven months a year when he attended a one-room school in Marion, Ohio, not far from the cabin of his aunt's homestead. And he describes the books he read again and again after exhausting his town's minuscule collection. From the schoolhouse, however, Ross at fifteen went on to the newly founded campus of Coe College—there were no College Board exams in those days—and after teaching at a private high school for two years, he set off one June day for Berlin. Five years later, Ross was lecturing on economics at Stanford and writing against the California railroad monopoly.

There were thousands of young men and women like Ross. In another autobiography of that period, *The Rebel Girl*, the labor organizer and women's activist Elizabeth Gurley Flynn remembers her grammar school on 138th Street in the South Bronx—PS 9—as "a decrepit old building . . . with toilets in the yard." But she also remembers one of her teachers, James A. Hamilton, "who fired me with ambition," she writes, "to become a constitutional lawyer and drilled us so thoroughly in the U.S. Constitution and . . . the Bill of Rights that I have been defending it ever since" (41). About ten years later and a thousand miles to the south, Zora Neale Hurston left her home to board at an all-black school in Jacksonville, Florida, where she found out that she "just had to talk back at established authority and that established authority hated back-talk worse than barbed-wire pie. . . . My immediate teachers were enthusiastic about me. It was the guardians of study-hour and prayer meetings who felt that their burden was extra hard to bear" (48).

Even under the regime of segregation, the system of schooling that produced a Zora Hurston and an E. A. Ross was fundamentally different from any that had preceded it, because educators of the time believed that its purpose was not to maintain unchanging standards but to transform social life, not to impose the form of a perfected civilization on those who could never be or do anything without it—the educational ideal in classical Greece as well as in Confucian China—but to displace the dead weight of tradition and to release, as John Dewey put it, "emotions, needs and desires so as to call into being . . . things that have not existed in the past" (245). Because there has never been a perfected civilization, because knowledge bears the impress of violence and exclusion, Dewey understood that the only possible measure of learning was the enlargement of lived experience and that no other standard could be erected as long as our society continued to pursue the universalization of freedoms reserved in ages past for the elite. Dewey knew that when we define what it means to read and write as though the nature of reading and writing must remain unchanged, we have halted the process of democratization that North alludes to in his essay. Was Hurston, for example, a "good writer"? Was she as good a writer as, say, Richard Henry Dana or Robert Louis Stevenson, prose "masters" often excerpted in the composition textbooks eighty years ago? Dewey might have answered that comparisons of this kind are fundamentally misguided because our collective sense of what good is will change—and must change—as more and more people like Hurston have the opportunity to read and write.

At the end of a century that has witnessed a fairly sweeping vindication of Dewey's argument, we might regard the growing emphasis on standardized assessment as a reversal with ominous consequences. Who benefits from the testing boom? Ideally, the answer is everyone—the students, the teachers, the institutions, the big-hearted funding agencies. But who really benefits? In New Jersey, where I live and teach, fourteen years of high school proficiency exams and college-level basic-skills entry tests have failed to produce any change in the performance of the state's students. But if assessment has done nothing to improve the performance of our students, it has helped to create a substantial new bureaucracy, and it has put many millions of dollars into the coffers of ETS. Formerly an active member of New Jersey's Basic Skills Council, which supervises the development and administration of the state's standardized college placement test, I have seen some of my worst fears realized: the irresponsible use of test results to discredit teachers and institutions; the strategic finessing of data for consumption by the press; the deliberate reversal, at least once, of the council's explicit resolutions by a representative from the state government; and the persistent refusal of ETS to modify the college test in response to criticisms by teachers in the field. While standardized testing has many possible uses—and while some of them might be consistent with a democratic culture—college-level testing in my state has primarily served to intimidate the masses of adjunct instructors who get "stuck" with the job of remediation. At the same time, the testing effort has greatly extended the reach of local and federal operatives, to say nothing of the private sector's rapidly expanding "education industry." In the darkest days of the New Jersey testing program, state officials began to override the normal practice of external review for academic departments and programs, directly intruding into classrooms and curricula. I have no doubt that we will someday see vigorous efforts to resume these dangerous policies, which New Jersey's five-year recession has temporarily halted.

Let me make my position as clear as I can: standardized testing is one of the most dangerous, invasive, and reactionary developments in the last hundred years of educational policy. We should not forget that for much of these hundred years, without the benefit of state and national testing programs, our society somehow managed to produce the world's most broadly educated citizenry. We did it by spreading a *culture* of literacy. In the 1940s and 1950s, for example, we opened up colleges and universities to millions of returning GIs whose parents had never made it past the ninth grade, and we treated those GIs as we had treated the sons and daughters of the wealthy at schools like Princeton and Bryn Mawr. The GIs read good books, talked about them, wrote, debated—participated in a way of life. We did not put the GIs on a "developmental" track. If the work of Sylvia Scribner and Michael Cole shows anything, it shows that literacy is no more a context-neutral "cognitive skill" than Balinese water rituals or adherence to the precepts of the *Imitatio Christi*. When we drag high school students into a classroom for seven hours a day, forcing them to read dreadful, demeaning, dumbed-down textbooks and testing the quality of their skills from month to month and grade to grade, we are not in any sense promoting literacy, no matter how much care or sensitivity we happen to bring to the task. We are promoting a new and different weltanschauung—a culture of normalization—and we can hardly be surprised when the test scores stay flat.

We need to appreciate more fully than we have the historical connections between the printed word and democracy. While it is true that some highly literate societies, the Third Reich most conspicuously, have been anything but democratic, it also seems likely that the spread of democracy across the globe has something to do with the free flow of information that print technology makes possible. In a recent book on the collapse of communism in Eastern Europe, the historian Gale Stokes argues that the rise of sub-rosa media—clandestine printing presses and even radio stations—enabled Czech and Polish opposition activists to create a virtual state within the state. These new states differed from the ones in power, though, by virtue of their uncontainable pluralism: no one faulted Lech Walesa for his occasional grammar mistakes. Literacy in this alternative sense, not a tidy little skill but an expansive way of life, has nothing to do with proficiency as our tests measure it. Yet perhaps if we promote *this* literacy—first of all by giving students greater access to the knowledge that impinges most directly on their lives—proficiency might take care of itself.

Sadly, access to knowledge hardly ever looms large in the plans of educators. What they care about most is their own legitimation. Unless my state makes significant changes in the unequal funding of its public schools, funding that starves poor school districts while engorging the ones already privileged, testing will not raise up the lowly but will help to naturalize economic disparities that grow wider every year. With test results in hand, authorities are in a position to retract even the vestigial appearance of equality that a high school diploma still confers on the marginal. Armed now with solid evidence, the best and the brightest can rest assured that the poor are stupid and undeserving. Given what I think about testing, am I persuaded that we could do it better by doing much less of it, as Peter Elbow maintains? Absolutely. But do I believe that Elbow's proposal will win out in the testing wars? It might, at least within universities like mine, but the alliance of industry and government administrators will scarcely be content with that solution, which leaves assessment in the hands of students and their teachers, the groups that testing advocates regard as least worthy of the public trust.

This last point, in my view, deserves particular emphasis. Tacitly or otherwise, the advocates of standardized testing have worked hard to promote the image of teachers as lazy and incompetent and of students as lazy and ignorant. On the evidence of contacts with the administrators from my state's government, I can testify to the contempt many of them feel for teachers and scholars at virtually every level. And teachers and scholars have in turn cultivated a truly ruinous naïveté about the forces poised to transform every aspect of their working lives. A complete knowledge of Fredric Jameson's oeuvre is hardly a substitute for understanding the real-world political terrain, which is crude, unlike high theory, and blatant rather than "unconscious." We know a great deal about semiosis and split subjectivity but little about politics as practiced in the legislatures and on the street. While the teachers of developmental English in New Jersey are required by law to prepare their students for the state's postremediation test, I doubt that more than five or ten percent of them know much about the state bureaucracy, the Basic Skills Council, or the policy-making bodies at their home institutions. And no one, I feel sure, could say anything of substance about the crucial legal issues that William Lutz outlines in his essay (in sec. 1).

We should understand those legal issues, but understanding does not go nearly far enough. Unless we can play an active role in the fashioning of policy, there is little chance that we will retain control over what we do as teachers or as scholars. On committees at the institution where I teach, I have made every effort to link discussions of assessment to the issues of intellectual diversity and faculty governance. On one such committee, I was able to block the appointment of a strong testing advocate, long allied with the Trenton bureaucracy, to the powerful position of director of our new Teaching Excellence Center. More recently, as a member of our state's Basic Skills Council, and subsequently as the chair—a position that it took me nearly seven years of mind-numbing meetings to land—I found allies within the state

bureaucracy who shared my opposition to uses of testing that undermine the credibility of teachers and programs. When understood as a
pragmatic instrument for the placement of students already accepted
by an institution, a test like New Jersey's basic-skills exam can help universities improve their retention efforts, as it has at my school. But every test lends itself to a variety of uses, many of them far from benign.

At this moment, however, the crucial issue may no longer be whether
to test or not but how we will choose to make sense of the test results—
and this too is a matter of policy. What we most need to emphasize on
every public occasion is the importance of having multiple criteria:
course grades as well as scores on standardized tests, performance in
subsequent classes as well as the acquisition of ostensibly quantifiable
basic skills. And what we most need to guard against is any effort to exclude programs, departments, and universities from the collecting and
interpreting of data on their own classes, since the parties that control
the spin put on this information will have the last word in every forum.
During my tenure on the Basic Skills Council, I was surprised to see
how often state administrators can produce exactly the data that will
garner for their branch or division abundant new attention—and new
financial support. We should remember that administrators who do
their jobs inconspicuously tend to be forgotten by their higher-ups.
Given this constant pressure to be seen as getting big things done, testing is a bureaucrat's dream come true, a publicly visible enterprise that
keeps growing larger—which is all the more reason for us to become
involved. Anyone who bothers to enter the debate will soon recognize
that assessment has, in the last remove, almost nothing to do with
meeting the needs of programs, teachers, or students. Testing is surveillance, first and last, and if we neglect to ask who is surveying whom
and for what ends, we will have no one to blame but ourselves.

Postscript 1996

During the four years when this volume was in preparation, the Repub-
lican governor of New Jersey abolished both the education bureaucracy and its elaborate testing program in a righteous —and highly
popular—frenzy of budget cutting. Such events, however, can have un-
foreseeable consequences. No one expected Governor Christine Todd
Whitman to support the public colleges with anything approaching
conviction, yet her moves may have inadvertently saved New Jersey's
developmental effort by giving its defenders new latitude.

In a climate increasingly hostile to the teaching of basic skills on the college level, developmental teachers initially feared that the end of the testing program would allow the state to return to the unhappy days of revolving-door admissions. By identifying "skills-deficient" students immediately after their admission, the old testing program had at least held the colleges and universities accountable for high failure rates. But at the same time that the teachers were determined to preserve basic-skills education, they understood that some future version of the test could become the rationale for a reconstituted bureaucracy— hence their call for a testing program operating independently, under the direction of the teachers. Instead of arguing against further testing *tout court,* teachers from every sector of higher education—the county colleges as well as the research universities—have formed a consortium to take control of basic-skills testing and the collection of outcomes data.

The consequences? As of this writing, no one can say.

Rutgers University, New Brunswick

NOTE

[1]Several decades earlier, the Carnegie Institution, loosely associated with the Carnegie Foundation for the Advancement of Teaching, had played an important role in IQ testing and the promotion of eugenic sterilization. See Chorover 40–43, 58–75.

PART IV

Issues of Inclusion and Equity

Introduction

Political decisions give status and power to some and confirm the weakness of others; they allocate rewards and punishments; and they limit the freedom of some individuals and expand that of others. Because of the privileges and penalties that may result from political decisions, individuals and groups actively endeavor to make those decisions or influence their character. The efforts of such individuals and groups are highlighted by Sandra Kamusikiri, Deborah Holdstein, and Liz Hamp-Lyons, who focus on issues of race, gender, and class in the assessment of writing.

In "African American English and Writing Assessment: An Afrocentric Approach," Kamusikiri examines an ongoing and as yet unresolved concern in the teaching of composition: How should African American English in student writing be assessed? As a result of the negative perception of African American English, Kamusikiri argues, "there exists a disjunction between the way we assess [African American English] in students' writing and what current composition theory and practice tell us about assessment." Kamusikiri proposes an Afrocentric approach to writing assessment to increase its fairness. Her approach tries to align the composition teacher's beliefs, philosophy, and pedagogical ideology with what is currently known about African American English and what is recommended by the research on composition.

Because the ways of assessing writing are sometimes grounded in the androcentric context of the university, test bias can be based on gender as well as on race or class. In "Gender, Feminism, and Institution-Wide Assessment Programs," Holdstein considers the potential for gender bias in assessment programs and in holistic scoring of student essays. Gender bias may be found, she asserts, "in the institutional interests that surround testing programs at the university level, in the writing and selection of prompts, in the varieties of student response (those of women *and* men) to those prompts, and in the responses of even well-trained readers to the writing itself." Holdstein believes that acknowledging the complexities introduced by gender into all aspects of the testing process will help us resolve some of the inconsistencies among theory, teaching, and testing.

Hamp-Lyons, in "The Challenges of Second-Language Writing Assessment," proposes the development of tests responsive to the special needs of nonnative English-speaking citizens and residents of this country. These assessment instruments "must be well designed and sensitive to the contexts of the learners to be tested and of their teachers, and its users must be conscious of the social environment that has engendered the demand for assessment." Such tests, she argues, are essential to learners' fair access to education and therefore to their integration as full citizens into society.

Marcia Farr's response looks closely at the options raised by the three essays and concludes that "opening up assessment—and, more generally, teaching—to increased tolerance of nonmainstream and female ways of knowing, thinking, and using language" does not have to lead to diminished clarity, style, or sense of community. Her attempt to keep the baby while throwing out the bathwater suggests that there is a way to value both diversity and commonality in writing assessment.

African American English and Writing Assessment: An Afrocentric Approach

Sandra Kamusikiri

During my twenty years of teaching college-level freshman composition, I've encountered a number of students who suffer from varying degrees of writing apprehension and writer's block. Several cases stand out in my mind. In one, Larry, a distraught student from another instructor's class, came to me with his in-class essay. He explained that the purpose of this impromptu, timed essay, written during the first session, was to enable the instructor to develop an instruction plan tailored to the writing needs of each student. The other students received their plans; Larry received his essay with a single comment at the bottom: "Quite frankly, this is hopeless."

In another instance, Debra, rough draft in hand, sat in my office and wept. This was her third attempt at English 101, and in a recent conference her instructor, having read her draft, informed her that she was the most incompetent writer the instructor had ever encountered and that there was no need for her to complete the essay; it would be best if she dropped the course. Still another student, a junior, sought advice about whether she should drop out of school. Her instructor, in response to the first draft of her research essay, said that the university system had clearly carried her along, because a student with her low writing competence could otherwise never have reached upper-division status.

I have heard similar stories from other students in a variety of settings: in my composition classes, draft conferences, tutoring sessions, advising sessions, and students' writing portfolio self-assessments. What links each of these cases is that the drafts of the students contained African American English (AAE), sometimes referred to as Black English Vernacular (BEV) or Ebonics. In the view of their instructors, the presence of AAE in an essay draft indicated writing incompetence and represented a pedagogical problem that could not be handled in the typical nonremedial freshman composition classroom. Furthermore, the presence of AAE appeared to some teachers as irremedial, as disqualifying and permanent as skin color: "Quite frankly,

187

this is hopeless." Such an attitude highlights an as yet unresolved issue in the teaching of composition: What constitutes an effective response to AAE in student writing in the freshman composition classroom? How should AAE in student writing be assessed?

Although America is a pluralistic society with various social, cultural, and language backgrounds, the educational system, especially on the college level, has tended to impose Anglocentric writing standards without sufficient appreciation of the cultural and linguistic expressions of other groups. AAE in particular, perceived by some as lacking political, social, and economic value, is stigmatized in the classroom as "nonstandard" and part of an "academic subculture" (Farr and Daniels 24). As a result, there exists a disjunction between the way we assess AAE in students' writing and what current composition theory and practice tell us about assessment. African American English is such a red flag for many composition instructors that they fail to stay the course of a process-based pedagogical approach; believing themselves to be in uncharted waters, they employ summative evaluation prematurely and assign outmoded, decontextualized grammar and usage exercises. The composition instructor becomes, often unwittingly, a gatekeeper, a destructive political force who assesses the AAE writer's competence prematurely, in the earliest stages of the composing process.

My essay addresses this issue and suggests an alternative approach that takes account of and appreciates the place of African American English in the assessment of writing in both the classroom and testing programs. I propose a new approach that bridges practice and theory and incorporates an Afrocentric linguistic perspective into the assessment of AAE in composition. The term *Afrocentric*, according to Molefi Asante in *The Afrocentric Idea*, does not refer to "merely an artistic or literary movement." An Afrocentric approach asserts that, in any analysis of African American culture, recognition must be given to that culture's retention of African culture as expressed through philosophy, behavior, ideas, artifacts, and language (124). It seeks to align the belief sets, worldview, philosophy, and pedagogical ideology of the composition teacher with what we currently know about African American English and the best practices recommended by research on composition.

Given the powerful and decisive role of the composition instructor as an evaluator, an Afrocentric approach is critical. Rather than create ethnically balkanized groups within the classroom and the assessment community, it contributes to the recognition of the value and integrity of different cultural traditions, seeks to create a polycentric assessment model, envisages an equity-based community of student writers modeled on a pluralistic society, and, overall, enables a composition instructor to enhance his or her fairness and effectiveness. Such an approach moves us closer to realizing the two-decade-old *College Composition and Communication* resolution "Students' Right to Their Own Language."

Teacher Attitude toward African American English

The adoption of an Afrocentric approach to writing assessment necessitates changes in the assessor's attitude toward and knowledge of AAE. Because language behavior is "affected by intrapsychic factors as well as by institutional arrangements and practices" (Haskins and Butts 11), an instructor's belief that AAE cannot provide a means for logical thought may adversely affect student performance (Hall 207; Labov, *Language* 230; T. Fox 73). When AAE is labeled negatively, teacher expectation is lowered and the student's performance conforms to teacher expectation (Haskins and Butts 52; Wolfram 269).

Teachers need to know something about the language of their students ("Students' Right"; see also Burling 3). To free themselves from "racial ethnocentrism" (Weaver 1–2, 9), teachers should become familiar with some of the grammatical, phonological, syntactic, and semantic characteristics of AAE (Simpkins 164; Weaver 9); study its history; and appreciate that it developed from a positive cultural tradition. Informing teachers about AAE can improve both teacher attitude and pupil performance (S. Lewis 85; T. Fox 73). A sense of the history of AAE helps students build the pride and self-esteem that facilitate the learning of Standard English (Burling 127) and that increase "linguistic self-confidence" (Angle 148). According to Burr Angle, there is more value in respecting AAE than in teaching patterns of Standard English (148). Shirley Lewis found that those AAE-dominant pupils "who held positive black cultural attitudes performed as well or better than either the Black or White standard English–dominant pupils on all tests" (91).

Another step in the development of an Afrocentric perspective is the recognition by those who assess writing that AAE is a rule-governed language system. African American English is a "linguistic term, not a social term," and it "refers to the highly consistent grammar, pronunciation and lexicon that is the first dialect learned by most black people throughout the United States" (Labov and Harris 6; see also Dillard). AAE, a product of the diaspora, is a Pan-African Language spoken throughout the Western Hemisphere (Twiggs 25). African in origin and international in scope, AAE is in many of its characteristics analogous to English-based pidgins and creoles that are still used today in the Caribbean, Africa, and South America. These include Guyanese Creole, Jamaican Creole, Sranan (the Creole English of Surinam in South America), and many West African pidgins, such as Nigerian Pidgin English (Smitherman, "From Africa" 412; Edwards 404; Haskins and Butts 42–43). In a 1949 study of Gullah, the AAE spoken mainly in the coastal regions of South Carolina and Georgia (Traugott 81, 87), Lorenzo Turner found clear correspondences among the grammar, syntax, phonology, and vocabulary of Gullah and twenty-one African languages, including Ewe, Fante, Twi, and Yoruba. Following Turner, other researchers have detailed linguistic parallels between AAE and traditional African languages. In AAE *d* or *f* replaces *th*, a sound that does not exist in West African languages. As a result, *this* becomes *dis* and *south* becomes *souf* (Smitherman, *Talkin* 7). In addition, clusters of consonants are rarely found in West African languages, and words are more likely to end in vowel or soft-consonant sounds than in hard-consonant sounds (Haskins and Butts 43). Consequently, in AAE the final sounds represented by *r* are eliminated; *dough* and *door* are pronounced the same (Haskins and Butts 42), *more* is pronounced *mo*, and *brother brotha*. As AAE developed, its speakers did what second-language speakers typically do; they used not the sounds of the foreign language but those sounds of their original tongue that they imagined to be equivalent (Strevens 112).

The first AAE speakers also applied the rules of their own African languages to syntax and morphology. In many African languages (e.g., Yoruba, Ewe, Kimbundu, and Kongo) it is grammatically correct to repeat the noun subject with a pronoun (Van Sertima 144); the AAE speaker will say, *My father, he work there* (Smitherman, *Talkin* 6). Many African languages (e.g., Ibo, Ewe, Fante, Yoruba, Ga, and Kongo) use the same form of the noun for singular and plural (Van Sertima 140–41); the AAE speaker will say *one boy* and *five boy* (Smitherman, *Talkin* 7). In addition, the AAE speaker may say *I go* and *he go*, on the model of the West African languages in which the same verb form is used for all subjects (7). In a number of West African languages, like Yoruba, the past- and present-tense verb forms are the same (Van Sertima 141); thus *I go* can signify either present or past action. Ewe, Yoruba, Twi, Fante, and Ga have no passive voice; in AAE, verb forms are always active (142). Many West African languages, such as Ibo, do not use possessive markers (140), which is another of the features of AAE. The AAE speaker may say *the girl book* instead of *the girl's book*. Ibo, Ga, Yoruba, and Ewe make no distinction between nominative and possessive forms of the personal pronoun (140); the AAE speaker may say *she house* rather than *her house*.

By understanding the features and rules of AAE and acknowledging the language as a legitimate linguistic system, we align our thinking with the findings of current research and abandon the misconception that AAE developed as a result of cultural deprivation and physical and cognitive deficiencies (Alexander; Smitherman, *Talkin*; Weaver; Baugh). We then can recognize that AAE does not reflect a thinking deficit that retards the speaker's capacity to learn (Alexander 21) and that AAE is not "an inferior method of speech" (Whiteman 18, citing *Martin Luther King Junior Elementary School Children v. Ann Arbor School District Board*, "Court Memorandum and Opinion," 1978).

Teacher Perception of the AAE Writer; Code Switching

The next change an Afrocentric approach advocates is in the assessor's perception of the AAE speaker. Some instructors who have not adopted an Afrocentric perspective tend to see the AAE speaker in the freshman composition classroom as a misplaced basic writer. AAE speakers may be perceived as what Tom Fox calls "initiates" (72). Because of dialectical or interdialectical forms in their writing, they are thought to be unfamiliar with academic discourse and its conventions. It is often believed that they "hear no standard grammar, see no standard grammar, speak no standard grammar, and must therefore begin at the beginning—must concentrate on words before sentences . . . must, in short, master the standard language in isolation before they are equipped to compose in that register" (Wilson 48).

But in fact the AAE speaker may be very knowledgeable of the conventions of Standard English. Many African Americans are adept at a linguistic phenomenon called code switching, which is the "ability to move back and forth among languages with ease, as demanded by the social situation" (Elgin 109). Code switching is a cognitive skill common to bilingual or polyglot speakers (Hall 201); it is often a carefully planned and controlled, if sometimes intuitive, communication strategy "by which the skillful speaker uses his knowledge of how language choices are interpreted in his community to structure the interaction so as to maximize outcomes favorable to himself" (Penalosa 77).

Code switching can provide a linguistic advantage for the AAE speaker in the composition classroom (Gilyard 33). The AAE speaker may have a language repertoire that includes "Black English, a productive (speaking) biloquialism, and a broader receptive (listening) bidialecticalism . . . [as well as] an adroitness at responding to the perceived need to match each dialect to different sets of social circumstances" (33). William Hall confirms this view, noting that black children show superiority in code switching, "which suggests that their total linguistic resources are greater than that of monolingual White children" (205).

Traditionalists typically view code switching as an unplanned, almost haphazard activity of which the bidialectal speaker is unaware. The implication is that African Americans do not know that they are code switching. Scholarship on the sociopsychological impact of being African American in the United States suggests the opposite. There is evidence that African Americans, from their early presence as enslaved people in the United States to the present, have always been astutely aware of the power of language as a means to minimize the effects of oppression and to construct a positive identity. This linguistic role-playing, of which the movement between African American English and Standard English is one example, is for many African Americans an essential strategy for survival in the United States. The belief that code switching from AAE to Standard English is an unconscious occurrence rather than a conscious—or at least intuitive—political choice echoes subtly the disempowering cognitive-deficit theories promoted by earlier twentieth-century scholars who sought to maintain Standard English as the dominant code.

Code switching is not merely a feature of speech, instructors must realize; it also plays a role in the AAE speaker's writing. Mina Shaughnessy observes that the AAE speaker's "intuitions about English are the intuitions of native speakers. Most of what they need to know has already been learned—without teachers. They can swiftly unscramble sentences that the foreign-language student would have to puzzle over" (129). Angle studied students selected from among the fifteen lowest scorers on the Michigan Test (a hundred-item test of Standard English grammar, vocabulary, and reading comprehension), students who came from "very segregated and very Black cultures (two from the all-Black Mississippi village of Mound Bayou)" (146–47). In the composition classroom he found that these AAE speakers already knew Standard English grammar, syntactic patterns, and pronunciation quite well. When he treated African American English as a respectable and intrinsically interesting linguistic and cultural phenomenon in the composition classroom, much of the students' defensiveness about language use disappeared. They were then able to sort out different levels of rhetorical appropriateness and eliminate so-called AAE grammatical and syntactic errors from their writing (147–48). Paralleling Angle's work, Daisy Crystal conducted a study in which incoming freshmen-level AAE speakers were given two tests, a timed, impromptu essay and a second test requiring students to change nonstandard dialect to Standard English in a list of sentences (135). Crystal found significant differences between the composition test and the sentence-rewrite test: although students had difficulty identifying and correcting the nonstandard features in the sentences, these features never appeared in their essays (136). Crystal's findings highlight the AAE speaker's code-switching facility and knowledge of Standard English, and they demonstrate clearly the known superiority of writing samples over decontextualized grammar tests. Studying the error patterns in students' essays, Marcia Farr and Harvey Daniels found a mix of AAE and Standard English features that suggested that students were familiar with Standard English yet were catching only a handful of the AAE features in the revision process. The student does not need an explanation of the past tense, they assert; "what is needed is for the student to understand the contrast in this particular feature between speaking and writing, and to practice editing for a form the student already is using in some contexts" (80). Researchers such as Sondra Perl ("Understanding Composing"), David Bartholomae ("Study"), and Patrick Hartwell have also suggested that AAE-speaking students "'know' Standard English features and can correct most of their nonstandard patterns to standard ones (and therefore that the teaching of Standard English grammar is unnecessary)" (cited in Farr and Daniels 20).

Identifying the AAE Writer: The Challenges It Presents and Its Effect on Assessment

In addition to understanding that AAE is a rule-governed language system and that the AAE writer may already know Standard English, an instructor who adopts an Afrocentric perspective needs to recognize that not all students of African American descent speak or write in AAE (Alexander 24). Some African Americans are AAE speakers, some are Standard English speakers, and some are Standard Black English (SBE) speakers. According to Orlando Taylor, Standard Black English conforms to Standard English grammar and phonology but has intonational patterns that mark the speaker as African American (cited in S. Lewis 85). Jerrie Scott has noted that "individuals vary in their usage of different language features: some Blacks use more of the non-structural features of Black language, e.g., discourse patterns associated with the Black Preaching Style," while other blacks use a combination of nonstructural features and such structural features as phonological, morphological, and syntactic patterns (131).

Both AAE and Standard English may appear in the first-draft writing of some African American students. This mixture can lead uninformed teachers to misjudge the AAE writer and adopt assessment policies designed to identify that student's "true" writing competency. For example, an instructor may be surprised by the presence of AAE in the writing of a student who has passed the placement exam for freshman composition; the instructor may conclude that since the student is not dialect-free, the student has been misplaced and cannot be taught at that level. Or an instructor may be surprised by the presence of AAE in a student's in-class writing and the utter lack of AAE in a student's work done outside class and hence suspect plagiarism where none has occurred.

Some instructors are also disconcerted when a student speaks Standard English or Standard Black English in class but writes using a mix of Standard English and AAE. An instructor may admonish such students "to write as they speak," perpetuating the notion that African American students are inherently verbally articulate but poor writers. An instructor may find that one mode of discourse elicits more AAE than does another or that in a single essay certain sections are dominated by AAE more than others are. This phenomenon may lead to the belief that AAE speakers are capable only of certain modes of discourse—narration and not analysis, for example. An instructor may become reluctant to assign certain kinds of writing and may adopt a "divergence avoidance" approach to assessment (Wilson 44), which on the one hand suggests that AAE speakers need not employ Standard English in written academic discourse and on the other implies that they may not be able to utilize it. Or an instructor may favor in-class writing assignments over out-of-class ones, believing that a timed, in-class assignment is a more valid way to assess the students' writing ability.

Toward a Process-Based Afrocentric Assessment Model

If we agree that the assessment practices described above are problematic because they ignore the facts that AAE is a rule-governed language system and that code switching is normal for the AAE writer, then what is the most equitable and effective way to assess AAE? First, teachers need to apply to the AAE writer the findings of current research on composition. Composition theorists maintain that students become better writers and have a more successful writing experience when they are encouraged to engage in prewriting activities, write multiple drafts, and revise (Odell, "Measuring"; Emig, *Processes*; Cooper, "Research Roundup"; Stallard; Hillocks; Bamberg; Faigley and Witte). Peer feedback is important throughout the drafting process (Bruffee; Elbow, *Writing*; Clifford, "Composing"; Beaven), and so are instructor commentary and conferences (Murray; Graves). In a process-based approach to writing, the draft versions of an essay may contain grammar and spelling errors; editing is reserved for the later phases of the composing process (after the student has resolved such issues as audience, focus, organization, development, and language choice); the final drafts or presentation versions of essays, from the most successful to the least, may contain a few editing errors in standard usage; and, finally, usage errors are assessed on the basis of frequency and type. Recent research advocates the moderate noting of surface errors, the focusing on sets or patterns of related errors, and the flexible and cumulative evaluation of student writing, an evaluation that stresses revision and is sensitive to variations in subject, audience, and purpose (Farr and Daniels 46).

Many teachers do not adopt such a process-based approach when they assess essays that contain AAE. The traditional conception of how black students should be taught to write equates "the teaching of writing with the eradication of deviant language patterns" (Lipscomb 149). For such teachers the teaching of writing has become synonymous with the teaching of subskills and "those surface features of the language which are not composing" (149). But in Edward White's view, "there is no evidence that writing quality is the result of the accumulation of subskills" (*Teaching* [1st ed.] 123). A focus on subskills violates one of the fundamental ideas about writing, that it is not a single act but involves a series of recursive activities. Linda Flower and John Hayes describe the process of writing as "a set of distinctive thinking processes which writers orchestrate or organize during the act of composing." Emphasizing the recursive nature of writing, they see it as involving "a hierarchical, highly embedded organization in which any given process can be embedded within any other" ("Theory" 366; see also Murray). On the whole, according to Farr and Daniels, an emphasis on the mechanics of writing "punishes—drastically and disproportionately—students whose home dialect happens to differ even slightly from the dialect approved by the school" (82).

For the typical Standard English speaker in freshman composition, the process approach to writing "dispels one of the key fears inexperienced writers suffer: the need to get everything right the first time" (Elbow, *Writing* 5). These students understand that they "can generate an imperfect rough draft, not worrying about gaps and errors, and then come back later to mend, expand, and revise" (Farr and Daniels 65). For the AAE speaker, however, the writing experience can be quite different. Because AAE is associated with incorrect forms, some AAE speakers are more reluctant than Standard English speakers to engage in the drafting process. They see drafting not as the liberating experience it is for many non-AAE speakers but as an activity that reveals what the teacher who assesses writing according to Standard English considers their incompetence. Such students, feeling that multiple drafts only multiply their negative assessment experiences, resist submitting essay drafts; and when they do submit them, concern with correct usage often impedes the development of their ideas. In timed, in-class writing situations, some AAE speakers experience a writer-anxiety syndrome that keeps them at the level of "false starts" (Scott 143). When we analyze their writing according to Mike Rose's categories, we find that their reluctance to write is so intense they become blocked in spelling, the motor-aesthetic area, basic conventions, topics and information, and revision (3).

In my own research I have found that many instructors comment on AAE during the drafting process, often as early as the first draft. Their comments range from the intolerant, as in the two cases described at the beginning of this essay, to the genuinely constructive, comments that suggest to the student the need to be aware of the necessity of changing the language from AAE to standard usage and that even recommend specific grammar exercises. In either situation, however, the instructor has interfered with and reversed the composing process for the student. Premature assessment has aborted the composing process for some AAE speakers. When we comment on AAE in the early drafts of a student's essay, we are in effect suggesting to the student that grammar is something that is not handled recursively, in a series of stages, throughout the composing process. We are suggesting, too, that issues of mechanics, usually reserved for editing, should precede those of focus, organization, and the development of the student's ideas. Finally, by suggesting that features of AAE need to be "corrected," we have moved, however unwittingly, into an arena of assessment generally reserved for the final, or presentation, version of a student's essay.

While it is certainly acceptable to ask for revisions at the paragraph or even the sentence level in early drafts, what happens with the revision of AAE differs from what happens with other kinds of draft work. Because of unfamiliarity with the features of AAE, many instructors fail to identify its syntactic, phonological, and morphological features, categorizing them all as grammar errors. To label incorrect the phrases *he done been gone* and *he gone* is to overlook the concept of time expressed in them and to misdirect the student. When we adopt an Afrocentric perspective, we recognize that a fundamental difference between Standard English and African American English is the special use of the verb *to be,* especially its use in what linguists call the "habitual tense," which has its roots in West African languages and in the Bantu languages of eastern and southern Africa (Haskins and Butts 42–43; Van Sertima 144–45). The mere "correction" of such an AAE feature by the instructor does not typically produce Standard English, and it often forces the student out of the composing process and into the realm of hypercorrection.

When we encounter (as I have) the consistent use of *are* for *our* in a draft, we understand that the student has not made an error but is engaged in the composing process, which for the AAE speaker includes the transference of AAE to Standard English. We understand that for the AAE speaker "are" is a phonological analog of "our." Verley O'Neal and Tom Trabasso have observed "that when we read we go from the print (the 'orthographic' representation) to sound (the 'phonological' representation) to meaning (the 'semantic' representation). When we write, we do the reverse, namely, we go from meaning to sound to spelling (or semantics to phonology to orthography)" (172). O'Neal and Trabasso found that for many AAE speakers "phonological representations do correlate with spelling and that, to some extent, phonological differences in lect lead to differences in spelling" (185). There are semantic differences between AAE and Standard English. For the AAE speaker, for example, the word *book* can mean "to leave quickly," as in "he booked out of there." To identify this semantic difference as an error overlooks the fact that the student is aware of the meaning of the term and is capable of code switching.

An Afrocentric approach requires a shift in the terminology teachers use in their responses to AAE in a student's writing. Walt Wolfram and Donna Christian suggest the term "influence" rather than "interference" to describe cross-dialect difference (Shuy 3). William Hall uses the term "translation" instead of "correction," explaining that when a person "furnishes a grammatical form in [AAE] for a Standard English sentence, we say a translation has occurred" (203). William Labov reports that "since the listener does perform the translation, it is clear that he does understand the standard sentence" and that a process of decoding, involving "perception, analysis, and storage of the sentence in some relatively abstract form," has taken place (*Language* 63). Labov's comments highlight the AAE speaker's code-switching ability and suggest the inappropriateness of seeing the presence of AAE as error. Jerrie Scott adopts the term "dialect transfer." Dialect interference, Scott explains, "draws attention to final competence in the target-lect [Standard English] while dialect-transfer calls attention to the processes involved in the movement from native [AAE] to target-lect structure" (139). Because of their emphasis on process instead of product and on revision instead of correction, "dialect transfer," "translation," and similar terms may be the most appropriate for a process-based, strategy-oriented approach to teaching and assessing the writing of the AAE speaker.

Besides changing the terminology by which AAE issues are addressed, the instructor needs to change the context in which AAE is assessed. I agree with Allison Wilson that AAE should not be assessed in the draft stages of a student's essay (52). I recommend that AAE be assessed only in the final version of a student's essay and that it be assessed not as error and not as dialect interference but as a matter of language choice. All writers must make language choices appropriate to the audience, subject, and purpose of an essay. These choices may include slang or colloquial English, jargon and technical English, and written Standard English. When we adopt an Afrocentric approach, we recognize that AAE is also one of those choices. We discuss the choices with the class. By including AAE in that discussion, we move away from the implication that AAE is wrong and must be discussed with the student in the privacy of the instructor's office—or simply avoided altogether, on the assumption that the student cannot help using AAE.

By presenting AAE as a matter of linguistic negotiation, we make students aware that there are many style and diction choices, none of them intrinsically wrong, each appropriate in its context. Michael Linn refers to the choice between AAE and Standard English as the "system of decorum which governs what varieties of speech are appropriate under what circumstances" (150–51). Assessment of AAE in the final version of a student's essay is based, therefore, not on the presence of AAE "errors" but on the appropriateness of AAE for the essay's subject, purpose, and audience. "Appropriateness" in this context becomes necessarily a political term, and the typical AAE speaker who has achieved college freshman status is certainly cognizant of both the political realities of the world in which he or she lives and the type of language demanded by college-level writing. Especially political are biracial situations where a negative instructor attitude can affect the performance of black college students (Epps 44, citing works by Atchison, Cohen, Epps, Perry, Roper, and Williams). E. G. Cohen and S. S. Roper, who refer to the stressful impact of such biracial situations as "interracial interaction disability," argue that in them societal expectations lead both blacks and whites to expect poor performance from blacks (cited in Epps 44).

By adopting the process-based Afrocentric assessment model, I have seen the incidence of AAE in essays change dramatically from draft to final version. I have seen drafts with a high frequency of AAE features and the final versions of the same essays with less than one percent of AAE in the essay's total word count. I have seen, too, a student choose to use AAE in a manner that was consistent, effective, and appropriate to subject, audience, and purpose in the final version of an essay. In a description of the basic writing student, Shaughnessy states that "correcting errors is an editorial rather than a composing skill and requires the writer to notice features of the sentence he would ordinarily have to ignore while composing. . . . Thus composing requires the writer to forget about the details that a proofreader must scrutinize" (128). In contrast, the transference of AAE to Standard English is not wholly an editorial activity; for the AAE speaker it is both an integral part of the composing process and, by implication, a political choice.

The Assessment Format

When we adopt an Afrocentric approach, we need to consider the assessment format, which includes what type of prompt is used and whether the essay is assigned to be written outside the class or given in a timed, in-class setting.

Decontextualized multiple-choice grammar tests we can dismiss immediately as a valid means of writing assessment. Those of us who have adopted a process-based pedagogical approach to composition certainly subscribe also to the findings of current research on the inappropriateness of such tests as an assessment format (Odell cited in Camp, "Changing" 48). Multiple-choice tests on mechanics and usage are ineffective and "do not sample the full range of knowledge and skills involved in writing" (White, *Teaching* [1st ed.] 1; see also Camp, "Changing" 48, citing works by Cooper, Gere, Lloyd-Jones, and Odell). Furthermore, multiple-choice tests disadvantage AAE speakers (Camp, "Changing" 48, citing works by Berstein, Cole, Heath, Linn, and Moss; White, *Teaching*; Wolfram 282). AAE speakers are not limited to one variety of speech, and skills-assessment tests produced only in Standard English do not always tap skills possessed by AAE-dominant students (S. Lewis 87).

Writing samples are a better measurement and fairer to minorities (White, *Teaching* [1st ed.] 70, 83). However, if we are to rely on writing samples produced in a timed exam setting, we must keep in mind that direct measures of writing ability are generally first drafts and that "first drafts are only the start of the writing process" (243). Such tests, therefore, may generate a mix of AAE and Standard English. We must consider also the demands and constraints of this assessment format. Does it interfere with effective dialect transfer? Have we devised an assessment procedure and scoring guide that identify patterns of AAE according to type and frequency?

If we adopt timed, in-class essays as an assessment format, the demands of the prompts are important. Prompts need to be clear about audience, purpose, and discourse mode (101) and evaluated in terms of their sociolinguistic and communicative assumptions to ensure against test bias. One discourse mode or essay purpose may not require the same skills and strategies as another (Camp, "Changing" 56, citing works by Freedman, Greenberg, Pringle, and Witte). Geneva Smitherman found that the incidence of AAE varied depending on the mode of discourse (*Black Student Writers* 7). She found a higher incidence of AAE in essays that called for description than in those that called for narration. The narrative essays, according to Smitherman, required the use of field-dependent cognitive skills (i.e., situational context, use of narrative sequence, and lack of distance between writer and reader), whereas the descriptive task required field-independent cognitive skills (use of categorical classification in written analyses and use of physical and psychological distance between writer and reader) (11).

Assessors need to define explicitly, by means of test guidelines, prompts, and scoring guides, the language and discourse styles that are acceptable. According to Orlando Taylor and Dorian Lee, it is the context-independent language style, a style that "is rigid, controlled and predictable [and whose] meanings of utterances are exact," that is preferred on many writing tests. They note that some African Americans tend to exhibit a lower frequency of preference toward this context-independent language style (76). Paralleling Taylor and Lee, Michael Linn has observed that a low-context response—consisting of a "formal or frozen style"—is expected for essay tests, but some AAE speakers will choose a high-context response that suggests personal familiarity with the topic and will use colloquial language and a highly personal and casual style (152). Taylor and Lee, who have discussed topic associating as an African American discourse style, note that it is the topic-centered style rather than topic associating that is usually expected by standardized tests. (73). The topic-associating style is often viewed by assessors as disorganized or pointless. The African American communicative style devalues responding to obvious questions with obvious information (72). According to Delsey Noonan-Wagner, features of black discourse style like free association as a generative principle, sermonizing, moralizing, and word choice present "the greatest difficulty in preparing students for college writing" (1, 4). If the observations of Taylor and Lee, Linn, Smitherman, and Noonan-Wagner are correct and given that African American discourse styles are rooted in a traditional African philosophy and worldview (Asante; Smitherman, *Talkin*), we need to be careful that prompts are not biased against certain legitimate communicative styles. A prompt that allows the student only to present a main point directly and immediately may be in conflict with a communicative style that has the writer present information indirectly, before the main point is stated. I am not arguing for a divergence-avoidance approach to assessment, nor am I suggesting that AAE speakers cannot produce context-independent, low-context, field-independent, topic-centered writing; they can. Rather, I am arguing for an increase in awareness, clarity, and explicitness in demands, expectations, and goals. I am asserting the need for the development of writing tests that "respect differences in modes of learning as well as expression" (White, *Teaching* [1st ed.] 246).

Because timed, in-class writing samples are first drafts (243), we need to adopt an assessment format that allows the writer to demonstrate more clearly and effectively what he or she knows. We need an assessment format that appreciates and takes into account differences in communicative style, code switching as a fundamental component of the AAE speaker's composing process, and the legitimacy of AAE as a tradition-based language system. Such a format may be the portfolio.

Portfolios are a more equitable means of evaluation because they contain multiple samples of student writing, on various subjects, for different audiences and for different purposes, samples composed and revised with the advice and support of teachers and peers. Unlike writing-sample tests, which minimize the role of revision (Wolcott 40), portfolios allow the writing process to be recursive. When used effectively, they may encourage assessors to be clear about the kind of writing required for a particular prompt. Portfolios provide a way for the AAE speaker to demonstrate his or her ability to manipulate successfully two communicative and language codes. If we perceive writing as a means of "identifying entities, categorizing objects and concepts, perceiving ideas and things, grasping the abstract, the concrete as well as the supernatural, and thinking about anything in whatever form" (Afolayan 174), then we recognize the need for an assessment format that will allow the writer to engage in these activities and will provide the assessor with a multifaceted and equitable vehicle to evaluate the writing.

Portfolios are particularly significant when we consider that current research has shown that "students from nonmainstream cultures may be especially disadvantaged by the lack of social and instructional context in traditional formats and conditions for assessment" (Camp, "Changing" 58, citing Johnston). Traditional assessment models typically lack explicit expectations for audience, purpose, and subject. In portfolio assessment the teacher has the opportunity to identify what the student knows and the student has the opportunity to choose the best representations of his or her writing. Through portfolios we can separate what is a matter of dialect transfer or dialect influence from what are sentence-level errors, observe the student writer in a variety of modes of discourse, and evaluate the writer's overall use of language, which may differ from essay to essay, depending on the subject, audience, and purpose.

The combination of portfolio assessment and an Afrocentric approach—in which both student and teacher are informed about the history and tradition of AAE and the student writer and his or her peers understand that AAE is a valid language choice when appropriate to the subject, audience, and purpose of the essay—may be the answer for the writing teacher who is seeking a sound pedagogical and assessment tool. Portfolio assessment is also a way to study the longitudinal development of AAE writers and to learn about the processes and strategies these students use. A portfolio approach designed according to Afrocentric principles may contribute to clarity, in that both audience and discourse mode are defined; validity, in that a good range of scores is produced; and reliability, in that an accurate scoring guide can be developed, resulting in agreement among scorers rather than in idiosyncratic scoring.

By adopting an Afrocentric approach to writing assessment, teachers can appreciate the linguistic virtuosity of AAE speakers and see them "as people who have brought, originated, and transmitted certain unique mores and values to create a culture that has survived continual efforts to annihilate it" (Haskins and Butts 14). Teachers also understand that knowing Standard English, in itself, does not guarantee the economic success, educational advancement, political advantage, or social acceptability of AAE speakers (Ogbu; Smitherman, *Talkin*). An Afrocentric approach can help students whose writing contains AAE develop a positive cultural identity by not requiring them to abandon AAE in favor of Standard English. At the same time, it can empower AAE speakers by enhancing their understanding of the traditional essay style and their ability to write in it. An Afrocentric approach calls for a change in pedagogy and assessment design to prepare both student and teacher for "life in a multilinguistic transnational world" (Smitherman, *Talkin* 219). It is a political program whose main goal is to have AAE writers benefit from what we know about teaching and assessment, to bring all writers to a high level of performance. Such an approach to assessment is bound to affect the training of teachers and the content of writing textbooks and handbooks. Not only can an Afrocentric approach increase the validity and reliability of our assessments, it can also help bring about a more fair and just society.

California State University, San Bernardino

Gender, Feminism, and Institution-Wide Assessment Programs

Deborah H. Holdstein

> *What she lacks in intelligence and maturity she more than compensates for through unbridled enthusiasm. . . . After an ignoble start—with a B- on her first paper—she moved from a B, to a B+, to several A's, and, finally, to an A+ on her last, and best, effort. . . . She was able to help me awaken a generally lackluster group of scholars at 9 every morning. . . .*
>
> Term evaluation

The evaluation of my performance as a sophomore in a Keats and Shelley course at Carnegie Mellon University, printed above, bears tremendous irony, given the institutional context of the assessment, a pass-fail system. The system, a product of the late-1960s movement to evaluate students qualitatively instead of quantitatively, was created to remove the stigma of traditional letter grades, to open the academy, freeing students and the process of learning from punitive ranking while retaining standards.

In the course of over twenty years of teaching and studying composition and literature, I began to understand—long after the experience of being evaluated myself—the full weight of bias possible in qualitative evaluations. Seen twenty years ago as less damaging than the traditional connotations of A or B, qualitative evaluations nevertheless often reflected—indeed, seemed to celebrate—the arrogance, insensitivity, and sexism of an instructor whose unquestioned authority shaped a student's intellectual potential and personal self-worth. Despite that era's plethora of bumper stickers demanding that we all question authority, few students were capable of that at such an intellectually vulnerable phase of their lives. My rather unscientific perusal of other qualitative evaluations finds loaded language used against women to minimize their accomplishments by emphasizing personality instead of work—"bright," "enthusiastic," "perky," and (my personal favorites) "energetic" and "vivacious." By saying that I was able to help "awaken a generally lackluster group of scholars," the instructor implied that I somehow stood outside that group, a cheerleader rather than a quarterback, an entertainer rather than a scholar. Ironically for the system that stood behind these remarks, a simple A—without commentary—would have been preferable to and more humane than the highly charged language that ultimately had nothing to do with my scholarly performance in the course.

I offer this gem from my personal history only to highlight an often-mentioned but infrequently explored complexity in any situation where a text is produced, read, and judged: the ingrained and yet slippery issues related to gender that permeate thinking, reading, and writing. Indeed, we as composition specialists have been remiss in leaving assessment all but untouched by the same social and critical theory and analysis that we readily merge with our other forms of practice, issues of gender being just one example of such merging. But let us turn to a form of evaluation more prevalent than the one I have discussed: the holistic assessment of student essays, where issues of gender transcend the obvious use of *he* as the universal pronoun. Holistic scoring is often seen as problematic because readers score "by impression" (Smitherman, *Black Student Writers* 11). I have observed a method that combines holism with primary trait scoring and have noted that even the set parameters conveyed to readers about ratings have little or no effect on gender-biased responses or, indeed, on the structures that govern the mechanics of testing (prompt design, selection, and so on). Nor do the various, standard ways of judging proficiency tests alleviate the additional difficulties of assessments grounded in the androcentric context of the university. The subtleties of gender bias and the potential for gender bias in assessment programs and holistic scoring of student essays seem ubiquitous: they exist in the institutional interests that surround testing programs at the university level, in the writing and selection of prompts, in the varieties of student response (those of women *and* men) to those prompts, and in the responses of even well-trained readers to the writing itself.

In the pages that follow, I mix personal and professional observation to point out the variety of ways in which gender might help us understand problems that result from how academic institutions perceive holistic and other forms of essay testing and rating. My observations stem from the political realities at my institution as well as at institutions where I have worked as a consultant. Administrators would love to see simple, "value-free," machine-scorable test results they can defend easily to irritated students and their parents and use to satisfy legislators who mandate quantitatively based forms of testing. If only the human and complex acts of writing and the reading of that writing were so simple.

By raising issues of gender, I hope to remind my colleagues in writing and from other fields participating in cross-disciplinary efforts that we must better educate ourselves and our students about what holistic techniques can and cannot do. We must also teach—indeed, publicize—that the complexity and difficulties of holistic assessments are acceptable, inevitable, and part of the best testing mechanism when we evaluate what Edward White and others in composition recognize as "first-draft composing." Testing programs as they are often constituted contradict the feminist principles and the issues of gender that permeate composition studies as a whole, and in composition scholarship there is little or no discussion of gender as it complicates test development, student writing, faculty reading, and the institutions that structure and administer assessment programs.

Gender stands with culture, race, class, sexual orientation, and other significant facts of difference as a subtle yet influential element in the testing process; it illustrates, with them, that holistic evaluation of writing, though valid, is a complex process that is beyond a merely statistical appreciation of validity. The act of reading student texts expands the notion of validity to include the following statements. Competent, trained readers may disagree, within limits, in their assessments of the same essay. A writing specialist may provide leadership for design and management of an assessment program and serve as last reader and final arbiter of contested judgment among a university's trained assessment team. In an interdisciplinary testing program, the specialist's decisions should not be regarded as serving the self-interest of the English department. Since the testing is of first drafts, one student may fail the exam because few of his sentences reached completion, while another may fail because she forgot to mark paragraphs and neglected to elaborate ideas. A student may be judged as having succeeded on one exam though he barely met the standards set for passing it, while the same student may be judged as having failed a second exam that seems comparable to the first but for various reasons isn't.

Some of our colleagues in other disciplines who take an interest and seek to participate in university-wide testing efforts do not always understand or appreciate these issues. Their misunderstanding can lead to a discrepancy between the reasons we test and institutional agendas, and that discrepancy can undermine the reasons we test. If we apply gender considerations and aspects of feminist criticism to the politics of holistic essay evaluation within institutions, we can use these perspectives to make ourselves and others aware of the necessarily (and acceptably) complex nature of the testing process and of holistic scoring. Such awareness will alleviate many of the controversies that typically plague essay testing (Holdstein). These issues might then lead us to alternatives to first-draft assessment in standard competency or proficiency exams.

Empowering Whom?
The Institutional Factor Makes Testing Complex

In a stirring address to those attending the 1989 meetings of the Conference on College Composition and Communication, Andrea Lunsford cited Kenneth Burke's phrase "perspectives by incongruity" to describe composition's ongoing yet vital and "more heterogeneous, more expansive and inclusive" dynamic as a discipline. "We will insist . . . on combining the private and the public, the personal and the professional, the political and the social . . . " ("Composing" 77). As the philosopher Sandra Harding has written:

> Feminist-inspired research in the natural and social sciences has challenged many beliefs that had been thought to be well-supported by empirical evidence, and, therefore, to be free of sexism and androcentrism. No longer is it non-controversial to assert that "man the hunter" created human culture . . . that women's destinies are determined by biology but men's are determined by history, and so on. (196)

While we might follow Lunsford's advice to "compose ourselves" and become nonhierarchical within composition studies and within our own classrooms in accordance with feminist principles, the institutions at which we teach and test remain very much hierarchical and androcentrically derived. Where assessment—holistic, for instance—is concerned, "incongruity" is a term best avoided when one must defend assessment practices within institutional hierarchies.

Yet feminism sees a wholeness in incongruity. For instance, asking students to write about the personal (the domestic aspects of their lives, perhaps) is political and often raises patriarchal hackles, even among women readers. I have observed in our own testing process that writers and readers, students as well as faculty members, become impatient with personal narrative where topics center on what is traditionally considered "women's experience" (the difficulties of balancing career, education, and family is one example). That women's economic, social, and cultural experiences make such an appealing prompt for my students (including a number of men in my classes) seems disreputable to many readers, even when such narrative is used in the service of "acceptable" academic argument.

Writing assessment that insists on one right answer (whether in multiple-choice tests or in dichotomizing essay questions that demand a one-draft response) disallows dialectical development of subtle answers and so forces students out of inquiry and into simple, nonexploratory argument. All this for the sake of administratively defensible results, a hierarchical, andocentric quality that, in its practical form, makes portfolio assessment (which openly relies and rests on human judgment) suspect at best. As Harding writes, "If there can be 'a' feminist standpoint, it can only be what emerges from the political struggles of 'oppositional consciousness'—oppositional precisely to the longing for 'one true story' that has been the psychic motor for western science" (199). The institutional perception, an example of that longing, is that any reader's disagreement invalidates the scoring process, that a trained third reader's judgment is human, subjective, and therefore easily discredited.

Gender differences that surface throughout the testing programs I've observed have led administrators to search for what I'll call absolute validity and reliability, a state of quantifiable perfection that reaches beyond even the relative strengths of .9 interrater reliability to seek some kind of irrefutably standardized production of texts and standardized evaluation of those texts: that is, no contested topics, no reader disagreement, and no nuances. This absolutism resembles one unfortunate legacy of applied New Criticism (which translated in the classroom seemed to demand that students somehow come up with the one true interpretation of a particular text) that feminist critics, among others, successfully challenged. The resilient, empowered hierarchy of academic administrators—men and what Patrocinio Schweickart has called "immasculated" women—often misguidedly demands that single truths emerge through structure in testing that lacks nuance or any juxtaposition of incongruity, a wish that goes against everything we as composition specialists know about writing as a recursive, complex process. Lunsford exalts us to oppositional greatness; Harding brings us to reality. Within the existing androcentric hierarchies that surround university-wide testing programs, administrators often impede the testing process by misperceiving the acceptability of disagreements among trained readers' judgments in response to student writing. Indeed, the institutional setting similarly fails to acknowledge the appropriateness of judging students' writing as an evolutionary process rather than as one-time product. In an evolutionary process, students learn to write for different occasions and different purposes; such a process permits exploratory forms of writing and thinking (through personal stories, for instance) that eventually lead to modes of conventional, academically "appropriate" argument.

Gender issues appear at every level of the text and in the context in which the text is produced. Making the andocentrically universal pronoun *he* into a plural or replacing it with *she*, using *chair* instead of *chairman*, and other editing-level corrections may have their long-term benefit in terms of how we generally view language and the gender bias in it, but they are also mere surface features of gender-related issues in writing. We can look at language in a "gynocentric" or "gynocritical" fashion, to adapt Elaine Showalter's term, just as one can look at writing in an Afrocentric fashion, saving commentary on African American English for the later, editing stages of drafts, after detailed discussion of audience and purpose to encourage students' ability to switch from one valid language dialect to another (see Kamusikiri's essay in this volume).

But, as with negative reader response to African American English, some manifestations of gender transcend the sentence level and the text itself and extend to the institutions in which the assessment is based. Design of prompts, choice of topic, genre, audience, rhetorical strategy, organizational principle, and so on are potentially sites of gender bias in writing. Geneva Smitherman speaks eloquently of unconscious racism on the part of readers (*Talkin*); yet when readers are given specific parameters to work in (primary-trait scoring, for example, or combinations of holistic and primary-trait scoring), such features as storytelling and coherence might be valued—features culturally attributed to speakers of African American English and, often, to women in general.

Even the preferences of a well-trained reader, whether conscious or unconscious, can have an influence, despite that reader's awareness of specific scoring parameters. Witness the following literary example of how gender influences judgment. Sydney Janet Kaplan notes the discomfort of Katherine Mansfield's male biographers, who "have certain difficulties coming to terms with her feminism and with her youthful struggles for independence. Their discomfort is most apparent when they describe her first experiences as a woman alone . . . " (125). Kaplan quotes Jeffrey Meyers, who categorizes Mansfield as the type of

daughter who "confirms a father's fears." He continues: "Though Katherine was afraid of her uncontrollable feelings, she believed she had to
'experience' life before she could write about it. But her raw emotion
was only thinly veiled by a pose of sophistication, and . . . a destructive
sexual extremism" (qtd. in Kaplan 125). Kaplan ponders "what Meyers
would have said about a young *male* artist's sexual activity. . . ." She
finds that most revealing is Meyers's assumption that Mansfield's "complex and serious-minded questioning of patriarchal standards of feminine behavior . . . establishes the father's position as more important"
than the daughter's (125). In the course of training readers of student
texts, I have heard other biased commentary based on assumptions
about the writer's gender (even though students use social security
numbers, not names, on the exams). Certainly our students shouldn't
have to learn to adopt a genderless (read "male") stance to avoid biased
judgments of first drafts, which often set the tone for their writing experiences at the university. They shouldn't have to neuter their experiences to pass an exam that bears little or no relation to the varieties and
forms of writing they will be asked to do later on.

Gender differences might reveal themselves in a text, but they also
permeate the institution that houses the processes of writing and assessing. Feminists often promote collaborative approaches in the generation and revision of texts, something to which we in composition studies
have given tremendous currency through peer-revision groups and
other activities. Yet in testing we don't allow collaboration or much time
for revision. Lunsford's postmodern emphasis on intensive collaboration between us and our students runs counter to the institutional practices of and assumptions about composition and the holistic assessment
of writing. Ironically, these same institutional practices, placing highest
value on the singly authored nature of a text, place it also on the text in
which Lunsford declares that we in composition are "non-hierarchical
and exploratory; we are intensely collaborative" ("Composing" 76).

As the philosopher Susan Sherwin writes in "Philosophical Methodology and Feminist Methodology: Are They Compatible?," "Psychologists have observed that women tend to prefer social, interactive
processes, unlike men, who long for the isolation of completely private
thought" (27). Psychologists have set the foundation for the institutionally valorized solitary scholar and the paradigm of the single-author text
that we demand in competency testing—even if we encourage, indeed
require, collaborative work in our classrooms. Sherwin further notes:

> The methodology of feminism is the methodology of women's
> thought: consciousness-raising begins with personal experience,

and then collectively moves to a broader analysis. Generalizations come after a number of particulars are presented. This is an interactive activity, and not the sort of private process Descartes envisioned.   (27)

Such male Cartesianism is not the vision with which we should design holistic essay scoring and other types of early- or first-draft testing. As in most kinds of institutionally informed holistic assessment, the emphasis in philosophy is on universal claims. This emphasis, Sherwin continues, "makes positive claims virtually impossible to prove and renders counterexamples potentially devastating; hence commenting on a philosopher's thought is often taken to require a furious search for the decisive counterexample, however hypothetical it may be" (28). Feminist scholarship also values logic, yet feminists are unlikely to tolerate a theory that wholly rejects or denies personal experience. In Sherwin's words, feminism "holds [on to] an ideal of cooperative, collective work. Scholarship in pursuit of a shared goal is to be undertaken as a collective enterprise . . . " (30). In holistic assessment and even in primary-trait scoring, the collaborative work of the readers best fits this vision; however, when institutions do not support the validity of collaborative work (with inevitable reader disagreements and third-reader arbitrations), then the collaboration may become an unfortunate form of institutionalized collusion.

Over the years, I have observed well-trained readers become overly concerned with types of personal evidence in an essay (usually it is an essay I will for simplicity call woman-centered), even when the evidence is used to support the student's assigned argument. In addition, these same readers are often concerned about how they will be perceived if they pass a certain number of papers or fail a certain number of papers. They do not trust their own, sincere judgments, judgments based on collaboratively derived criteria, because of an administrative desire for a mathematics of value judgment. But the phenomenon of assessment, though rule-governed, is not reducible to the types of formulas institutions want. That something isn't exact does not make it irrational, and even science is full of probabilities. The reasonable nature of an essay must conform to some expectations of genre and rhetoric, but part of the point of the writing process is to express difference—the self. And so gender differences in writers and readers should be not only expected but also accepted. Perhaps we must change the framework within which students write and we as readers judge that writing, thereby opening for discussion and alleviating the most potentially damaging forms of bias in test making, writing, and evaluating.

In "Feminism, Marxism, Method, and the State," Catherine A. Mac-Kinnon persuasively reconfigures and defines feminist philosophical methodology as a form of consciousness-raising: "Consciousness-raising is the major technique of analysis, structure of organization, method of practice, and theory of social change of the women's movement" (22). MacKinnon does not suggest that anything goes. She suggests, rather, that feminist methodologies lead us toward the political significance and importance of personal experience—for women *and* men. When applied to composition, these methodologies might simply encourage exploration of the personal as part of a student's writing process, in a portfolio of writings that also use the personal, as I've said above, to support academic argument. Perhaps the value of feminist theory within the institutional paradigm of testing lies, for now, in our using feminist theory to assert and explain more effectively to the existing hierarchy the various validities that mark acceptable differences, differences yielding complexities in the testing process that often seem intangible and vague to the administrative eye. To be remiss in so asserting and explaining might subject our students once again to the multiple-choice, scannable writing tests that we in the profession assumed had been discredited long ago. My institution and several other institutions I visited have come dangerously close to reinstating such tests.

Testing on the Margins:
The Need to Acknowledge the Conflicts

Whenever a woman sits down to write, she is engaged in a complex political act in which the self and the world struggle in and through the medium of language.   (Annas 360)

The dominance of . . . academic literacy is challenged by people who have made their way into the schools but whose native tongues are at a relatively greater remove from the academic dialect, whose preferred modes of developing ideas conflict with the linear logic and impersonal posture of academic debate, and whose cultural treasures are not included in the academic canon.
(Bizzell, "Arguing" 141)

But I did well in school . . . and there was the idiotic testimony of those peculiar witnesses, IQ tests: those scores invented me. Those

scores were a decisive piece of destiny in that they affected the way
people treated you and regarded you; they determined your authority; and if you spoke oddly, they argued in favor of your sanity.
(Brodkey 222)

Theorists of writing and its teaching, concerned with gender, race,
and class, with students marginalized, with issues of canonicity—
Pamela Annas and Patricia Bizzell are two such theorists—have fruit-
fully merged social, feminist, and critical theory with composition
theory, actively putting good theory into good practice in the writing
classroom and within the writing program at large. While it might tug
at the limits of open-mindedness to type the writer Harold Brodkey as
gender-sensitive (but who, in his own sphere, writes of being marginalized), I include this excerpt from his autobiographical short story to remind us how our students are affected by testing and its processes—and
to remind us that feminist issues are not limited to women. If students
"speak oddly" (use African American English, for instance) or go somewhat against the grain (get too personal) in the essays they write, how
do traditional forms of institutionalized assessment invent or compose
those students—or deny who they are?

The three brief excerpts above show that gender has been prominent
in classrooms, in notions of academic literacy, yet all but neglected as a
factor in scholarship and research on assessment, even holistic assessment. Why should gender not be discussed in assessment too? Concerns associated with gender dominate virtually every other aspect of
composition theory and practice. If gender becomes an issue for the
readers of text and their relation to text, what of gender in the writing
of text and in the creation of prompts? Even the most recent scholarship—save one interesting study, which I discuss in the pages that follow—skirts or entirely ignores the issue.

It appears that at the crux of the problem is, once again, the institution. Our methods for testing and evaluating writing owe more to institutional philosophies that narrowly define accountability than they do
to the specialists who are at the helm of writing programs and often
have a different view of accountability. Perhaps those of us involved in
college-level writing and testing programs have been remiss, assuming
that our unchallenged autonomy in our classrooms and the open nature of our pedagogy will transfer to the complex policies of university-
wide testing programs, whether English department–based or not. We
have little published theory with which we might arm ourselves to correct the perception that the nonquantitative judgments inherent in
evaluation are suspect.

Concentrating on language arts and secondary school English classrooms, Nancy Mellis McCracken and Bruce C. Appleby promote discursive values in their collection *Gender Issues in the Teaching of English*. As noted in a review of the book by Catherine Hobbs Peaden:

> [One of the] primary "issues" referred to by the title is a call to reform the [composition] field's false "gender blindness," especially as expressed by composition in the period of the 1970s and early 1980s. . . . For composition, the repeated message is that composition's past effort to eliminate sexism by ignoring gender has failed, and it is time to pay attention to differences caused by students' previous socialization. (261)

In that volume, Duane H. Roen's essay "Gender and Teacher Response to Student Writing" elaborates numerous concerns that transfer implicitly to reader evaluations of proficiency essays. Detailing the results of his study on gender-coded persuasive letters, Roen finds that male and female secondary school English teachers respond differently to "*as yet unidentified* linguistic and rhetorical features of discourse, with male teachers giving significantly higher scores to males on the persuasive letters and female teachers females, regardless of the labeled gender of the papers" (Peaden 262; emphasis added). In Peaden's words, Roen "also finds that teachers bring powerful gender stereotypes to reading student papers" (262). Roen affirms something many of us involved in testing programs have suspected, through the responses of our colleagues during training sessions and through our observations of the ways in which individual raters evaluate specific essays. Roen declares that "reading and evaluating student writing may be more hazardous than we usually consider it to be" (Roen 137).

In another essay in *Gender Issues,* one might be wary of Jean Sanborn's tendency to polarize, identifying "good" organic forms of writing as feminine and constructive of knowledge and "bad" linear, academic essays as masculine and authoritarian, but she also calls for teachers to recognize difference as "multiplicity" rather than "dominant/other" (146). Roen's and Sanborn's work reflects and elaborates my concerns about writing assessment. Issues of gender so permeate reading, thinking, and writing that other essays in McCracken and Appleby's collection suggest that we "re-gender" the reading of literature, teaching boys to read as girls and girls to read as boys. And yet none of these essays explicitly goes beyond the classroom level—or to the university level—to inform institutionalized assessment practices.

Published scholarship regarding the authority of the writing specialist offers little help. Annas's authority in her classroom to reconfigure writing processes and acknowledge the complex political acts of writing evidently does not extend outside the classroom—nor does the authority even of writing-program administrators, those to whom we would turn for help in changing institutional forms of testing. Gary A. Olson and Joseph M. Moxley underscore the powerlessness of most directors of composition. Although they do not specifically mention programs in evaluation, it seems to follow that the "limits to the extent of writing program administrators' authority and power of persuasion" (53; qtd. from Polin and White) are greater in the university-wide arena of testing. If we cannot even influence policies that concern the teaching of writing in our own departments, then what resources have we to demonstrate that issues like gender generally infect the complex structure of testing writing? As a start, I suggest that we teach our colleagues the conflicts and the complexities (to adapt Gerald Graff's well-circulated phrase) that are inevitable in testing—gender being only one of those contested complexities. As in the now legendary canon debates in English literature, an airing of these complexities might promote their acceptance and incite vitality in the empirically driven (read "dry") world of assessment. We might indeed learn to live with conflicted assessments; but, better yet, open discussion might well lead to revised notions and multiple strategies—assessment, altering Pound's phrase, made new.

But published airings especially would help in reconfiguring the assumptions about testing that have been made and have gone awry at the institutional level. As Bizzell points out, between 1975 and 1986 only two "important collections on the testing of writing ability had been published" ("What Can We Know" 575). In that period, of course, we welcomed the collections by Charles Cooper and by Cooper and Lee Odell. In an essay in the coedited volume, Cooper notes, in regard to holistic scoring and what it measures, "There is, of course, a serious reliability problem" ("Holistic Evaluation" 21). Bizzell observes, of publications by Edward White and by Karen Greenberg, Harvey Wiener, and Richard Donovan that came after those of Cooper and Odell, that

> the White and Greenberg books acknowledge the historical association of testing and politics and the paucity of empirical research on testing; but neither subjects its own arguments to political analysis. Instead, both tend to talk about the writing sample test they advocate as if the superiority of these tests had been empirically established.   ("What Can We Know" 577)

Why not open up the debate more publicly than we have, then, to acknowledge that we misrepresent essay samples scored holistically when we disavow, by our silence, any notion of dissent? Why not make acceptable various forms of dissent about holistic evaluation and its necessarily human factors, dissent that runs counter to what Sherwin calls the "style of philosophy that is characteristic of the Anglo-American approach, a method that has its roots in analytic philosophy and prizes a 'scientific' approach to thought" (27)? If feminists have aligned themselves with the time-honored philosophic tradition that encourages "radical rethinking of [philosophy's] underlying assumptions" (31), then why not use feminist theory as the basis for rethinking our own underlying assumptions about testing and, more significant, those of our institutions—regarding gender, race, and other issues—to inform better and reconfigure the parochial views of people who seek impossibly clean, empirical agreement relatively untouched by human intellect (much less human hands)? As Sandra Kamusikiri writes, in this volume, about issues surrounding African American English, "A prompt that allows the student only to present a main point directly and immediately may be in conflict with a communicative style that has the writer present information indirectly, before the main point is stated. . . . I am arguing for an increase in awareness, clarity, and explicitness in demands, expectations, and goals." Quoting White, Kamusikiri asserts "the need for the development of writing tests that 'respect differences in modes of learning as well as expression.' " Such an assessment format, she suggests, may be the portfolio, "a more equitable means of evaluation because [it contains] multiple samples of student writing, on various subjects, for different audiences and for different purposes, samples composed and revised with the advice and support of teachers and peers." In my own and other institutions, however, I have observed that administrators trust more in statistical evidence than in faculty judgment. They oppose a portfolio system that empowers both student and teacher-facilitator by its emphasis on individual and collective judgment, judgment that is not quantifiable or at least not easily quantifiable. Moreover, machine-scored tests are relatively inexpensive, particularly when administrators compare their price with the price of additional faculty salaries and released time for less immediate, more qualitative forms of assessment.

There are other arguments encouraging composition specialists to reexamine most institutionally based forms of writing assessment. We can rethink (or, in political terms, put a new spin on) Gordon Brossell's 1986 conclusion that research on testing has been "widely scattered,

disparate, and unsystematic" and has developed "little or no cumulative knowledge base" (169). Brossell, here concerning himself with empirical research, apparently assumes that quantitative assessment is
the only appropriate measure of a testing effort; he does not consider
any form of testing that might offer alternative contexts acknowledging
the complexities of student writer and essay reader. Indeed, perhaps
the "scattered, disparate" nature of such research reflects exactly those
complexities that I suggest we now simply acknowledge and open up to
debate while we attempt, as composition specialists, to influence institutional policies regarding assessment.

Even White, a thorough, proficient defender of holistically scored
writing samples, inadvertently demonstrates the ironies of testing and
reveals exactly those conflicts, gender among them, that we must air.
Coauthor of an essay reporting the results of a survey that indicates the
relative powerlessness of writing-program administrators (White and
Polin), White nonetheless misses the opportunity to link that important information to his other, well-publicized work on testing. Without
going on to consider the complexities of the testing process when the
issue of gender is raised, he does note that testing as it is most usually
conducted—testing that attributes skill, power, and proficiency to what
is in effect first-draft composing—betrays "in practice what we say
about revision and the entire composing process" (*Teaching* [1st ed.]
243). In *Assessing Writers' Knowledge and the Processes of Composing*,
Lester Faigley and his coauthors run the risk of serious understate-
ment when they note, "Of necessity, practice has far outrun theory in
writing assessment" (576). It is no wonder, then, that our literature
contains little or no acknowledgment of those issues—gender among
them—that further complicate assessment, a literature that could assist those seeking to inform the testing process.

To his credit, White does spend an entire chapter of his book *Teaching and Assessing Writing* raising the specter of critical theory, indicat-
ing only by implication the ways in which critical theory complicates
the testing methods we live by. He essentially validates what we know
as composition specialists and what is a denial of most of the forms of
testing practice we permit. White aptly quotes Vincent Leitch ("Two
Poststructuralist Modes of Inter[Textuality]") on the subject of the de-
stabilization of the test, the relocation of the reader from the outside of
the reading process to the center of the process:

> What are texts? Strings of differential races. Sequences of floating
> signifiers. Sets of infiltrated signs, dragging along numerous in-

tertextual elements. Sites for the free play of grammar, rhetoric, and illusory reference, as Paul de Man puts it. What about the "meaning" and "truth" of a text? . . . No text utters the truth: the truth lies elsewhere—in a reading. Constitutionally, reading is misreading.   (*Teaching* [1st ed.] 91)

White might take his use of Leitch's work further, acknowledging that if reading is indeed misreading, then issues of gender certainly make that reading—and consequently the assessing—even more intangible and complex. White's work provides excellent fuel for reconditioned testing debates (like the debates on the literary canon), in which the canon of assumptions about testing and the way it is conducted is challenged and aired. At the same time, airing the conflicts of assessment might link them to other issues of power and powerlessness within the institution—for instance, White's awareness of the limits of authority in composition programs.

White concludes his brief examination of reader-response and other critical theories with the statement "Our obligation is to help students see what other, highly sophisticated readers have made of the text so that they can enrich the text with various readings" (92). He affirms that part of the difficulty in evaluating writing comes "out of our deep understanding that we need to consider the process of writing as well as the product before us and that much of what the student is trying to say did not get very clearly into the words on the page" (93). He notes that the problem in the systematic measurement of writing is one of reading. Process theories of writing, therefore, accompany process theories of reading to invite readers and different judgments as part of the evaluation process. And yet the prescriptive nature of the rest of White's informative and necessary book conforms to the institution's rather than to the composition specialist's views of testing. It seems to negate, if not betray, the complexities that are implied by White's very mention of critical-theoretical contexts for even the best process-based testing programs.

A landmark study by Richard H. Haswell and Janis E. Tedesco begins to address several of these issues and contributes to the possibilities for our airing the conflicts, for rethinking institutional assumptions about the evaluation of writing, and for redirecting efforts in assessment.[1] Haswell and Tedesco note that

there has been no empirical study of "gendership"—how readers form a picture of the author's sex—and how gendership affects the pedagogical appraisal of student writing.   (1)

> Most of these [previous studies about gender] do not . . . pursue the possibility that contextual factors must be interacting with gender to effect the critique of student writing, factors such as those identified by the investigation of social value-judgment practices at large. (4)

The authors focus their investigation on one particular area of concern suggested by gender, yet the implications of the term *gender* and its relation to evaluation practices are many and mind-boggling. Publications in the 1990s have enriched a long history of gender-based study in psychology that began in the late 1960s: Haswell explores the interaction of the writer's sex and personal development (*Gaining Ground*); D. L. Rubin and K. Greene explore the interaction of the writer's sex and gender-role orientation; and Alan Purves ("Reflections") finds that raters say they can tell the sex of the writer from handwriting (Haswell and Tedesco 4). Robert J. Connors and Andrea Lunsford's extensive study of teacher marking of errors in student writing ("Frequency"), according to Haswell and Tedesco, "left sex of teacher and student unrecorded and therefore could only raise 'tantalizing implications about men's and women's ways of knowing and about gendered response'" (4).

Investigating the question of gender ascription, Haswell and Tedesco write:

> Initially we ask if female and male readers form an image of the author's sex as they critique a student essay. We call this reader's construction of the author's sex "gendership," coining the term in parallel with "authorship" as defined by post-structuralist discourse theory. Just as the reader's sense of an author is constructed by personal knowledge . . . ideology . . . and community discourse conventions, . . . so the reader's sense of an author's sex is multiply constructed. (5–6)

The study holds tremendous implications for holistic evaluation—again, less to dismantle such processes than to inform those who practice them and to correct the public image that often undermines even the best testing efforts. The authors note that "masking writers' names . . . does not work well, that spontaneously most readers form their picture of the writer's sex anyway." Moreover, they suggest that "holistic rating may be implicated in quite blatant self-fulfilling prophecies." That is, teachers often hold the gender stereotype that female students write better than male students, with results "that merely entrench the original stereotype" (43). Having observed each of these phenomena in our own testing program at Governors State University, I find that the resulting question is an essential one: If gendership cannot be untangled from the work of critique, then what does one do with it? The only possible response, in my view, is a simple one: Acknowledge it as a way to affirm the innate and acceptable imperfections of holistic testing, where the complex human acts of writing and reading transcend statistics. And, where possible, rework the institutionalized first-draft testing process toward a methodology that, to Kamusikiri and others, truly offers clarity, validity, and reliability—the portfolio.

Haswell and Tedesco's research proves useful in yet another way that has implications for both classroom evaluation and essay evaluation procedures. It shows that teachers' expectations that female and male students will write differently and that females will write better than males leads to a mirroring student response, "because [students] are alert to what teachers want and because their culture has taught them the same expectations" (44). At my institution I presided over a discussion about an ETS-sanctioned prompt concerning the difficulties of balancing work, family, and going to college full- or part-time. Despite the attempt to make the prompt "gender-neutral" (rather than openly acknowledge the potentials for difference at a variety of levels for both sexes), the question was primarily chosen by women, who clearly stated their gender in their responses. The group of readers for this particular question (with interrater reliability hovering around .8), male and female, professed their boredom with the responses and hence with the prompt. They asked that I not use it in the future, as the writers all said the same things, things of little intellectual interest. Students, it seems, are punished for being interested in such a question. The prompt, ideal in permitting them to use experience important to them in the service of an argument, nonetheless penalizes the students—mostly female—who choose it. Haswell and Tedesco ask:

> How much of the teachers' expectations that women students will write on interpersonal and homey topics such as friendships and family ties is based on the fact that women students actually tend to do this . . . and how much on the fact, supported by the present study, that the students intuit that the teachers expect them to do it?   (44)

In my observation, any way such a student turns, we penalize her for it: as testers, by providing a prompt that she finds conducive to writing and then, as readers, by not valuing the response because it's based on female, personal experience. Wanting that kind of prompt eliminated, the readers ironically disenfranchise those whose experience (particularly in an institution such as mine, populated with returning adult learners) might find its voice through such an essay. Haswell and Tedesco's students further illuminate this dilemma:

> Victoria is caught in the double-bind of writing in an improved masculine vein and then being punished for it because she is a woman—an infamous trap hypothesized by feminists of the last decade and supported by evidence in this study. But we also found support for a similar but less-publicized bind, the one suffered by Kevin, who cannot speak honestly about his interest in friends and family ties without paying for it. (44)

The criteria for argument demand that students not tell a story, that they use stories as examples to prove a point of view, but for these writers, mostly women, the value of their writing often is in their stories. The attempt to make personal stories important, to value them, is not new in literary criticism, in the writing classroom, as a new legacy of scholarship aptly demonstrates (see, e.g., Sherwin; Tompkins, "Sentimental Power"). But in the light of traditional prejudices that accompany even the best-trained readers, how do we make room for more personal types of writing? How do we encourage both men and women to use friendship, families, and other "typically female" forms of experience in the service of academic argument, valorizing prompts that elicit those forms of experience?

In another vein, how might Kevin and Victoria have responded to a prompt uncritically presented by a handout I use, a page from an essay entitled "Principles of Genetics: Inheritance of Acquired Characteristics"? The prompt read as follows: "The blacksmith in the village had huge muscles in his arms and chest from pounding iron all day with his sledgehammer. Three of his children are girls and do not have muscular builds." Does this prompt have to do with genetics, sex-linked traits, culture, or, simply, those who exercise and those who do not? What acceptable direction might a response to this prompt take? What should readers look for? What does the Haswell and Tedesco study imply about this type of writing situation?

Through Haswell and Tedesco's extensive observations, we can fault essay readers, the types of questions to which students respond, and the testing institution itself—or we can acknowledge the problems as inevitable conditions in the writing and reading of texts. Hélène Cixous's words might serve as a trope for, and be in ironic counterpoint to, the community of interpreters who score students' writing samples.

Her "Laugh of the Medusa" underscores the ironies described by Haswell and Tedesco, the double bind for women (and men), the essayist influenced by culture, the reader influenced by culture, and the agendas of institutional hierarchies.

> Where is the ebullient, infinite woman who, immersed as she was in her naivete, kept in the dark about herself, led into self-disdain by the great arm of parental-conjugal phallocentrism, hasn't been ashamed of her strength? And why don't you write? Write! Writing is for you, you are for you. . . . I know why you haven't written. (And why I didn't write before the age of twenty-seven.) Because writing is at once too high, too great for you, it's reserved for the great—that is, for "great men," and it's "silly." (1091)

In addition to shedding light on a student writer's assumptions and fears about audience, about giving the readers—those evaluating first-draft texts—what they want, Cixous's tirade reveals the complexities of a powerful institutional process:

> Write, let no one hold you back, let nothing stop you: not man; not the imbecilic capitalist machinery, in which publishing houses are the crafty, obsequious relayers of imperatives handed down by an economy that works against us and off our backs; and *not yourself.* Smug-faced readers, managing editors, and big bosses don't like the true texts of women—female-sexed texts. That kind of scares them. (1091)

Considering the implications of Cixous's words within the context of the Haswell and Tedesco study, we might wonder to what extent we as readers and as participants in a testing process become "smug-faced readers," nothing more than "crafty, obsequious relayers of imperatives handed down by an economy"—in this case, part of an institution that does not appreciate or understand or promote understanding of the complexities inherent in writing and a person's thoughtful response to it.

In an essay appearing in a collection in 1985, the year of White's important work on writing assessment (*Teaching and Assessing Writing;* yet there was little mutual influence between her and White), Showalter evaluates the influence of psychoanalytically oriented feminist concepts on literary criticism and notes that such critics as Sandra Gilbert, Susan Gubar, Nancy K. Miller, and Elizabeth Abel emphasize "the constancy of certain emotional dynamics depicted in diverse cultural situations" ("Feminist Criticism" 259). Indeed, in her discussion of theories of culture Showalter maintains that the "female psyche can be studied as the product or construction of cultural forces" (259). If "women writing are not . . . inside and outside of the male tradition, they are inside two traditions simultaneously" (264) and potentially penalized for both, as Haswell and Tedesco demonstrate. Showalter notes:

> One of the great advantages of the women's culture-model is that it shows how the female tradition can be a positive source of strength and solidarity as well as a negative source of powerlessness; it can generate its own experiences and symbols which are not simply the obverse of male tradition.   (264)

By reconfiguring the ways testing is perceived within our institutions, we might be able to evaluate properly "what women actually write, not in relation to a theoretical, political, metaphoric, or visionary ideal of what women ought to write" (264) but various forms of what Haswell and Tedesco call code switching. Such new perception would be to the benefit of women and men—of Victoria and Kevin and of the women and men who read what they write. We can use the oppositional worldview of scholars such as Susan Jarratt, bell hooks, and Gayatri Spivak, whose work ironically has left assessment untouched, to convey to our administrators, to our essay readers, and to our students precisely how complex and necessarily human our collective work can be. We are at best negligent (at worst irresponsible) if we permit these issues to remain unacknowledged; we then leave unchallenged the misperceptions of those who hold the institutional authority and continue driving the assessment machine in ways that ultimately disempower our students—and that potentially discredit composition studies as a viable part of the academy.

Are There Practical Solutions?

The institutional constraints on composition specialists who attempt to foster change are immense. Putting aside for a moment the writing-program administrator's limited power to influence institutionalized testing processes, one cannot ignore that portfolio evaluation of student writing, which I recommend, is not without its difficulties. Yet Kamusikiri tells us that an "Afrocentric approach proposes not a radical reconstruction of the teaching of writing but a new way of seeing that facilitates an equitable application of those demonstrated successful pedagogical and assessment practices that already exist, to foster an appreciation of the language diversity in our society."[2] In this environment, African American English is viewed, in White's words, "as a social and communicative act, an interactive and inherently meaningful, motivated activity" (*Teaching* [1st ed.] 181). Kamusikiri's view, arguing for difference and for the appropriateness of portfolios that encourage writing for a variety of situations and with a variety of purposes, is also gynocritical. The portfolio allows the writer to demonstrate most clearly and effectively what she or he knows, and it permits teachers and peers to evaluate the writer as she or he uses different forms of discourse. I do not deny that students ultimately must learn the ways of the academy; I do not suggest that traditionally androcentric forms of argument in academic essay writing are bad. I do, however, insist that considerations of gender permeate institutions, the testing program itself, and the awareness of student writers and their readers. We must allow our students' own voices and discourses to mark our students' path toward writing for that "other purpose"—the academy—and we must give currency to their doing so. Portfolios allow us that option.

Our creating a productive set of perspectives on class atmosphere, assignments, and evaluation of portfolios increases rather than diminishes the responsibility of writing-program administrators and composition faculty members. Instructor preparation will foreground any program-wide portfolio effort; the best interests of all students demand that instructors be educated on a wide variety of concerns, of which this essay has mentioned just one or two. While most composition instructors believe they are able to rework their thinking on language structures and evaluation from a variety of perspectives—the Afrocentric perspective discussed by Kamusikiri, for instance, or a new perspective on the term "basic" in "basic writing"—most are surprised to find that their self-described progressive views of pedagogy need refreshing. This need seems particularly apparent when they confront the subtle yet powerful restrictions in gendered and gender-biased reading, writing, testing, and evaluating. In addition, many instructors who use portfolios in their classes offer extensive written responses. If we neglect careful preparation for instructors, we risk reinforcing the more subtle, perhaps, but equally oppressive progeny of those blatantly dismissive evaluations that so blighted my education in the late 1960s and early 1970s.

If we must test, and it seems we must, then let us make our peace with and publicize well the inevitable inconsistencies among theory, teaching, and testing, or let us reinvent assessment itself. Acknowledging the complexities introduced by gender to all aspects of the testing process will help us do either. On the one hand, we can continue to acknowledge and defend that in early-draft testing and holistic scoring we look merely at a student's ability to write under pressure, even if the course after placement emphasizes writing as process through multiple drafting. On the other hand, we can develop a model that incorporates drafting and revision yet still preserves the question of rhetorical forms and readers' responses. We can argue that, yes, those in the workplace will always have that twenty-five-minute memo to write, something to get perfect the first time. But critical theory—and the various forms of feminist theory in particular—underscores the inconsistencies in most institutional forms of testing (especially the holistic evaluation of writing) in a way that the empirical research Faigley, Brossell, Bizzell, and others demand cannot. We must accept and debate publicly these inconsistencies. The result, I suspect, will be as intriguing as the canon wars and might further indicate to us, in ways more fully than our colleagues have explored, the oxymoronic nature of the term "writing assessment," as it is most often perceived and as administrators demand it, and the biases that complicate the writing of texts and our attempts to score them uniformly. These biases form not only along racial and cultural lines but also along lines involving gender—shortchanging students and faculty members, women and men in the process. Because we have become "nonhierarchical" and "heteroglossic" (Lunsford's words) in our theory and our classrooms, it is imperative that we turn our attention now to institutions and their testing practices, where first- or early-draft products, forms of bias, and illusions of gender neutrality retain their strong hold.

Governors State University

NOTES

[1]The quotations of Haswell and Tedesco are from an early manuscript, titled "Gender Bias, Gendership, and Critique of Student Writing." For the final version of this essay, see Haswell and Haswell.

[2]The quotation is from an early draft of the essay by Sandra Kamusikiri that appears in this volume.

The Challenges of Second-Language Writing Assessment

Liz Hamp-Lyons

The language minority population (not including international students) makes up about ten percent of the school-age population nationally, yet nowhere in President Bush's (now President Clinton's) America 2000 report, the spur for the current intense activity in the development of models and proposals for national competency testing in literacy, was there any mention of that ten percent. Those of us who are concerned about the well-being of nonnative English-speaking citizens and residents of this country see the development of tests that are responsive to the special needs of this large group as essential to its equitable access to education at all levels and thus essential to the integration into our society of nonnative English speakers as fully functioning citizens. In this paper I look closely at the assessment of second-language writing and describe some of its best practices and some of the challenges it poses. I conclude by reasserting the need to find assessment methods and measures whose fairness to language minority test takers can be shown.

The Context

The multiplicity of terms used for nonnative speakers and writers of English is potentially confusing and blurs an important distinction between two groups. The first group consists of overseas visitors from non-English-speaking countries who come to the United States to attend college (often as graduate students in technical subjects) and then return to their home countries. The second, much larger group is composed of the various immigrant groups that have entered and continue to enter the United States. Students in this group are often called bilingual, but many of them came here as children or have been in this country for many years, and many are the second or third generation of their family to be born here. Thus, they may not be literate in the language of their heritage. Furthermore, their social circumstances coupled with

226

the inadequate attention they receive in schools may cause them to graduate from high school with poor English literacy skills. Overseas visitors, in contrast, usually arrive with strong literacy skills in their first language and a strong orientation to the values of formal education. They take the ESL courses they need, pursue their degrees, usually successfully, and return home. The challenges of second-language writing instruction and assessment, then, are not from the first group but from the second.

The United States government refers to the students of the second group in K-12 education as "limited English proficient," or LEP, a term that has been found objectionable by many educators and students. In this paper I prefer to use the more neutral ESL (English as a second language) or to describe such a student as NNS (nonnative speaker, the opposite of which is NS, native speaker) or as a second-language or first-language writer. There is astonishingly little attention paid to writing assessment for NNS citizens and NNS future citizens; states and school districts are generally satisfied to base their decisions for tracking and special provision on standardized tests. Colleges and universities are usually satisfied to apply the TOEFL (Test of English as a Foreign Language), another standardized test, to international students. Educational Testing Service's TOEFL Program developed the Test of Written English (TWE) and introduced it in 1986, but we still do not know how many schools consider TWE scores when making acceptance decisions or assigning students to language courses. Furthermore, because of privacy laws, students not holding overseas-student visas are not identified as potentially having special needs. The larger and more needy group of nonnative writers I describe above, then, are unidentified, or they are identified as underachieving without attention to the cause of their underachievement.

At the college level, some international students go through an English language institute and then into required mainstream composition courses; some have high enough TOEFL scores to go straight into the composition sequence. Few "bilingual," that is, resident-status, students go through English language institutes, though there is increasing provision for these students in special programs at colleges. But typically our writing programs find, in the lowest levels, a disproportionately high number of students for whom English is not a first language. Most composition teachers have no training in teaching second-language writing; most of them learn to be sensitive to their second-language writers through trial and error, which is not the best way when the errors are mistakes made in individual students' lives.

The Challenges

I have argued elsewhere ("Basic Concepts") that the assessment of second-language writing shares many problems with the assessment of first-language writing but adds some new ones. In the field of writing assessment generally, we accept that if assessment is to have positive effects, its instruments must be well designed and sensitive to the contexts of the learners to be tested and of their teachers, and its users must be conscious of the social environment that has engendered the demand for assessment. The purpose of the assessment, the objectives to be tested, the test format, question types, and so on must all be clear to those affected by the test—test takers, their families, teachers, school administrators, and the people and agencies who will receive scores. Because the anecdotal evidence for "curricular alignment" (changes in what is taught made in conscious or subconscious response to what is tested) is strong, the test developers must know what the curricular consequences of their test instruments are likely to be. In addition to taking such general considerations into account, second-language writing assessments must respond to the diversity of the test population. But there are many special considerations that developers of writing assessments must be aware of as they design instruments for writers for whom English is a second language.

Probably the first thing that the untrained reader of NNS writing notices is the prevalence of certain linguistic features. Until fluency in English is quite advanced, second-language writers may not master features such as agreement of subjects and verbs, correct choice of prepositions, correct use of definite or indefinite articles, or maintenance of proper time relations. Studies by Terry Santos; by Roberta Vann, Frederick Lorenz, and Daisy Meyer; and by Michael Janopoulos have shown that college faculty members are generally more tolerant of NNS errors in writing than they are of NS errors. Nevertheless, the existence of persistent linguistic errors in nonnative writing may result in miscommunication between student and reader and from that lead to lowered grades on subject-area papers. Having to spend extra time and effort reading papers may negatively affect professors' judgments of their NNS students. Vann, Meyer, and Lorenz find that the less exposure faculty members have to NNS writing, the more affected they are by grammatical errors in that writing. In all three studies, errors found to be most serious include incorrect word order and incorrect relative clause structure, while errors such as incorrect article and preposition usage are treated more tolerantly. Janopoulos questions whether nonnative speakers who have been allowed to pass through composition courses with lower standards of language accuracy in coursework will suffer when they find themselves in test settings where they are judged by the same standards as NS writers. In large-scale testing where NS and NNS writers are tested together, NNS writers may be disadvantaged by readers' paying excessive attention to the multiple occurrences of fossilized local errors in their writing. Robert Carlisle and Eleanor McKenna found that readers at the University of Michigan could ignore surface errors and attend to the quality of ideas and argument in NNS students' essays, even when NNS and NS essays were mingled together in a reading day. However, these were well-trained readers using a multiple-trait scale that emphasized ideas and coherence over correctness, and they were supported by reading leaders with strong backgrounds in second-language writing instruction. It is not known whether this finding would transfer to other contexts. Nor is it known how much more readers would be influenced by global language errors (errors that affect sentence and text comprehension rather than merely obtrude momentarily at the phrase level), such as incorrect relative clause construction and inappropriate word choice, on a large-scale test of the writing of mixed NS and NNS writers. While our current tendency is to place greater weight on the command of ideas, the ability to form and develop an argument, and other higher-order text-making skills than on sentence grammar and surface accuracy, it is not clear how much weight should be placed on the various aspects of writing competence. It is perhaps worth noting that the current trend in writing assessment and in the teaching of writing is in the opposite direction to the current trend in educational politics; before long we may find ourselves obliged to pay more attention to external accountability for accuracy in writing. If so, the question of accuracy versus expression of ideas and knowledge will become more problematic for teachers and testers of second-language writing than it is at present.

Another element that potentially intrudes, though more subtly, into essay readers' judgments of second-language writing is the question of rhetorical structure and rhetorical style. Teachers of second-language writing generally accept that those who are literate in their own language bring to writing in English a set of writing habits, patterns, and perceptions that affect the way they structure their texts in English: we call the study of such differences "contrastive rhetoric." Spanish-speaking and Spanish-influenced students, for example, have been found by Rosario Montano-Harmon to rely more on "additive, explicative, or resultative relationships between ideas," whereas Anglo students in the same study rely more on deductive and enumerative relations (254). Paul Lux finds that essays by Anglo-American students have significantly fewer supporting points than do those by Latin American students but that in the Anglo-American essays there is more detail for each point. His findings echo those of earlier studies, which show that students of Spanish-speaking background prefer a style that privileges long sentences with heavy subordination, whereas students of English background prefer a style that privileges "efficiency" (96). Phillip Elliott finds that writers of Spanish background and writers of English background even seem to prefer different approaches to an essay prompt (topic). Cross-cultural differences in handling essay prompts and in constructing text can importantly influence raters' judgments of essays. Examining the writing subtest of the British Council's English Language Testing Service, I found that raters' judgments were affected by the rhetorical choices made by writers and that, depending on the rater's background and knowledge, the rhetorical choices transferred from some languages might be more favored than those transferred from others. Japanese patterns were favored by raters who had taught in Japan and disfavored by those who had not; Greek patterns were generally favored and Arabic patterns generally disfavored ("Raters Respond"). Terry Santos describes some key differences between the educational cultures of first-language composition teachers and second-language writing teachers. She points out that rhetorical modes are still commonly taught in ESL composition courses, that the focus is still on form, and that discussion of rhetorical differences between English writing and writing in other languages is very common (2). In the philosophy and practice of basic writing courses, emphasis is more likely to be placed on fluency and confidence of self-expression. Because rhetorical structure is so closely allied with coherence, a key criterion for strong writing in English, international students may have an advantage over bilingual immigrant and ESD (English as a second dialect) students, who have not been overtly taught the conventional expectations of formal English text and who do not have an alternative set of recognizable conventions that they can apply instead. This point is discussed by Miriam Chaplin, who found that the writing of black students was often recognizable to essay raters because it had many features of oral style. Chaplin recommended that black students be specifically taught the conventions of formal academic writing style. Perhaps a similar strategy could usefully be applied to students from immigrant backgrounds.

The two aspects of ESL writing discussed so far require attention in testing and teaching contexts equally; I turn now to issues specifically applicable to testing contexts. The first issue is task, that is, prompt, development. Good essay prompts are difficult to develop, and this difficulty is compounded, in tests for a diverse population, by the problem of avoiding culture bias. Probably the most important component of culture bias is the assumption of shared background knowledge. The Test of Written English (TWE), testing the writing of a quarter of a million international students annually, necessarily puts great emphasis on avoiding topics that assume certain kinds of cultural background or information that will not be shared by all the test takers, who come from hundreds of countries. Even though the TWE uses a panel of composition experts to develop prompts, it accepts for pretesting only about one of every eight prompts prepared, and of every three or four prompts accepted perhaps one pretests successfully. There are always surprises, as when the term *theater* was interpreted by a number of students as "operating theater." Avoiding problems of background knowledge is vital on an essay test because an essay test is usually a one- or two-item test. Students who happen to know a lot about the topic are lucky, and while variations in background knowledge can never be completely avoided, a lack of knowledge is especially problematic for ESL and bilingual writers who are being treated as basic NS writers and given the kinds of questions found on typical composition-program placement tests. The solution to this problem is likely to look like that used by the TWE and the Michigan English Language Assessment Battery (MELAB): anodyne prompts that are of limited interest and stimulation to all students. Although the jury is still out on the benefits versus the disadvantages of offering students a choice of prompt (Hamp-Lyons, "Second Language Writing"), many composition programs have decided that they must offer a choice in order to try to combat the bias likely to result when only a single prompt is offered to their diverse student populations.

Another challenge for ESL writing assessment is the training of readers to rate ESL student essays. There has been no serious investigation of the question whether NNS writing needs to be evaluated by raters who are specially trained in ESL writing or have experience teaching ESL students. The faculty studies cited above (Santos; Janopoulos; Vann, Lorenz, and Meyer) suggest that familiarity brings tolerance. Is the opposite true? At the moment we don't know. Some researchers found that, in the context of the TWE, scores given by an ESL-trained rater and a composition-trained rater correlated as trongly as scores given by two raters of the same cultural background.

Yet looking in depth at raters' reasons for assigning scores, I found that familiarity with the writing of some cultures affected raters' judgments ("Raters Respond"). Rosemary Hake found that the race, the gender, and the language background of raters could predict their scoring behaviors; according to Hake, black raters were harsher than white, women harsher than men, and southerners harsher than northerners.

The search for appropriate scoring methods also poses special problems in second-language writing assessment. As Davida Charney points out, holistic scoring, because it has single-score outcomes and is not designed to offer correction, feedback, or diagnosis, is problematic in ESL writing assessment contexts. Diagnostic feedback and correction, while useful to every student, is especially valuable for NNS writers. First, many overseas ESL students have had only limited exposure to instruction in English and are only partway through their individual process of mastering the language. If they are given the right guidance, continued growth in writing is a real possibility for most of these learners. Second, many immigrant NNS students have been allowed to move through school with little opportunity to write, and teachers' expectations of their writing, when such students do write, have been low. If the students then find themselves in a program that places high value on writing, whether in a secondary or postsecondary institution, they will need a great deal of support. A single score does not provide sufficient information for either kind of student, for the teacher, or for the administrator who must decide on the optimal use of courses as curricular options and must set up special services like tutoring, conferencing, or workshops. Such services can be especially helpful to both international and immigrant ESL students. Further, a second-language writer often acquires the different components of written control at different rates. Every teacher of ESL writing has seen students who have fluency without accuracy and students who have accuracy but little fluency. Some writers will have a wide vocabulary but markedly less syntactic control, some will have syntactic control but little rhetorical control, and so on. From second-language writers who already have some mastery of a specialized discipline, it is common to encounter texts that show very strong content while their grammatical and textual competence lags far behind.

A better choice of scoring method for such students might be primary-trait scoring, where a single trait is defined and the writer's performance on that trait carefully described. When a student is given several primary-trait tasks, the several scores that result can provide a rich diagnostic picture of where that student's strengths and weaknesses lie, information that is very useful to teachers and administrators as well as to the students themselves. But primary-trait assessments are expensive and so have generally been used only in extremely large-scale assessments such as the National Assessment of Educational Progress.

In my view, the best option for assessing ESL writing and the writing of all minority students is the multiple-trait method. A multiple-trait assessment instrument builds up a scoring guide that permits a reader to respond to the salient features of the writing whether they are all at the same quality level or not. The essential characteristics of the multiple-trait instrument are its grounding in judgments and discussions of essays in the context where decisions will be made; the selection of salient features of writing quality within that context, which selection in turn focuses the reader's attention on contextually salient features in future assessments; and the provision of scores on each of these features for use in such decision making as acceptance into a program or placement within a program or for use in the instructor's diagnosis of specific writing problems. When proponents of holistic scoring object to methods that give separate scores for various traits in an essay, they are usually reacting against the analytic scoring used in the 1960s and 1970s, which focused on relatively trivial features of text (grammar, spelling, handwriting) and which did indeed reduce writing to an activity apparently composed of countable units strung together—hence the label "analytic," which came to have a derogatory connotation in writing assessment. What I am calling multiple-trait procedures are quite different from the old analytic scoring (Hamp-Lyons, "Scoring Procedures"). Measures very like multiple-trait assessment have been used for over a decade now to assess the writing of second-language English writers (see Jacobs, Zinkgraf, Wormuth, Hartfiel, and Hughey; Weir; Purves; Hamp-Lyons, *Assessment Guide*). Like primary-trait scoring, a multiple-trait procedure is an approach to the whole writing assessment process, not only to the scoring. Reader training is the norm in all writing assessment these days, but a multiple-trait procedure goes beyond other procedures by including reader involvement as a vital component in instrument development. Like primary-trait instruments, multiple-trait instruments are grounded in the context of their use; they are therefore developed on-site for a specific purpose, for a specific group of writers, and with the involvement of the readers who will make judgments in that context. Each is also developed as a response to actual writing on a single, carefully specified topic type. Containing no content specifications, they can be applied to a range of prompts, as long as those prompts fulfill the initial design criteria and as long as the context remains essentially unchanged. It is therefore easy for small but committed groups of teachers to use, develop, pilot, and monitor them in the teachers' own context, adding new prompts and making sure that the new prompts pursue the same writing goals as the original prompts. Of course, multiple-trait instruments can be developed that do include content specifications, but the amount of work to develop such instruments and to train readers for their scoring is much greater.

Multiple-trait scoring also helps ensure that scores reflect the salient facets of ESL writing in a balanced way. As we saw above, NNS writing typically contains significantly more language errors than does NS writing, and the danger is that a reader might respond negatively to the large number of grammatical errors found in the second-language text and not reward the strength of ideas and experiences the writer discusses. Holistic scoring obscures a pattern of consistent overemphasis or underemphasis on basic language control, but a multiple-trait instrument, in which language control is a trait to be judged together with other traits found salient in the context, and in which the reader is free to attend to the multidimensionality of ESL writing, is likelier to facilitate a balanced response to the strengths and weaknesses of the writer's text.

All this careful test development and reader training would ultimately go to waste without profile score reporting. This is the reporting of all the separate trait scores rather than, or in some contexts in addition to, a composite score. Scores exist not simply to assign decisions but also to communicate useful information that can be shared with the writers, their academic advisers, and other concerned parties. As I have argued above, detailed information is especially useful for second-language writers. When the writing in any one sample looks similar from different perspectives and has no noticeable peaks or troughs of skill, I call the resulting set of multiple-trait scores a flat profile. Such writing performance may reasonably be expressed as, for example, a single score of 6 on a nine-point scale without significant loss of information. But sometimes—and often with ESL writers, for the reasons discussed above—the writing quality looks different from different perspectives. I call the set of scores that show this unevenness a marked profile. By looking at the score profile, the writer, the class teacher, and the program administrator can make informed decisions about which course offering or other kind of service will most help the individual writer make progress. And when a writer has generally sound writing skills but a weakness in just one area, a single-number score will almost certainly fail to reflect the extremely marked aspect of the writing performance, whereas multiple-trait scores will reveal it. While the overall score may not indicate that the writer needs any special help, program administrators, college counselors, the teacher, and the writer as well can see the unusual pattern and decide whether to take action about it. Second-language users of English are particularly likely to be in this category.

The need to design better contextualized and more informative measures of NNS writing has led to multiple-trait assessments. At the same time, innovations in measurement theory have begun to liberate us from some of the constraints of classical testing practices, which have been problematic in first-language writing assessment but even more so in second-language writing assessment. Instead of classical measures, generalizability theory can be applied to estimate the effect of multiple sources of error. Using g-theory, we can begin to assess the effect of all sources of error rather than express error variance merely as an estimate of interrater reliability, as though the rater were the only source of error. With the development of item response theory and particularly with the recent introduction of multi-faceted Rasch analysis, we can account statistically for the effect of different raters, topics, and other factors and place all students' performances on the same relative metric. These procedures will eventually enable us to identify topics that are especially problematic for NNS writers (or any other special group) within an assessment of a mixed population, raters who are unduly harsh or lenient toward ESL writers, and other kinds of special factors that need to be accommodated. Multiple-trait analysis will be more useful in writing assessment than are the existing differential item functioning (DIF) procedures presently used to attempt to identify test items that are functioning differently for members of specifiable groups (by gender, race, ethnicity), and it will avoid test bias by eliminating such items. These procedures require a large number of existing items to act as criterion measures for making the decisions. In writing assessment, of course, we rarely have large numbers of items that have been administered to comparable populations.

Portfolio Assessment for ESL Writers

Portfolio assessment has become the assessment of choice in many fields, but it has yet to be widely accepted in second-language writing classes. In part I think this is because the influence of language testing on ESL instruction has been much greater than the influence of educational measurement on first-language writing instruction (the ESL community's flagship journal, *TESOL Quarterly*, regularly publishes serious articles on language testing and other quantitative research). In part too I think the lack of acceptance of portfolio assessment relates to the different, more conservative paradigm Santos describes ESL-writing teachers as inhabiting (the first-language writing community's flagship journal, *College Composition and Communication,* where post-modernism is the flavor of the decade, seems quite far from the concerns of most ESL teachers). Whatever the reasons, this relative lack of use of and research on portfolios in the ESL-writing context seems to me a matter for regret.

Portfolios are thought to be especially suitable for use with NNS students because they provide a broader measure of what those students can do and because of the elimination of the timed-writing context, which has long been claimed to be particularly discriminatory against nonnative writers. There is some evidence for this view. When I was at the University of Michigan, we found that after we introduced portfolios, more ESL students tested out of Practicum (the lowest-level mainstream writing class) the first time. There seem to be two reasons for this: first, students have time to revise. They don't have to turn in papers that are full of fossilized errors that pop out when time pressures are on; they can take the time to find and correct their errors, to go to the writing center and get tutorial help with problems of expression, to write in the computer and use spell-checker programs, and so on. These are all strategies that any writer is free to use in normal writing environments but is denied in the setting of a timed impromptu exam. The portfolio method of evaluation is more realistic, and in its realism it appears not to penalize ESL students relative to other students as much as timed writing tests do. A second reason may be that ESL students are encouraged to do more than zip out a quick, short text and work on getting its language correct. They know that papers may come around again and that any paper may be one they choose to put in a portfolio to represent them to outside readers. They can see the paper in layers and work on different layers at different times. It is often the need to focus on competing textual needs simultaneously that overwhelms uncertain writers, NNS or NS, in timed situations. In the portfolio assessment context, ESL writers can be convinced that concentrating on ideas, content, support, text structure, and so on is worthwhile because they don't have to fear that such concentration will be at the cost of attention to technically correct language—which most of them have been conditioned to believe that teachers value most.

Although I have rarely heard the issue discussed, it seems to me that portfolios can reveal the differences between novice and skilled writers. In narrow writing contexts, novice writers always have the excuse of time pressure to account for their single-draft writing approach, for sticking to simple ideas and simple sentences, for editing instead of revising: all those features of novice writing that have been identified by Sondra Perl ("Composing Processes"), Janet Emig (*Composing Processes*), and others in the first language and confirmed by Vivian Zamel, Ann Raimes, and others in the second language. Such an excuse isn't possible in a portfolio assessment. Novice writers, or experienced ESL writers who have chosen novice strategies for their ESL-writing survival, have time to see that their teachers expect more and that those expectations are reasonable given the time available. Thus, when we find a portfolio that displays novice writing skills, we know that the writer is truly there, at that point in growth toward writing excellence, rather than driven there by time and context pressures. For long-term residents even more than for international students the portfolio, once they understand it, provides a motivation, or at least a prod, they haven't had before. These students often need to be motivated; they often have figured out ways to survive in the society, in jobs, and even in most courses in college, with very poor writing skills. But faced with a portfolio assessment, they begin to realize they will have to become skilled, for this assessment mode does not allow them to pump out the same old, barely acceptable, formulaic, extremely short writing that has got them through high school. Teachers' expectations are higher; they dig more deeply; there are no excuses for weak writing, no "Well, it isn't that bad, he is ESL after all." Failure to work, failure to listen to peer input and revise to meet it, failure to put the teacher's comments into practice in the revision, failure to go to the writing center and get special help when the teacher asks—all these failures are not hidden, not washed away in a quick test at the end. Questions such as "Did the writer follow through?" and "Did the writing really get better?" play an important part in deciding pass/fail and/or grades. Improvement, the ability to act on input, can be expected of every writer however weak she or he is at the outset. In this way portfolios are a tougher form of assessment. That many ESL writers do better on portfolio assessment tells me that most of them are indeed motivated and will still learn even after years in this country.

When we began to introduce portfolios at the University of Colorado, Denver, we had a lot of discussion about what type of portfolio we should use. Some teachers wanted everything to be in the portfolio; others wanted a limited set of texts, as at the University of Michigan or the State University of New York, Stony Brook. My experience made me suggest that to read all the writing of another class of students would be too time-consuming, and I convinced my colleagues to go with a limited portfolio, which we called the show portfolio by analogy with an artist's portfolio. But nearly half the teachers require a full portfolio as well, which they use to confer with students on their future writing needs, to discuss grades with them as the semester's end approaches, and sometimes to have them critique their portfolio and propose their own grade. Students are amazed when they see their whole portfolio, all that writing gathered together and presented neatly; they can't believe how much they've accomplished and how far they've moved. Even students who have to be told that they haven't moved far enough to reach the level where they can move on are impressed and encouraged by their visible development, so that they are less unhappy about repeating the level. They are likelier to accept the argument, which we think an honest one, that they are making progress but need more time and more professionally guided, intensive practice and that another semester of such progress will benefit them. Since we introduced portfolios as the exit assessment from our composition classes, issues of ESL writing have repeatedly come up and have had to be centrally addressed. In two major meetings to discuss portfolio criteria and standards, a serious topic of discussion for many teachers was what skills ESL students should show to pass a level, what skills they can be expected to gain in a single semester, and whether expectations for regular students and ESL students should be different. The consensus seemed to be that expectations should be the same but that certain perceptions need to be revised. For example, teachers may respond to fossilized linguistic errors in portfolios as negatively as they do to them in timed essays. When teachers discuss the ESL writers in their own classes in the general portfolio meetings and in the meetings of their portfolio teams, opportunities arise to talk about how significant those ESL writers' problems are in comparison to the level of their ideas, the level of their ability to provide appropriate support for ideas, the level of their macrostructural control, and so on. Useful discussion about portfolios necessitates sharing a good deal of contextual information such as the kinds of assignments given, the writing skills taught and practiced, the role of reading in the course, and the challenges posed as stimulus to writing. Teachers, thinking at length about the special needs and problems of ESL students, strengthen one another's skills in looking at ESL writing. In most composition programs, where there are a small number of ESL students and only maybe three or four ESL-trained teachers out of thirty, that sharing of skills and knowledge is important.

In portfolio assessment, the advantages of multiple-trait methods in traditional writing assessment are taken further: contextualization, teacher involvement, meeting over texts, and opportunities to provide detailed feedback that can inform not only pass-fail and placement decisions but also the availability and variety of support services. Not all the potential advantages of portfolio assessment have yet been implemented: portfolio readings typically result in single-score and single-element decisions rather than in diagnostic information, for example. Some classroom teachers have begun exploring the tremendous possibilities of student self-assessment, which is a logical corollary of portfolio practices (see, e.g., Ballard), but self-assessment has yet to make its way into large-scale assessments.

Sandra Murphy and Barbara Grant (in this volume) describe positivist and constructivist approaches to portfolio assessment, seeing them as oppositional. I consider it essential that we reconcile these apparently unreconcilable views rather than choose one over the other. The portfolio is a concept rather than an entity, and its chameleon nature, although confusing to some, is for me its greatest strength. For each context we need to understand the purpose for which we are using a portfolio and to decide the type of portfolio that best meets the needs of that context.

We must also remember that evidence for the benefits of portfolios for NNS writers is more rational and anecdotal than empirical. There is an urgent need for empirical investigation of how portfolio assessment affects differently the measured writing performances of NNS students and NS students. Using portfolios does not necessarily mean that ESL and other minority populations will suddenly find themselves on a level playing field. Robert Linn, Eva Baker, and Stephen Dunbar see no reason why issues of fairness and bias should not loom as large for performance assessments as for traditional testing; they remind us that "results from the NAEP indicate that the difference in average achievement between Black and White students is of essentially the same size in writing (assessed by open-ended essays) as in reading (assessed primarily, albeit not exclusively, by multiple-choice questions)." Gaps in performance among groups exist, they say, "because of [the influence of] difference in familiarity, exposure, and motivation on the tasks of interest" as well as because of unfair assessments (18). Rebecca Zwick has referred to evidence of bias in high-stakes portfolio assessment. Daniel Koretz has pointed out that scores on portfolios cluster and therefore do not discriminate, obscuring actual differences between strong and weak writers: not only does that lack of discrimination jeopardize classical reliability, it also means that strong and weak writers may receive the same scores. The advantage to weaker writers—among them, perhaps, ESL writers—may entail disadvantaging stronger writers. We must ask ourselves how equitable that would be and also what empirical evidence will be necessary before we know for sure whether portfolios allow readers to see the best of what ESL writers can do or whether portfolios simply depress real differences.

Second-language writing assessment, along with first-language writing assessment, has developed in several exciting ways in the last twenty years. But we still have a long way to go. Beyond the assessment methods themselves, we need better programs for identifying non-international students whose first or dominant language is not English; we need greater acknowledgment at federal, state, and local levels of the existence of these students; and we need funding for their educational support beyond initial language-survival programs, including funding at the college level. We also need, in our training programs for writing teachers, much more attention paid to the special needs of ESL (and, indeed, other minority) students. Above all, we need to remember, and to remind the politicians, that although the decisions we make about testing practices are highly political, a good test is not necessarily good politics. And assessments were never meant to be instruments of social engineering. I believe that those who look to assessments to solve social problems, even relatively benevolent assessments like portfolio assessment, are misguided. Turning to writing tests as the big stick to beat the nation into universal literacy is more than dangerously naive: it is disastrous. We develop improved assessments to better reflect what students are learning, with the minimum intrusion into the teaching-learning miracle. We are still learning how to do that well.

Hong Kong Polytechnic University

NOTE

This paper was written while the author was an associate professor at the University of Colorado, Denver.

Response:
Awareness of Diversity

Marcia Farr

Issues of diversity permeate recent academic discourse, within and beyond this group of chapters and this volume as a whole. The recent focus on diversity comes as university faculties confront the changing demographics in the United States and other traditionally European-dominant nations. In another time and place, this volume's theme—the politics involved in assessing student writing—might not have been proposed at all, or brought to publication, although such issues, like diversity itself, have always existed. What has not existed until recently is the increasingly widespread awareness of diversity and the political implications of dealing with that diversity within the educational domain.

The three chapters to which I respond address various facets of diversity. Sandra Kamusikiri presents an Afrocentric rather than the traditional Eurocentric approach to teaching and assessing the writing of African Americans. This approach is based on respect for the dialectal and cultural differences evidenced in the writing of some African American students. Calling for an attitude among writing teachers and assessors that recognizes difference rather than deficit, Kamusikiri specifies the African origins of many of these linguistic and cultural features. Deborah Holdstein makes a similar argument for the recognition of gender differences that are evidenced in student writing, although unfortunately she does not discuss the complex relation between gender and ethnic identity: What if a writer is both African American and female? Whereas Kamusikiri discusses both grammatical and rhetorical-cultural reflections of difference, Holdstein restricts her discussion to features of women's writing at the level of rhetoric and culture (i.e., "women's culture") and Liz Hamp-Lyons restricts her discussion of nonnative English speakers' writing to grammar. But Holdstein goes beyond arguing for an attitude that recognizes difference: she, like other feminists, calls for profound change in the larger institutional systems in which writing is assessed. Here difference cannot simply be recognized and granted equity. Holdstein challenges the fundamental, and androcentric, assumptions that underlie testing in its entirety in educational institutions. Such a challenge is radical indeed.

Hamp-Lyons treats the issues arising with students who are non-native speakers of English; she correctly points out that the bulk of this population is composed not of international students but of students from non-English-speaking (both resident and citizen) families. Unlike the approaches of the other two essays in this section, Hamp-Lyons's approach is more pragmatic than philosophical, although clearly it too is based on a recognition of difference. Difference, of course, is more easily acknowledged at the level of grammar, especially in cross-linguistic contrasts, than at the level of culture or gender, where difference tends to be expressed in discourse styles and thus is more fluid and less concrete.

Putting aside for the moment a justifiable concern about promoting the acceptance of mediocrity, we will find it useful to consider the implications of promoting the acceptance of ethnic and gender differences in student essays. Most contemporary composition scholars would agree that such differences deserve respect and understanding, even though unfortunately many otherwise liberal academics do in fact and in daily action disagree with this premise. Yet all students, until they learn "school" ways of thinking and using language, call on their accustomed ways of thinking and speaking when they write essays in school, and it simply is not equitable to privilege some ways of thinking and speaking over others. Kamusikiri and Holdstein strongly argue for a broader acceptance of nonprivileged discourse styles, and Kamusikiri and Hamp-Lyons urge us to allow more leeway, at least in initial stages of composing, to nonprivileged grammatical features as well, namely, those characteristic of African American English and of nonnative English use. Although Kamusikiri misunderstands code switching between languages and dialects (it is not carefully planned and consciously controlled; like language use in general, it is patterned, but largely unconsciously), her central recommendation is cogent and convincing: that AAE be assessed only in the final version of a student's essay and that it be assessed not as error or even as dialect interference but as language choice. Such an approach truly undermines the privilege enjoyed by some dialects over others.

Undealt with in these chapters, however, are questions regarding how most teachers and assessors determine which features in student writing, whether of AAE or another nonstandard dialect, are occasioned by language choice and which features are the result of imperfect learning of the written code. Such a judgment is not as simple as it appears and it requires some knowledge of language variation and linguistics. A similar problem is acknowledged by Hamp-Lyons when she points out that scores on nonnative English speakers' portfolios tend to cluster and thus not discriminate between weak and strong writers. Both Kamusikiri and Hamp-Lyons call for increased use of portfolio assessment because it allows more time for revision, which, while important for all writers, is especially important for nonnative and non-standard-dialect speakers. Portfolio assessment, however, may not clarify for the teacher which aspects of standard written English (whether grammatical features or discourse styles) a particular student is having difficulty with.

These concerns raise a thorny issue, which is embedded in relativism: the promotion of cultural and linguistic relativity (whereby no dialect or discourse style is privileged over any other) is based on an impulse to equity, but if everything is relative, on what basis do we judge inequity? Are we simply saying that anything goes? Are we relinquishing important ideals, some of which are based on notions of fairness and equity, and settling for the mediocre mean? I would argue that there is a way out of this apparent dilemma. Opening up assessment—and, more generally, teaching—to increased tolerance of nonmainstream and female ways of knowing, thinking, and using language does not necessarily entail the loss of a style of communal discourse that emphasizes explicit and accessible language and the inclusion of alternative points of view, as in the best of what has been termed essayist literacy. After all, as John Trimbur has pointed out, the historical turn toward "plain style" English discourse that was more broadly accessible was a move toward democracy ("Essayist Literacy").

We don't have to throw out the baby with the bathwater. Just as there often is value in maintaining formal procedures (e.g., decision-making procedures in institutions) when informal ones too easily perpetuate bias and privilege, so there is value in maintaining a public discourse style through which people from diverse backgrounds can learn to communicate clearly and honestly. Such a discourse style, of course, would not be monolithic and without linguistic and cultural variation, especially since so-called minority discourse styles already are influencing and will continue to influence mainstream discourse. Yet an effective public discourse style would not be so metaphorical or full of allusions that it is virtually inaccessible to some groups of people. Such inaccessibility is precisely the criticism by feminists and multiculturalists of much postmodern discourse: just as minorities and women begin to be included in academic discourse, truth in discourse is declared to be uncertain, and some valuable insights from deconstruction and other recent philosophy are written about in such a way, even, as to exclude many of the academic community's newcomers. What, one might ask, is going on here?

Thus I concur with the thrust (although not with all the particularities) of all three of the chapters in this section: We must enlarge our understandings and acceptance of difference. As Johnetta Cole, the president of Spelman College and an anthropologist, said in an address at the American Anthropological Association, we must focus on difference until difference no longer makes a difference. In this focus, however, we must also work to maintain clarity and responsibility in our public discourse, so that honest communication is facilitated, not obscured, and the implicit contradictions and tacit assumptions embedded in public discourse can be brought to the surface for open discussion. Clear, explicit, and accessible public discourse is a goal that may not always be reached, as there are very real cultural and linguistic differences among various groups; I would argue, nevertheless, that it is a goal well worth keeping. Of utmost importance in the reaching of this goal are methods of explicit teaching, as called for by Hamp-Lyons here and by others elsewhere. Precisely because of difference, explicit teaching of an evolving mainstream discourse style is crucial, not instead of the process approach to composition instruction but along with it.

PART V

A Look to the Future

Introduction

What about the future of writing assessment? How do those in the assessment community view the sort of change needed and the proper tactics to achieve that change? The authors in this section offer answers to these questions and in so doing present a range of perspectives, diverse methodologies, and varied problems and solutions. Hunter Breland; Donald Daiker, Jeff Sommers, and Gail Stygall; Richard Larson; and Sandra Murphy and Barbara Grant suggest approaches to writing assessment that have not as yet become established practices. Breland traces the reasons why grading essays by computer has not caught on. Some of the lack of interest in computer-assisted writing assessment he attributes to the conflict between C. P. Snow's "two cultures"—the sciences and the humanities. Is the grading of essays by computer the province of the sciences or of the humanities? Since some standardization, especially in writing mechanics, is a basic part of both writing and writing assessment, Breland asserts, computers are "at least *potentially* better suited to dealing with them than are English teachers." In Breland's view, "a political stance that denies the importance of writing mechanics and resists all forms of technology and science is not good for writing instruction."

Daiker, Sommers, and Stygall focus on the politics and policies of portfolio assessment, which, they say, "is part of a democratizing and egalitarian educational trend." They demonstrate the impact that one type of portfolio assessment, a college-placement program, had on teachers and senior students in high school English classes. "Like the movement from product to process in the composition classroom, the gradual replacement of multiple-choice tests and impromptu writing samples by portfolio assessment" "is a promising sign," representing, "among other things, at least a partial power shift from testing authority to student."

Larson illustrates the ways in which power and the authoritative assertion of values are crucial ingredients in the making of political decisions. Focusing on portfolio assessment in large-scale settings, he asks who should hold the power to compel examination of teacher-nurtured student writings, who should determine what kinds of writing are included in the portfolio, and who should say how these writings are to be viewed. Larson takes us through the ways that using portfolios can disrupt the private relationship between student and teacher and create difficulties among teachers, students, administrators, and people on the governing boards in schools and colleges. He proposes ways to make a constructive linkage between "the power of authority and the beliefs and feelings of teachers."

Murphy and Grant reflect on the growing interest in portfolio assessment and warn that educators may be re-creating more of the same problems that plagued traditional assessment. Like all forms of assessment, portfolios have a social context, and how we assess reveals our awareness of the distribution of power and authority. We may choose to construct a portfolio model that promotes collaborative and contextualized assessment or a positivist one that "leads to standardized, top-down assessments—assessments that erode teachers' authority as professional educators and that fail to provide students with opportunities to take control of their own literacy learning." Murphy and Grant warn against assessment that follows the less flexible, positivist paradigm.

Edward M. White's response to these essays concludes this volume. He looks back on the political questions he raised in his opening essay, now with the perspective of this section and, indeed, the entire volume. Will portfolios or computers or other innovations dramatically affect the politics, policies, and practices of writing assessment, involved as they are with issues of power? Perhaps, but only insofar as new approaches take account of the political issues that lurk just below the surface of assessment.

Computer-Assisted Writing Assessment: The Politics of Science versus the Humanities

Hunter M. Breland

> We will *soon be grading essays by computer, and this develop-*
> *ment* will *have astonishing impact on the educational world.*
>
> Ellis Page

> *The non-scientists have a rooted impression that the scientists*
> *are shallowly optimistic, unaware of man's condition.*
>
> C. P. Snow

Three decades have passed since Ellis Page startled the educational world with the controversial claim that essays could be graded by computer (238). Page, a psychologist, had once been an English teacher; knowing well the staggering burden of work placed on English teachers, he wanted to help. What Page did was show, through correlational analysis, that four human judges of a set of essays seemed indistinguishable from a fifth judge of the essays, a computer. Human judges disagree in their evaluations of written work; the correlational analyses showed that the computer disagreed with the human judges no more than they disagreed among themselves. Since Page's study, the world has been overwhelmed by computers in many areas of work. The word-processing revolution has touched almost every student and office worker, almost every field from architecture to medicine. Professional writers use computers extensively, as do writing students. But for some reason, Page's vision of grading essays by computer has not caught on. Why not?

It is certainly not for lack of trying. Since 1966, other articles have appeared supporting the use of computers in grading essays, some of these by Page himself. In 1995, Page and Nancy Petersen published a paper documenting a blind test of computer grading in which a computer program predicted human judgments of essay quality even better than had been possible in 1966. In 1992, Niki McCurry and Alan Mc-Curry described the successful use of a computer program for evaluating student writing in Alaska. Despite these successes, William Wresch reviewed in 1993 the progress of computer evaluation of essays since 1966 with some skepticism. Wresch concluded: "Computer essay grading actually may be less imminent than it was twenty-five years ago" (57). In another recent review of the use of technology in language assessment, a review whose focus is much broader than the computer grading of essays, Jill Burstein, Lawrence Frase, April Ginther, and Leslie Grant note the potential of technology in language assessment but conclude that the dialogue is only beginning. It is important to emphasize that this dialogue will involve not only scientists, engineers, and computer programmers but also writers, teachers of writing, and other humanists with a less technological bent.

Patrick Finn has observed that a fundamental conviction among some teachers of writing is that "writing is a product of intelligence and creativity and that a computer cannot evaluate this product." Finn suggested that this kind of conviction is "symbolic of a basic struggle between engineers and humanists" (69). C. P. Snow generalized the struggle to that between scientists and nonscientists, "the two cultures," as he called them. Snow, a physicist by training but a writer by vocation, participated in both cultures. He noticed that the two cultures had a "curious distorted image of each other." Between them was a "gulf of mutual incomprehension, lack of understanding, and noncommunication" (4). Moreover, he noted, "intellectuals, particularly literary intellectuals, are natural Luddites" (23). To make any sense out of the thirty-year struggle over computers and writing assessment, it is important to understand who the players are. Do they represent science or the humanities? And in the humanities, what convictions about rules, order, and standardization—all essential to science—are held?

Some of the early confrontations are well represented by two reviews of Page's work that appeared in the fall 1969 issue of *Research in the Teaching of English.* Ken Macrorie's response was particularly negative. Macrorie's opinion was that Page had analyzed student essays written under extreme time pressure and that his results were thus meaningless: "Rating this writing involved making distinctions between papers without distinction. And no one has ever done well at that job" (232). Macrorie clearly saw no potential for computers in writing assessment: "The computer would have to anticipate too much in order to make itself ready to perceive not only the brilliant creative ability of the human mind but simply the hard particulars of uniqueness in every person" (235). I suspect that many English teachers agree with Macrorie. Don't impose any rules or standards on the writer; just let the creative juices flow, and you will be making a great contribution to education. Or just let students work hard (while the teacher does nothing but assign work), and they will become stronger writers in time.

In an accompanying review, Don Coombs took a different view of what Page had done. Coombs, a researcher in communications, cited a report by Page and Dieter Paulus and said:

> Page and Paulus are on the right track; they seem to have isolated a number of indicators of student writing quality which instructors utilize. There is nothing suspect about the approach, since at one level or another indicators are all that we deal with in our lives. Without indicators, we would be swamped with stimuli.   (225)

This statement suggests that in the communications profession there are at least some who are slightly afflicted with scientific values.

In 1971, Henry Slotnick, a scientist, and John Knapp, an English professor, attempted to bridge the two cultures. They described an application of computers to writing assessment that was somewhat different from simple grading (80). They proposed that a student receive a copy of a computer analysis of his or her paper before it is submitted, make whatever corrections seem reasonable, and give the paper to the instructor along with the computer analysis. This is not computer grading, of course; it is merely computer-generated editing advice.

In 1980, Alden Moe concluded:

> The analysis of text by computers has been demonstrated to be both feasible and practical. Computers are readily available and the programs are rapidly improving. The versatility and the efficiency of computers for text analysis should convince educators that computers are enormously useful tools for studying language.
>
> (31)

In 1981, a team of researchers at Bell Laboratories observed:

> Some processes of writing continue to resist analysis, hence we need more research to build sophisticated instructional programs that address not just detection and revision skills, but higher level processes involved in effective writing. Even so, current text analysis programs provide a rich and flexible resource for approaching this task.   (Frase et al. 24)

Lawrence Frase and his colleagues developed a system of computer programs that they called *Writer's Workbench*, a system that found its way into numerous schools but ultimately led to some shaking of heads (among English teachers) about the use of its programs in instruction. In 1989, J. W. Bowyer, an English professor, examined *Writer's Work-*

bench and two additional writing-analysis programs (*RightWriter* and *Grammatik* 3) and concluded: "Clearly, these writing analysis aids do not belong in the repertoire of serious linguists; moreover, composition instructors must recognize the potentially pernicious effects of using the programs as grading instruments" (95). Bowyer's statement suggests how far Page's idea of grading essays by computer had advanced up through 1989—not very far. Other critics such as Margret Hazen (cited in Bowyer 90) reject such programs because the programs do not analyze content and organization. It is a rather high expectation to have of a computer, that it analyze content and organization.

But still other critics make positive statements about these computer programs. Preston Gralla, a senior editor of *PC/Computing*, describes how *Writer's Workbench* is used in English composition courses at Colorado State University. One professor there "feels that the overall quality of his students' writing has improved since they started using *Writer's Workbench*" (156). Guy Pace, a journalist, reviewing a version of *RightWriter* more recent than that examined by Bowyer, proclaims that "Strunk and White never had it so good!" (5). Pace observes that "the value of the program is in what you learn as you work with it and in improving your ability to communicate" (6). Jo Zuppan (cited in Bowyer 90) views computer programs as highly useful in editing.

There are computer programs under development that are more sophisticated than those examined by Bowyer. IBM's *Critique,* for example, "differs from *Writer's Workbench* in that it checks for grammatical errors instead of simply assessing style and diction" (Gralla 146). Houghton Mifflin's *CorrecText* uses artificial intelligence to parse sentences; it knows the difference between *who* and *whom,* flags incorrect uses of adjectives and adverbs, and detects split infinitives and subject-verb disagreement. "In short, using *CorrecText* is a bit like having Edwin Newman look over your shoulder as you write" (Gralla 153). Although some research in text production argues that premature editing damages writing by distracting the writer from ideas, such a program could be helpful once an initial draft has been completed. A program called *WordMAP* has been developed by Eldon Lytle, formerly a professor of linguistics at Brigham Young University, and it is marketed to school systems, colleges, and graduate schools. One graduate school of business has offered *WordMAP* as a service to students, who have paid for its use.

Analyses that Lytle and I have done with *WordMAP* indicate the potential of such systems (Breland and Lytle). In an earlier study, I and others collected writing samples from first-year English composition courses in six colleges (Breland et al.) This data collection is unique because the students sampled, about three hundred, each wrote six different essays during their first semester; all students in all six colleges wrote on the same six topics; and none of the essays were written under extreme time pressure—some were written in the forty-five minutes of class time, and others were take-home assignments that were discussed in draft form with other students and then rewritten. Two of the topics were narrative, two expository, and two persuasive. These essays were each graded three times, each time by a different experienced reader. The sum of all the grades on all the essays was thus a good indication of each student's writing ability (writing ability defined here as skill in performing the kinds of tasks usually required in a first-year college composition course). For the computer analyses using *WordMAP*, a subsample of one of the six essays written by ninety-two students, an expository essay, was keyed into the computer. These ninety-two texts were then analyzed.

WordMAP produced a number of scores, including a count of words written, passive verbs flagged, *to be* verbs flagged, subject-verb disagreements flagged, danglers flagged, spelling errors flagged, fuzzy words flagged, capitalization errors flagged, and punctuation errors flagged. A flag simply indicates the possibility of an error, since even the most sophisticated system cannot tell for certain that an error has occurred. The flag scores were combined to produce grammar, style, structure, and usage scores, which were in turn used to predict the scores assigned to the essays by the human readers. "Predict" does not imply some kind of mystical foretelling; it means only that variables are combined in an equation in a certain way to estimate something else, here, the holistic scores. Good predictors of the readers' scores were the subject-verb-disagreement, dangler, spelling, and word-count scores. Interestingly, scores for passive verbs, *to be* verbs, and punctuation did not help predict the readers' scores on this essay very well at all.

Another analysis was conducted in which the computer-generated scores were combined with scores from three multiple-choice tests: the Test of Standard Written English (TSWE), the English Composition Test (ECT), and the Scholastic Aptitude Test verbal score (SAT-V). These scores had been obtained when the students applied for college, probably a number of months before they wrote the essays. The best predictor of readers' scores was the TSWE, followed by the ECT, SAT-V, and count of words written, in that order. When these multiple-choice scores were combined with the computer-generated scores, a very good prediction of the readers' scores was obtained. The computer-generated scores were substantially more accurate than the estimations obtained when the multiple-choice scores alone were used.

A more significant analysis predicted the sum of all readers' scores on five of the six essays that the students wrote (the scores on the essay that had been analyzed by computer were not included). This sum is essentially an index of the students' writing ability, at least as it was represented by the students' performance in those particular English composition courses studied. Other analyses showed that the sum was a very reliable indicator. The best predictor of this writing-ability index was the sum of three readers' scores on the essay that was withheld from the index, followed closely by the TSWE and ECT scores and less closely by the SAT-V score and the word count. Of the computer-generated scores, the best predictors were, in this order, the spelling-error, subject-verb-disagreement, and dangler flags scores. The passive-verb, *to be*–verb, fuzzy-word, and punctuation scores did not help to predict the writing ability index.

In statistical analysis, predictive effectiveness is evaluated by the multiple-correlation coefficient, R. An R equal to 1.0 indicates perfect predictive effectiveness, and an R of .00 indicates none. In the estimation of writing ability, as defined by the five-essay standard of the Breland and Lytle study, we can use the R value to give a relative indication of the predictive effectiveness of various types of writing assessment. Let us assume that we have a single essay written by a student, we have three experienced readers of essays (English teachers), we have a computer analysis program like *WordMAP*, and we have some multiple-choice test scores (TSWE, ECT, and SAT-V). Which of these devices and in which combination will do the best job of predicting future performance of that student in writing? The accompanying table gives predictive effectiveness in R values.

Predictive Effectiveness of Various Types of Writing Assessment

Predictor(s)	R Value
One teacher	.64
Computer	.66
Two teachers	.72
TSWE and ECT	.73
Three teachers	.74
Two teachers and computer	.75
Two teachers and TSWE	.80
TSWE, ECT, SAT-V, and computer	.82
One teacher, TSWE, ECT, and computer	.84
One teacher, TSWE, ECT, SAT-V, and computer	.85

These results will surprise some people. If an evaluation of a student's writing is made on the basis of one expository essay written during class time and read by only one English teacher, the assessment is not likely to be accurate. In other words, one might just as well use a computer. Having two teachers evaluate the student's essay is better, but even better assessments can be made by combining the teachers' judgments with computer analyses of the essay and with the student's scores on multiple-choice tests of writing skills. The multiple correlations obtained indicate that the computer can contribute to assessment. It can contribute even when only one essay is assessed. The assessment of more student essays might tell a different story, because, unlike teachers, who get tired, computers can analyze as many essays as are available.

None of the above-mentioned analyses suggest that essays can be graded by computer. Grading is a high-stakes event that can affect other important events, such as college admission; accordingly, grading seems an unlikely task for the computer. But computers can help students as well as teachers. They can help students prepare and edit written work, and they can help teachers by providing information about the students' writing that the teachers may have overlooked. Such information, however, needs to be mediated by human judgment. Computers can assist in instruction planning by contributing to the prediction of students' writing abilities; thus they can help determine the numbers and types of teachers and the numbers and types of classrooms that will be needed. Computers can assist in counseling, guidance, and placement of students in courses of instruction. The number of computer programs that have been developed for the purpose of analyzing written work attests to the widespread belief that they are or can be useful.

Will the two cultures of science and the humanities ever come together? Perhaps they already have. There are signs that a rapprochement is occurring at least in some areas. Consider these organizations: the Association for Computers and the Humanities, the Association for Literary and Linguistic Computing, the Consortium for Computers in the Humanities, the Society for Conceptual and Content Analysis by Computer, and the Association for Computational Linguistics. Moreover, these associations regularly invite older, more traditional organizations to participate in their conferences. The American Historical Association, the American Philological Association, the American Philosophical Association, the Linguistic Society of America, and the National Endowment for the Humanities have participated in recent conferences sponsored by the Association for Computers in the Humanities. There is a *Humanities Computing Yearbook,* and the Modern

Language Association has a Committee on Computers and Emerging Technologies. It seems doubtful that C. P. Snow, were he alive today, would call literary intellectuals "natural Luddites." The two cultures appear to be coming together more and more, at least in those fields that have traditionally worked with words. And the computer is what is bringing them together.

Some humanities professionals, however, still fear the order, rules, and standardization that computers, and science more generally, require. These fears have been voiced by English teachers like James Zebroski, who asserts, "I nurture in myself and my students a healthy skepticism toward new advances generally and toward new advances in the technology of literacy specifically" (84). And Beth Daniell writes of rigid pedagogies that "hinder rather than advance the right to literacy" (205). While there is merit in these arguments, there is also a hint of the same sort of reaction that the Cherokee had when Sequoya introduced them to his syllabic writing system: "[T]heir first inclination was to put him to death for dabbling in an evil magic" (Knoblauch 75).

A certain amount of standardization, particularly in writing mechanics, is an essential part of writing and writing assessment. Computers, which have no theoretical problems with such matters, are at least *potentially* better suited to dealing with them than are English teachers. If computers were allowed to handle some of the more menial tasks of writing instruction, teachers would have more freedom to concentrate on the more important aspects. A political stance that denies the importance of writing mechanics and resists all forms of technology and science is not good for writing instruction.

Educational Testing Service

The Pedagogical Implications of a College-Placement Portfolio

Donald A. Daiker, Jeff Sommers, and Gail Stygall

Although college writing portfolios have been variously defined, they tend to share five common characteristics. Most portfolios

- include multiple samples of writing from a number of occasions;
- require a variety of kinds or genres of writing;
- provide opportunities for revision and request evidence of the revision process;
- ask students for their reflections—on their portfolio, on their writing process or history, or on themselves as writers; and
- offer important choices to the writer.

Each of these characteristics carries significant pedagogical implications.

The requirement that a portfolio contain several pieces of writing implies that no single writing sample can adequately measure writing ability, either for a course or for large-scale assessment. The related requirement that the writing be done on different occasions recognizes the truth that writers perform better on some days than on others. The implication here is that because changing physical and psychological factors affect performance, even multiple writing samples, if they are collected at the same time, cannot adequately measure writing ability.

The second characteristic of most portfolios—that several different kinds of writing be included—reflects the widespread belief that writing is a complex, multifaceted activity that cannot be appropriately represented by a single genre: not by exposition, not by argument, not by critical analysis. This requirement implies both that writing competence varies from genre to genre—certainly no surprise to anyone who has read Hemingway's poetry, Keats's plays, or Milton's prose—and that schools should encourage different kinds of writing. To ensure that various genres are included, portfolio programs often specify what is wanted—sometimes in general and sometimes in more restrictive terms: the exit portfolio of State University of New York, Stony Brook, requires an expressive piece or informal essay, an academic essay of any sort, and an academic essay that analyzes another essay; the business writing portfolio of California State University, Fullerton, requires a proposal, a report, a memo, a letter, and a summary. (For a fuller description of these and other portfolio programs, see Belanoff and Dickson.)

Portfolio programs imply strong endorsement of the revision process. Indeed, portfolio assessment has become popular largely because standard testing programs deny opportunities for meaningful revision. Thus most portfolio programs openly encourage students to revise their work at various stages of the composing process. For example, Miami University's placement-portfolio guidelines stipulate that papers revised after being returned by a teacher are acceptable. A further implication of endorsing revision is that writers are encouraged to take constructive criticism from their teachers—and from their classmates —more seriously, since they have the option of using that criticism in revising their work. Thus portfolio assessment invites collaboration between student and teacher as well as among students, both in structured workshops and in less formal contexts, and it implies that there is special educational value in collaboration and community. Finally, portfolio assessment's encouragement of revision helps create an environment in which students are more likely to take risks and try exploratory writing. After all, if they stray too far through experimentation, there's always the chance to begin again.

Portfolios characteristically require a piece of reflective writing, because research has made it increasingly clear that thinking about what we have learned or are learning leads to future learning. The portfolio thus becomes a form of assessment that, unlike the multiple-choice examination or the impromptu essay, itself stimulates learning and in this way models the education process at its best—a process in which assessment is inseparable from learning. The reflective piece usually invites writers to evaluate their own work, either the contents of their portfolio or their development as writers or both, and thus implies the value of self-assessment. Students who evaluate their work gain practice in formulating and applying evaluative criteria, a process that helps them not only to read and respond to the writing of others, both professionals and classmates, more thoughtfully but also to develop their own set of standards for use once they have left school. We need to remind ourselves again and again that we assess students today so that they can assess themselves tomorrow.

The last and perhaps most important characteristic of college writing portfolios is that they offer a series of significant choices. Writers must consider (1) which of their pieces they should submit, a choice that sometimes means deciding whether to use a piece on hand or to compose a new one; (2) how extensively, if at all, they should revise each piece; and (3) when and where they should do their writing and revising. In granting students a large measure of control over their work, in giving them essential ownership of it, portfolio programs treat them as real writers. And when students are treated as writers and given significant choices to make, it follows that they will gain self-confidence both as writers and as persons. They will develop critical thinking and evaluative skills, and they will become more independent and self-reliant. One major implication of writing portfolios is that the opportunity to make choices leads to learning and growth.

There are several other important implications of college writing portfolios. The first is that portfolios encourage sustained thinking and continuing effort. Unlike timed impromptu essays, which reward students who think fast and reach quick, often glib, conclusions, portfolios allow students to think long and deep about an issue. With a course portfolio, students will often have a full fifteen-week semester for thinking and writing; with an admission or placement portfolio, they may have even longer. Whereas students get only one chance with multiple-choice examinations or timed impromptu essays, portfolios allow as many chances as a student wants—and in this way they convey the positive message that continuing effort can lead to improvement.

The emphasis on improvement through continuing effort is not the only implication of portfolio assessment that has direct bearing on classroom instruction. Portfolios also help teachers focus more on texts than on grades: if all texts may be revised, as is generally assumed with portfolio assessment, then all grades before the final submission must be tentative ones. And since most students, when offered the chance, will work to strengthen their papers so as to improve their grade, portfolios encourage students and teachers to be allies rather than antagonists, especially if the portfolios are to be submitted to evaluators other than the teachers.

Finally, portfolios carry two strong implications for evaluation. The first is that it makes sense to evaluate students on the basis of their best work, not their average work. Critics follow the same principle in evaluating professional writers: they judge Melville to be a great writer because of the achievement of *Moby-Dick, The Confidence-Man,* and *Billy Budd*; they do not average these works in with *Typee, Omoo,* and *Timoleon.* The second implication is that portfolios make possible local control of evaluation, since with training and practice teachers at all levels can create a portfolio program and score portfolios reliably. It is no longer necessary to rely on the Educational Testing Service, as one must for the administering and scoring of multiple-choice tests or essay examinations.

These are, at least in theory, some of the broader pedagogical implications of college writing portfolios. In the paragraphs that follow we explore the effects of one kind of portfolio assessment—in a college-placement program—on a limited audience: teachers and senior students in high school English classes.

Portfolio Effects on High School Writing Programs

The Miami University Portfolio Writing Program, begun in 1990, encourages entering students to submit a collection of their best high school writing in order to earn college credit and advanced placement in composition. Students are asked to include four pieces of writing in their portfolio: a reflective letter; a story or a description; an explanatory, exploratory, or persuasive essay; and a response to a written text. To ascertain the implications of Miami's portfolio program for high school instruction, we asked five high school English teachers to keep logs of their teaching activities during the first year and a half of the Miami University Portfolio Writing Program. We asked them to record any effects of Miami's portfolio program on their teaching and on their students' behavior and attitudes. Some teachers asked their students to evaluate the portfolio program and included students' responses in the log. In addition, we conducted a forty-five-minute videotaped interview with each of the teachers. Most questions asked during the interview focused on the effect a college writing portfolio has on high school teaching and learning. All five participating teachers teach senior English classes at high schools that each year send at least several students to Miami University. The teachers are Marilyn Elzey, of Talawanda High School in Oxford; D. J. Hammond, of Madeira High School in Cincinnati; John Kuehn, of Fairmont High School in Kettering; Teri Lee Phillips, of Mount Healthy High School in Cincinnati; and Doris Riddle, of Norwood High School in Cincinnati.

Teacher interviews, teacher logs, and student testimony included in the logs reveal how warmly students welcome the opportunity portfolios provide to submit several different kinds of writing composed on different occasions and how decisively they reject the impromptu, one-sitting, critical-analysis model of the advanced placement (AP) program of the Educational Testing Service. One of Kuehn's students, Stacy Jarrett, wrote that her world "bloomed" when she encountered the portfolio system.

> Portfolios gave me a chance to spread out. I was able to write about what I wanted when I wanted and revise and edit for the entire time. Some days you just can't write. This gave me a chance to collect ideas for a long period of time, reevaluate my writing on a daily or weekly basis. Portfolios have tremendously increased my writing ability and reinforced the idea that writing is a process and takes time, effort, and a great deal of work (blood, sweat, and tears work too!).

Kuehn's student Steve Mallorca summarized the strengths of portfolios in relation to timed, impromptu testing with the comment "Instead of rating the skills of a student's work in three hours (like the AP test), it [portfolio assessment] rates a student's lifework." Steve recognized that a portfolio-placement program, by requiring samples written at different times, directly challenges the validity of the nation's most venerable college placement test. The Educational Testing Service recommends levels of college placement based on its evaluations of three essays, all written at a single sitting and none evaluated by more than a single reader.

A clear implication of this reception of a portfolio-placement program, then, is that participating students—and teachers—are growing increasingly skeptical that a one-shot, timed essay written on a surprise topic adequately measures writing competence. A second implication is that high school teachers feel challenged to assign different kinds of writing for their students. A third implication is that high school students are coming more and more to practice revision and to believe in its value. Kuehn reported in his teacher's log that a student of his "was amazed to find that one of her pieces had gone through five drafts, each one heavily rescribbled. She said that before this year it was one draft and a few changes and a clean copy." Several of Phillips's senior students asked if they could revise a piece of writing from their junior year to include in their semester's work and in Miami's portfolio. One major reason portfolios help students value revision, according to Hammond's student Brandy Burns, is that portfolios "show how our writings have improved from draft to draft. They motivate us to do the best we can on our papers."

Teaching Revision

In part because portfolios demonstrate that students like Brandy and Stacy are able to dramatically improve their writing through revision, teachers find themselves more motivated than ever before to spend classroom time on the teaching of revision. In an early entry in her log, Elzey noted this change:

> When I think about it, I am much more conscientious about making sure kids know how to *revise.* If this portfolio thing is going to work, kids have got to learn how to do more revising on their own! I'd like to have one of our English department meetings dedicated to just that—what do other teachers do to get their kids to revise!?

Midway through the term, Elzey decided to ask her students to freewrite for ten minutes on how they went about revising a paper before submitting it. The results, she explained, were "discouraging."

> Most kids said they are so glad to get something "done" that they don't have the time or don't want to have the time to revise. It is boring to them!! A few people said they would do it, but they didn't know how. Ah ha! Confirms what I always thought—we've never really taught these kids how to revise.

Elzey's end-of-the-quarter log entry makes clear that she had hit on another successful strategy for teaching revision: "I've decided the key (one of them) is to spend more time teaching kids revision—showing them the differences between different versions." Elzey also noted that one requirement for next year's seniors would be to teach a junior how to revise one of the junior's papers.

Kuehn suggested in his log that because portfolios encourage teachers to emphasize the process of revising, of moving a piece of writing from one stage to another, they help students not only to grow as writers but also to see their own growth.

> For me, the key to our success is that these kids come in with so little knowledge of their own writing, of organizing their work, of having others read it and offer critiques, even ignorant of very elementary editing skills—that as they learn the processes and learn to work together and learn from Strunk and White and Kuehn up to a hundred editing strategies—they put writing and conferencing

and revising and editing together—and over a period of 2–3–4 weeks, they *see* the growth, something they have rarely if ever seen before.

If the process of revising pieces for their portfolio enables students to see that they have grown as writers, the reflective essay invites them to consider not only the ways they have grown but the reasons for their growth. Typically, the reflective essay allows students to move in one of several related directions: to assess the strengths and weaknesses of their portfolio; to explain the key choices they made in assembling their portfolio; to contrast their most successful and least successful piece; to describe their writing process, either in general terms or for one specific portfolio piece; to discuss their evolution as writers or the place of writing in their life; or to formulate their writing goals for the future. In part inspired by Miami University's requirement of a reflective letter, Phillips decided that one of her goals was

> to promote letter writing as a valid form of communication. Letters allow students to reflect upon experience and to express themselves honestly; but, unfortunately, teachers often dissuade student letter writing, seeing the exchange of letters as nothing more than classroom disruption. Therefore, today I asked students to write their first "Dear Ms. Phillips letter," anonymously if they preferred, to tell me how they are faring in/liking/disliking English class (and school in general) this year. I collected these letters and shared my letter to them at the end of the bell.

This reflective-writing assignment proved so successful that Phillips began starting each quarter by handing out portfolios and asking students to look over pieces they had written the previous quarter.

> I then asked them to write a "Dear Ms. Phillips" letter in which they discuss their writing: the types of pieces they had written, which pieces they feel were successful and why, and which pieces they feel need further revision and how they plan to revise them. I also asked them to assess their writing growth last quarter and to set writing goals this quarter. They might consider, in addition, the process used in creating any or all of their pieces.

What is common to reflective writing, regardless of which topic students choose, is self-assessment: students examine their writing products, their writing process, or their writing history to find patterns of development and success. Kuehn wrote in his log:

> The portfolio in general and the reflective piece in particular make it possible, actually inevitable, that kids grow as writers and see themselves grow. They may not have a grip on a great draft, but they all know a rough draft is a long way from a polished piece, and they know how to get from rough to polished a whole lot better.

Self-Assessment and Reflective Writing

The self-assessment integral to reflective writing is built into the portfolio process itself. At Mount Healthy High School, for example, students in consultation with Phillips or another teacher select a piece of writing each quarter for inclusion in their permanent portfolio: deciding which piece to include obviously involves self-assessment. And, as Hammond noted in her log, there is a close connection between self-assessment and critical thinking.

> One of the main appeals of portfolio assessment seems to me to be the amount of sustained thought it requires. Done properly, students spend a year thinking about the pieces in their folder, deciding which pieces to revise and which to include in the final portfolio. Certainly this evaluation would call for some critical-thinking skills on the part of the kids. Which pieces are my favorites? Which are the "best"? Are those pieces which are my favorite most likely to appeal to an "unknown" audience of graders? That reflection seems an enormously valuable learning technique.

Hammond's observations echo the findings of Thomas L. Hilgers, whose research suggests that self-assessment is "the cornerstone upon which rest the successful writer's composing skills. This is true whatever the age of the writer and whatever the writer's definition of success" (36).

Each of the twin processes of reflection and self-assessment depends on choice: the portfolio writer's freedom to make key decisions before, during, and after writing. Kuehn believes that choice is the reason so many of his students are drawn toward portfolios. And according to Kuehn's students themselves, choice is the crucial element in portfolios. "I like it," Brian Damewood wrote. "The portfolio system gives me the freedom to work on up to three topics at a time rather than concentrating on one paper or topic. I'm finding that I don't have the burnout or mental block while writing that I used to experience." Kuehn said in his interview that portfolios influenced his class not only by giving students more choices but also by allowing him to offer more student choices and options.

It was partly because students welcomed the opportunity for choice that Kuehn judged his classroom use of portfolios an extraordinary success and a major source of the "triumphant feelings" he experienced during the term. "Using portfolios has affected my role dramatically, positively," he wrote in his log. "I am writing coach 95% of the time, evaluator only a tad. I like that." Similarly, Miami University's portfolio writing program helped change Hammond's role in the classroom and her relationship to her students. She noted in her log that college portfolios encourage conferencing between students and teachers. "Of course, students can compile a portfolio on their own, but there is that opportunity for really meaningful dialogue." Even more important, according to Hammond, is that portfolios enable teachers to become partners with their students rather than adversaries.

Riddle reported in her log that portfolios also had a salutary effect on her relationships with her students. She wrote:

> We became closer, much, much closer. I'm talking in terms of relating as writers primarily, rather than so much as teacher-pupil. And they were, I think, less bothered by comments than they might have been. Students often tend to be defensive regarding their writing and I think they were less defensive, much more open.

Did portfolios help students write better? This is a more complex question.[1] Kuehn and Phillips saw clear signs of improvement. Kuehn was especially impressed by the clear presence of voice in his students' portfolios. "In 80 to 90% of the portfolios I read, I needed no name to tell me the author. You talk about VOICE!" Phillips became "absolutely, absolutely" convinced that the portfolio program helped her students improve as writers. She explained why in her interview.

> Because I think they're more willing to keep revising, to keep *adding*, and adding more than editing. I mean, editing is not the biggest deal. I think they're willing to expand and explain and add descriptive details and *examples* to illustrate their points. And that's, that's the biggest problem with writers—getting enough descriptive details, illustrative examples. You know, show me; don't just tell me about it. And I think the fact that they have someone else out there to impress has caused them to become better revisers, better editors.

Improved Student Attitudes

Even clearer to the participating teachers was the effect of portfolios on student attitudes. All five teachers reported that the portfolio program helped students develop positive attitudes toward writing in general and toward their own writing in particular. Hammond believes it is the real audience provided by portfolios that encourages students to re-value their own work. She said:

> The notion of a "real" audience is a powerful one. So what am I, chopped liver, the old joke goes. But it's true. When Miami University is willing to give college credit for papers written in high school, those papers are suddenly raised from the status of another dumb assignment to something valuable since somebody else values it. Interestingly, I find this true even for students not planning on attending Miami University. Because you value high school writing, they value high school writing.

The other teachers agreed that working on papers that may be included in a college portfolio helps students take a more serious and responsible attitude toward their writing. Riddle was convinced that the portfolio program made her students more conscientious about revising. Elzey said in her interview that her students, like Riddle's, asked her more questions about writing than ever before, a sure sign of increased interest, and that they were "much more serious, much more conscientious, spending more time in revision." They realized, Elzey said, that "there was more of a purpose for what they were doing."

It seems likely that students' conscientiousness increased as students were given added responsibility. Kuehn said that one of the major effects of the portfolio program was that it "turned responsibility more toward the student to think, and to write, and to use her time well." Elzey reported that using portfolios meant that she "did a lot more stressing than ever before of students' being more responsible for the work they submitted." And it appears that assuming more responsibility for their work helped students gain in confidence. Another obvious explanation for their confidence is that a college portfolio program tells them that their work matters, that it counts. Hammond said in her interview that "the portfolio program tells students that high school writing is important. I mean, I tell them, but they don't necessarily believe me all the time. I don't know why. Portfolios reinforce that idea of importance: this isn't simply a paper you are doing for me."

Some of the major pedagogical implications of a college writing portfolio program for high school teaching and learning, then, appear to be skepticism on the part of students and teachers alike that a one-shot, impromptu writing examination is a valid measure of writing competence; teacher willingness to assign and accept more different kinds of writing; the value of increased instruction in revision by teachers and increased practice of revision by students; the value of more attention to self-assessment through various forms of reflective writing; the desirability of more choices for student writers before, during, and after writing; the likelihood of a redefined role for teachers, with new emphasis on the teacher as mentor or coach rather than as evaluator; and the likelihood of heightened student motivation and self-confidence. Significantly, the five teachers in our study ultimately decided to use portfolio assessment in their classrooms. Hammond wrote in her log, "The advantage of portfolios is that they transform the institution, not just dance on its edges."

The Politics of Portfolios: Gender

Miami University's portfolio writing program has proved particularly attractive to female students. In each of the program's first three years, significantly more entering women than men chose to submit a portfolio to earn college credit and advanced placement. Of a total 1,111 portfolios received, 739, or 66.5% of them, were submitted by women. Equally important, women had a significantly higher success rate than men in two of the program's first three years. The combined result of more submissions and higher success rate is that seven out of every ten students to earn credit or advanced placement are women. (See table.)

By looking at selected reflective letters, we can begin to understand why portfolios attract more women than men and why portfolios submitted by women tend to receive higher scores. Portfolios provide a sense not merely of the student's writing—conceived as a set of definable, discrete, and reified skills—but also of the student as a writer. That is, portfolios invite students to present a more holistic, complex view of their writing, their reading, and themselves, and it seems that women are far more likely to welcome that invitation than are men (Black). Women's and men's reflective letters differ significantly and in ways that suggest both why women feel especially comfortable with portfolio assessment and why they score so well.

Reflective letters written by women show that they see their writing

Gender Differences in Portfolio Submissions and Success Rates

Year		Women	Men
1990			
Portfolios submitted	277	175 (63.2%)	102 (36.8%)
Portfolios earning credit	121	83 (69.1%)	38 (30.9%)
Success rate	42.6%	48.1%	37.4%
1991			
Portfolios submitted	369	253 (68.6%)	116 (31.4%)
Portfolios earning credit	164	125 (76.4%)	39 (23.6%)
Success rate	44.4%	49.4%	33.6%
1992			
Portfolios submitted	465	311 (66.9%)	154 (33.1%)
Portfolios earning credit	211	138 (65.4%)	73 (34.6%)
Success rate	45.4%	44.3%	47.3%
Totals			
Portfolios submitted	1,111	739 (66.5%)	372 (33.5%)
Portfolios earning credit	496	346 (69.9%)	150 (30.1%)
Success rate	44.6%	46.8%	40.3%

in more personal terms than men do. Women are more likely than men to use writing both as therapy and for sharing joy and happiness. Because women see their writing more closely related to their selves, they are more likely to fear criticism of their writing, to take it personally, and to be hurt by it. And although in their reflective letters men and women both identify themselves as writers, women more often than men depict themselves as writers: they show themselves in the act of confronting the empty page or working obsessively through the night. Finally, women more often than men say that they write from choice, and they list the forms their writing takes—journals, diaries, notes, poetry, fiction—more frequently than men do. Not only do more women than men assert that writing is important in their life, but they also illustrate its importance more often.

Since women perceive a closer connection between writing and the self than men do, it follows that they respond more positively than men to an assessment program that allows them to present their writing in a personal and holistic setting. It also follows that they welcome the opportunity for writing a reflective letter whose stated purpose is to give readers a clearer understanding of who they are as writers and as persons. And since the Miami University scoring guide characterizes an excellent portfolio as one in which there is "a close connection between the writer's sense of self and the writing" (Daiker et al., 1992: 112), it is understandable why women's portfolios earn credit more often than men's do.

According to Edward M. White (*Teaching* [1st ed.] 10–17), there has been from our national beginnings an ideological conflict between two views of why we teach writing in the schools. The first view holds that the central purpose of writing instruction is to socialize and civilize students; to help introduce them to the accepted truths, history, myths, and manners of their culture; and to encourage them to conform to societal and scholastic rules and conventions. The second view holds that the major reason for teaching writing is not to socialize but to individualize: not to teach students to adhere to rules and conventions but to encourage them to question and examine rules and conventions; not to teach students to conform to what others have thought but to encourage them to think for themselves.

Of course, virtually every writing teacher, every teaching strategy, and every assessment program combine in varying degrees the socializing and individualizing views of writing instruction. But it seems clear that college portfolio-placement programs and high school portfolio programs ally themselves much more closely with the individualizing view. Portfolio programs encourage students to think for themselves in all sorts of ways: in selecting their topics for writing; in choosing which pieces to include in their portfolio; in deciding how, how much, and when to revise; in choosing which suggestions from teachers and fellow students to follow and which to ignore; and in determining whether to focus their reflective piece on their writing products, their writing process, or their writing history. The reflective piece itself is clearly linked to writing as an individualizing force, since it asks students to convey a sense of who they are, of their unique identity. Moreover, many portfolio programs either state or imply that creativity rather than conventionality will be rewarded. In its portfolio brochure Miami University announces, "Students will be rewarded for originality and variety so long as the guidelines for the four pieces of writing are observed" (*Miami* 6). Portfolio proponents accept White's assertion that "if the principal rule for socialization is to perform conventionally, the overriding motivation for good writing is to think for oneself" (*Teaching* [1st ed.] 13–14).

Like the movement from product to process in the composition classroom, the gradual replacement of multiple-choice tests and impromptu writing samples by portfolio assessment represents, among other things, at least a partial power shift from testing authority to student. It is part of a democratizing and egalitarian educational trend that is a promising sign as we turn away from the age of Reagan and Bush.

Miami University, Oxford

NOTES

For support in conducting the research that made this article possible, we thank the Fund for the Improvement of Postsecondary Education, United States Department of Education. And for their cooperation, insights, and friendship, we are grateful to five wonderful high school teachers: Marilyn Elzey, of Talawanda High School, Oxford; D. J. Hammond, of Madeira High School, Cincinnati; John Kuehn, of Fairmont High School, Kettering; Teri Lee Phillips, of Mount Healthy High School, Cincinnati; and Doris Riddle, of Norwood High School, Cincinnati.

[1]For indications of the quality of writing inspired by the Miami University Portfolio Writing Program, see the six volumes of *The Best of Miami's Portfolios*, for the years 1990–95. For free copies of any of these volumes, please write to Donald Daiker, Dept. of English, Miami Univ., Oxford, OH 45056.

Portfolios in the Assessment of Writing: A Political Perspective

Richard L. Larson

One might well ask, Why an essay on the politics of such a popular practice as gathering and reading portfolios of students' work for assessment? Mainly because using portfolios for assessment can bring distinct difficulties into the interpersonal relationships among teachers, students, administrators, and members of the governing boards in schools and colleges.

We can begin by recognizing that the use of tests for the large-scale assessment of writing ability, whether the instruments be multiple-choice or essay or a combination of the two, is a comparatively impersonal process. Except of course for tests constructed by an individual teacher for an individual class or classes, tests of writing are administered in a nonpersonalized context. The test makers are probably not known to the students, and they construct the tests usually without any reference to the work of individual classes in writing. The persons who preside at the testing sessions may well not include the students' teachers. The persons who score the tests—by machine or in large-scale, controlled essay readings—are typically not the students' teachers; if they are, they are not acting in that role. Scores are reported impersonally—on a computerized note, on a list posted outside a departmental office, or through an office for student advisement. Frightening and formidable for students and worrisome to teachers (who have a stake in seeing their students perform well), such tests of writing usually do not look significantly into the close, day-to-day working relationships of students and teachers. In preparing for such tests, students and teachers alike often confront a faceless educational bureaucracy, a system operated by anonymous authorities at some distance from them.

When portfolios are used as instruments—or, more properly, as artifacts—for assessment, quite the opposite is usually true. Portfolios usually bring together writings that students have produced not at a special testing session but over time and usually in response to the specific tutelage of one or more teachers. Furthermore, as teachers increasingly collaborate with students in the process of composing, the writings in the students' portfolios may come into final form with the teachers' active help. The objects being assessed are therefore often the products of an interchange between teacher and student; they are, one might say, the written displays of the student's learning process and of the teacher's teaching process as well. The portfolio, in other words, is not simply a gathering of a student's performances; it is also a part of the record of a teacher's performance, especially if annotated early drafts of the student's writings are included. To use a portfolio as an object of assessment, then, is almost to eavesdrop on the discussions, the dialogue, between teacher and student—much as one might eavesdrop on the conversations between attorney and client. To do so seems, in some respects, like an invasion of privacy—an invasion of the teacher's classroom—because the student's performance is not given in the anonymity of a room full of fellow students giving similar performances; it is a performance given in the comparative intimacy of a one-on-one conversation.

The political implications of such an assessment procedure, therefore, are strikingly different from those of large-scale (or even small-scale) testing. When I use the word *political* here, I have in mind the relationships between the people who wield power in a given setting—those who have, or have asserted, authority over what happens in that setting—and the people whose behavior is directed or influenced by the people in power. For those directed, the question is whether their willing consent has been obtained or whether they must act as directed regardless of whether they agree with what is directed. Power is often wielded in accordance with some sort of governance document, but it is equally often wielded informally, by those who through a process of acquiring or asserting influence have come to control events. In the use of portfolios for assessment, the central questions of politics apply to sensitive personal relationships: Who holds the power—the power to compel examination of the carefully nurtured student writings and to say how those writings should be viewed—and where does that power come from? Who controls the processes of judging the writings? Who establishes the bases for deciding the value of students' work, and who has authority to decide what actions will occur as a result of those judgments? At what point, if ever, do those in control obtain, or care about, the consent of those whose private professional relationships are being scrutinized? From the perspective of these questions my essay looks at the use of portfolios for assessment of writing and offers advice to those who use them. It focuses on ways to make a bridge between the power of authority and the beliefs and feelings of teachers, so that the behavior of those teachers in portfolio assessment will be fully voluntary and not grudging or surly or simply resistant.

Such political questions usually do not arise when portfolios are employed by individuals as a technique for teaching, as a kind of specialized writing assignment or sequence of assignments. (I pass over the question of the political relationships between teacher and students.) The teacher asks the students to write on an assigned subject or on a subject of their choosing; the students, dutifully playing their role as students, draft and revise, often—if the teacher encourages them to respond to one another's work (not yet a seriously disputed activity)—with the advice of classmates. The teacher may comment on the students' work and may even give evaluations. The students retain their papers, may revise them further later on, and compile them in folders or binders with other papers written earlier or later, also quite possibly with notes, outlines, and earlier drafts. Students are often encouraged to comment in writing, as time passes, on their papers and on their overall progress and perhaps to exchange portfolios to help their fellows track their progress or decide which writings are most effective. To earn a final grade at the end of the semester, they may select the writings they think best display their accomplishments, resubmitting them often with their own written evaluations. The teacher determines the grade, or perhaps occasionally fellow students determine it. The writers and the teacher know each other well; the processes are collegial, often comfortable, and private. It is when this privacy is compromised that political disturbances erupt. This essay explores such potential disturbances.

There is no question that portfolios, just as they can be an effective procedure for instruction, can also be a valuable tool for assessment, especially when the assessment is principally a private taking of inventory of students' abilities and accomplishments—a taking of inventory within the confines of the writing class, perhaps with the agreed-on participation of some students and teachers from outside the class. (A former staff member of the American Association for Higher Education highlights the origin of the term *assessment* in the Latin *ad-* plus *sedere* 'to sit near'; a person doing the assessment almost literally sits beside the learner and observes the learner's strengths and weaknesses as a writer.) Portfolios can be full compilations of students' work. If the teacher requests and the students agree, portfolios can include, besides drafts and revisions of principal papers, the notes that preceded those papers, other documents such as journal entries produced during the writing course, and varieties of other materials, such as those enumerated by Maria Valeri-Gold, James Olson, and Mary Deming. They can even include, as my colleague Judith Entes has suggested, records of consultations between student and instructor and records of group discussions in class.

If we view assessment as a private taking of inventory (even assuming that a summary statement of what the inventory shows will be made part of the students' record), we can see that portfolios allow teachers to gather complex and instructive information about students' progress (or lack of it). The large number of writings in a portfolio may be arranged chronologically or collaterally across courses and subjects of study or both. (A current staff member of the American Association for Higher Education compares such a portfolio to a motion picture of a student's abilities, in contrast to the snapshot obtained from a single, time-limited test of those abilities.) Teachers can see the markers that show students' progress in the various activities included in writing; they can see, for example, if students write with greater insight, force, and clarity about history or social science than about the sciences or the humanities. Teachers recognize the operation of important cognitive processes and see the results of that cluster of evaluative acts we call critical thinking. Teachers tell when students are developing a productive way of going about composing or are constrained by counterproductive habits. In portfolio assessment, teachers often ask students to evaluate their writing (Murphy and Smith, "Talking"). Such self-evaluations become the bases for student-teacher consultations, which help students verbalize the qualities they think their writing displays. Such verbalization in turn helps them develop ways of reading, of judging, their own writing—and thus they learn how to strengthen it through revision. If strengthening one's ability to write is partly a process of learning to read one's writing, then portfolios contribute mightily to students' learning by helping them assess their own work.

When students make comparisons among several pieces of their writing while the pieces are directly before them and the teacher, they come to see what in their writing works well and what works less well. In the discussions of these comparisons and of criteria for judging different kinds of writing, students may even influence the teacher's evaluation of their work. They are, in short, contributing to the teacher's "official" assessment of their writing. Such an assessment is therefore collaborative or consultative; judgments are reached, but the emphasis of the process is on describing, not on categorizing or ranking (Elbow, "Ranking"), even if some sort of grade emerges.

These procedures for using portfolios in assessment are usually initiated by the teacher. They may also be negotiated by a group of teachers (for instance, members of a department) working with a common purpose and by consensus—indeed, in the same spirit evoked when the portfolios are developed by students and discussed with teachers. This spirit was shown by the writing teachers at the State University of New York, Stony Brook; it is described by Peter Elbow and Pat Belanoff in their essays on the use of portfolios in that writing program. This spirit also evolved among the teaching staff at the University of Cincinnati (Roemer, Schultz, and Durst). Concurrence among participants is essential. As Elbow and Belanoff and the teachers at Cincinnati amply demonstrate, using portfolios even for local assessment—within a course or a program—changes teachers' outlooks: the discussion that leads to agreement on the content of portfolios and on how they should be read can change teachers' ways of viewing themselves, their roles, and writing. But teachers must actively want, or at least be willing, to put those changes into practice.

That willingness cannot be taken for granted, even among the volunteer members of a collaborative group. In a project conducted a few years ago in cooperation with the Educational Testing Service—a project I had the opportunity to observe closely—leaders of the Institute for Literacy Studies at Lehman College, City University of New York, elected to use portfolios to interpret the progress of seventh- and eighth-grade student writers in an extramurally funded teacher development activity known as the Middle Schools Writing and Learning Project. (The funding agency wanted a systematic evaluation before it considered whether to renew funding.) I observed many activities of the project and participated in meetings of teachers and in meetings of project leaders and ETS staff. The attention given during the project to the guidelines for the makeup of students' portfolios and to the portfolios themselves as sources of information about students' progress rapidly came to affect the classroom work of participating teachers, the assignments they gave to students, and their ways of handling students' writing. One result was a substantial increase in the teachers' workload. As the assessment project developed, not all the participating teachers, it appeared, were ready to expend the extra effort required, though they had joined the project voluntarily, even willingly, and the project leaders had taken pains to consider the feelings and the energies of all. The project approached the line between willing involvement and resigned acquiescence of its participants. Though the project dealt with teachers and writings in the middle schools, I see a parallel between what happened in it and what may happen when leaders of college programs attempt to introduce portfolios into the assessment of college writing and into writing instruction.

I have suggested that using portfolios for assessment, particularly for assessment as the taking of inventory to strengthen teaching and enhance students' learning, can be relatively unproblematic if faculty members are consenting participants: if they buy into the goals and values of the project and are willing to work collegially. But what of the tougher political issues of authority and consent? What happens, for instance, if the decision to use portfolios is not the teachers' decision? In the Lehman College project, leaders of a staff development program decided, at the urging of an outside agency, to use portfolios as a tool to assess that program. And what happens when the decision virtually requires, as we have seen that it can, that teachers make major changes in their teaching style? To look further along in the scenario, what happens if the ways of reading portfolios ("scoring" may be the word here) are not the teachers' decisions? What happens if the people who use the scores or judgments based on the students' compilations, those judging the judgments, are not people the teachers trust? What happens if reporting the results serves a purpose other than helping individual students progress? What happens, that is, if the introduction of portfolios is legislated and the ways they are employed and scored are mandated or heavily influenced from outside the classroom? What happens if an unwilling majority, or even an unwilling minority, is simply directed to use portfolios or if the recorded results of the readings are taken from teachers' hands, for use by school authorities or project leaders? If faculty members are not allowed to make their own choices and consensus is replaced by legislation, the use of portfolios becomes acutely, sometimes painfully, political. When authority directs the day-to-day activities of the individual teacher in the classroom, the teacher's autonomy is compromised. In such a situation, the potentially effective use of portfolios for teaching and for finely nuanced formative evaluation in the classroom may be brushed aside for the convenience of those who demand assessment. The remainder of this essay addresses these questions.

My many conversations with teachers in secondary schools and in colleges highlight the issues that arise when the use of portfolios is not by the choice of all or most teachers but is imposed as an approach to assessment or to teaching by people outside the classroom. These issues become particularly acute when portfolios are introduced primarily as a means for assessing students systematically, at arm's length, rather than for judging students' work as part of the process of instruction. When a school administrator or a college department chair asks teachers to collect portfolios of students' work as a part of the teaching process, teachers who are not convinced of the value of portfolios may complain (as many have complained to me) that eliciting, collecting, handling, judging, and even storing portfolios add a great deal of work to their load, besides threatening teachers' authority over the management of their professional time. Teachers convinced of the value of portfolios may resent the imposition but grudgingly agree to accept the extra work; others may simply resist or comply in a superficial, half-hearted way that reduces the value of the assessment. The literature on uses of portfolios amounts mostly to declarations of preference by some teachers, reports of teachers' experiences, and informed recommendations from teachers and professional leaders. But thus far that literature does not offer cogent evidence from systematic research of the instructional value of portfolios, let alone evidence of their validity or reliability as foci of assessment of students. Indeed, at this writing the one published study that has systematically examined the educational outcomes of using portfolios—an article by Nancy Baker, of Southeast Missouri State University—reports limited effects from a trial of portfolios in first-year composition.

Some years ago the director of a composition program at a college tried to insist, without consulting the staff, that all teachers in one of the courses collect and, in teams of two or three, exchange portfolios at midsemester and at the end of the semester; this procedure was to be part of the process of informing students about their progress and of arriving at final grades. Many members of the staff resisted, citing both the extra work and the erosion of their authority to evaluate their students. (Some instructors were clever: they encouraged students to proclaim, stridently, that they did not want persons other than their own instructors to have a hand in determining their final grades.) The director's mandate had to be softened until it became little more than a suggestion to teachers, and today no teachers at that institution work in teams to evaluate students' portfolios (though some use portfolios in assessment as a matter of personal choice).

Colleagues at various universities confirm one of the major reasons for teachers' resistance to efforts to impose portfolios: busy faculty members perceive that even if they believe that portfolios may be useful for teaching and assessment, the time required to develop assignments and read the students' writings would be too great, making portfolios impractical as a teaching tool or as the sole or principal basis for evaluating student progress. Furthermore, building a writing course around portfolios is not a procedure one automatically knows how to use; faculty members, as the teachers in the Lehman College middle schools project discovered, often need to reconsider their entire approach to writing and teaching, and such reconsideration takes time and intellectual effort. Old ways of envisaging the teaching of writing are not quickly discarded, especially not if new ways of teaching are dictated by those in authority. The implication seems clear: an institution whose leaders want to see portfolios used for assessment or for teaching must engage faculty members in adequate, open, and democratic discussions of what is involved; the leaders should not rely on mandates or indoctrination.

Surely as controversial as efforts to require the use of portfolios in instruction or local assessment of student progress are efforts to install portfolios as a tool for large-scale assessment of students, teachers, and programs, particularly if the assessment is conducted for the information of persons outside the teaching faculty. Those who resist such moves contend that a portfolio gives the reader much greater access, undue access, to a student's work than does a standardized test or even holistically scored samples of writing, and access therefore to what the teacher has been assigning, so that those in power can observe, then perhaps try to dictate, how writing is taught and judged. In my conversations with teachers who expressed this view, the resistance was not to accountability but rather to the invasion of their private professional reflections and responsible decisions about how to do their jobs. Further, since validated scoring rubrics for use with portfolios are not widely available, mandated assessment by portfolios carries with it the danger of mandated criteria for making that assessment and thus the danger of teachers' being coerced to conform to what administrators or policy-making boards think should be taught and how. At Lehman College we risked the charge of coercion when we made an assessment of our 1984 curriculum for general education and distribution—an assessment we carried out partly by collecting and reading, according to an assessment profile we had devised for ourselves, portfolios containing samples of students' work from several courses outside English composition (Larson). When we reported our findings to the college community at large, therefore, we had to do so tentatively and gently, lest we be accused of judging the work of our students by standards they had not been helped to understand and taught to meet.

Arguments against the use of portfolios in large-scale assessment do not come only from teachers, or from all teachers. Some teachers actually prefer using portfolios (if the teachers set the ground rules) over more impersonal methods of assessment. But people interested in educational accountability, some teachers have told me, resist the suggestion that teachers should be allowed to base assessment of students and programs on student portfolios, using their own standards to judge them. The teachers report that some school administrators and governing boards view the judging of portfolios as "soft," inexact, not rigorous (particularly when the portfolios include personal retrospection and commentary or essays that express feelings)—too mushy or slippery to furnish information about students' performance that is solid and can be compared with the performance of students in other districts or states. Such administrators, though they might not acknowledge the justness of this language, ignore the messiness, the labyrinthine complexity of composing processes; they prefer to see in composing a neat regularity that will lend itself to an equally neat description and a quantitative assessment. This preference of many administrators raises not only the question of who controls assessment but also the even thornier questions of who controls the kinds of writing that students are asked or allowed to do in school and how that writing should be viewed. Schools and school systems considering the use of portfolios need to be alert to such political questions and their implications. These questions must be dealt with before the decision is made to assess through portfolios.

Working ostensibly against grade inflation and other sorts of unjustified overstatement of students' abilities, advocates of accountability, teachers say, prefer instruments such as tests holistically scored by teams of trained readers, tests that can be judged according to precisely formulated criteria that are widely accepted and understood among those with experience in testing. As Edward White has argued (*Teaching*), portfolios have yet to be shown to permit the kinds of reliable, consistent, criterion-referenced scoring that makes possible firm judgments about students. (Individual writing samples permit such scoring.) The use of portfolios in teaching and judging students' writing, that is, can encounter political resistance from those in power in a college, school, or school system who demand a precise determination of what individual students or groups of students have accomplished. Those authorities want an assessment that will permit comparisons of local students with students across a state or across the country and enable the authorities to answer a question frequently asked by constituents: How do we stack up? The purpose sought, to use Elbow's distinction, is not to describe but to rank.

But let's assume that a school or college faculty has at least agreed on a plan to collect portfolios from students as a basis for assessment. What problems of authority and control then arise? How does the administration (or the faculty majority) arrange for the collection of portfolios? If all the teachers are asked to elicit from students the same kinds of writings in order to ensure comparable portfolios, some teachers will object. Such a practice, one experienced and respected teacher told me, deflects teachers' attention from getting students to do their best work, regardless of genre, and prevents the students from selecting their best work for inclusion in their portfolios. Good portfolios, my informant said, will not necessarily emerge from a good teacher's classroom if rules are imposed about what can and cannot be included in them and demands are made about what must be included. (The well-known program at Miami University—described in this volume in the essay preceding mine—that encourages incoming students to submit a portfolio to earn advanced placement in or exemption from the university's writing sequence appears to avoid this difficulty. Though the portfolio must contain specific kinds of writing, students *volunteer* their portfolios in hopes of winning a reward. Portfolios are not systematically gathered from particular classes. No effort is made to evaluate students' secondary school instruction, and no effort is made to generalize about students from specific schools.) Another informant observed that the best portfolios come from students who are in control of their content and feel ownership of them. Yet from an administrator's perspective, having students decide what to put into their portfolios will most likely mean judgments made about work that is not comparable from student to student. Resolving this issue will require negotiation between administrators and teachers, with the result, one hopes, that the portfolios will contain much that teachers and students want as well as some of what administrators say they need.

Once the content of the portfolios and the processes for collecting them have been negotiated, with due regard to the teachers' professional judgment, the next issue arises: What procedures are to be followed in the reading of the portfolios? Faculty members can legitimately resist the requirement that they devote time to develop a scoring rubric and to do the scoring itself without compensation. Scoring, moreover, is a complex activity that requires extensive training for readers—that training being only part of the process of faculty development made necessary by the introduction of portfolios. Even the offer of real compensation (dollars) may not be enough to ensure faculty members' willing cooperation in the reading of portfolios. Teachers may also resist having students' work turned over for assessment to outsiders unfamiliar with the school's writing program. The administration (or faculty majority) thus faces the political problem of winning faculty consent. Great respect for individual faculty members' views would seem to be required, as would considerable tact and negotiating skill to build bridges between what the administration prefers and how the faculty wishes to teach.

As an important initial step in bridge building, the administration should consult with the faculty to establish the bases on which portfolios are to be judged. Teachers often dislike having to abandon their criteria in favor of someone else's, and the thought of sharing the evaluation of portfolios with those who teach differently can arouse passionate objections from some teachers. Such feelings need to be taken into account, since it is the teachers' work with their students that is being assessed, and it is the teachers who will arrange for and collect the portfolios. If administrators (maybe also trustees, board members, and even parents) can talk freely with faculty members about ways of reading portfolios, each group may learn useful things about what the other group values and needs to know—and why. But, as Liz Hamp-Lyons and William Condon have demonstrated, agreement in principle about the scoring of portfolios often does not translate easily into agreement about scores on individual portfolios. Specific scoring criteria need to be carefully negotiated.

Having obtained the participation of faculty members in the reading of portfolios, the organizers of a portfolio assessment program next confront the question of who should see the results and what responses should be made to them. If the results are to be used by administrators or institutional researchers to reach summative judgments about students as individuals and about groups of students, teachers may resist, arguing (as Elbow often does) that such judgments are inexact and misleading because they take into account neither the complexity of writing nor the ways in which writers develop. Pointing to institutions like Evergreen State College, in Washington, where teachers do not grade students but write descriptive paragraphs about students' work at the end of a semester, many teachers argue against the summative judgments of grades, particularly in the area of writing. Yet administrators and campus leaders accountable to legislators and taxpayers may demand access to such judgments (especially if they have arranged for them) and may insist on being able to make comparisons between the students at their institution and comparable students elsewhere. Negotiating a resolution to that conflict is not easy.

Even if administration and faculty agree to have summative assessment of the writing in portfolios and agree on how to score the portfolios and report the results to administrators, the question remains of how those results will be interpreted. The level of generality used in reporting results may be a significant issue. From the performance of a small group of students, will judgments be made about the abilities of a large group or an entire student body? Will judgments be made about the effectiveness of faculty members, about their commitment to their work, about their attentiveness, about their teaching techniques, the skill with which they assign and respond to writing? Although we do not have research data to support the efficacy of making students' portfolios a tool to evaluate teachers, portfolios do indicate what teachers ask of students and how they respond to student writing. In any case, the temptation to assess teachers' performance on the basis of data in student portfolios will prove strong. Such judgments, as one colleague told me, can sharply threaten the self-confidence and morale of teachers.

The kinds of inferences and comparisons that are legitimate in interpreting scores on student portfolios (if scores are assigned to them) are very much open to debate. Will administrators claim that the student body ranks above or below that of another institution in some particular ability? Generalizations made from test scores of groups of students are often cited to support proud claims or apprehensive prophecies. Will the results of this complex kind of assessment be reported in quick summary form to parents, as if those results were definitive statements about students? Will the results encourage persons with political agendas—perhaps persons who are not informed enough about writing and testing to have anything other than a superficial and possibly unfair response to those results—to broadcast invidious conclusions to newspapers, legislators, and college associations? Will thoughtful explanation of the significance of the findings accompany the findings when they are disseminated? Wise administration of assessment procedures requires that these questions be confronted in advance of the assessment and that agreement be reached among all interested persons about who besides students and faculty members sees the results.

Finally, I suggest that those planning to use portfolios for assessment need to make clear in advance, to teachers and maybe to students, what kinds of actions are envisaged after the results are known. Will the results be used by a school board, dean, or college president to justify imposing a change in the curriculum? Will they be used to justify a demand that the awarding of grades or credit reflect higher standards? Will they be used to justify higher or lower funding for a writing program? Will they be used to justify personnel actions regarding faculty members (on the easy but, as noted, misleading assumption that students' achievements in their portfolios reveal the effectiveness of teachers)? Will they be used, in other words, to support an exercise of administrative power or control? The answers to such questions are hard to predict, and they are often not considered in advance. They depend on the political climate of a particular school. But the questions need to be anticipated.

Any assessment plan, of course, raises the question of what is to be done with the findings beyond the central purpose of characterizing students' work and helping teachers improve the effectiveness of their teaching. To see whether students are learning what teachers think and hope has been taught is probably the main reason that any kind of assessment is done. Other purposes for which the results will be used, even if the purposes are limited to strengthening an institution's general self-knowledge, should be identified before the assessment and discussed with the people who will be affected, to obtain their concurrence. And once those purposes are agreed to, all concerned parties (including administrators and legislators) must abide by the agreement and not use the results for unannounced political purposes. In assessment, mutual trust and good faith are essential; without them, corrosive antagonisms arise.

If the political problems identified here are addressed, people responsible for the assessment of writing can gain from studying portfolios a great deal that other means of assessment do not provide. Portfolios of students' work can furnish richer data than one- or two-question essay tests do, and supply more detail than time-limited tests do. From students' portfolios one learns much about the kinds of guidance the students have received, about what they have been asked to do, and about the extent and the range—not to mention the development—of their abilities. Such knowledge confers power, and power used without the consent of those affected can be divisive, even explosive. Wise administrators will recognize that the possible benefits of portfolio assessment will not be achieved without the cooperation of the faculty and maybe of the students, too. They will consult with the faculty and students, explore the assessment techniques to be used, make clear the processes of gathering and interpreting data, identify the persons who will receive those data, and specify the purposes to be served—all before introducing the substantial new approach to assessment that reading portfolios represents. When administrators oversee humanely the introduction of portfolios for assessment (that use of portfolios going beyond the private purposes of the classroom), they will realize substantial benefits: they will bring into the open, for departmental and even campus-wide discussion, questions about what constitutes literacy, what the term "writing" embraces, how "ability to write" may be understood, and even what "reading" includes. They will discover that in this process portfolio assessment becomes for all participants not threatening, not political, but educative.

And wise administrators will furnish continuing support and encouragement to faculty members to use portfolios well: support in the form of facilitative meetings, discussions, and other staff development activities and support in the form of time allowed as well as monetary compensation for faculty efforts. Such support is not cheap, but the task is not easy, because using portfolios to assess does invade the private space in which teachers and students engage in their sensitive consultations. If administrators win informed consent from all those affected by the use of portfolios and provide continuing support for that use, they will maximize the benefits of portfolio assessment and minimize resistance and opposition to it. In such circumstances, portfolios can be a valuable assessment tool, and reading them can help to promote improved learning.

Lehman College, City University of New York

Portfolio Approaches to Assessment: Breakthrough or More of the Same?

Sandra Murphy and Barbara Grant

> *I worry that whoever thought up the term "quality control"*
> *thought if we didn't control it, it would get out of hand.*
> Lily Tomlin

Since the mid-1980s, as educators have become increasingly dissatisfied with traditional assessment measures, there has been an escalating interest in portfolio assessment, so much so that portfolio assessment is now in danger of becoming the latest educational bandwagon. Yet bandwagons, however alluring and brightly lit, have been known to ensnare rather than transport the unsuspecting rider. The danger of a portfolio bandwagon is that educators may simply re-create more of the same difficulties that plague traditional assessments. While portfolio assessment does appear to offer solutions to many of the inadequacies of traditional assessment constructs and procedures, in fact the word *portfolio* by itself means little. It is the individual decisions concerning what to put in a portfolio, who evaluates it and how, and what to do with the results, as well as the assumptions that underlie those decisions, that determine the value of an assessment for teaching and for learning. In this chapter we focus on decisions concerning portfolio contents and ownership.

We begin with the relations among assessment procedures, underlying models or paradigms of learning, and the social structures through which learning occurs. Contrasting positivist approaches to assessment with constructivist approaches, we discuss the limitations of traditional assessment procedures. We introduce readers to the ways portfolio programs are enacted in different contexts and for different purposes, and we analyze how practical decisions—the choices people make as they construct their projects—locate programs on the continuum between top-down and collaborative designs and on the continuum between standardization and contextualization. We assert that decisions based on a constructivist paradigm promote collaborative and contextualized assessments, while a positivist model leads to standardized, top-down assessments—assessments that erode teachers' authority as professional educators and that fail to provide students with opportunities to take control of their own literacy learning. We point out that portfolios are not by definition constructivist. Although portfolios offer opportunities for constructivist assessment, in practice they may reflect a positivist paradigm. We conclude that a constructivist paradigm is more likely to provide a flexible and useful framework for creating assessments that will enhance learning and empower rather than impede teachers and students.

Positivist Assessment

Most traditional assessment measures are anchored in a positivist paradigm, a paradigm that is dominant in education in general and to some degree in the field of writing assessment. Positivism treats knowledge as skills, as information that can be divided into testable bits, or as formulaic routines. With positivism there is a truth, a correct interpretation, a right answer that exists independently of the learner. As Janet Emig points out, "the positivist believes that a one-to-one correspondence exists or can be established between a phenomenon and an interpretation of that phenomenon" ("Inquiry Paradigms" 67). Within a positivist framework, there is no room for the idea that several equally valid interpretations might be possible.

A positivist perspective calls for a context-free, laboratory-oriented model of evaluation that is located outside the learning process. Within such a model, assessment procedures are employed to measure products and previously learned behaviors elicited in response to stimuli presumed to be uniform and presented under uniform conditions so that educators can obtain reliable results from tests. Lawrence Stenhouse notes:

> *Behavior,* as a concept, implies human action as it appears to an observer who denies himself access to the reflective, retrospective testimony of the actor whom he observes. Behaviors are the data of a psychology which aspires to be an observational science in the positivist tradition. (22–23)

Echoing the tradition of experimental design and statistical analysis developed by Ronald A. Fisher and deployed in the field of agricultural research (Stenhouse), the assumption of uniform conditions in traditional assessment mirrors the assumptions of experiments conducted in laboratories. Students are compared with one another, sorted into categories, and labeled.

The labels often take on a life of their own, funneling students into ability groups, tracks, and remedial programs; thus some students, ethnic and linguistic minority students in particular, are left with inadequate access to quality schooling and with a legacy of differential instruction (Deyhle; Duran). Although many worthwhile programs employ formal assessments to identify students needing assistance, when programs impede upward mobility and when tests are used as gatekeepers, traditional assessment approaches may limit access to knowledge for students who do not perform well. Further, since traditional assessments are supposedly objective, failure to do well on a test may be viewed as an individual's deficiency or, for minority groups, as a group deficiency. Thus positivist assessment can function to rank and sort children (often according to socioeconomic status) while at the same time making this function appear legitimate. Positivist assessment, then, like any other kind of assessment, is inherently political, though it claims to operate outside of social contexts.

Assessment often determines what counts as knowledge in school settings. For example, the prespecified outcomes of positivist assessment could be seen as symptomatic of an educational system that relies on a knowledge-transmission model of education and that decides in advance which knowledge will be made available (and which not made available) to students. Michael Apple argues that by determining which knowledge will be seen as socially legitimate, schools help "create and recreate forms of consciousness that enable social control to be maintained without the necessity of dominant groups having to resort to overt mechanisms of domination" (*Ideology* 3). According to Apple, one way social control is accomplished is through the "selective tradition" in which "certain meanings and practices are chosen for emphasis, certain other meanings and practices are neglected and excluded" (7). In this way, schools preserve and distribute "symbolic property"—the "cultural capital"—of the dominant culture (3). An assessment system anchored in a positivist tradition by its reliance on prespecified questions and assignments lends itself to an educational system based on such a knowledge-transmission model, a model that raises serious questions about the latent ideological content of schooling. As Apple asks about curriculum design, "Whose knowledge is it? Who selected it? Why is it organized and taught in this way?" (7), one might ask about assessment, Who decides what knowledge to assess? Why is it organized and assessed in this way? How we choose to go about assessment reveals our perspective on the distribution of power and authority. Positivist kinds of assessment help place that authority not with teachers and students but with experts. Clearly, what we choose to assess reveals what we value as educational activity and what the dominant culture counts as legitimate knowledge.

Like other forms of assessment, writing assessment influences how knowledge is defined in schools. Indirect measures of writing, such as multiple-choice tests, focus on discrete skills: how to recognize agreement between subject and verb or identify a complete sentence. Thus they encourage a view of learning that focuses on grammatical items instead of on strategies for writing. Traditional essay tests, unlike multiple-choice tests, do require students to use writing strategies; yet they may reflect the limitations of a positivist perspective, in particular when students are tested under tightly controlled, standardized conditions removed from those under which they normally write.

Standardizing collection procedures enhances statistical reliability. It is ironic that such techniques, employed to ensure equal opportunity and statistical reliability in traditional large-scale assessments, are now calling into question their own validity and value (Camp, "Changing"; P. Moss, "Can There Be?"); see also, in this volume, Roberta Camp's essay "New Views of Measurement and New Models for Writing Assessment"). A single writing sample is insufficient to represent the wide variety of kinds and purposes of writing (Emig, "Inquiry Paradigms"). Research tells us that writing done for one purpose requires processes and strategies different from those required for another purpose (Witte; Matsuhashi). Given this reality, there is little ground for the all too common practice of generalizing from a single sample to a student's ability in other kinds of writing. In addition, writing processes and strategies are used differently by writers who have different personal and cultural histories (Flower and Hayes, "Cognitive Process Theory"; Applebee; O'Connor; see also the three essays in part 4 of this volume). Yet this diversity is ignored by the product orientation of traditional direct methods for assessing writing and by the current propensity to compare writing produced in timed conditions by different writers. A view of writing complicated by ideas about cultural diversity and about the varying demands of different audiences and purposes is not compatible with traditional, positivist approaches to assessment.

A Constructivist Perspective

The positivist view of learning and assessment reflected in traditional forms of assessment stands in stark contrast to the constructivist view. In a constructivist framework, knowledge is seen not as something to be transmitted but as something that students actively collaborate to build. Learning takes place through interaction; it exists in the transactions between student and student, student and text, student and teacher. In the constructivist perspective, assessment procedures are inevitably a part of the dialectic of teaching and learning, part of the process that defines what is learned and what knowledge is. Thus a constructivist perspective acknowledges the role of assessment in defining the curriculum. Placed at the service of instruction, writing assessment helps teachers hear individual students' voices, discover the strategies students are using, and discover the knowledge students have already constructed. Assessment becomes an opportunity for planning the next move in the conversation. Further, assessment provides a means for engaging students in self-reflection and for acknowledging their role as collaborators in the learning process.

In addition to being collaborative, constructivist assessment is contextualized, reflecting and supporting what students and teachers are actually doing in classrooms. As described by Sheila Valencia, William McGinley, and P. David Pearson, contextualized assessment is continuous, multidimensional, and grounded in knowledge. It reflects the dynamic nature of learning, provides views of learning from different angles, and anchors itself in current theory, best practice, and tasks that have genuine purposes.

Current theories of writing and writing development are in consonance with the constructivist viewpoint. Writing is conceptualized as a process, not a product, so that assessment, instead of obliging teachers to compare written products, becomes an opportunity for them to learn what students know and are able to do. For students, assessment becomes an opportunity to practice authorship, that is, to assume ownership of and authority over their work rather than fulfill the expectations of others. Current models see writing embedded in social interaction (Dyson) and stress the importance of regarding the classroom as a community of writers and readers (Graves; Atwell). Receiving peer response, being published, interacting in writing conferences, having a teacher who is a writing coach, and keeping a dialogue journal are all ways that students may become active participants in the learning community and authors with readers.

By emphasizing the effect of assessment on learning, we do not mean to imply that constructivist assessment cannot occur outside the classroom. Rather, we suggest that a variety of assessment purposes can be met while student learning is simultaneously enhanced. Assessments that are well grounded in current theory and that reflect exemplary classroom practice are most likely to enhance student learning. Because constructivist portfolios are often collections of classroom work, they offer a unique opportunity to conduct contextualized assessment on a larger scale.

Portfolio Assessment in Theory

Portfolio approaches appear to offer constructivist solutions to many of the inadequacies of traditional assessments, since they

○ provide collections of student writing, addressing the problem of overgeneralizing from single samples collected on single occasions;
○ include writing produced in natural settings, addressing the problem of asking students to write in artificial situations that have little similarity to those in which writers actually write;
○ reflect an ongoing curriculum rather than external, and perhaps irrelevant, purposes;
○ document the drafting and revising processes used by students, providing information that is directly useful in instruction; and
○ include the students' own reflections on their writing and on their needs for further instruction, addressing the problem of the lack of student involvement in the assessment process.

But portfolios are not always constructivist. Educators are well aware of the age-old slip 'twixt cup and lip, 'twixt theory and practice. In practice, constructivist theory is often not realized in pure form, in perfectly contextualized, smoothly collaborative assessments. Portfolio programs often reveal a positivist orientation.

Moving from Theory to Practice: Diversity of Portfolio Projects

There is no guarantee that people all mean the same thing when they use the word *portfolio*. In fact, some publishers have applied the word to its antithesis, collections of worksheets. Spectrum Educational Media, for example, advertises a "grammar portfolio" with the following description:

> Greatly extends the number of exercises available to supplement the traditional grammar book. Asks students to identify sentence parts, fill in the blanks, distinguish between grammatical elements, and determine how words, phrases, and clauses are used. . . . Fifty reproducible worksheets, answer key. Grades 7–12.

Beyond such obvious departures from the notion of portfolios as collections of real writing, portfolio approaches to the assessment of writing vary widely. The National Writing Project, a staff development program to improve the teaching of writing in the nation's schools, with 159 sites in 44 states and Puerto Rico, has identified within its network over 50 portfolio assessment projects in 17 states (M. Smith). Because these projects (and their portfolios) have been developed for a variety of reasons and in a variety of contexts, they are very different from one another. Project purposes range from tracking student development over time, showcasing student response to a range of assignments, evaluating student work across the curriculum, motivating students, promoting learning through reflection and self-assessment, evaluating students' thinking and writing processes—to program implementation, program assessment, curriculum evaluation, and the establishment of exit requirements. In addition, portfolio projects differ in scale. Some are classroom-based; some are grade- or department-based. Some are initiated at the interdepartmental level; others are schoolwide, districtwide, or university-wide in their scope.

Although portfolio projects reflect diverse contexts and purposes, every project presents its implementers with the same key problems or situations that require decision making. The decisions, which sometimes appear merely practical or even trivial, often have profound implications, because practical decisions reflect theoretical orientations as well as different distributions of authority and power among the various parties in both teaching and assessment. In effect, practical decisions locate projects along the continua shown below:

Positivism	⟷	Constructivism
Standardization	⟷	Contextualization
Top-Down Decisions	⟷	Collaboration

In the sections that follow, we discuss the tensions represented in these continua. It is our view that as projects move toward constructivism, contextualization, and collaboration, opportunities for learning from the assessment process are enhanced, teachers regain professional prerogatives and authority, and students are encouraged to take responsibility for their own literacy.

Decisions concerning Standardization and Contextualization

Making decisions about how portfolio folders will be filled requires balancing between standardization and contextualization. By standardization we mean the degree to which the contents of portfolios are specified in advance as well as the degree to which the conditions for writing are the same for all students. By contextualization we mean the degree to which portfolios are individualized to reflect local curricula—including the curriculum of a particular classroom or the curriculum designed for an individual student—as opposed to districtwide, statewide, or university-wide curricula. At the standardization end of the continuum lie publishers' portfolios; at the contextualization end, portfolio projects designed by teachers and students to reflect the actual classroom curricula of particular schools. For example, the *Integrated Assessment System* offered by the Psychological Corporation is a package of materials designed for elementary schools. The "Reading/Writing" activities included in the package come with "handy blackline masters . . . so that teachers may make clean copies of directions and writing templates for each student" (7). Each writing task comes with a corresponding scoring guide and model anchor papers for each score point. The assumption is made that certain reading passages are appropriate for certain grade levels. Activities "may be administered 'out-of-level,'" but model papers for scoring are based on the designated grade level. Thus, although the package claims that teachers can choose those activities that are appropriate for their students and their curricula, clearly the thrust here is standardization and independence from the curriculum of the school or the teacher. In schools that use these materials, students in the same grade probably read the same passages, respond to identical prompts for writing, and perform under identical conditions.

The positivist orientation reflected in standardized tasks and conditions for writing is not confined to publishers' portfolios or to elementary school. Portfolio assessments in secondary and postsecondary institutions can also reflect a positivist orientation—for example, when portfolio contents are limited to department-wide, narrowly pre-scribed, standard tasks: assignment number 1, assignment number 2, and so on. Paradoxically, in these situations, portfolio assessment can operate to standardize a richly diverse curriculum, influencing teach-ers to "teach to the test," to focus on perfecting performance in relation to a few kinds of assignments rather than on providing students with diverse audiences and purposes for writing.

In contrast, consider a contextualized portfolio. Its contents are se-lected from the curriculum that is actually in place at the school, not from activities scripted by publishers. For example, teachers at Mount Diablo High School in Concord, California, ask students to select pa-pers for their portfolios from their ongoing coursework. If the class studying Shakespeare is writing diary entries from the point of view of Romeo, then students might choose to include such papers in their portfolios. In brief, some portfolios tap what students are learning and doing in school; others tap someone's idea of what students typically should be learning and doing, given their year in school, without re-gard to the particular classroom or curriculum.

Along the continuum between standardization and contextualiza-tion, different schools, colleges, and universities have reached different compromises. At the standardization end, particularly in schools where a competency-based model of basic skills has been implemented, port-folios may include a rich array of evidence, but student choice is not likely to be a factor. For example, at Seattle Central Community College, assignments completed as part of a course were included in portfolios evaluated for evidence of student competence in areas directly related to the Washington State Core Competencies. The portfolios included both timed and open-ended writing assignments, journal topics, gram-mar quizzes, reading quizzes, videotaped speaking and listening activi-ties, and a mock job interview. Thus, while the portfolios included a rich array of evidence, student choice was not a factor in this portfolio pro-gram, because all the students completed the same course assignments and all the assignments were included in their portfolios. Toward the contextualization end of the continuum are individualized programs such as the one at Hampshire College at Amherst, where students gather with a faculty committee and collaboratively plan a program of study and establish the requirements for their portfolios.

Some portfolios designed to avoid narrowly defined tasks or require-ments for specific kinds of evidence have used categories of entries that allow students some freedom of choice. During the first year of the California Assessment Program's Portfolio Project, teachers at Mount Diablo asked students to make selections from broad categories of writing emphasized in the curriculum (for example, writing about opinions or writing about personal experience). Students could select from any number of papers as long as the papers they selected fit within the categories. A similar approach is employed in the portfolio program at Miami University (see the essay by Daiker, Sommers, and Stygall in this volume). Students who submit a portfolio are asked to include a reflective letter, a story or a description, an explanatory or exploratory essay, and a response to a written text. Thus, while required categories ensure that a range of genres are included, specific assignments are not required.

A focus on strategies is yet another alternative to highly specific portfolio guidelines. In a strategy-oriented portfolio, some of the teachers at Mount Diablo asked students to select work that demonstrated particular abilities, such as knowing how to revise and knowing how to use writing to learn, analyze, and reflect. Another open-ended approach, which was field-tested in the New Standards Project, a collaborative effort by several states and school districts to develop new ways to assess learning, asked students to demonstrate their range, versatility, technical command, use of literacy processes, and ability to reflect and analyze. Guidelines for students in the Arts PROPEL project (a project sponsored by the Rockefeller Foundation, dedicated to fostering the artistic development of middle and secondary school students in Pittsburgh) are similarly open-ended. Students are invited to include a diverse range of works, from journal entries, poems, essays, and letters to reflections on the evolution of a work and on their progress as writers (Wolf, "Opening Up"). Students are evaluated on their accomplishment in writing, their use of processes and resources for writing, and their development as writers. These more flexible kinds of guidelines for portfolio contents and evaluation invite students to reflect on their work and to exercise judgment; such guidelines emphasize learning while at the same time allowing a more diverse curriculum.

Although portfolios offer the opportunity to create constructivist assessment, contextualized portfolios inevitably express the political and theoretical views embedded in a curriculum, whether that curriculum has been adopted on a schoolwide basis or whether it is confined to an individual classroom. Contextualization is not in itself a virtue. The curricula in some schools and classrooms may be quite positivist in orientation. Emig points out that writing assignments reflect a positivist point of view when "the instructor sets a task, often discrete and decontextualized, from the frame of his own rhetorical reference or from the frame of a given rhetorical theory (or rhetoric text)" and when the assignments do not "emanate from the student writer [or] from the students' prior writing such as free writings, journal entries, or response-to-text papers" ("Inquiry Paradigms" 68).

The alternative, Emig suggests, is a process-oriented approach to the teaching of writing, one that fosters students' ability to generate their own topics for writing and to think critically about significant issues. Yet even in some ostensibly process-oriented classrooms, instruction may reflect a positivist orientation. As Arthur Applebee notes, process-oriented instruction "stresses the student's role as author with something of value to say" (104). Applebee also points out that if instruction does not make explicit links between process and product, it can easily degenerate "into an inappropriate and lockstep formula." In this case, instead of "suggesting a range of strategies for solving problems," process-oriented instruction "will become just another series of practice exercises" (102–03).

Thus some writing programs, and by extension some portfolios, reconceptualize even process-oriented instruction in positivist terms, as formulaic routines—day 1, first draft; day 2, revise; day 3, final draft—that students perform in response to decontextualized, artificial tasks set by others and given simultaneously to everyone in the class. Making process a routine, such standardized programs disregard the facts that writing processes vary from individual to individual and that writing for different purposes requires different strategies.

Whether standardization occurs in the classroom or in large-scale assessment, from a constructivist perspective it is equally problematic. In traditional assessments, or for that matter in portfolio assessments that require standardized conditions, writing is stripped of its social context both in the classroom, where to varying degrees it is a collaborative undertaking, and outside the classroom. Further, standardized conditions are not consistent with an effective process model of instruction since timed work usually means that there is time for at most a jotted outline and a single draft, not time for prewriting or reflection between drafts. Nor are standardized conditions consistent with a process model that respects the ways in which processes vary from individual to individual.

From a constructivist perspective, the idea of standardizing writing tasks is also problematic. Indeed, the practice of giving everyone the same task can be considered standardization only under the positivist assumption that the task will be interpreted in the same way by every student, an assumption open to doubt. Rather, one would hope that students approach writing tasks in diverse rather than uniform ways, showing individual voice and the integration of varied experience. When portfolios consist of standardized assignments collected under standardized conditions, they do not accommodate instruction that emphasizes diversity and individualization, nor do they lend themselves to authorship models that give students a measure of control in generating portfolio contents and in deciding how their work will be presented to an audience. In sum, any assessment, portfolio or not, that requires that tasks and conditions for writing be standardized is likely to undermine rather than support a writing program based on effective writing-process or authorship models.

Decisions about Authority: Top-Down or Collaborative Assessment

Unlike constructivist assessment, which is contextualized in the practice and theory of the classroom, traditional assessments often originate outside the classroom and are imposed on teachers and students by administrators and policy makers. This top-down quality of traditional assessments guarantees that what is tested is taught, so that they often have the effect, inadvertently or not, of standardizing the curriculum and thus, to use Apple's term, "deskilling" teachers.

> The concept of deskilling refers to the process by which workers' control over timing, over defining appropriate ways to do a task, and over criteria that establish acceptable performance are all slowly taken on as the prerogatives of management personnel who are usually divorced from the actual place in which the work is carried out.   (*Teachers* 209)

Apple argues that testing, along with "management systems, reductive behaviorally based curricula, pre-specified teaching 'competencies' and procedures and student responses," leads to a "loss of control and a separation of conception from execution" (32). Traditional assessments thus contribute to a climate that deskills the teacher, because they appropriate planning and evaluating functions. In this climate, teaching becomes a kind of low-level management or perhaps pink-collar job in which teachers have little autonomy but nevertheless have the responsibility of supervising and managing workers—the students. Instead of acting as an expert guide to students moving toward independence, the teacher is reduced to implementing prepackaged programs, administering tests, and keeping records.

If, as Apple suggests, deskilling pressures teachers to assume a low-level management or supervisor role, the even lowlier students are then cast as factory workers who churn out consumer goods. Like factory workers, students have little say in product design, the manufacturing process, or marketing. Thus deskilling works to disempower them as well as teachers. When students are disempowered, when they play no active role in the assessment process, merely responding to tasks designed by others, they are cut off from an opportunity to learn from that process.

Constructivist evaluation, in contrast, is collaborative and put together from the inside out. Instead of responding to externally designed and mandated requirements, those who have the most at stake in the assessment—teachers and students—play active roles in all phases of it. As Evon Guba and Yvonna Lincoln point out, "The involvement of stakeholders . . . implies more than simply identifying them and finding out what their claims, concerns and issues are. Each group is required to confront and take account of the inputs from other groups" (56). In constructivist assessment, outcomes emerge by consensus and are created through an interactive process (Guba and Lincoln). Moreover, assessment is itself a learning process; how students see a problem and the path they follow to its solution are as important as the solution itself.

The Portfolio as a Collaborative Process

Portfolios provide opportunities for collaboration in assessment. Groups of educators can discuss and compare standards both for the range of writing skills a student is expected to demonstrate and for the criteria important to the evaluation of writing skills. Educators can reflect together on individual student development in relation to curriculum goals and teaching practices. Students can be included in the assessment process, and learning through reflection can be promoted.

However, just as portfolio programs fall along a continuum between standardization and contextualization, they vary in the degree to which students and teachers are involved in collaborative program design. Some portfolio programs are top-down; others are grass-roots affairs, developed entirely by teachers and students. Still others fall somewhere in between: perhaps mandated by external authorities but designed with input from teachers, sometimes with the assistance of consultants.

Practical decisions about the degree of collaboration affect every other aspect of the project, including, we believe, its longevity and its influence on teaching and learning. Projects in which teachers ask the questions the assessment purports to answer and projects that are teacher-designed (rather than administrator- or consultant-designed) lead to professionalization rather than the deskilling of teachers and consequently to beneficial changes in curricula and teaching. Projects that are entirely top-down are likely to be short-lived and of questionable utility.

When teachers participate directly in an assessment, the assessment becomes a learning process. In the middle school writing-across-the-curriculum project described by Sandra Murphy and Mary Ann Smith ("Talking") in 1990, teachers read portfolios in pairs during the scoring session at the end of the year. As they read the portfolios, they found themselves explaining to one another how they designed and taught the writing tasks and how students responded to both the assignments and the teaching process. Thus scoring sessions provided teachers with an opportunity to trade successful assignments and teaching strategies across departmental boundaries, learn more about the goals and methods particular to each discipline, and become more aware of the ways individual students were responding to the varied demands of a middle school curriculum. Similar benefits have been reported in college programs. Peter Elbow and Pat Belanoff, describing the portfolio assessment program at the State University of New York, Stony Brook, note that the

> portfolio system encourages collaboration among teachers. . . .
> Our profession lacks any firm, theoretical, discipline-wide, basis
> for deciding the right interpretation or evaluation of a text. . . .
> The only way to bring a bit of trustworthiness to grading is to get
> teachers negotiating together in a community to make some col-
> laborative judgments. That the portfolio promotes collaboration
> and works against isolation may be, in the end, its main advantage.
> ("Portfolios" 338)

Whether or not staff development is an acknowledged goal of a project, such dialogue will occur where teachers are making important decisions. Dialogue is especially useful when teachers have the opportunity to explore their own questions about curriculum issues and student development, thus linking theory and practice to student work. Whether at case conferences where student portfolios are presented and discussed, at scoring sessions where portfolios are evaluated in relation to curriculum, or during sessions devoted to hashing out the purposes of the assessment or to creating scoring guides and response sheets, teachers find themselves weaving concerns about individual students' strengths and areas for improvement with concerns about teaching methods and curricula. Teachers benefit from these opportunities to link their rich experience and knowledge of students to other teachers' experiences and to theory.

Students, like teachers, are potential collaborators, and project implementers must make decisions about the degree of their involvement, in selecting entries for the portfolios, for example. In the more standardized portfolio projects described above, no choice is possible, because all the students write to the same assignments. Sometimes they are allowed to choose among a number of specific assignments. In some projects (mostly at the elementary school level) teachers make the selections, in others students make them, and in still others selection is collaborative. When students are allowed to make their own selections, they are encouraged to engage in the self-reflective process of reviewing and evaluating their writing and themselves as writers. Teachers can promote self-reflection in any number of ways, with questions (Camp, *Stimulating Reflection*), with a regular audit (Kirby and Kuykendall), with assignments like reflective letters, afterwords, and forewords (Murphy and Smith, *Writing*). When students are encouraged to choose, they are encouraged to exercise judgment and to take responsibility for their own learning.

The basic decisions of who makes selections for the portfolios and what goes into the portfolios have important consequences. They also reflect underlying philosophies. If project designers hold to a positivist perspective, they will treat students as most traditional assessments do: as merely the objects of assessment. Students will have little voice in the decisions that are made about what goes into the portfolios. But if project designers adopt a constructivist point of view, they will acknowledge that students have the most at stake and therefore the most right to have their voices heard. Constructivist portfolios are more likely than positivist ones to be used to display student work, to document progress toward individualized goals within a broadly defined curriculum framework, and to promote collaboration between students and teachers. They are less likely to be used to sort students into categories or to provide scores based on data from overly prescribed programs of instruction.

Observing teachers and administrators wrestle with the issues of degree of contextualization and degree of collaboration has led us—in our nightmares—to imagine a standardized national portfolio, everyone marching to the same drummer: every student at each level across the nation dutifully completing a specified number of preassigned writing tasks. The standardized contents, collected under standardized conditions (timed and with surprise topics) would be scored, and students, teachers, schools, districts, and states would be compared with one another along exactly the same dimensions. Numbers would be generated; resources allocated; administrators, teachers, and students publicly judged on the basis of student performance. The prospect is chilling because of the potential for a negative impact on the curriculum, on teachers, and on students.

This nightmare portfolio may seem easy to dismiss as unlikely. But top-down, standardized portfolio programs are proliferating. We think it imperative, therefore, that policy makers carefully analyze their decisions, because decisions about project design inevitably affect the most important parties in assessment, teachers and students.

In the rush to leap on the bandwagon, it may be tempting to mandate portfolio assessment and standardize contents and collection procedures. But portfolio assessment, under such circumstances, resembles the managerial programs decried by Apple; it deskills teachers by removing from them the planning and decision-making functions of their profession. P. David Pearson and Sheila Valencia point out, "If the responsibility for assessment and instructional decision-making is placed with the teacher, we will produce more capable, concerned teachers. Take this away, and we create teachers who are just managers rather than educational professionals" (6).

When teachers engage in focused dialogue concerning the practical and theoretical issues raised during a portfolio project, they are creating knowledge along with a climate that can lead to curricular reform. And when students and teachers are given authority to make decisions, the assessment process merges with the instruction process. These benefits alone would seem an adequate reason for adopting a collaborative framework in the design of portfolio projects.

Yet such a framework alone may not be enough to ensure real reform. Even teacher-designed portfolios, by nature contextualized, defined by the curriculum and the underlying paradigms of that curriculum, will be more of the same if they reflect a positivist orientation toward students and learning. In a production-line classroom context, student writing and teacher reading become routinized and dull.

Constructivist teaching, however, cannot be scripted. In process-oriented classrooms that follow a constructivist learning model, teachers must constantly invent and refine teaching practices and constantly respond to student needs and interests as they implement broad curriculum goals. In such classrooms the focus is on students as individuals and as authors who are writing to explore important issues, to create compelling imagined worlds, or to exercise judgment. In such classrooms portfolios are used to help students seriously engage in writing that uncovers and develops authentic voice and disciplined thinking.

Portfolios offer opportunities to develop contextualized and collaborative assessments, assessments that enhance and articulate learning. Yet, like all forms of assessment, portfolios are anchored in social contexts. And the choices educators make as they move between the poles of standardization and contextualization, between top-down and collaborative designs, will inevitably reflect their underlying assumptions.

University of California, Davis (SM)
Saint Mary's College of California (BG)

Response:
Assessment as a Site of Contention

Edward M. White

The first question likely to occur to readers looking for new directions in this section is, Why do the new directions seem so old? One might ask the same about this book as a whole and the field of writing assessment as a whole. Why is change in assessment policy and practice so slow when every writer, whatever his or her angle of vision, sees what is wrong with assessment as usual? While the essays in part 5 register the usual dissatisfaction with current practice, the changes they propose seem modest and uncertain. Hunter Breland points out that the computer revolution has not particularly affected writing assessment, and Sandra Murphy and Barbara Grant remain suspicious that portfolios may turn out to be "more of the same." Why is writing assessment so resistant to new directions?

I think the answer to this question emerges from the different and sometimes conflicting demands placed on assessment by different interest groups, as my opening essay in this volume asserts. The book contains many examples of the complex demands writing teachers make: Peter Elbow wants assessment to get out of the way of the individual teacher working with the individual student; Richard Larson suggests that teachers may resist the intrustion of portfolio assessment into their classrooms; the teachers in part 4 confront the insensitivity of most assessment to issues of race, class, and gender. In short, teachers want assessment to be personal, individual, supportive of their own teaching styles and curricula, and—most important—not coercive. But ruling bodies and the publics they represent want from assessment the opposite. As Gordon Brossell and Maurice Scharton point out, they want normative numbers, success rates of groups, and ways of identifying failing students and incompetent teachers. Students make yet a different set of demands: they ask for immediate feedback from tests that seem fair and reasonable, that examine what they have been taught. Like the teachers, students resist assessment that interferes with learning or is merely bureaucratic or punitive; like the government, they want consistent measures that are determined not by teacher subjectivity but by clear standards. The statistician Doug Shale observes how complex the problem of consistency turns out to be when examined as a technical phenomenon. Meanwhile, test professionals such as Breland focus on what he calls "accurate" scoring, a matter of statistical and bureaucratic accounting with high credibility in a scientifically oriented world but without much concern about the effects of the scoring on teaching and learning.

We must learn to live with assessment as a site of contention. Every innovation proposed on behalf of one set of interests is likely to be opposed by people coming from a different perspective. Many writing teachers may recoil from the computer and multiple-choice assessment models that seem so reasonable to Breland, while the portfolios proposed by several of our other contributors as a support for teaching are bound to seem unresponsive to the needs of test professionals and governing bodies. Competing interests of this sort are probably healthy and beneficial, part of the political process that requires painful consensus building and slow progress. With such different views of writing and hence of writing measurement, the various interest groups will see to it that no one group predominates. Whatever direction assessment takes, it will not rush headlong down new paths; progress is likely to be a matter of backing and filling, overcoming obstacles and objections along the way.

So it should not be surprising that the new directions look so much like the old ones: some computer editing or computer grading of mechanics, some movement of portfolios from individual classrooms (where they have been in use for decades) to a wider field of assessment.

Breland's concept of writing differs from that of most of the writing teachers in this book, who privilege writing as related to discovery, cognition, and imagination. In common with a large segment of the public, he takes writing to be a measurable skill like many others: "A certain amount of standardization, particularly in writing mechanics, is an essential part of writing and writing assessment." Since computers are efficient and tireless in dealing with mechanics and simple error, he proposes that the machines handle those matters in both instruction and measurement so that "teachers [will] have more freedom to concentrate on the more important aspects." Breland does not state what those more important aspects are; they do not figure in his argument. Furthermore, he respects on practical grounds the multiple-choice tests, such as the Test of Standard Written English, that many writing teachers condemn since those tests tend to predict how the essays are scored.

In private correspondence, I mentioned to Breland that many English teachers see the standardization he supports as a danger, that their opposition is not to science but to a political stance inhospitable to racial and class difference as well as to creativity. His reply focused the issue: "Your argument that standardization is viewed as a form of oppression by some English teachers convinces me that the idea [of the two cultures] is still alive. Rules, order, standardization and the like are what science is about" (Breland). I am not sure that every scientist would agree with such a statement, but I do know that many college professors believe that writing is a much more simple and measurable matter than writing teachers imagine it to be. However much we may resist the view that writing should measure up to a known mechanical standard, that view is widely shared, even among our English colleagues.

Many of us find Breland's new direction to be a move backward to an exclusionary world that uses machines to measure written products and editing skill, to classify students, and to discourage independent thought. We should not condemn his stance out of hand, however, since evidence shows that some mechanical measures in fact evaluate student writing much as essay readers do (at least for Breland's research sample), and Breland does reserve the "more important aspects" for teacher judgment. Furthermore, we cannot dispute his claim that the warm reception writers and writing teachers have given to computers suggests that science has a role to play in the future of writing assessment.

The definition of writing expressed in the rest of part 5 seems much more in tune than Breland's essay with composition theory in the 1990s; the new direction here is away from mechanics—though not from measurement or standards—and toward multiple examples of written work evaluated by trained professionals. Writing is defined as a complex, multifaceted activity that includes revision, and writing assessment is defined as an activity that should encourage student writing, even a willingness to take risks and try exploratory writing. The Miami University's directions to students place its program in opposition to the Breland ideal of standardization: "Students will be rewarded for originality and variety." The reason for assessment is pedagogical: to enable students to learn self-assessment. Most significant, portfolios return assessment to local control, shifting power from testing authority to student.

Teachers reading this book will surely find the portfolio descriptions rich with promise and responsive to their needs. But what about the other constituencies? What will those looking for hard data have to say about expensive, individualized assessments with uncertain reliability and wispy statistics? We should remain alert to the problems that will be encountered by those traveling in the new direction—if it is a new direction—indicated by portfolios.

Finally, we must note that writing assessment remains a site of contention among competing power groups, each group seeking to define writing and the measurement of writing in ways suited to the group's own interests. Since I am a teacher, my sympathies lie with the portfolio and that abbreviated version of the portfolio, the essay test. But the Breland essay is a sharp reminder that teachers are but one among many interested parties in writing assessment and by no means the most powerful. As we debate issues in writing assessment, we are also jockeying for political power and attempting to steer the field in what we want its new direction to be. The politics of writing assessment lies directly behind the policies of writing assessment, and both guide its practice.

Works Cited

Adams, Peter Dow. "Basic Writing Reconsidered." *Journal of Basic Writing* 12 (1993): 22–36.

Afolayan, Adebisi. "African Languages and Literature in Today's World." *African History and Culture.* Ed. Richard Olaniyan. Nigeria: Longman Nigeria, 1982. 169–83.

Albernarle Paper Co. v. Moody. 422 US 405. 1975.

Alexander, Clara Franklin. "Black English Dialect and the Classroom Teacher." Brooks 20–29.

American Psychological Association. *Standards for Educational and Psychological Tests.* 2nd ed. Washington: Amer. Psychological Assn. and Natl. Council on Measurement in Educ., 1974.

Angle, Burr. "Freshman English Applications of Current Research in Black English." Luelsdorff 143–54.

Annas, Pamela. "Style as Politics: A Feminist Approach to the Teaching of Writing." *College English* 47 (1985): 360–71.

Anson, Chris M. "Response Styles and Ways of Knowing." Anson, *Writing* 332–66.

———, ed. *Writing and Response: Theory, Practice, and Research.* Urbana: NCTE, 1989.

Apple, Michael. *Ideology and Curriculum.* London: Routledge, 1979.

———. *Teachers and Texts: A Political Economy of Class and Gender Relations in Education.* New York: Routledge, 1986.

Applebee, Arthur. "Problems in Process Approaches: Toward a Reconceptualization of Process Instruction." *The Teaching of Writing: Eighty-Fifth Yearbook of the National Society for the Study of Education, Part II.* Ed. Anthony Petrosky and David Bartholomae. Chicago: U of Chicago P, 1986. 95–113.

Archbald, Doug A., and Fred M. Newmann. *Beyond Standardized Testing.* Madison: Natl. Center on Effective Secondary Schools, School of Educ., U of Wisconsin, Madison, 1988.

Argyris, Chris. *Increasing Leadership Effectiveness.* New York: Interscience-Wiley, 1976.

Armstead v. Starkville Municipal Separate School District. 316 US 535. 1942.

Arts PROPEL: A Handbook for Imaginative Writing. Princeton: Educ. Testing Service; Cambridge: Harvard Project Zero, 1993.

Arts PROPEL: An Introductory Handbook. Princeton: Educ. Testing Service; Cambridge: Harvard Project Zero, 1991.

Asante, Molefi. *The Afrocentric Idea.* Philadelphia: Temple UP, 1987.

Atwell, Nancie. *In the Middle: Writing, Reading, and Learning with Adolescents.* Portsmouth: Boynton, 1987.

Baker, Nancy W. "The Effect of Portfolio-Based Instruction on Composition Students' Final Examination Scores, Course Grades, and Attitudes toward Writing." *Research in the Teaching of English* 27 (1993): 155–74.

Ballard, Leslie. "Portfolios and Self-Assessment." *English Journal* 81 (1992): 46–48.

Bamberg, Betty J. "Composition Instruction Does Make a Difference: A Comparison of the High School Preparation of College Freshmen in Regular and Remedial English Classes." *Research in the Teaching of English* 12 (1978): 47–59.

Baron, Joan B. "Strategies for the Development of Effective Performance Exercises." *Applied Measurement in Education* 4 (1991): 305–18.

Barrs, Myra, Sue Ellis, Hilary Hester, and Anne Thomas. *The Primary Language Record: Handbook for Teachers.* London: Centre for Lang. in Primary Educ., 1989.

Bartholomae, David. "Inventing the University." Rose 134–65.

———. "The Study of Error." *College Composition and Communication* 31 (1984): 253–69.

———. "The Tidy House: Basic Writing in the American Curriculum." *Journal of Basic Writing* 12 (1993): 4–21.

Baugh, John. *Black Street Speech.* Austin: U of Texas P, 1983.

Beason, Larry. "Feedback and Revision in WAC Classes." *Research in the Teaching of English* 27 (1993): 395–422.

Beaugrande, Robert de. "Psychology and Composition: Past, Present, Future." *What Writers Know: The Language, Process, and Structure of Written Discourse.* Ed. Martin Nystrand. New York: Academic, 1982. 211–67.

Beaven, M. H. "Individualized Goal Setting, Self-Evaluation, and Peer Evaluation." Cooper and Odell 135–56.

Beckwith, Lewis D. "Constitutional Requirements for Standardized Ability Tests Used in Education." *Vanderbilt Law Review* 26 (1973): 789–821.

Belanoff, Patricia, and Marcia Dickson, eds. *Portfolios: Process and Product.* Portsmouth: Boynton-Heinemann, 1991.

Belanoff, Patricia, and Peter Elbow. "Using Portfolios to Increase Collaboration and Community in a Writing Program." *WPA: Writing Program Administration* 9.3 (1986): 27–40. Rpt. in Belanoff and Dickson 17–29.

Bennett, Randy E., and William C. Ward, eds. *Construction versus Choice in Cognitive Measurement: Issues in Constructed Response, Performance Testing, and Portfolio Assessment.* Hillsdale: Erlbaum, 1993.

Bennis, William G., et al. *The Planning of Change.* 3rd ed. New York: Holt, Rinehart, 1976.

Berlak, Harold, et al. *Toward a New Science of Educational Testing and Assessment.* Albany: State U of New York P, 1992.

Berlin, James. "Rhetoric and Ideology in the Writing Class." *College English* 50 (1988): 477–94.

———— . "Rhetoric and Poetics in the English Department: Our Nineteenth-Century Inheritance." *College English* 47 (1985): 521–33.

———— . *Rhetoric and Reality.* Carbondale: Southern Illinois UP, 1987.

———— . *Writing Instruction in Nineteenth-Century American Colleges.* Carbondale: Southern Illinois UP, 1984.

Biennial Survey of Education, 1930–1932. Washington: GPO, 1935.

Bizzell, Patricia. "Arguing about Literacy." *College English* 50 (1988): 141–53.

———— . "What Can We Know, What Must We Do, What May We Hope: Writing Assessment." *College English* 49 (1987): 575–84.

———— . "What Happens When Basic Writers Come to College." *College Composition and Communication* 37 (1986): 294–301.

———— . "What Is a 'Discourse Community'?" Summer Conf. on Rhetoric. Pennsylvania State U, University Park. 1987.

Black, Laurel. "Writing like a Woman and Being Rewarded for It: Gender, Assessment, and Reflective Letters from Miami University's Student Portfolios." Black, Daiker, Sommers, and Stygall 235–47.

Black, Laurel, Donald A. Daiker, Jeff Sommers, and Gail Stygall, eds. *New Directions in Portfolio Assessment: Reflective Practice, Critical Theory, and Large-Scale Scoring.* Portsmouth: Boynton-Heinemann, 1994.

Blok, H. "Estimating the Reliability, Validity, and Invalidity of Essay Ratings." *Journal of Educational Measurement* 22 (1985): 41–52.

Board of Curators of the University of Missouri v. Horowitz. 435 US 78. 1978.

Board of Regents v. Roth. 408 US 564. 1972.

Bowyer, J. W. "A Comparative Study of Three Writing Analysis Programs." *Literary and Linguistic Computing* 4 (1989): 90–98.

Braddock, Richard, Richard Lloyd-Jones, and Lowell Schoer. *Research in Written Composition.* Urbana: NCTE, 1963.

Breland, Hunter M. Letter to Edward M. White. 28 Aug. 1992.

Breland, Hunter M., Roberta Camp, Robert J. Jones, Margaret M. Morris, and Donald A. Rock. *Assessing Writing Skill.* Coll. Board Research Monograph 11. New York: Coll. Entrance Examination Board, 1987.

Breland, Hunter M., and Eldon Lytle. "Computer-Assisted Writing Skill Assessment Using *WordMAP*." Meeting of the Amer. Educ. Research Assn. and the Natl. Council on Measurement in Educ. Boston. 1990.

Brennan, Robert L. *Elements of Generalizability Theory.* Iowa City: Amer. Coll. Testing Program, 1983.

Britton, James, et al. *The Development of Writing Abilities (11-18).* London: Macmillan Educ., 1975.

Brodkey, Harold. "A Story in an Almost Classical Mode." *Stories in an Almost Classical Mode.* New York: Vintage, 1989. 219–67.

Brooks, Charlotte K. *Tapping Potential: English Language Arts for the Black Learner.* Urbana: NCTE, 1985.

Brossell, Gordon. "Current Research and Unanswered Questions in Writing Assessment." Greenberg, Weiner, and Donovan, *Writing Assessment* 168–82.

Brossell, Gordon, and Barbara Hoetker Ash. "An Experiment with the Wording of Essay Topics." *College Composition and Communication* 35 (1984): 423–25.

Brown, Penelope, and Stephen C. Levinson. *Politeness: Some Universals in Language Usage.* Cambridge: Cambridge UP, 1987.

Brown, Rexford. "A Personal Statement on Writing Assessment and Education Policy." Greenberg, Weiner, and Donovan, *Writing Assessment* 44–52.

Bruffee, Kenneth A. *A Short Course in Writing.* Boston: Little, 1980.

Bullock, Richard, and John Trimbur, eds. *The Politics of Writing Instruction: Postsecondary.* Portsmouth: Boynton, 1991.

Burling, Robbins. *English in Black and White.* New York: Holt, Rinehart, 1973.

Burstein, Jill, Lawrence T. Frase, April Ginther, and Leslie Grant. "Technology and Language Assessment." *Annual Review of Applied Linguistics* 1996 (in press).

Burt, Cyril. "Test Reliability Estimated by Analysis of Variance." *British Journal of Statistical Psychology* 8 (1955): 103–18.

Camp, Roberta. "Assessment in the Context of Schools and School Change." *Redefining Student Learning: Roots of Educational Change.* Ed. Hermine H. Marshall. Norwood: Ablex, 1992. 241–63.

———. "Changing the Model for the Direct Assessment of Writing." Williamson and Huot 45–78.

———. "The Place of Portfolios in Our Changing Views of Writing Assessment." Bennett and Ward 183–212.

———. "Portfolio Reflection in Middle and Secondary School Classrooms." Yancey 61–79.

———. *Stimulating Reflection in Arts PROPEL Portfolios.* Princeton: Educ. Testing Service, 1989.

———. "Thinking Together about Portfolios." *Quarterly of the National Writing Project and the Center for the Study of Writing* 12.2 (1990): 8+.

Camp, Roberta, and Denise Levine. "Portfolios Evolving: Background and Variations in Sixth- through Twelfth-Grade Portfolios." Belanoff and Dickson 194–205.

Cardinet, Jean, Yvan Tourneur, and Linda Allal. "The Symmetry of Generalizability Theory: Applications to Educational Measurement." *Journal of Educational Measurement* 13 (1976): 119–35.

Carlisle, Robert, and Eleanor McKenna. "Placement of ESL/EFL Undergraduate Writers in College-Level Writing Programs." Hamp-Lyons, *Assessing* 197–214.

Cast, B. M. D. "The Efficiency of Different Methods of Marking English Compositions." *British Journal of Educational Psychology* 9 (1939): 257–69; 10 (1940): 49–60.

CCCC Committee on Assessment. *Post-secondary Writing Assessment: An Update on Practices and Procedures.* Urbana: Conf. on Coll. Composition and Communication, 1988.

Chaplin, Miriam T. *A Comparative Analysis of Writing Features Used by Selected Black and White Students in the National Assessment of Educational Progress and the New Jersey High School Proficiency Test.* Research report 88-42. Princeton: Educ. Testing Service, 1988.

Charney, Davida. "The Validity of Using Holistic Scoring to Evaluate Writing: A Critical Overview." *Research in the Teaching of English* 18 (1984): 65–81.

Cheong, Jacqueline, and Mary A. Barr. "Portfolio Assessment and Chapter 1: The California Learning Record." Achieving Schools Conf. California Dept. of Educ. Los Angeles. 1992.

Cherry, Roger D., and Paul R. Meyer. "Reliability Issues in Holistic Assessment." Williamson and Huot 109–41.

Chittenden, Edward, and Rhoda Kanevsky. "Documenting Young Children's Science Learning: School-Based Inquiry." Conf. Action Research and the Reform of Mathematics and Science Educ. Chatham. 1992.

Chittenden, Edward, and Vivian Wallace. "Reforming School Assessment Practices: A Case in Point." A Mature Restructured School: Three Perspectives of Central Park East Elementary School. Annual Meeting of Amer. Educ. Research Assn. San Francisco. 22 Apr. 1992.

Chorover, Stephan. *From Genesis to Genocide: The Meaning of Human Nature and the Power of Behavior Control.* Cambridge: MIT P, 1979.

Christensen, Francis, and Bonnijean Christensen. *Notes toward a New Rhetoric.* 2nd ed. New York: Harper, 1978.

Cintron, Ralph. Pues Aqui: *Language and Power in Angelstown.* Forthcoming.

——— . "The Use of Oral and Written Language in the Homes of Three Mexicano Families." Diss. U of Illinois, Chicago, 1990.

Civil Rights Act of 1964. 42 USC. Sec. 2000d. 1976.

Cixous, Hélène. "The Laugh of the Medusa." *The Critical Tradition: Classic Texts and Contemporary Trends.* Ed. David H. Richter. New York: St. Martin's, 1994. 1090–1102.

Clifford, John P. "Composing in Stages: The Effects of Collaborative Pedagogy." *Research in the Teaching of English* 15 (1981): 37–53.

——— . "The Subject in Discourse." Harkin and Schilb 38–51.

Clifford, John, and John Schilb, eds. *Writing Theory and Critical Theory.* New York: MLA, 1994.

Coffman, William E. "On the Reliability of Ratings of Essay Examinations." *NCME Measurement in Education* 3 (1972). 1–7.

Cohen, E. G., and S. S. Roper. "Modification of Interracial Interaction Disability: A Modification of Status Characteristic Theory." *American Sociological Review* 37 (1972): 643–57.

Cole, Nancy, and Pamela Moss. "Bias in Test Use." R. Linn 201–19.

Coles, William. *The Plural I—and After.* Portsmouth: Boynton-Heinemann, 1988.

Coles, William E., Jr., and James Vopat. *What Makes Writing Good: A Multiperspective.* Lexington: Heath, 1985.

Conlan, Gertrude. "'Objective' Measures of Writing Ability." Greenberg, Weiner, and Donovan, *Writing Assessment* 109–25.

Connors, Robert J. "Rhetoric and the Modern University: The Creation of an Underclass." Bullock and Trimbur 55–84.

———. "The Rise and Fall of the Modes of Discourse." *College Composition and Communication* 32 (1981): 444–63.

Connors, Robert J., and Andrea Lunsford. "Frequency of Formal Errors in Current College Writing; or, Ma and Pa Kettle Do Research." *College Composition and Communication* 39 (1988): 395–409.

———. "Teachers' Rhetorical Comments on Student Papers." Forthcoming.

Coombs, Don H. "Roundtable Review." *Research in the Teaching of English* 3 (1969): 225–29.

Cooper, Charles R. "Holistic Evaluation of Writing." Cooper and Odell 3–31.

———, ed. *The Nature and Measurement of Competency in English.* Urbana: NCTE, 1981.

———. "Research Roundup: Oral and Written Composition." *English Journal* 62 (1973): 1201–03.

Cooper, Charles R., and Lee Odell, eds. *Evaluating Writing: Describing, Measuring, Judging.* Urbana: NCTE, 1977.

———. Introduction. Cooper and Odell, *Evaluating Writing* vii–xii.

Cox, Roy. "Reliability and Validity of Examinations." *World Book of Education, 1969: Examinations.* Ed. J. A. Lawreys and D. G. Scanlon. London: Evans, 1969. 70–78.

Cronbach, Lee J. *Essentials of Psychological Testing.* 3rd ed. New York: Harper, 1970.

———. "Five Perspectives on Validity Argument." *Test Validity.* Ed. Howard Wainer and Henry I. Braun. Hillsdale: Erlbaum, 1988. 3–17.

Cronbach, Lee J., G. C. Gleser, H. Nanda, and N. Rajaratnam. *The Dependability of Behavioral Measurements: Theory of Generalizability for Scores and Profiles.* New York: Wiley, 1972.

Cronbach, Lee J., N. Rajaratnam, and G. Gleser. "Theory of Generalizability: A Liberation of Reliability Theory." *British Journal of Statistical Psychology* 16 (1963): 137–63.

Crystal, Daisy. "Dialect Mixture and Sorting Out the Concept of Freshman English Remediation." Luelsdorff 131–42.

Daiker, Donald A., et al., eds. *The Best of Miami's Portfolios.* 6 vols. Oxford: Miami U, 1990, 1991, 1992, 1993, 1994, 1995.

Daniell, Beth. "The Situation of Literacy and Cognition: What We Can Learn from the Uzbek Experiment." Lunsford, Moglen, and Slevin 197–207.

Darling-Hammond, Linda, and Carla Ascher. *Creating Accountability in Big City School Systems.* New York: ERIC Clearinghouse on Urban Educ.; Natl. Center for Restructuring Educ., Schools, and Teaching, Teachers Coll., 1991.

Davis, Barbara Gross, Michael Scriven, and Susan Thomas. *The Evaluation of Composition Instruction.* 2nd ed. New York: Teachers Coll. P, 1987.

Davis v. Washington. 348 F. Supp. 15. DDC. 1972.

Debra P. v. Turlington. 474 F. Supp. 244. MD FL. 1979.

Delandshere, Ginette, and Anthony R. Petrosky. "Capturing Teachers' Knowledge: Performance Assessment." *Educational Researcher* 23.5 (1994): 11–18.

Dewey, John. "Creative Democracy—The Task before Us." *The Political Writings.* Ed. Debra Morris and Ian Shapiro. Indianapolis: Hackett, 1993. 240–45.

Deyhle, Donna. "Learning Failure: Tests as Gatekeepers and the Culturally Different Child." *Success or Failure? Learning and the Language Minority Student.* Ed. Henry T. Trueba. Cambridge: Newbury, 1987. 85–108.

Diederich, Paul Bernard. *Measuring Growth in English.* Urbana: NCTE, 1974.

Diederich, Paul Bernard, John W. French, and Sibyl T. Carlton. *Factors in Judgments of Writing Ability.* Research Bulletin RB-61-15. Princeton: Educ. Testing Service, 1961.

Dillard, J. L. *Black English.* New York: Random, 1972.

Dixon, Kathleen G. "Intellectual Development and the Place of Narrative in 'Basic' and Freshman Composition." *Journal of Basic Writing* 8 (1989): 3–20.

Dixon v. Alabama State Board of Education. 294 F. 2d 150. 5th Cir. Cert. denied. 368 US 930. 1961.

Duran, Richard P. "Testing of Linguistic Minorities." R. Linn 573–87.

Dyson, Anne Haas. *The Multiple Worlds of Child Writers: A Study of Friends Learning to Write.* New York: Teachers Coll. P, 1990.

Eble, Kenneth, and William J. McKeachie. *Improving Undergraduate Education through Faculty Development.* San Francisco: Jossey-Bass, 1987.

Edwards, Walter F. "Two Varieties of English in Detroit." Smitherman, *Black English* 393–408.

Eisenstadt v. Baird. 405 US 438. 1972.

Eisner, Elliot W. "The Primacy of Experience and the Politics of Method." *Educational Researcher* 17.5 (1988): 15–20.

Elbow, Peter. Foreword. Belanoff and Dickson ix–xvi.

———. "Ranking, Evaluating, and Liking: Sorting Out Three Forms of Judgment." *College English* 55 (1993): 187–206.

———. "Reflections on Academic Discourse: How It Relates to Freshmen and Colleagues." *College English* 53 (1991): 135–55.

———. "Writing Assessment in the Twenty-First Century: A Utopian View." *Composition in the Twenty-First Century: Crisis and Change.* Ed. Lynn Bloom, Donald Daiker, and Edward White. Carbondale: Southern Illinois UP, 1995. 83–100.

———. *Writing without Teachers.* New York: Oxford UP, 1973.

Elbow, Peter, and Pat Belanoff. "Portfolios as a Substitute for Proficiency Examinations." *College Composition and Communication* 37 (1986): 336–39.

———. "State University of New York: Portfolio-Based Evaluation Program." *New Methods in College Writing Programs: Theories in Practice.* Ed. Paul Connolly and Teresa Vilardi. New York: MLA, 1986. 95–105. Rpt. in Belanoff and Dickson 3–16.

Elgin, S. H. *What Is Linguistics?* 2nd ed. Englewood Cliffs: Prentice, 1979.

Elías-Olivares, Lucia. "Hablar con sinceridad: Variedad discursiva del español mexico-americano." 11th Intl. Congress of ALFAL. State U of Campinas, Campinas, Brazil. 1990.

Elliot, Norbert, Maximino Plata, and Paul Zelhart. *A Program Development Handbook for the Holistic Assessment of Writing.* Boston: UP of Amer., 1990.

Elliott, Phillip. "Spanish and English Opinion Essays: A Study in Contrastive Rhetoric." Unpublished paper.

Emig, Janet. *The Composing Processes of Twelfth Graders.* Research report 13. Urbana: NCTE, 1971.

———. "Inquiry Paradigms and Writing." *College Composition and Communication* 33 (1982): 64–75.

Engelhard, George. "Examining Rater Errors in the Assessment of Written Composition with a Many-Faceted Rasch Model." *Journal of Educational Measurement* 31 (1994): 93–112.

Epperson v. Arkansas. 393 US 97 (1968).

Epps, Edgar G. "Situational Effects in Testing." Miller 41–51.

Etzioni, Amitai. *A Comparative Analysis of Complex Organizations.* Rev. ed. New York: Free, 1975.

Evans, Peter J. A., ed. *Directions and Misdirections in English Evaluation.* Ottawa: Canadian Council of Teachers of English, 1985.

Faigley, Lester. "Judging Writing, Judging Selves." *College Composition and Communication* 40 (1989): 395–412.

Faigley, Lester, Roger D. Cherry, David A. Jolliffe, and Anna M. Skinner, eds. *Assessing Writers' Knowledge and the Processes of Composing.* Norwood: Ablex, 1985.

Faigley, Lester, and Stephen Witte. "Analyzing Revision." *College Composition and Communication* 32 (1981): 400–14.

Farr, Marcia. "Biliteracy in the Home: Practices among *Mexicano* Families in

Chicago." *Adult Biliteracy in the United States.* Ed. David Spener. Washington: Center for Applied Linguistics, 1994. 89–110.

——— . *"En los Dos Idiomas:* Literacy Practices among *Mexicano* Families in Chicago." *Literacy across Communities.* Ed. Beverly Moss. Cresskill: Hampton, 1994. 9–47.

——— . "Essayist Literacy and Other Verbal Performances." *Written Communication* 10 (1993): 4–38.

Farr, Marcia, and Harvey Daniels. *Language Diversity and Writing Instruction.* New York: ERIC Clearinghouse on Urban Educ.; Urbana: NCTE, 1986.

Farris, Christine. "Disciplining the Disciplines: The Paradox of Writing across the Curriculum Claims." Conf. on Coll. Composition and Communication Convention. San Diego. 1993.

Fiacco v. Santee. 72 A. 2d 652. 421 NYS 2d 431. 1979.

Fiedler, Frank E. "The Contingency Model and the Dynamics of the Leadership Process." *Advances in Experimental Social Psychology.* Ed. L. Berkowitz. Vol. 11. New York: Academic, 1978. 59–112.

——— . "The Effects of Leadership Training and Experience: A Contingency Model Interpretation." *Administrative Science Quarterly* 17 (1972): 453–70.

Finlayson, Douglas S. "The Reliability of the Marking of Essays." *British Journal of Educational Psychology* 21 (1951): 126–34.

Finn, Patrick J. "Computer-Aided Description of Mature Word Choices in Writing." Cooper and Odell 69–89.

Fish, Stanley. "Anti-foundationalism, Theory Hope, and the Teaching of Composition." Koelb and Lokke 65–79.

——— . Interview. Koelb and Lokke 80–98.

——— . *Is There a Text in This Class? The Authority of Interpretive Communities.* Cambridge: Harvard UP, 1980.

Fisher, Ronald A. *The Design of Experiments.* Edinburgh: Oliver, 1935.

——— . *Statistical Methods for Research Workers.* London: Oliver, 1925.

Flower, Linda S., and John R. Hayes. "A Cognitive Process Theory of Writing." *College Composition and Communication* 32 (1981): 365–87.

——— . "The Dynamics of Composing: Making Plans and Juggling Constraints." *Cognitive Process in Writing.* Ed. L. W. Gregg and E. R. Steinberg. Hillsdale: Erlbaum, 1980. 31–50.

Flynn, Elizabeth Gurley. *The Rebel Girl: An Autobiography.* Rev. ed. New York: Intl., 1973.

Fox, Helen. *Listening to the World.* Urbana: NCTE, 1994.

Fox, Tom. "Basic Writing as Cultural Conflict." *Journal of Education* 172 (1990): 65–83.

Frase, Lawrence T., et al. "Computer Aids for Text Assessment and Writing Instruction." *NSPI Journal* Nov. 1981: 21–24.

Frederiksen, John R., and Allan Collins. "A Systems Approach to Educational Testing." *Educational Researcher* 18.9 (1989): 27–32.

Frederiksen, Norman, Robert Glaser, Allan Lesgold, and Michael G. Shafto, eds. *Diagnostic Monitoring of Skill and Knowledge Acquisition.* Hillsdale: Erlbaum, 1990.

Frederiksen, Norman, Robert J. Mislevy, and Isaac I. Bejar, eds. *Test Theory for a New Generation of Tests.* Hillsdale: Erlbaum, 1993.

Freedman, Sarah Warshauer, and William Robinson. "Testing Proficiency in Writing at San Francisco State University." *College Composition and Communication* 33 (1982): 393–98.

Frick, Ted, and Melvin I. Semmel. "Observer Agreement and Reliabilities of Classroom Observational Measures." *Review of Educational Research* 48 (1978): 157–84.

Fulwiler, Toby. "Evaluating Writing across the Curriculum Programs." *Strengthening Programs for Writing across the Curriculum.* New Directions for Teaching and Learning 36. San Francisco: Jossey-Bass, 1988. 61–75.

———. "How Well Does Writing across the Curriculum Work?" *College English* 46 (1984): 113–25.

———. "Writing to Reform the English Major." Conf. on Coll. Composition and Communication. Cincinnati. 1992.

Gardner, Howard. "Assessment in Context: The Alternative to Standardized Testing." Natl. Commission on Testing and Public Policy. Berkeley. 1988.

Gaspar v. Bruton. 513 F. 2d 843. 10th Cir. 1975.

Geertz, Clifford. *Works and Lives: The Anthropologist as Author.* Stanford: Stanford UP, 1988.

Gere, Anne Ruggles. "Empirical Research in Composition." McClelland and Donovan 110–24.

———, ed. *Into the Field: Sites of Composition Studies.* New York: MLA, 1993.

Gilyard, Keith. *Voices of the Self: A Study of Language Competence.* Detroit: Wayne State UP, 1991.

Gitomer, Drew H. "Performance Assessment and Educational Measurement." Bennett and Ward 241–64.

Glaser, Robert. "Cognitive and Environmental Perspectives on Assessing Achievement." *Assessment in the Service of Learning: Proceedings of the 1987 ETS Invitational Conference.* Princeton: Educ. Testing Service, 1988. 37–43.

Godshalk, Fred I., Frances Swineford, and William E. Coffman. *The Measurement of Writing Ability.* Research Monograph 6. New York: Coll. Entrance Examination Board, 1966.

Gold, Susan E. "Increasing Student Autonomy through Portfolios." Yancey 20–30.

Goodman, Kenneth S., Yetta M. Goodman, and Wendy J. Hood, eds. *The Whole Language Evaluation Book.* Portsmouth: Heinemann, 1989.

Gosling, G. *Marking Compositions.* Victoria: Australian Council for Educ. Research, 1966.

Goss v. Lopez. 419 US 565. 1975.

Gould, Stephen Jay. *The Mismeasure of Man*. New York: Norton, 1981.

Graff, Harvey J. *The Legacies of Literacy: Continuities and Contradictions in Western Culture and Society*. Bloomington: Indiana UP, 1987.

Gralla, Preston. "Grammar Checkers: Prose and Cons." *PC/Computing* Oct. 1988: 146–56.

Graue, M. Elizabeth, ed. *A Case Study Observing the Development of Primary Children's Composing, Spelling, and Motor Processes during the Writing Process, Final Report*. NIE grant G-78-0174. Durham: U of New Hampshire, 1981. [Ed 218 653.]

———. "Integrating Theory and Practice through Instructional Assessment." *Educational Assessment* 1 (1993): 283–310.

Graves, Donald H. *Writing: Teachers and Children at Work*. Exeter: Heinemann Educ., 1983.

Greenberg, Karen. Foreword. Elliot, Plata, and Zelhart ix.

———. "The Politics of Basic Writing." *Fourth National Basic Writing Conference Pleneries*. Spec. issue of *Journal of Basic Writing* 12.1 (1993): 64–71.

Greenberg, Karen L., Harvey S. Wiener, and Richard A. Donovan. Preface. Greenberg, Wiener, and Donovan, *Writing Assessment* xi–xvii.

———, eds. *Writing Assessment: Issues and Strategies*. New York: Longman, 1986.

Greenberg, Karen, and Stephen Witte. "Validity Issues in Direct Writing Assessment." *Notes from the National Testing Network in Writing* 8 (1988): 13–14.

Grego, Rhonda, and Nancy Thompson. "The Writing Studio: Reconfiguring Basic Writing / Freshman Composition." Unpublished essay, 1966.

Griggs v. Duke Power Co. 401 US 424. 1971.

Gronlund, Norman E. *Constructing Achievement Tests*. 3rd ed. Englewood Cliffs: Prentice, 1982.

Guba, Evon G., and Yvonna S. Lincoln. *Fourth Generation Evaluation*. Newbury Park: Sage, 1989.

Guerra, Juan C. "An Ethnographic Study of the Literacy Practices of a Mexican Immigrant Family in Chicago." Diss. U of Illinois, Chicago, 1992.

Guttman, Louis. "Measurement as Structural Theory." *Psychometrika* 36.4 (1971): 329–47.

Haisty, Donna B. "The Developmental Theories of Jean Piaget and William Perry: An Application to the Teaching of Writing." Diss. Texas Christian U, 1983.

Hake, Rosemary. "Composition Theory in Identifying and Evaluating Essay Theory." Diss. U of Chicago, 1973.

Hake, Rosemary, and Joseph Williams. "Some Cognitive Issues in Sentence Combining: On the Theory That Smaller Is Better." *Sentence Combining: A*

Rhetorical Perspective. Ed. Donald A. Daiker, Andrew Kerek, and Max Morenberg. Carbondale: Southern Illinois UP, 1985. 86–106.

Hall, William S. "Black and White Children's Responses to Black English Vernacular and Standard English Sentences: Evidence for Code-Switching." Harrison and Trabasso 201–08.

Hamp-Lyons, Liz, ed. *Assessing Second Language Writing in Academic Contexts.* Norwood: Ablex, 1991.

——— . *Assessment Guide for ELTS M2 Writing.* London: English Lang. Testing Service of the British Council, 1987.

——— . "Basic Concepts." Hamp-Lyons, *Assessing* 5–18.

——— . "Raters Respond to Rhetoric in Writing." *Interlingual Processes.* Ed. Hans Dechert and Gunther Raupach. Tubingen: Narr, 1989. 229–44.

——— . "Scoring Procedures for ESL Contexts." Hamp-Lyons, *Assessing* 241–78.

——— . "Second Language Writing: Assessment Issues." *Second Language Writing: Research Insights for the Classroom.* Ed. Barbara Kroll. New York: Cambridge UP, 1990. 69–87.

Hamp-Lyons, Liz, and William Condon. "Questioning Assumptions about Portfolio-Based Assessment." *College Composition and Communication* 44 (1993): 176–90.

Haney, Walt, and George Madaus. "Standardized Testing: Harmful to Educational Health." *Phi Delta Kappan* 70 (1989): 683–87.

Harding, Sandra. "Feminist Justification Strategies." *Women, Knowledge, and Reality: Explorations in Feminist Philosophy.* Ed. Ann Garry and Marilyn Pearsall. Boston: Unwin, 1989. 189–202.

Harkin, Patricia, and John Schilb, eds. *Contending with Words: Composition and Rhetoric in a Postmodern Age.* New York: MLA, 1991.

Harrison, Deborah Sears, and Tom Trabasso, eds. *Black English: A Seminar.* Hillsdale: Erlbaum, 1976.

Hartog, P., E. C. Rhodes, and C. Burt. *The Marks of Examiners.* New York: Macmillan, 1936.

Hartwell, Patrick. "Grammar, Grammars, and the Teaching of Grammar." *College English* 47 (1985): 105–27.

Haskins, Jim, and Hugh F. Butts. *The Psychology of Black Language.* New York: Barnes, 1973.

Haswell, Richard H. *Gaining Ground in College Writing: Tales of Development and Interpretation.* Dallas: Southern Methodist UP, 1991.

Haswell, Richard H., and Janis E. Haswell. "Gender Bias and Critique of Student Writing." *Assessing Writing* (1996, forthcoming).

Haswell, Richard H., and Susan Wyche-Smith. "Adventuring into Writing Assessment." *College Composition and Communication* 45 (1994): 220–36.

Hays, Janice N. "Models of Intellectual Development and Writing: A Response to Myra Kogen." *Journal of Basic Writing* 6 (1987): 11–27.

Hazen, Margret, et al. *Report on* Writer's Workbench *and Other Writing Tools.* Chapel Hill: U of North Carolina Microcomputing Support Center, 1986. ERIC ED 277015.

Heath, Shirley Brice. *Ways with Words: Language, Life and Work in Communities and Classrooms.* Cambridge: Cambridge UP, 1983.

Herrington, Anne. "Teaching, Writing, and Learning: A Naturalistic Study of Writing in an Undergraduate Literature Course." *Writing in Academic Disciplines.* Ed. David Jolliffe. Norwood: Ablex, 1989. 133–66.

Hilgers, Thomas L. "How Children Change as Critical Evaluators of Writing." *Research in the Teaching of English* 20 (1986): 36–55.

Hill, Jane. "Language, Culture and World View." *Linguistics: The Cambridge Survey.* Ed. Frederick Newmeyer. Vol. 4. Cambridge: Cambridge UP, 1988. 14–36.

Hillocks, George, Jr. *Research on Written Composition: New Directions for Teaching.* Urbana: ERIC Clearinghouse on Reading and Communication Skills; Natl. Conf. on Research in Teaching, 1986.

Hirsch, E. D., Jr. *The Philosophy of Composition.* Chicago: U of Chicago P, 1977.

Hoetker, James, and Gordon Brossell. "The Effects of Systematic Variations in Essay Topics on the Writing of College Freshmen." *College Composition and Communication* 40 (1989): 414–21.

———. "A Procedure for Writing Content-Fair Essay Examination Topics for Large-Scale Writing Assessments." *College Composition and Communication* 37 (1986): 328–35.

Holdstein, Deborah H. "Collaboration and Writing Assessment." Reagan, Fox, and Bleich 77–88.

Holland, Norman. *Five Readers Reading.* New Haven: Yale UP, 1975.

Hopkins, Kenneth D. "Generalizability Theory and Experimental Design: Incongruity between Analysis and Inference." *American Educational Research Journal* 21 (1984): 703–12.

Hopkins, T. L. *The Marking System of the College Entrance Examination Board.* Harvard Monographs in Educ., Ser. 1, No. 2. Cambridge: Graduate School of Educ., Harvard U, 1921.

Howard, Kathryn. "Making the Writing Portfolio Real." *Quarterly of the National Writing Project and the Center for the Study of Writing* 12.2 (1990): 4+.

———. "Portfolio Culture in Pittsburgh." *Fire in the Eyes of Youth.* Ed. Randolph Jennings. Saint Paul: Occasional, 1993. 89–94.

Hoyt, C. J. "Test Reliability Estimated by Analysis of Variance." *Psychometrika* 6 (1941): 153–60.

Huddleston, Edith M. "Measurement of Writing Ability at the College-Entrance Level: Objective vs. Subjective Testing Techniques." *Journal of Experimental Psychology* 22 (1954): 165–213.

Hughes-Wiener, Gail, and Susan Jensen-Cekalla. "Organizing a WAC Evaluation Project: Implications for Program Planning." *Writing across the Curricu-*

lum in the Community College. Ed. Linda Stanley and Joanne J. Ambron. New Directions for Community Coll. San Francisco: Jossey-Bass, 1991. 65–70.

Hughes-Wiener, Gail, and Gerald R. Martin. "Results of Instructional Research in a Writing across the Curriculum Staff Development Program." Amer. Educ. Research Assn. Conf. San Francisco. 1989.

Hunt, Kellogg W. "Early Blooming and Late Blooming Syntactic Structures." Cooper and Odell 91–104.

Huot, Brian. "The Influence of Holistic Scoring Procedures on Reading and Rating Student Essays." Williamson and Huot 206–36.

Hurston, Zora Neale. *I Love Myself When I Am Laughing: A Zora Neale Hurston Reader.* Ed. Alice Walker. New York: Feminist, 1979.

Hymes, Dell. "Ways of Speaking." *Explorations in the Ethnography of Speaking.* Ed. Richard Bauman and Joel Sherzer. Cambridge: Cambridge UP, 1974. 433–51.

Ingraham v. Wright. 430 US 651. 1977.

Jacobs, Holly L., Stephen A. Zinkgraf, Deanna Wormuth, V. Faye Hartfiel, and J. B. Hughey. *Testing ESL Composition: A Practical Approach.* Rowley: Newbury, 1981.

Janopoulos, Michael. "University Faculty Tolerance of NS and NNS Writing Errors." *Journal of Second Language Writing* 1.2 (1991): 109–22.

Jenness v. Fortson. 403 US 431. 1971.

Jenseth, Richard. "Surveying the Writing Minor: *Que Es Eso?*" Conf. on Coll. Composition and Communication Convention. Boston. 1991.

Johnson, Burges. *Good Writing.* An Inquiry into the Efficacy of the Teaching of Written Composition in American Colleges and a Search for the Criteria of "Good Writing." N.p.: Carnegie Foundation for the Advancement of Teaching, n.d.

Johnston, Peter H. *Constructive Evaluation of Literate Activity.* New York: Longman, 1992.

Kaplan, Sydney Janet. *Katherine Mansfield and the Origins of Modernist Fiction.* Ithaca: Cornell UP, 1991.

Kerek, Andrew, Donald Daiker, and Max Morenberg. "Sentence Combining and College Composition." *Perceptual and Motor Skills* 51 (1980): 1059–1157.

Kirby, Dan, and Carol Kuykendall. *Mind Matters: Teaching for Thinking.* Portsmouth: Boynton-Heinemann, 1991.

Kirsch, Irwin S., and Ann Jungeblut. *Literacy: Profiles of America's Young Adults.* Natl. Assessment of Educ. Progress report. Princeton: Educ. Testing Service, 1986.

Kitzhaber, Albert R. *Themes, Theories, and Therapy: The Teaching of Writing in College.* New York: McGraw, 1963.

Knoblauch, C. H. "Literacy and the Politics of Education." Lunsford, Moglen, and Slevin 74–80.

Knoblauch, C. H., and Lil Brannon. *Rhetorical Traditions and the Teaching of Writing*. Upper Montclair: Boynton, 1984.

Koelb, Clayton, and Vergil L. Lokke, eds. *The Current in Criticism*. West Lafayette: Purdue UP, 1987.

Koenig, Judith, and Karen Mitchell. "An Interim Report on the MCAT Essay Pilot Project." *Journal of Medical Education* 63 (1988): 21–29.

Koretz, Daniel. "The Evaluation of the Vermont Portfolio Assessment Programs: Interpretations and Implications of Initial Findings." Meeting of the Natl. Council on Measurement in Educ. Atlanta. 1993.

Labov, William. *Language in the Inner City: Studies in the Black English Vernacular*. Philadelphia: U of Pennsylvania P, 1972.

———. "The Logic of Nonstandard English." *Language and Social Context*. Ed. Pier Paolo Giglioli. Harmondsworth: Penguin, 1972. 179–215.

Labov, William, and W. Harris. "De Facto Segregation of Black and White Vernaculars." Conf. of New Ways of Analyzing Variation in English. Montreal. 1983.

Lane, Suzanne, Carol Parke, and Barbara Moskal. "Principles for Developing Performance Assessments." Meeting of the Amer. Educ. Research Assn. San Francisco. 1992.

Lane, Suzanne, and D. Sabers. "Use of Generalizability Theory for Estimating the Dependability of a Scoring System for Sample Essays." *Applied Measurement in Education* 2 (1989): 195–205.

Larry P. v. Riles. 495 F. Supp. 926. ND CA 1979. 343 F. Supp. 1306. ND CA 1972. Affirmed 502 F. 2d 963. 9th Cir. 1974.

Larson, Richard. "Using Portfolios in the Assessment of Writing in the Academic Disciplines." Belanoff and Dickson 137–49.

Lau v. Nichols. 414 US 563. 1974.

Lauer, Janice M., and J. William Asher. *Composition Research: Empirical Designs*. New York: Oxford UP, 1988.

Lauter, Paul. "The Literatures of America: A Comparative Discipline." *Redefining American Literary History*. Ed. A. LaVonne Brown Ruoff and Jerry W. Ward, Jr. New York: MLA, 1990. 9–34.

Lederman, Marie Jean. "Why Test?" Greenberg, Wiener, and Donovan, *Writing Assessment* 35–43.

Lederman, Marie Jean, Susan Ryzewic, and Michael Ribaudo. *Assessment and Improvement of the Academic Skills of Entering Freshmen: A National Survey*. New York: Instructional Resource Center, City U of New York, 1983.

Leitch, Vincent. "Two Poststructuralist Modes of (Inter)Textuality." *Critical Texts* 2 (1982): 3–5.

LeMahieu, Paul G., JoAnne T. Eresh, and Richard C. Wallace. "Using Student Portfolios for a Public Accounting." *School Administrator* Dec. 1992: 8–15.

LeMahieu, Paul G., Drew H. Gitomer, and JoAnne T. Eresh. "Using Student Portfolios in Large-Scale Assessment: Difficult but Not Impossible." *Educational Measurement: Issues and Practice* 14.3 (1995): 11–28.

Lerner, Barbara. "Good News about American Education." *Commentary* 91 (1991): 19–25.

——— . "The Minimum Competence Testing Movement: Social, Scientific, and Legal Implications." *American Psychologist* 36 (1981): 1057–66.

Lesh, Richard, and Susan J. Lamon, eds. *Assessment of Authentic Performance in School Mathematics*. Washington: AAAS, 1992.

Levine, Denise S. "The Four P's of Context-Based Assessment: Evaluating Literacy across the Curriculum." *Literacy across the Curriculum*. Ed. Carolyn Hedley, Patricia Antonacci, and Dorothy Feldman. Norwood: Ablex, 1992. 167–76.

Lewis, Donald Marion. "Certifying Functional Literacy: Competency Testing and Implications for Due Process and Equal Educational Opportunity." *Journal of Law and Education* 8 (1979): 145–83.

Lewis, Shirley A. R. "Teacher Attitude Change: Does Informing Make a Difference?" Whiteman 85–92.

Lieberman, Ann. "The Meaning of Scholarly Activity and the Building of Community." *Educational Researcher* 21.6 (1992): 5–12.

Linacre, John M., and Benjamin D. Wright. *A User's Guide to FACETS: Rasch Measurement Computer Program*. Chicago: MESA, 1994.

Linn, Michael D. "Black Rhetorical Patterns and the Teaching of Composition." *College Composition and Communication* 26 (1975): 149–53.

Linn, Robert, ed. *Educational Measurement*. 3rd ed. New York: Macmillan, 1989.

Linn, Robert L., Eva I. Baker, and Stephen B. Dunbar. "Complex, Performance-Based Assessment: Expectations and Validation Criteria." *Educational Researcher* 20.8 (1991): 5–21.

Lipscomb, Delores. "Introduction: Writing." Brooks 149–53.

Lloyd-Jones, Richard. "Primary Trait Scoring." Cooper and Odell 33–68.

Lucas, Catharine Keech. "Toward Ecological Evaluation." *Quarterly of the National Writing Project and the Center for the Study of Writing* 10.1 (1988): 1+.

——— . "Toward Ecological Evaluation, Part Two: Recontextualizing Literacy Assessment." *Quarterly of the National Writing Project and the Center for the Study of Writing* 10.2 (1988): 4–10.

Lucas, Catharine, and Sybil B. Carlson. *Prototype of Alternative Assessment Strategies for New Teachers of English*. San Francisco: California New Teacher Project, 1989.

Luelsdorff, Philip, ed. *Linguistic Perspectives on Black English*. Münster: Regensberg, 1975.

Lunsford, Andrea. "Cognitive Development and the Basic Writer." *College English* 41 (1979): 38–46.

————. "Composing Ourselves: Politics, Commitment, and the Teaching of Writing." *College Composition and Communication* 41 (1990): 71–82.

————. "The Past—and Future—of Writing Assessment." Greenberg, Wiener, and Donovan, *Writing Assessment* 1–12.

Lunsford, Andrea A., Helene Moglen, and James Slevin, eds. *The Right to Literacy*. New York: MLA, 1990.

Lunsford, Ronald, and Richard Straub. *Twelve Readers Reading*. Cresskill: Hampton, 1994.

Lux, Paul. "Discourse Styles of Anglo and Latin American College Student Writers." Diss. Arizona State U, 1991.

MacKinnon, Catherine A. "Feminism, Marxism, Method, and the State." *Feminist Theory*. Ed. Nannerl O. Keohane, Michelle Z. Rosaldo, and Barbara C. Gelpi. Brighton: Harvester, 1982. 5–26.

Macrorie, Ken. "Roundtable Review." *Research in the Teaching of English* 3 (1969): 228–36.

Mahala, Daniel, and Michael Vivion. "The Role of AP and the Composition Program." *WPA: Writing Program Administration* 17.1–2 (1993): 43–56.

Mahiri, Jabari. "Discourse in Sports: A Study of African-American Preadolescents." Diss. U of Illinois, Chicago, 1991.

Maimon, Elaine P., and Barbara F. Nodine. "Measuring Syntactic Growth: Errors and Expectations in Sentence-Combining Practice with College Freshmen." *Research in the Teaching of English* 12 (1978): 233–44.

————. "Words Enough and Time: Syntax and Error One Year After." *Sentence Combining and the Teaching of Writing: Selected Papers from the Miami University Conference*. Ed. Donald A. Daiker et al. Akron: U of Akron P, 1979. 101–08.

Matsuhashi, Ann. "Explorations in the Real-Time Production of Written Discourse." *What Writers Know: The Language, Process, and Structure of Written Discourse*. Ed. Martin Nystrand. New York: Academic, 1982. 269–90.

McCarthy, Lucille Parkinson. "A Stranger in Strange Lands: A College Student Writing across the Curriculum." *Research in the Teaching of English* 21 (1987): 233–65.

McCarthy, Martha M. "Court Cases with an Impact on the Teaching of Reading." *Journal of Reading* 23 (1979): 205–11.

McCleary, William J. "A Note on Reliability and Validity Problems in Composition Research." *Research in the Teaching of English* 13 (1979): 274–77.

McClelland, Ben W., and Timothy R. Donovan, eds. *Perspectives on Research and Scholarship in Composition*. New York: MLA, 1985.

McClung, Merle. "Competency Testing Programs: Legal and Educational Issues." *Fordham Law Review* 47 (1979): 651–712.

McCracken, Nancy Mellis, and Bruce C. Appleby. *Gender Issues in the Teaching of English*. Portsmouth: Boynton, 1992.

McCurry, Niki, and Alan McCurry. "Writing Assessment for the Twenty-First Century." *The Computing Teacher* 19 (1992): 35–37.

McKendy, Thomas. "Locally Developed Tests and the Validity of Holistic Scoring." *Research in the Teaching of English* 26 (1992): 149–66.

Messick, Samuel. "Meaning and Values in Test Validation: The Science and Ethics of Assessment." *Educational Researcher* 18.2 (1989): 5–11.

———. "Validity." R. Linn 13–104.

Miami University Portfolio Writing Program. Brochure. Oxford: Miami U, 1995.

Miller, Lamar P., ed. *The Testing of Black Students.* Englewood Cliffs: Prentice, 1974.

Mishler, Elliot G. "Meaning in Context: Is There Any Other Kind?" *Harvard Educational Review* 49 (1979): 1–19.

Mislevy, Robert. *On Inferential Issues Arising in the California Learning Assessment System.* Princeton: Center for Performance Assessment, Educ. Testing Service, 1995.

Mitchell, Karen, and Judith Anderson. "Reliability of Essay Scoring for the MCAT Essay." *Educational and Psychological Measurement* 46 (1986): 771–75.

Mitchell, Ruth. "Sampler of Authentic Assessment: What It Is and What It Looks Like." California Assessment Program Conf. Sacramento. 1989.

———. *Testing for Learning.* New York: Free, 1992.

Moe, Alden J. "Analyzing Text with Computers." *Educational Technology* July 1980: 29–31.

Montano-Harmon, Rosario. "Discourse Features in the Compositions of Mexican English as a Second Language, Mexican-American Chicano, and Anglo High School Students: Considerations for the Formulation of Educational Policy." Diss. U of Southern California, 1988.

Moran, Michael G., and Ronald F. Lunsford, eds. *Research in Composition and Rhetoric: A Bibliographic Sourcebook.* Westport: Greenwood, 1984.

Morenberg, Max, Donald Daiker, and Andrew Kerek. "Sentence Combining at the College Level." *Research in the Teaching of English* 12 (1978): 245–56.

Moss, Beverly. "The Black Church Sermon as a Literacy Event." Diss. U of Illinois, Chicago, 1988.

Moss, Pamela A. "Can There Be Validity without Reliability?" *Educational Researcher* 23.2 (1994): 5–12.

———. "Shifting Conceptions of Validity in Educational Measurement: Implications for Performance Assessment." *Review of Educational Research* 62 (1992): 229–58.

———. "Validity in High Stakes Writing Assessment: Problems and Possibilities." *Assessing Writing* 1 (1994): 109–28.

Moss, Pamela A., et al. "Portfolios, Accountability, and an Interpretive Approach to Validity." *Educational Measurement: Issues and Practice* 11.3 (1992): 12–21.

Mufwene, Salikoko S., ed. *Africanisms in Afro-American Language Varieties.* U of Georgia P, 1993.

Murphy, Sandra, and Roberta Camp. "Toward Systemic Coherence: A Discussion of Conflicting Perspectives on Portfolio Assessment." *Writing Portfolios in the Classroom: Policy and Practice, Promise and Peril.* Ed. Robert Kelsey. Hillsdale: Erlbaum, in press.

Murphy, Sandra, and Leo Ruth. "The Field Testing of Writing Prompts Reconsidered." Williamson and Huot 266–302.

Murphy, Sandra, and Mary Ann Smith. "Looking into Portfolios." Yancey 49–60.

———. "Talking about Portfolios." *Quarterly of the National Writing Project and the Center for the Study of Writing* 12.2 (1990): 1+.

———. *Writing Portfolios: A Bridge from Teaching to Assessment.* Markham, ON: Pippin, 1991.

Murray, D. M. *A Writer Teaches Writing.* Boston: Houghton, 1986.

Nardini, Gloria. "Writing English as a Second Language: Second to What?" Peer Tutoring in Writing Conf. Purdue U, West Lafayette. 1987.

National Assessment of Educational Progress. *The Reading Report Card, 1971–88.* Princeton: Educ. Testing Service, 1989.

———. *The Writing Report Card, 1984–88.* Princeton: Educ. Testing Service, 1989.

Newmann, Fred. "Linking Restructuring to Authentic Student Achievement." *Phi Delta Kappan* 72 (1991): 458–63.

Noonan-Wagner, Delsey. *Black Writers in the Classroom: A Question of Language Experience, Not Grammar.* ERIC 183 599. 1980. 1–4.

North, Stephen M. *The Making of Knowledge in Composition: Portrait of an Emerging Field.* Upper Montclair: Boynton, 1987.

Nystrand, Martin, A. S. Cohen, and N. M. Dowling. "Assessing Reliability Problems in the Portfolio Assessment of Writing." *Educational Assessment* 1 (1993): 53–70.

Ochsner, Robert S. *Physical Eloquence and the Biology of Writing.* Albany: State U of New York P, 1990.

O'Connor, Mary Catherine. "Aspects of Differential Performance by Minorities on Standardized Tests: Linguistic and Sociocultural Factors." *Test Policy and Test Performance: Education, Language, and Culture.* Ed. Bernard R. Gifford. Boston: Kluwer Academic, 1989. 129–81.

Odell, Lee. "Defining and Assessing Competence in Writing." Cooper, *Nature* 95–138.

———. "Measuring the Effect of Instruction on Pre-writing." *Research in the Teaching of English* 8 (1974): 228–40.

―――― . "Piaget, Problem-Solving, and Freshman Composition." *College Composition and Communication* 24 (1973): 36–42.

Odell, Lee, and Dixie Goswami, eds. *Writing in Nonacademic Settings*. New York: Guilford, 1985.

Ogbu, John U. "Literacy and Schooling in Subordinate Cultures: The Case of Black Americans." *Perspectives on Literacy*. Ed. Eugene R. Kintgen, Barry Kroll, and Mike Rose. Carbondale: Southern Illinois UP, 1988. 227–42.

Ohmann, Richard. *English in America: A Radical View of the Profession*. New York: Oxford UP, 1976.

Olson, Gary A., and Joseph M. Moxley. "Directing Freshman Composition: The Limits of Authority." *College Composition and Communication* 40 (1989): 51–59.

O'Neal, Verley, and Tom Trabasso. "Is There a Correspondence between Sound and Spelling? Some Implications for Black English Speakers." Harrison and Trabasso 171–90.

Pace, Guy. "Grammar and Style Checking; or, Strunk and White Never Had It So Good!" *Text Technology* 1 (1991): 5–6.

Page, Ellis B. "The Imminence of Grading Essays by Computer." *Phi Delta Kappan* 47 (1966): 238–43.

Page, Ellis B., and Dieter H. Paulus. *The Analysis of Essays by Computer*. Final report of US Office of Educ. project 6-1318. Storrs: Bureau of Educ. Research, U of Connecticut, 1968.

Page, Ellis B., and Nancy S. Petersen. "The Computer Moves into Essay Grading: Updating the Ancient Test." *Phi Delta Kappan* 76 (1995): 561–65.

Paris, Scott G., Theresa A. Lawton, Julianne C. Turner, and Jodie L. Roth. "A Developmental Perspective on Standardized Achievement Testing." *Educational Researcher* 19.2 (1991): 12–20.

Patton, Michael Q. *Qualitative Evaluation Methods*. Beverly Hills: Sage, 1980.

Paulson, F. Leon, Pearl R. Paulson, and Carol A. Meyer. "What Makes a Portfolio a Portfolio?" *Educational Leadership* 48.5 (1991): 60–63.

Peaden, Catherine Hobbs. Rev. of *Gender Issues in the Teaching of English*, by Nancy Mellis McCracken and Bruce C. Appleby. *Journal of Advanced Composition* 13 (1993): 260–63.

Pearson, P. David, and Sheila Valencia. "Assessment, Accountability, and Professional Prerogative." *Research in Literacy: Merging Perspectives; Thirty-Sixth Yearbook of the National Reading Conference*. Rochester: Natl. Reading Conf., 1987. 3–16.

Penalosa, F. *Introduction to the Sociology of Language*. Rowley: Newbury, 1981.

Perl, Sondra. "The Composing Processes of Unskilled College Writers." *Research in the Teaching of English* 13 (1979): 317–36.

―――― . "Understanding Composing." *College Composition and Communication* 31 (1980): 363–69.

Perrone, Vito, ed. *Expanding Student Assessment*. Alexandria: Assn. for Supervision and Curriculum Dev., 1991.

Perry, William. *Forms of Intellectual and Ethical Development in the College Years*. New York: Holt, 1968.

Phelps, Louise Wetherbee. "Cross-Sections in an Emerging Psychology of Composition." Moran and Lunsford 27–69.

Pilliner, Albert E. G. "Applications of Analysis of Variance to Problems of Correlation." *British Journal of Statistical Psychology* 5 (1952): 31–38.

Pinckney, H. B. "Florida's Minimum Competency Program: Two Years Later and the Judge's Decision." *Clearing House* 53 (1980): 318–22.

Pitkin, Willis. "Discourse Blocs." *College Composition and Communication* 20 (1969): 138–48.

Polin, Linda, and Edward White. "Speaking Frankly: Writing Program Administrators Look at Instructional Goals and Faculty Retraining." *WPA: Writing Program Administration* 9.1–2 (1985): 19–30.

Popham, W. James. *Educational Evaluation*. Englewood Cliffs: Prentice, 1975.

Psychological Corporation. *Integrated Assessment System: Language Arts Performance Assessment; Language Arts Portfolio*. San Antonio: Harcourt, 1990.

Purnell, Rosentene. "A Survey of the Testing of Writing Proficiency in College: A Progress Report." *College Composition and Communication* 33 (1982): 407–10.

Purves, Alan. "Reflections on Research and Assessment in Written Composition." *Research in the Teaching of English* 26 (1992): 108–22.

Raimes, Ann. "What Unskilled ESL Students Do As They Write." *TESOL Quarterly* 19 (1985): 229–58.

Reagan, Sally Barr, Thomas Fox, and David Bleich, eds. *New Directions in Collaborative Teaching, Learning, and Research*. Buffalo: State U of New York P, 1994.

Reed v. Reed. 404 US 71. 1971.

Reif, Linda. "Finding the Value in Evaluation: Self-Assessment in a Middle-School Classroom." *Educational Leadership* 47.6 (1990): 24–29.

Resnick, Daniel P., and Lauren B. Resnick. "The Nature of Literacy: An Historical Exploration." *Harvard Educational Review* 47 (1977): 370–85.

———. "Standards, Curriculum, and Performance: A Historical and Comparative Perspective." *Educational Researcher* 14.4 (1985): 5–20.

Richardson, Joan. "Graduates with No Degrees Call WSU Essay Test Biased." *Detroit Free Press* 27 Nov. 1992: 1A+.

Riesman, David. *On Higher Education: The Academic Enterprise in an Era of Rising Student Consumerism*. San Francisco: Jossey-Bass, 1981.

Roemer, Marjorie, Lucille Schultz, and Russell Durst. "Portfolios and the Process of Change." *College Composition and Communication* 42 (1991): 455–69.

Roen, Duane H. "Gender and Teacher Response to Student Writing." McCracken and Appleby 126–41.

Rogers, Everett M. *Diffusion of Innovations*. New York: Free, 1983.

Rose, Mike, ed. *When a Writer Can't Write: Studies in Writer's Block and Other Composing Problems*. New York: Guilford, 1985.

Rosenblatt, Louise M. *Literature as Exploration*. 1938. 4th ed. New York: MLA, 1983.

——— . "The Transactional Theory: Against Dualisms." *College English* 55 (1993): 377–86.

Ross, Edward Alsworth. *Seventy Years of It: An Autobiography*. New York: Appleton, 1936.

Rothman, Robert. "Auditors Help Pittsburgh Make Sure Its Portfolio Assessment Measures Up." *Education Week* 5 Aug. 1992: 27–28.

Rowley, Glenn L. "The Reliability of Observational Measures." *American Educational Research Journal* 13 (1976): 51–59.

Rubin, D. L., and K. Greene. "Gender-Typical Style in Written Language." *Research in the Teaching of English* 26 (1992): 7–20.

Ruth, Leo, and Sandra Murphy. *Designing Writing Tasks for the Assessment of Writing*. Norwood: Ablex, 1988.

Sanborn, Jean. "The Academic Essay: A Feminist View in Student Voices." McCracken and Appleby 142–60.

Santos, Terry. "Ideology in Composition: L1 and ESL." *Journal of Second Language Writing* 1 (1991): 1–16.

Scardamalia, Marlene, and Carl Bereiter. "Research on Written Composition." *Handbook of Research on Teaching*. 3rd ed. Ed. M. Wittrock. New York: Macmillan, 1985. 708–803.

Scharton, M. A. "Models of Competence: Responses to a Scenario Writing Assignment." *Research in the Teaching of English* 23 (1989): 163–80.

Schon, Donald. *Educating the Reflective Practitioner*. San Francisco: Jossey-Bass, 1987.

Schumacher, Gary M., and Jane Gradwohl Nash. "Conceptualizing and Measuring Knowledge Change Due to Writing." *Research in the Teaching of English* 25 (1991): 67–96.

Schweickart, Patrocinio P. "Reading Ourselves: Toward a Feminist Theory of Reading." *Gender and Reading*. Ed. Elizabeth A. Flynn and Patrocinio P. Schweickart. Baltimore: Johns Hopkins UP, 1986. 31–62.

Scollon, Ron, and Suzanne B. K. Scollon. *Narrative, Literacy, and Face in Interethnic Communication*. Norwood: Ablex, 1981.

Scott, Jerrie. "Black Language and Communication Skills: Recycling the Issues." Smitherman, *Black English* 130–45.

Scribner, Sylvia, and Michael Cole. *The Psychology of Literacy*. Cambridge: Harvard UP, 1981.

Shaughnessy, Mina P. *Errors and Expectations: A Guide for the Teacher of Basic Writing.* New York: Oxford UP, 1977.

Sheingold, Karen, Joan Heller, and Susan Paulukonis. *Actively Seeking Evidence: Shifts in Teachers' Thinking and Practice through Assessment.* Princeton: Center for Performance Assessment, Educ. Testing Service, 1994.

Shepard, Lorrie A. "The Place of Testing Reform in Educational Reform: A Reply to Cizek." *Educational Researcher* 22.4 (1993): 10–13.

Sherwin, Susan. "Philosophical Methodology and Feminist Methodology: Are They Compatible?" *Women, Knowledge, and Reality: Explorations in Feminist Philosophy.* Ed. Ann Garry and Marilyn Pearsall. Boston: Unwin, 1989. 21–36.

Showalter, Elaine. "Feminist Criticism in the Wilderness." Showalter, *New Feminist Criticism* 243–70.

———, ed. *The New Feminist Criticism.* New York: Pantheon, 1985.

Shuy, Roger W. "Vernacular Black English: Setting the Issues in Time." Whiteman 1–9.

Simpkins, Edward. "Equitable Policy." Smitherman, *Black English* 163–70.

Sims, Verner Martin. "The Essay Examination as a Projective Technique." *Educational and Psychological Measurement* 8 (1948): 15–31.

Slattery, Patrick. "Applying Intellectual Development Theory to Composition." *Journal of Basic Writing* 9 (1990): 54–65.

Slotnick, Henry B., and John V. Knapp. "Essay Grading by Computer: A Laboratory Phenomenon?" *English Journal* 60 (1971): 75–87.

Smagorinsky, Peter, and Michael W. Smith. "The Nature of Knowledge in Composition and Literary Understanding: The Question of Specificity." *Review of Educational Research* 62 (1992): 279–305.

Smith, Mary Ann. Personal communication from the codirector of the Nat'l. Writing Project to Sandra Murphy and Barbara Grant.

Smith, William. "Assessing the Reliability and Adequacy of Using Holistic Scoring of Essays as a College Composition Placement Technique." Williamson and Huot 142–205.

Smitherman, Geneva, ed. *Black English and the Education of Black Children and Youth.* Detroit: Center for Black Studies, Wayne State U, 1981.

——— . *Black Student Writers, Storks, and Familiar Places: What Can We Learn from the National Assessment of Educational Progress?* ERIC, 1984. 259–328.

——— . "From Africa to the New World and into the Space Age." Smitherman, *Black English* 409–23.

——— . *Talkin and Testifyin: The Language of Black America.* Detroit: Wayne State UP, 1977.

Snow, C. P. *The Two Cultures and the Scientific Revolution.* New York: Cambridge UP, 1961.

Sommers, Nancy. "Responding to Student Writing." *College Composition and Communication* 33 (1982): 148–56.

———. "Revision Strategies of Student Writers and Experienced Adult Writers." *College Composition and Communication* 31 (1980): 378–88.

Spandel, Vickie, and Richard J. Stiggins. *Direct Measures of Writing Skill: Issues and Applications.* Portland: Northwest Regional Educ. Laboratory, Clearinghouse for Applied Performance Testing, 1980.

Spectrum Educational Media, Inc. Advertising flier for *Grammar Portfolio.* Mattoon: Spectrum Educ. Media, 1984.

Stallard, C. K. "An Analysis of the Writing Behavior of Good Student Writers." *Research in the Teaching of English* 8 (1974): 206–18.

Stanley, Julian C. "Analysis-of-Variance Principles Applied to the Grading of Essay Tests." *Journal of Experimental Education* 30 (1962): 279–83.

———. "Reliability." *Educational Measurement.* Ed. R. L. Thorndike. Washington: Amer. Council on Educ., 1971. 356–442.

Steele, Joe M. "The Assessment of Writing Proficiency via Qualitative Ratings of Writing Samples." Meeting of the Natl. Council on Measurement in Educ. San Francisco. 1979.

Stenhouse, Lawrence. "Case Study and Case Records: Towards a Contemporary History of Education." *British Educational Research Journal* 4.2 (1978): 21–39.

Stewart, Murray F. "Syntactic Maturity from High School to University: A First Look." *Research in the Teaching of English* 12 (1978): 37–46.

Stiggins, Richard J. "Revitalizing Classroom Assessment: The Highest Instructional Priority." *Phi Delta Kappan* 69 (1988): 184–93.

Stokes, Gale. *The Walls Came Tumbling Down: The Collapse of Communism in Eastern Europe.* New York: Oxford UP, 1993.

Street, Brian. *Literacy in Theory and Practice.* Cambridge: Cambridge UP, 1984.

Strevens, Peter D. "Pronunciation of the English Language in West Africa." *Papers in Language and Language Teaching.* London: Oxford UP, 1965.

"Students' Right to Their Own Language." *College Composition and Communication* 25 (1974): 1–32.

Swales, John M. *Genre Analysis: English in Academic and Research Settings.* Cambridge: Cambridge UP, 1990.

Tannen, Deborah. *Talking Voices: Repetition, Dialogue, and Imagery in Conversational Discourse.* Cambridge: Cambridge UP, 1989.

Tate, Gary, ed. *Teaching Composition: Twelve Bibliographical Essays.* Fort Worth: Texas Christian UP, 1987.

Taylor, Orlando, and Dorian Latham Lee. "Standardized Tests and African-American Children: Communication and Language Issues." *Negro Educational Review* 38 (1987): 67–80.

"Testing the Test." *Detroit Free Press* 8 Dec. 1992: 1A.

Thompson, Richard F. "Is Test Retest a Suitable Reliability in Most Composition Studies?" *Research in the Teaching of English* 14 (1980): 154–56.

Thorndike, R. L. "Reliability." *Testing Problems in Perspective*. Ed. A. Anastasi. Washington: Amer. Council on Educ., 1967. 284–91.

Tierney, Robert J., Mark A. Carter, and Laura E. Desai. *Portfolio Assessment in the Reading-Writing Classroom*. Norwood: Gordon, 1991.

Tompkins, Jane. "Fighting Words: Unlearning to Write the Critical Essay." *Georgia Review* 17 (1988): 585–91.

———— . "Sentimental Power: *Uncle Tom's Cabin* and the Politics of Literary History." Showalter, *New Feminist Criticism* 81–104.

Tormakangas, Kari. "The Validity, the Reliability, and the Generalizability of the Ratings of the Written Composition." Meeting of the Amer. Educ. Research Assn. Washington. 1987.

Traugott, Elizabeth Closs. "Pidgins, Creoles, and the Origins of Vernacular Black English." Harrison and Trabasso 57–94.

Trimbur, John. "Essayist Literacy and the Rhetoric of Deproduction." *Rhetoric Review* 9 (1990): 73–86.

———— . "Literacy and the Discourse of Crisis." Bullock and Trimbur 277–95.

Turner, L. D. *Africanisms in the Gullah Dialect*. Chicago: U of Chicago P, 1949.

Twiggs, Robert D. *Pan-African Language in the Western Hemisphere, PALWH [paelwh]: A Re-definition of Black Dialect as a Language and the Culture of Black Dialect*. Hanover: Christopher, 1973.

Valencia, Sheila, William McGinley, and P. David Pearson. "Assessing Literacy in the Middle School." *Reading in the Middle School*. 2nd ed. Ed. Gerald Duffy. Newark: Intl. Reading Assn., 1990. 124–41.

Valeri-Gold, Maria, James R. Olson, and Mary Deming. "Portfolios: Collaborative Authentic Assessment Opportunities for College Developmental Learners." *Journal of Reading* 35 (1991–92): 298–305.

Vann, Roberta J., Frederick O. Lorenz, and Daisy M. Meyer. "Error Gravity: Faculty Response to Errors in the Written Discourse of Nonnative Speakers of English." Hamp-Lyons, *Assessing* 181–96.

Van Sertima, Ivan. "My Gullah Brother and I: Exploration into a Community's Language and Myth through Its Oral Tradition." Harrison and Trabasso 123–48.

Vitanza, Victor. "Three Countertheses; or, A Critical In(ter)vention in Composition Theories and Pedagogies." Harkin and Schilb 139–72.

Walters, Keith. "Language, Logic, and Literacy." Lunsford, Moglen, and Slevin 173–88.

———— . "Writing and Its Uses." *Schrift und Schriftlichkeit / Writing and Its Use*. Ed. H. Gunther and O. Ludwig. Vol. 1. Berlin: de Gruyter, 1994. 638–45.

Walvoord, Barbara E., and Lucille P. McCarthy. *Thinking and Writing in College: A Naturalistic Study of Students in Four Disciplines.* Urbana: NCTE, 1990.

Washington v. Davis. 426 US 229. 1976.

Weaver, Constance. *Black Dialect? Or Black Face?* ERIC, 1974. 091–713.

Weiland, Jeanne. "An Analysis of the Speech Genres of a Tutorial Session: 'Do You Know What I Mean?'" Conf. on Coll. Composition and Communication Convention. Nashville. 1994.

Weir, Cyril. "The Specification, Realisation and Validation of an English Language Proficiency Test." *Testing English for University Study.* Ed. Arthur Hughes. ELT Documents 127. Oxford: Modern English, 1988.

West Virginia State Board of Education v. Barnette. 319 US 624. 1943.

White, Edward M. *Developing Successful College Writing Programs.* San Francisco: Jossey-Bass, 1989.

———. "Language and Reality in Writing Assessment." *College Composition and Communication* 41 (1990): 187–200.

———. *Teaching and Assessing Writing: Recent Advances in Understanding, Evaluating, and Improving Student Performance.* 1985. 2nd ed. San Francisco: Jossey-Bass, 1994.

White, Edward M., and Linda Polin. *Research in Effective Teaching of Writing: Final Report.* NIE grants G-81-0011 and G-82-0024. Washington: Natl. Inst. of Educ., 1986. ERIC ED 275 007.

White, Edward M., and Leon L. Thomas. "Racial Minorities and Writing Skills Assessment in the California State University and Colleges." *College English* 43 (1981): 276–83.

Whiteman, Marcia Farr, ed. *Reactions to Ann Arbor: Vernacular Black English and Education.* Arlington: Center for Applied Linguistics, 1980.

Wiggins, Grant. "A True Test: Toward More Authentic and Equitable Assessment." *Phi Delta Kappan* 70 (1989): 703–13.

Williamson, Michael M. "An Introduction to Holistic Scoring: The Social, Historical and Theoretical Context for Writing Assessment." Williamson and Huot 1–43.

Williamson, Michael M., and Brian A. Huot, eds. *Validating Holistic Scoring for Writing Assessment: Theoretical and Empirical Foundations.* Cresskill: Hampton, 1993.

Willner v. Committee on Character and Fitness. 373 US 96. 1963.

Wilson, Allison. "Black Dialect and the Freshman Writer." *Journal of Basic Writing* 4 (1985): 44–54.

Winchell, Donna Haisty. "Developmental Psychology and Basic Writers." *Research in Basic Writing: A Bibliographic Sourcebook.* Ed. Michael G. Moran and Martin J. Jacobi. Westport: Greenwood, 1990. 31–48.

Winston, Gordon C. "Hostility, Maximization, and the Public Trust: Economics and Higher Education." *Change* July–Aug. 1992: 20–27.

Wisconsin v. Constantineau. 400 US 433. 1971.

Witte, Stephen P. "The Influence of Writing Prompts on Composing." Conf. on Coll. Composition and Communication Convention. Saint Louis. 1988.

Witte, Stephen P., Roger D. Cherry, Paul Meyer, and Mary Trachsel. *Holistic Assessment of Writing: Issues in Theory and Practice.* New York: Guilford, forthcoming.

Witte, Stephen P., and Lester Faigley. *Evaluating College Writing Programs.* Carbondale: Southern Illinois UP, 1983.

Wolcott, Willa. "Writing Instruction and Assessment: The Need for Interplay between Process and Product." *College Composition and Communication* 38 (1987): 40–46.

Wolf, Dennie Palmer. "Assessment as an Episode of Learning." Bennett and Ward 213–40.

———. "Opening Up Assessment." *Educational Leadership* 45.4 (1988): 24–29.

———. "Portfolio Assessment: Sampling Student Work." *Educational Leadership* 46.7 (1989): 35–39.

Wolf, Dennie Palmer, Janet Bixby, John Glenn III, and Howard Gardner. "To Use Their Minds Well: Investigating New Forms of Student Assessment." *Review of Research in Education, 17.* Ed. G. Grant. Washington: Amer. Educ. Research Assn., 1991. 31–73.

Wolfram, Walt. "Levels of Sociolinguistic Bias in Testing." Harrison and Trabasso 265–88.

Wresch, William. "The Imminence of Grading Essays by Computer—Twenty-Five Years Later." *Computers and Composition* 10 (1993): 46–58.

Yancey, Kathleen B., ed. *Portfolios in the Writing Classroom: An Introduction.* Urbana: NCTE, 1992.

Young, Arthur, and Toby Fulwiler, eds. *Writing across the Disciplines: Research into Practice.* Upper Montclair: Boynton, 1986.

Young, Virginia. "Politeness Phenomena in the University Writing Conference." Diss. U of Illinois, Chicago, 1992.

Zamel, Vivian. "The Composing Processes of Advanced ESL Students: Six Case Studies." *TESOL Quarterly* 17 (1983): 165–88.

Zebroski, James Thomas. "The English Department and Social Class: Resisting Writing." Lunsford, Moglen, and Slevin 81–87.

Zessoules, Reineke, and Howard Gardner. "Authentic Assessment: Beyond the Buzzword and into the Classroom." Perrone 47–71.

Zuppan, Jo. "Electronic Editorial Advice." *Scholarly Publishing* 17 (1985): 77–87.

Zwick, Rebecca. "The Technical Requirements of High-Stakes Performance Assessments: Answers to Your Questions." Panel discussion at the Annual Meeting of the Natl. Council on Measurement in Educ. Atlanta. Apr. 1993.

Index

Abel, Elizabeth, 222
Adams, Henry, 58
Adams, Peter Dow, 131
Afolayan, Adebisi, 201
Alexander, Clara Franklin, 191
Allal, Linda, 86, 87
Althusser, Louis, 48
Anderson, Judith, 22, 67
Angle, Burr, 189, 192
Annas, Pamela, 212–13, 215
Anson, Chris M., 152
Apple, Michael, 286–87, 295, 299
Applebee, Arthur, 143, 287, 294
Appleby, Bruce C., 214
Archbald, Doug A., 140, 142
Argyris, Chris, 165
Asante, Molefi, 188, 201
Ascher, Carla, 100, 101, 142
Ash, Barbara Hoetker, 25
Asher, J. William, 57
Atwell, Nancie, 288

Baker, Eva I., 138, 139, 239
Baker, Nancy, 277
Ballard, Leslie, 239
Bamberg, Betty J., 195
Baron, Joan B., 142
Barr, Mary A., 141
Barrs, Myra, 141
Bartholomae, David, 110, 131, 193
Baugh, John, 191
Beach, Richard, 133
Beason, Larry, 158
Beaugrande, Robert de, 143
Beaven, M. H., 195
Beckwith, Lewis D., 35, 40
Bejar, Isaac I., 143
Belanoff, Patricia, 57, 124, 132, 133,
    141, 145, 149, 150, 258, 274, 297
Bennis, William G., 165
Bereiter, Carl, 143
Berlak, Harold, 135, 140, 142
Berlin, James A., 9, 47, 59, 113, 149
Bixby, Janet, 101, 135
Bizzell, Patricia, 113, 152, 212–13, 215,
    225
Black, Laurel, 132, 267
Blok, H., 91
Bowyer, J. W., 251–52

Braddock, Richard, 58, 121, 166
Brannon, Lil, 155
Breland, Hunter M., 19, 83, 101, 121,
    247, 249, 252, 254, 301, 302–03, 304
Brennan, Robert L., 85–86
Bridwell, Lillian S., 133
Britton, James, 152
Broad, Robert, 122, 125, 132, 134
Brodkey, Harold, 212–13
Brossell, Gordon, 7, 25–26, 29, 45,
    216–17, 225, 301
Brown, Penelope, 116
Brown, Rexford, 57
Bruffee, Kenneth A., 195
Buley-Meissner, Mary Louise, 132
Burke, Kenneth, 207
Burling, Robbins, 189
Burns, Brandy, 261
Burstein, Jill, 250
Burt, Cyril, 77, 83
Butts, Hugh F., 189, 190, 197, 202

Camp, Roberta, 19, 51, 57, 62, 97, 99,
    100, 101, 102, 105, 106, 121, 135, 136,
    141, 142, 144, 145, 199, 200, 202, 287,
    298
Cardinet, Jean, 86, 87
Carlisle, Robert, 229
Carlson, Sybil B., 143–44
Carr, George C., 31–32
Carter, Mark A., 141, 145
Cast, B. M. D., 83
Chaplin, Miriam T., 230
Charney, Davida, 57, 59, 90, 133, 232
Cheong, Jacqueline, 141
Cherry, Roger D., 101, 144
Chittenden, Edward, 141, 142
Chorover, Stephan, 157
Christensen, Bonniejean, 16, 151
Christensen, Francis, 16, 151
Christian, Donna, 197
Cintron, Ralph, 115
Cixous, Hélène, 221–22
Clanchy, M. T., 109
Clifford, John P., 4, 155, 195
Coffman, William E., 19, 65, 81–82
Cohen, A. S., 57
Cohen, E. G., 198
Cole, Johnetta, 244

Cole, Michael, 178
Cole, Nancy, 136, 137
Coles, William E., 111, 153
Collins, Allan, 99, 137–38, 139, 142, 143
Condon, William, 122, 127, 133, 281
Conlan, Gertrude, 57
Connors, Robert J., 16, 47, 153, 219
Coombs, Don H., 251
Cooper, Charles R., 57, 195, 199, 215
Cox, Roy, 77
Cronbach, Lee J., 24, 63, 78, 79, 80, 82, 83, 85, 86–87, 136
Crystal, Daisy, 192–93

Daiker, Donald A., 132, 133, 141, 145, 151–52, 247, 257, 270, 293
Damewood, Brian, 264–65
Dana, Richard Henry, 176
Daniell, Beth, 256
Daniels, Harvey, 111, 188, 193, 195–96
Darling-Hammond, Linda, 100, 101, 142
Davis, Barbara Gross, 158
Degenhart, R. E., 133
Delandshere, Ginette, 96
de Man, Paul, 218
Deming, Mary, 273
Desai, Laura E., 141, 145
Despain, LaRene, 122, 123, 133
Dewey, John, 176–77
Deyhle, Donna, 286
Dickson, Marcia, 57, 133, 141, 258
Diederich, Paul Bernard, 19, 24
Dillard, J. L., 189
Dixon, Kathleen G., 152
Donovan, Richard A., 130, 144, 215
Donovan, Timothy R., 4
Dowling, N. M., 57
Dunbar, Stephen B., 138, 139, 239
Duran, Richard P., 286
Durst, Russell, 145, 275
Dyson, Anne Haas, 288

Eble, Kenneth, 166
Edwards, Walter F., 190
Eisner, Elliot W., 95
Elbow, Peter, 10, 12, 24, 59, 105, 106, 114, 120, 124, 131, 133, 141, 145, 149, 150, 179, 195, 274, 279, 281, 282, 297, 301
Elgin, S. H., 191
Elías-Olivares, Lucia, 115
Elliot, Norbert, 150
Elliott, Phillip, 230
Ellis, Sue, 141
Elzey, Marilyn, 260, 262, 266, 270

Emig, Janet, 195, 237, 285, 287, 293–94
Engelhard, George, 102
Entes, Judith, 273
Epps, Edgar G., 198
Eresh, JoAnne T., 100, 102, 142, 144, 145, 146
Etzioni, Amitai, 165

Faigley, Lester, 111, 144, 158, 159, 163, 195, 217, 225
Farr [Whiteman], Marcia, 105, 108, 111, 115, 186, 188, 191, 193, 195–96, 241
Farris, Christine, 158
Fiedler, Frank E., 166
Finlayson, Douglas S., 77, 83
Finn, Patrick, 250
Fish, Stanley, 57–58, 93–94
Fisher, Ronald A., 83, 286
Flower, Linda, 143, 155, 195, 287
Flynn, Elizabeth Gurley, 176
Fox, Helen, 153
Fox, Tom, 189, 191
Frase, Lawrence T., 250, 251
Frederiksen, Norman, 99, 137–38, 139, 142, 143
Freedman, Sarah Warshauer, 127, 128, 133, 149, 200
Frick, Ted, 78
Fulwiler, Toby, 158–59

Gardner, Howard, 101, 135, 140, 141, 145
Geertz, Clifford, 108
Gere, Anne Ruggles, 4, 9, 16, 199
Gilbert, Sandra, 222
Gilyard, Keith, 191–92
Ginther, April, 250
Gitomer, Drew H., 100, 102, 140–46
Glaser, Robert, 140, 143
Glenn, John, III, 101, 135
Gleser, G. C., 78, 79, 80, 83, 85, 86–87
Godshalk, Fred, 19, 65, 68
Gold, Susan E., 145
Goodman, Kenneth, 143
Goodman, Yetta M., 143
Gorman, Thomas P., 133
Gosling, G., 80
Goswami, Dixie, 155
Gould, Stephen Jay, 19, 133
Graff, Gerald, 215
Graff, Harvey J., 110
Gralla, Preston, 252
Grant, Barbara, 141, 142, 145, 239, 247, 248, 284, 301
Grant, Leslie, 250

Graue, Elizabeth, 99, 101, 140
Graves, Donald H., 152, 195, 288
Greenberg, Karen L., 130, 131, 132, 136, 144, 150, 200, 215
Greene, K., 219
Grego, Rhonda, 130
Gronlund, Norman E., 55
Guba, Evon 15, 99, 100, 101, 296
Gubar, Susan, 222
Guerra, Juan C., 115
Guttman, Louis, 94–95

Haisty [Winchell], Donna B., 152
Hake, Rosemary, 151, 232
Hall, William S., 189, 191–92, 197
Hamilton, James A., 176
Hammond, D. J., 260, 261, 264, 265, 266, 267, 270
Hamp-Lyons, Liz, 122, 127, 133, 185, 186, 226, 228, 230, 231, 232, 233, 241, 242–43, 244, 281, 287
Haney, Walt, 140
Hanson, F. Allan, 133
Harding, Sandra, 207, 208
Harkin, Patricia, 4
Harris, W., 189
Hartfiel, V. Faye, 233
Hartog, P., 77
Hartwell, Patrick, 193
Haskins, Jim, 189, 190, 197, 202
Haswell, Richard H., 24, 124, 152, 153, 154, 156–57, 218–22, 223, 225
Hayes, John R., 143, 155, 195, 287
Hays, Janice N., 152
Hazen, Margret, 252
Heath, Shirley Brice, 112–13
Heller, Joan, 100, 102, 144
Herrington, Anne, 153
Hester, Hilary, 141
Hilgers, Thomas, 122, 123, 133, 264
Hill, Jane, 113
Hillocks, George, Jr., 57, 151, 153, 158, 166, 195
Hirsch, E. D., Jr., 91–92
Hoetker, James, 25–26, 29
Holdstein, Deborah, 185, 204, 207, 241, 242, 287
Holland, Norman, 16
Hood, Wendy J., 143
hooks, bell, 223
Hopkins, Kenneth, 83, 84–85
Hopkins, T. L., 77
Howard, Kathryn, 100, 144, 145
Hoyt, C. J., 83
Huddleston, Edith M., 77

Hughes, Gail, 105, 106, 158, 164
Hughey, J. B., 233
Hunt, Kellogg, 16, 151
Huot, Brian, 60, 133
Hurston, Zora Neale, 176–77
Hymes, Dell, 114, 117

Jacobs, Holly L., 233
Jameson, Fredric, 179
Janopoulos, Michael, 228, 231
Jarratt, Susan, 223
Jarrett, Stacy, 261
Jensen-Cekalla, Susan, 164
Jenseth, Richard, 156
Johnson, Burges, 174–75
Johnston, Peter H., 101, 141–42, 143, 202
Jolliffe, David A., 144
Jones, Robert J., 19, 83, 101, 121
Jungeblut, Ann, 116

Kamusikiri, Sandra, 22, 185, 187, 209, 216, 220, 223–24, 225, 241, 242, 243
Kanevsky, Rhoda, 141
Kaplan, Sydney Janet, 209–10
Kerek, Andrew, 151–52
Kirby, Dan, 298
Kirsch, Irwin S., 116
Kitzhaber, Albert R., 153
Knapp, John, 251
Knoblauch, C. H., 155, 256
Koenig, Judith, 22
Koretz, Daniel, 239
Kuehn, John, 260, 261, 262–63, 264–65, 266, 270
Kuykendall, Carol, 298

Labov, William, 112, 189, 197
Lamon, Susan J., 140
Lane, Suzanne, 88, 142
Larson, Richard, 247–48, 271, 278, 301
Lauer, Janice M., 57
Lauter, Paul, 108–09
Lavendel, Brian, 132
Lederman, Marie Jean, 57, 130
Lee, Dorian Latham, 200–01
Leitch, Vincent, 217–18
LeMahieu, Paul G., 100, 102, 142, 144, 145, 146
Lerner, Barbara, 32
Lesh, Richard, 140
Lesgold, Allen, 143
Levine, Denise, 145–46
Levinson, Stephen C., 116
Lewis, Donald Marion, 37–38

Lewis, Shirley A. R., 189, 193
Lieberman, Ann, 95
Linacre, John M., 102
Lincoln, Yvonna S., 19, 99, 100, 101, 296
Linn, Michael D., 198, 200–01
Linn, Robert L., 138, 139, 239
Lipscomb, Delores, 195
Lloyd-Jones, Richard, 58, 121, 166, 199
Lorenz, Frederick, 228, 231
Lucas, Catharine Keech, 133, 141, 142, 143–44
Lunsford, Andrea A., 56, 152, 153, 207, 208, 210, 219, 225
Lunsford, Ronald F., 24, 152
Lutz, William, 7, 33, 45, 179
Lux, Paul, 230
Lytle, Eldon, 252, 254

MacKinnon, Catherine A., 212
Macrorie, Ken, 59, 250
Madaus, George, 140
Mahala, Daniel, 12
Mahiri, Jabari, 115–16
Maimon, Elaine P., 151, 152
Mallorca, Steve, 261
Mansfield, Katherine, 209–10
Martin, Gerald R., 164
Matsuhashi, Ann, 287
McCarthy, Lucille P., 153, 157
McCarthy, Martha M., 31
McCleary, William J., 76
McClelland, Ben W., 4
McClung, Merle, 36–37
McCracken, Nancy Mellis, 214
McCurry, Alan, 249
McCurry, Niki, 249
McGinley, William, 141, 142, 288
McKeachie, William J., 166
McKendy, Thomas, 101
McKenna, Eleanor, 229
Melville, Herman, 259
Messick, Samuel, 24, 63, 136, 137
Meyer, Carol A., 145
Meyer, Daisy, 228, 231
Meyer, Paul R., 101
Meyers, Jeffrey, 209–10
Miller, Nancy K., 222
Mishler, Elliot G., 93
Mislevy, Robert J., 102, 143, 146
Mitchell, Karen, 21–22, 67
Mitchell, Ruth, 135, 140, 145, 146
Moe, Alden, 251
Montano-Harmon, Rosario, 229
Moran, Michael G., 152
Morenberg, Max, 151–52
Morris, Margaret M., 19, 83, 101, 121

Moskal, Barbara, 142
Moss, Beverly, 115
Moss, Pamela A., 53, 63, 78, 99, 101, 129, 136, 137, 139, 141, 143, 144, 145, 287
Moxley, Joseph M., 215
Murphy, Sandra, 1, 59, 69, 99, 100, 101, 113, 141, 142, 143, 145, 166, 239, 247, 248, 274, 284, 297, 298, 301
Murray, Donald M., 59, 195

Nanda, H., 78, 80, 83, 85, 86–87
Nardini, Gloria, 105, 108, 117
Nash, Jane Gradwohl, 17
Newman, Edwin, 252
Newmann, Fred M., 140, 142
Nodine, Barbara F., 151, 152
Noonan-Wagner, Delsey, 200–01
North, Stephen, 13, 105, 106, 148, 174, 176
Nystrand, Martin, 57

O'Connor, Mary Catherine, 287
O'Neal, Verley, 197
Ochsner, Robert S., 152, 156
Odell, Lee, 57, 62, 152, 155, 195, 199, 215
Ogbu, John U., 202
Ohmann, Richard, 47, 111
Olson, Gary A., 215
Olson, James R., 273

Pace, Guy, 252
Page, Ellis, 249, 250, 251, 252
Paris, Scott G., 95–96
Parke, Carol, 142
Patton, Michael, 172
Paulson, F. Leon, 145
Paulson, Pearl R., 145
Paulukonis, Susan, 100, 102, 144
Paulus, Dieter H., 251
Peaden, Catherine Hobbs, 214
Pearson, P. David, 141, 142, 288, 299
Penalosa, F., 191
Perl, Sondra, 193, 237
Perrone, Vito, 140, 142
Perry, William, 152
Petersen, Nancy, 249
Petrosky, Anthony, 96
Phelps, Louise Wetherbee, 153
Phillips, Teri Lee, 260, 261, 263, 264, 265, 270
Pilliner, Albert E. G., 83, 85
Pinckney, H. B., 31
Pitkin, Willis, 151
Plata, Maximino, 150

Polin, Linda, 16, 215, 217
Popham, W. James, 64
Pound, Ezra, 215
Purnell, Rosentene, 149, 150
Purves, Alan, 113, 133, 219, 233

Raimes, Ann, 237
Rajaratnam, N., 78, 79, 80, 83, 85, 86–87
Reif, Linda, 145
Resnick, Daniel P., 140
Resnick, Lauren B., 140
Rhodes, E. C., 77
Ribaudo, Michael, 130
Richardson, Joan, 44
Riddle, Doris, 260, 265, 266, 270
Riesman, David, 120
Robinson, William, 149
Rock, Donald A., 19, 83, 101, 121
Roemer, Marjorie, 145, 275
Roen, Duane H., 214
Rogers, Everett, 165
Roper, S. S., 198
Rose, Mike, 196
Rosenblatt, Louise, 121
Ross, E. A., 175–76
Rothman, Robert, 100
Rowley, Glenn L., 79
Rubin, D. L., 219
Ruth, Leo, 1, 59, 69, 101, 113, 143, 166
Ryzewic, Susan, 130

Sabers, D., 88
Sanborn, Jean, 214
Santos, Terry, 228, 230, 231, 236
Scardamalia, Marlene, 143
Scharton, Maurice, 41, 51, 53, 69, 71, 79, 80, 96, 97, 98, 99, 102, 133, 136, 301
Schilb, John, 4
Schoer, Lowell, 58, 121, 166
Schon, Donald, 100
Schultz, Lucille, 145, 275
Schumacher, Gary M., 17
Schweickart, Patrocinio, 208
Scollon, Ron, 108
Scollon, Suzanne B. K., 108
Scott, Jerrie, 193, 196, 197–98
Scribner, Sylvia, 178
Scriven, Michael, 158
Semmel, Melvin I., 78
Shafto, Michael G., 143
Shale, Doug, 41, 51, 67, 76, 97, 98, 99, 102, 143, 302
Shaughnessy, Mina, 153, 156–57, 192, 199
Sheingold, Karen, 100, 102, 144
Shepard, Lorrie A., 95

Sherwin, Susan, 210–11, 216, 221
Showalter, Elaine, 209, 222–23
Shuy, Roger W., 197
Simpkins, Edward, 189
Sims, Verner Martin, 77
Skinner, Anna M., 144
Slattery, Patrick, 152
Slotnick, Henry, 251
Smagorinsky, Peter, 94
Smith, Barbara Herrnstein, 133
Smith, Mary Ann, 100, 141, 145, 274, 290, 297, 298
Smith, Michael W., 94
Smith, William, 101, 124
Smitherman, Geneva, 190, 191, 200–01, 202–03, 205, 209
Snow, C. P., 247, 250, 256
Sommers, Jeff, 24, 132, 141, 145, 247, 257, 293
Sommers, Nancy, 92, 152, 153, 155
Spandel, Vickie, 144
Spellmeyer, Kurt, 107, 174
Spivak, Gayatri, 223
Stallard, C. K., 195
Stanley, Julian C., 77, 79, 80, 81, 83, 85
Steele, Joe M., 88, 90
Stenhouse, Lawrence, 285–86
Stevens, John Paul, 37
Stevenson, Robert Louis, 176
Stewart, Murray F., 151
Stiggins, Richard J., 140, 144
Stokes, Gale, 174, 178
Straub, Richard, 24
Street, Brian, 109–10
Strevens, Peter D., 190
Stygall, Gail, 132, 247, 257, 293
Swales, John M., 117
Swineford, Frances, 19, 65

Tannen, Deborah, 119
Tate, Gary, 153
Taylor, Orlando, 193, 200–01
Tedesco, Janis E., 218–22, 223, 225
Thomas, Anne, 141
Thomas, Leon L., 12, 21
Thomas, Susan, 158
Thompson, Nancy, 130
Thompson, Richard F., 76
Thorndike, R. L., 81
Tierney, Robert J., 141, 145
Tompkins, Jane, 108, 221
Tormakangas, Kari, 88
Tourneur, Yvan, 86, 87
Trabasso, Tom, 197
Traugott, Elizabeth Closs, 190
Trimbur, John, 1, 7, 45, 108, 243

Turner, Lorenzo, 190
Twain, Mark, 110
Twiggs, Robert D., 189

Valencia, Sheila, 141, 142, 288, 299
Valeri-Gold, Maria, 273
Van Sertima, Ivan, 190, 197
Vann, Roberta, 228, 231
Vitanza, Victor, 155
Vivion, Michael, 12
Vopat, James, 111

Wallace, Richard C., 100, 142, 145
Wallace, Vivian, 141, 142
Walters, Keith, 108, 113
Walvoord, Barbara E., 153
Weaver, Constance, 189, 191
Weiland, Jeanne, 118
Weir, Cyril, 233
White, Edward M., 7, 9, 12, 15, 16, 21, 45,
    52, 56, 69, 92, 93–94, 132, 144, 149, 150,
    166, 195, 199–200, 201, 206, 215, 216,
    217–18, 222, 224, 248, 269, 279, 301
Whitehead, Alfred North, 156
Whitman, Christine Todd, 180
Wiener, Harvey S., 130, 144, 215
Wiggins, Grant, 140, 142

Williams, Joseph, 151, 198
Williamson, Michael M., 16, 76, 101,
    136
Wilson, Allison, 191, 194, 198
Winston, Gordon C., 151
Witte, Stephen, 136, 158, 159, 163, 195,
    200, 287
Wolcott, Willa, 201
Wolf, Dennie Palmer, 101, 102, 135, 140,
    145, 293
Wolfram, Walt, 189, 197, 199
Wormuth, Deanna, 233
Wresch, William, 249–50
Wright, Benjamin D., 102
Wyche-Smith, Susan, 124

Yancey, Kathleen B., 132, 141
Young, Arthur, 158
Young, Virginia, 116

Zamel, Vivian, 237
Zebroski, James, 256
Zelhart, Paul, 150
Zessoules, Reineke, 145
Zinkgraf, Stephen A., 233
Zuppan, Jo, 252
Zwick, Rebecca, 239